Mark Antony

To my friend Stephanie Poletti

Mark Antony

A Plain Blunt Man

Paolo de Ruggiero

Pen & Sword
MILITARY

First published in Great Britain in 2013 by
Pen & Sword Military
an imprint of
Pen & Sword Books Ltd
47 Church Street
Barnsley
South Yorkshire
S70 2AS

ISBN 978 1 78346 270 4

A CIP catalogue record for this book is available from the British Library

Typeset in Ehrhardt by
Mac Style, Bridlington, East Yorkshire
Printed and bound in the UK by CPI Group (UK) Ltd,
Croydon, CRO 4YY

Pen & Sword Books Ltd incorporates the imprints of Pen & Sword
Archaeology, Atlas, Aviation, Battleground, Discovery, Family History,
History, Maritime, Military, Naval, Politics, Railways, Select,
Social History, Transport, True Crime, and Claymore Press,
Frontline Books, Leo Cooper, Praetorian Press, Remember When,
Seaforth Publishing and Wharncliffe.

For a complete list of Pen & Sword titles please contact
PEN & SWORD BOOKS LIMITED
47 Church Street, Barnsley, South Yorkshire, S70 2AS, England
E-mail: enquiries@pen–and–sword.co.uk
Website: www.pen–and–sword.co.uk

Contents

List of Maps

List of Plates

1. Lucius Cornelius Sulla, Glyphotech, Munich
2. Gaius Julius Caesar
3. Marcus Tullius Cicero
4. Ptolemy XII Auletes smashing enemies with a mace. Relief from the first pylon in the Temple at Edfu
5. The Forum today (Photo Tavares)
6. Octavian Augustus (statue known as the "Augustus of Prima Porta") Rome, Museo Chiaramonti (Photo Nierman)
7. Mark Antony
8. Marcus Iunius Brutus, Palazzo Massimo alle Terme, Rome
9. Dionysos and Satyrs, Paris, Bibliotheque Nationale
10. Cleopatra VII Théa Philopator, Berlin, Altes Museum
11. Coinage of Fulvia Flacca Bambula (Photo Classical Numismatics Group Inc)
12. Silver Denarius by Sextus Pompey (Classical Numismatics Group Inc)
13. Herod the Great conquers Jerusalem, Jean Fouquet 1470-75 (Paris, Bibliotheque Nationale)
14. A Parthian mounted archer, Turin, Palazzo Madama (Photo Chadrin)
15. Coin of Phraates, King of Parthia (Photo PHGCOM)
16. Octavia the Younger, Rome, Ara Pacis (Photo Dell'Orto)
17. The Apis Bull, Indianapolis Museum of Art, Indianapolis
18. The battle of Actium by Lorenzo Castro, 1672
19. The death of Cleopatra by Guercino (Genova, Galleria di Palazzo Roso)

'Biography lends to death a new terror.'

Oscar Wilde

Introduction

"I am no orator, as Brutus is,
But, as you know me all, a plain, blunt man,
that love my friend ..."

In Shakespeare's Julius Caesar, these are the few concise words that Mark Antony uses to introduce himself to the congregation of mourning Romans two days after the Ides of March. It is the one-sweep-of-a-brush self portrait of an understated simpleton, someone of good heart and simple feelings, but with a flat personality and nothing of interest to read between the lines. At best, the opener could signify the loyalty of a faithful subordinate, of scarce intellectual capacity and reach. But Shakespeare had something more in store for us: the rapid transformation of a man once he makes it to the stand, from subdued and mellow to powerful and inflammatory, so subtle in outsmarting Brutus and Cassius of their initial momentum, and in turning the tide of public sentiment against them. When the mask is removed, the plain man reveals himself to be sharp, psychologically shrewd and capable of charismatic delivery, and he outwits the intellectually refined and arrogant conspirators.

Which of these two men was really Mark Antony?

Born and raised in Rome, I still have vivid recollections as a child of my father and others in my family using the characterization of "Marco Antonio" to describe a man of an unusually tall, strong, and generally very athletic build. The expression could be taken at face value, and I don't think it carried any negative connotations, nor was it an example of the often traditionally held view that a man who stood out because of his physical appearance must therefore be intellectually lacking in some way. The expression has since fallen from common use as successive generations of Romans have become more and more oblivious to their heritage. As a modest but passionate amateur of the classical period, I, of course, find this regrettable. On the other hand, I have often asked myself if history has done Mark Antony a disservice by delivering to posterity a character that lent itself to the Hollywood big screen for the spectacular Cleopatra romance, a character that was praised, even by his enemies, for individual courage and good swordsmanship, but that was fundamentally lacking core leadership skills, had no strategic vision, was easily manipulated, especially at the hands of strong-willed women, was prone to excessive self indulgence and debauchery, and, most importantly, was driven by a blind thirst for personal power and self assertion. Brutus' words in Shakespeare's play sum it all up, when the plotters are debating and finally rejecting the possibility of assassinating him alongside the dictator:

"He cannot do more than Caesar's arm
  when Caesar's head is off."

Are we to believe that Marcus Brutus was fundamentally right, and that a couple of extra blows of his and Cassius' daggers would have made no difference to the course of history? The biographer is faced with the commonplace tradition, inherited from mainstream historiography, of the man who moved up in the shadow of more exalted leaders, and who, when invested with power, misuses it for his own personal motives and for excessive indulgence and extravagance. Supposedly, he is faced with a man whose limited personality exposes his weakness for the adulation of devious courtesans, who is easy prey for strong willed women (who influence him adversely), and who in the end, motivated by insatiable and naked ambition, makes a bid for power with a devious and malicious oriental queen, and, who, when systematically outsmarted by his opponents has no other exit but a downward spiral of vice and moral laxity, and eventually suicide when all other options are exhausted.

Furthermore, the commonly accepted view is that of a man who is dwarfed by the other great personalities of the period, who tower over him in terms of intellectual calibre, rectitude, piety, loyalty, sense of the State, bravery, leadership, and generalship.

Common sense suggests that, paralleling the signature subtlety of Rome's first Princeps, Augustan and imperial historiography did not operate a brutal *damnatio memoriae* of Mark Antony, but rather sought to attach elements of scorn, mockery, and caricature to the most visible traits of the personality of the Triumvir and denigrate his achievements while emphasizing the lack of judgment that caused his defeats. Shakespeare, on the surface, adheres to the stereotyped version of Antony's persona that is delivered to us by Plutarch – a plain, blunt man – and clearly reflects such widespread views through the mouths of his foes. But time and again, both in *Julius Caesar* and in *Antony and Cleopatra*, Shakespeare shows us a different man, passionate and impulsive, for sure, but with a noble soul and a certain intellectual finesse, charisma and elegance.

The life of this man, which was both at the very heart of the western hemisphere for over two decades – and two troubled decades for that matter – and absolutely central to all the events that shaped the Roman world through the end of the Republic, deserves one more look in an attempt to paint a portrait which does him more justice than we have seen so far. The aim of this work is to dispel the clichés appended to his image by the disinformation campaign carried out by Augustus' sycophantic historians and poets, which have blighted his image and stalked his legacy over the centuries.

The accusations of ostentation levelled at him have also tarnished his image. His detractors dwell – Cicero first and foremost – on his flashy Italian displays during Caesar's dictatorship: sporting treasures from his convoys, parading with lions on a harness, for example. But these anecdotes have also been read and interpreted as the superficial manifestation of a deeper and deliberate scorn for a status quo, a political class, and a social order that had outlived its times. Subscribing to this point of view, this book aims to collate, interpret, and further substantiate many of the arguments which support it. Superficial behaviour and mere anecdotes became hooks on which it has been too easy for imperial historiography to hang more substantive accusations and historical condemnations. Here is the historian Florus[2] on the relationship with Cleopatra, and on the terminal part of his life:[3]

"The madness of Antony, which could not be allayed by ambition, was at last terminated by luxury and licentiousness. After his expedition against the Parthians, while he was disgusted with war and lived at ease, he fell in love with Cleopatra, and, as if his affairs were quite prosperous, enjoyed himself in the queen's embraces.

"The Egyptian woman demanded of the drunken general, as the price of her favours, nothing less than the Roman Empire. This Antony promised her; as though the Romans had been easier to conquer than the Parthians. He therefore aspired to sovereignty, and not indeed covertly, but forgetting his country, name, toga, and fasces, and degenerating wholly, in thought, feeling, and dress, into a monster. In his hand there was a golden sceptre; a scymitar by his side; his robe was of purple, clasped with enormous jewels; and he wore a diadem, that he might dally with the queen as a king."

The stereotypical traits of Mark Antony's traditional persona are all reflected in these few lines: the love of luxury, the drinking habits, the disrespect for values and tradition, the licentiousness, the extravagant dress code, all of which support the accusations of squandering the assets of the Roman Republic and make them perfectly plausible. Once all the superficial manifestations of excess and the magnifying of his vices have been crystallized into character flaws, and his image has been vilified and tarnished, it is easier to be sceptical of the paramount importance of his deeds as a Statesman, and to condemn his actions and his political vision as dictated solely by exaggerated ambition and a thirst for power and wealth. In order to acquire a clear and more sophisticated understanding of Mark Antony's importance, it is, of course, necessary to frame his life and political career within the historical and social context of the late Roman Republic, which was one of the most explosive, fast-paced, and violent periods of classical antiquity.

The critical years of his upbringing and his early steps in the *cursus honorum* – the Roman citizen's career path in the service of the Res Publica – took place in a period of constant unrest, preceded and concluded, like two bookends, by two bloody Civil Wars. The first war ended with Sulla's final conquest of Rome and the end of Cinnan and the Marian faction. The second saw Antony as co-protagonist in the shakeout of Rome's ailing Republican institutions.

The intervening years were marked by an endless sequence of riots and internal strife, ridden with open rebellion against the State (Sertorius, Spartacus), revolutionary conspiracy (Catilina, Lepidus Snr.), and ongoing smaller scale sedition on the part of small-time rabble rousers (Clodius, Milo, Dolabella), which mostly involved patricians attempting to ride on popular discontent to ascend to power or benefit in one way or another. In the background, the scene is populated with some of the most imposing beacons of *romanitas*, on the surface incarnating Republican virtues, stoic values and morals, and towering over the corruption of the contemporary scene. In reality, the Catos, the Ciceros, the Pompeys, seem only to be the sentinels of institutions which, for over seventy years, had failed to solve the problems of a mutating society in a rapidly changing world, and were, in reality, just waiting for a final push to make way for a new rule. If we want to get tough with these men, we can make a compelling case that they were the guardians of a decayed status quo and of the privileges of the senatorial order and the landowners. At any rate, it is important to consider that civil strife in this period was not driven by a clash of ideologies but by bids for power on the part of individuals that tried to exploit the feelings of the masses, who were faced with the blatant inadequacies of the ruling class who endorsed policy agendas that went from land distribution to total forgiveness of all individual debts. It is important to keep this in mind to avoid yielding to the temptation of drafting lists of good and bad, and taking at face value statements which need to be carefully weighted. For example, Cicero's Philippics are a masterpiece of oratory and literature in general, but their vitriolic content stems from personal motives as much as from partisan political intent.

The later part of his life, when the late phase of this struggle ended with the advent of the Second Triumvirate, marked the beginning of the reconstruction of the State. The shakeout, in terms of the players if not of the formal institutions, had taken place already, and the reconstruction process had formally begun. The western part of the Roman dominions, including the Eternal City itself, went through a period of traumatic transformation, where the advent of the autocracy and the Principate were only partly masked by demagogy, but where the problems of the commoners were not resolved, or, for that matter, even addressed.

On the other hand, when the Caesaricides showed how easy it had been to bring the east, with its enormous riches and huge population, under their control and to their side, Rome woke up to the problem of integrating this vast world and establishing an effective control mechanism, which also could provide some degree of safety on the dangerous Parthian border, thus securing Syria and the Middle East. Rome had been faster at annexing huge territories, such as the former Seleucid Empire, Armenia, the whole lot of the bite-size Hellenistic kingdoms in Asia Minor, than reaching a consensus on how to govern them, protect them, and secure a revenue stream (on which there was great reliance) to the capital.

The Roman Republic was faced with a dual transformation problem: the transformation of its demographics and the structure of its society, with the consequence that it continued to rely on its institutions, and the huge expansion of its borders, creating the need to find more effective ways to control an increasingly complex world. Mark Antony's importance in both transformation processes was second to none, and it is genuinely quite incredible that the image of such a central figure at such a crucial time in the history of the Mediterranean basin could have been vilified to such a great extent.

When searching through the sources, the general feeling that official history has not been fair to Antony keeps surfacing time and again. Even reading between the lines of the openly hostile, we can sense some hidden admiration for his greatness amongst the harsh criticism and disapproval.

The theorem of this work is that the real Antony has been buried under centuries of stereotypes and the authority of the official sources, swamped in malicious propaganda attacks and hostile political disinformation campaigns which were carefully orchestrated in such a way as to make them echo through history. The disinformation campaign conducted at capillary levels has left very few gaps through which the modern reader can clearly view the real Mark Antony without the distorting screen of historical bias. It is normal to fall victim to this bias. For example, Antony makes a perfect scapegoat for the purge operated in Rome when the Second Triumvirate rolled into motion and violently eliminated all possible sources of further political instability, yet Octavian's image remains unscathed. Gory images of Cicero's severed head and hands have dogged Antony, and the episode of his wife Fulvia piercing the dead orator's tongue with a hairpin adds the touch of colour that leaves Antony mired in the blame and lets the first Augustus off the hook, leaving him untainted by the brutality of these *proscriptiones*. But, in reality, this is an improbable scenario, as the sources, and common sense, clearly point out. It is puzzling how some historical figures have been absolved by posterity for bloodshed and ruthlessness in a completely arbitrary manner, which is something very difficult to rationalize. Caius Marius' purges are the mirror image of Lucius Cornelius Sulla's, but the latter has been stigmatized to a much greater extent, maybe because the former's populist agenda inspired more sympathy than the latter's conservatism and full endorsement of the *optimates* agenda. Pompey Magnus, who carried out a substantial part of Sulla's dirty work to the point of being nicknamed "the adolescent butcher", is not usually associated with the brutal settlement of factional scores, but rather with that of balance, legitimacy, fairness, and respect for the law and the institutions.

The main sources have to be handled with great care, as they are linked to one another in a long chain of hostility, which can be easily tracked to the political ends of Antony's greatest foe, Octavian. In the course of the struggle which opposed them for fourteen years, and afterwards, when he became Rome's first Emperor with the name of Caesar Augustus, he had to strengthen his legitimacy and ground his ascent to sole power on historical necessity. However, with time the truth always finds a way to surface, no matter how deeply it is buried. Or, at least, if it is not the absolute truth, enough evidence can emerge to generate reasonable doubts about the official, dogmatic version of the contemporary historians. It is so that when we put together the whole body of documents from the original sources, we often find that the bias is blatant and contradicts proven facts, or that it clashes with common sense or with the most logical and probable flow of events. On other occasions, the sources, who, it must be remembered, are never first hand observers, involuntarily give us points of data which also contradict official conclusions, or at least enable us to re-elaborate the historical analysis and draw a different set of conclusions. Either way, implicitly, we can form a more independent reading of the events. As a byproduct, the second reading invariably sheds a more favourable light on Mark Antony.

It is in this way that the critical and careful use of a negative tradition can reveal to the biographer a man who incites the greatest admiration for his fundamental role in one of the most important transformations of the western world, and for the conception of a new order for the Eastern Mediterranean, in a visionary model which could have synchronized the best traditions of the Hellenistic kingdoms, the local cultural heritage, and the need for control of the Eternal City. This exercise does not need to be scholarly, or worse, pedantic. Besides, it will easily yield as a byproduct a much more accurate portrait of this man, with his burden of visible yet superficial weaknesses and defects, which make it all the more real and tangible, but more importantly, with his value system, his personality, his motivations, and his *modus operandi*. Sifting through the large mass of data provided by, it is worth underlining again, a hostile historiography, it is possible to identify some clear personality traits, and to sketch the profile of a man of great intellectual and moral integrity, of remarkable generosity and liberality, and of great human passion.

His first biographer Plutarch cannot help openly contradicting himself as he passes value judgment about the man. While it is clear that he tries hard to be seduced by Antony's fine qualities of courage, generosity, and integrity, he still cannot get beyond the alleged accusations of cruelty, vanity and exaggerated ambition. While one can sense a deep sympathy for the man Antony, appreciation for many of his deeds and behaviours, and moral forgiveness for many others, the conclusions drawn in the comparison with Demetrios, son of Antigonous, are extremely harsh, as if his first biographer, after giving proof of the nobility of his soul and of his many merits, wanted to comply with the official historiography in his overall conclusion, even at the cost of coherence.

On cruelty and ambition:

> "Antony, who enslaved the Roman people, just liberated from the rule of Caesar, followed a cruel and tyrannical object. His greatest and most illustrious work, the successful war against Brutus and Cassius, was done to crush the liberties of his country and of his fellow citizens."

On his enslavement to Cleopatra:

> "Antony, like Hercules in the picture where Omphale is seen removing his club and stripping his lion's skin, was over and over disarmed by Cleopatra, and beguiled away, while great actions and enterprises of the first necessity fell … And in the end, like another Paris, he left the battle to fly to her arms … he fled first, and abandoned his victory."

And there is much more, as we shall see.

As pointed out, the biographer has to deal with a largely hostile body of historiography. The palm for the most blindly hostile historian, if we want to call him that, goes to Velleius Paterculus, who should be handled with extreme care. Since he served as a military Tribune under Gaius Caesar, nephew of Octavian Augustus, and later as a General under Tiberius, his work is impregnated with gratitude towards the Julio-Claudians, and is particularly deferential with regards to his three patrons, mentioned above. He devoted special care to obtaining the moral acquittal of Octavian for his crimes during the proscriptions, to the detriment of Lepidus, but especially of Antony. He is a definite sycophant, and carefully stays away from fact-based discussions of events, dwelling instead on value judgments, stereotypical comments on character, and corny morals. For example, he entirely skips the campaign of Philippi, to ensure that Octavian, undeservedly, got some of the credit. He ignores the reality of the victory, which was a landmark accomplishment in the elimination of the last bastion of the old Republic and in the establishment of the unchallenged rule of the Second Triumvirate, and it had been solely to Antony's merit. On the other hand, he let himself go in a long tirade about the execution of Cicero. Still, his work can be useful for our purposes, as an instrument of contrast with more reliable sources, and to exemplify the extent to which the imperial disinformation campaign had distorted the reality of the facts.

Also, those who collected and re-elaborated the echoes of the propaganda for ease, or because it provided some spectacular material, can provide interesting angles on particular situations.

In some cases, the official version has been accepted because it had probably been endorsed by very authoritative historians, such as Titus Livy. Livy's work on this period is almost entirely lost. It is difficult to place the bar of expectations on how fairly he had treated Antony. Most of his work was completed under Augustus, which does not augur well for impartiality. As a matter of fact, young Livy had moved to Rome from provincial Padua right after the battle of Actium, and his work ends with the death of Augustus. It is of no doubt that his intent was celebrative. We have inherited a few fragments on this period from a fourth-century transcript called "Periochae" and just enough to ascertain that his contribution was well within the mainstream tradition. As Livy carried more weight than others, it is probable that his damnation influenced other historical compilers, and contributed to establishing and reinforcing the tradition. Other secondary historians such as Florus and Orosius do not really add much to the research among the sources, apart from a clear perception of how the official version prepared by servile historians such as Velleius had propagated over time and geography in the centuries. The tones of such chroniclers, if possible, become even more dogmatic, and the condemnation so univocal as to lose any significance from a critical historical perspective. There is nothing of interest there other than a few poetic images, such as the waves of Actium washing gold and purple ashore after the naval battle.

While his work is largely lost, another landmark intellectual who endorsed the Augusteal party line was Nicolas of Damascus, who had previously lived in close quarters with Antony and Cleopatra. In fact, it might have been Herod who placed the scholar at the court of Alexandria, originally charged with the upbringing of Alexander and Cleopatra Selene, but possibly also with a secret espionage mission. After 30 BC, he returned to his true master, Herod, in Jerusalem, to become one of the loudest squawk boxes of the Augustan propaganda, investing himself heavily in tasks such as the denial of Cesarion's paternity by Julius Caesar.

Upon reviewing the sources, the two authors who provide us with the deepest insights and the richest material are Appian and Cassius Dio. We expect fairer treatment from Appian, and this is exactly what we get. A member of Alexandria's affluent and intellectual Greek community during the Trajan golden age, he must have grown up amidst the echoes of the last years of the Ptolemaic dynasty and the remnants of Antony's passage. Appian is the author who, more than any other, tries to interpret Antony's actions in the most lucid and impartial way, and frequently he gives us the means to counter some of the stereotypical accusations with facts.

Antony conducted a love affair with the Near East as much as he did with Cleopatra. And it is perhaps impossible to say with any certainty that his contemporaries across the Mediterranean got to see his best side more so than those in Rome, because of his natural affinity with the Hellenistic style, or because he had breathed enough of the corrupt atmosphere of the Eternal City. At any rate it is clear that:

"Antony wore the tragic mask when in Rome, and the comic mask in Alexandria."[4]

The suspicion that here we have found a Roman who could not relate to Rome but felt more at home in an exotic environment grew steadily as this work progressed. And Antony's attempts to import touches of Rome to Hellenistic Egypt must not be derided. Even the famous triumph he celebrated in Alexandria upon his return from Parthia, which has been widely criticized as a carnival, should not just be written off as an extravagance. The atmosphere of this city, suspended between Egypt and the outside world, was clearly as unique and as fascinating as its queen. Egyptian rulers would call themselves "King of Egypt and of Alexandria", and it is not uncommon in narratives to find the locution "… he went from Alexandria to Egypt" as if the capital of Ptolemaic Egypt was extraterritorial. Its inhabitants were extremely cosmopolitan, and this melting pot was more unruly and difficult to govern than the traditional Egyptian population.

While part of the cause for his interest in this region was political necessity and his own vision for the east on which we shall elaborate later, recent historical work has highlighted this side of Antony's personality,[5] which was in all probability nurtured by progressive disaffection with the Roman scene, as well as a fascination with an Hellenistic Middle East in which he thrived, and where he had achieved some of his early career successes.

The layout of Appian's work is also very telling. On one side, we have the Civil War, which spans from the Gracchi to the elimination of Sextus Pompey, the last domestic war episode. But onwards, if the sequel to the story had survived to our days, we would have had to go back to the library, put back the books "XLVII–XLIX" or "the Civil War" and open a totally different treatise, which is known as "the Egyptian War" (books XLX–XLXIV), which unfortunately did not survive to the present day. The point, though, is that the late stages of the conflict are a war between sovereign powers, or maybe a war of independence, but not the closing act of Rome's Civil Wars. Appian is also interesting for our purposes because of his peculiar habit of including in his narration some summary transcripts of important speeches, which give us a good cross section of Antony's oratory skills, and which cannot possibly have been as poor as Cicero suggests[6] if we judge by their impact on some noteworthy occasions, the most famous being, of course, the one delivered after Caesar's assassination. Although we all have in our ears Shakespeare's revisiting, where a shrewd and calculating Antony, weary of the conspirators' lingering threat, disguises his vengeful message under subtle irony, Appian gives a much more inflammatory version, filled with extreme characterizations, such as portraying the Gallic Wars as just revenge for the raid against Rome brought by Brenno's Gallic tribes 160 years before. It mattered little that Brenno's Gauls were probably Ligurians from Cispadanic Gaul, and had little to do with their northern cousins. Interestingly enough, Cassius Dio also gives us a full transcript, and the two, as we will see, don't even look alike. Appian is unique and extremely precious for the biographer. His work is insightful, his political analysis brilliant, his conclusions exude independence of judgment and originality. Also, he dipped heavily into some sources emanating from Antony's inner circle, such as the intellectual General Asinius Pollio, thus making his commentaries all the more enriching. Unfortunately, he leaves us at the death of Sextus Pompey, the event which in his view marked the end of the Civil War's *strict sensu*.

Cassius Dio earned his stripes as an historian with a monumental compilation that starts with the landing of the Trojans on the Latium shores, and ends with the *Principatus* of the Severans. Dio was a high ranking officer in the imperial administration, and he took to writing relatively late in his life. The importance of this work lies in the fact that it relays a number of original sources which have been lost over the centuries. So, while his own contribution is minimal, he does give us a rather structured and thorough reorganization of detailed information from other sources.

While he follows the mainstream version of the facts, and the conclusions are very much in line with the official version, Dio provides such a wealth of factual information that the careful reader is able to see through the bias of the sources he had used for his synopsis. His narration remains sufficiently factual for the reader to discard at times the official conclusions, and use the detailed information provided to draw his own conclusions and extrapolate independently from the main data points provided.

Josephus Flavius' work on the other hand (the Jewish wars, the Jewish antiquities) is a masterly exercise to reconcile his *captatio benevolentiae* towards the Flavians with the celebration of Jewish bravery and leadership. In other words, the turncoat Jewish rebel general[7] had to prove that the *Pax Romana* could be reconciled with national pride and values. And until a few years earlier, this view had been incarnated by the Herodian dynasty, of which Herod the Great had been the founder and doubtlessly the most representative member. As we will see, the Herodian rule that stamped out the intestine wars was established on the battlefield, but these successes were fostered, supported and legitimized by Rome through Mark Antony. There is a strong indication that the relationship between the two leaders went beyond political opportunity, and that Herod truly befriended the Triumvir and felt genuine loyalty and admiration for him.[8] At any rate, from his narration we get a full appreciation of the historical context and objective difficulties which Antony tackled, as he manoeuvred to obtain a level of stability for a region ravaged by internal strife, which at the time involved an area that extended from Egypt to Syria. Josephus, while he is obsessed with his goal of justifying to his countrymen the rule of the Herodians and the pro-Roman stance, is very important for us, because he provides the point of view of a satellite kingdom on Antony's new order in Asia. While King Herod the Great was undoubtedly a true sycophant, and he and his family prospered under the Julio Claudians, Josephus gives us a line of sight on how deep Antony's understanding of his client kingdoms was, and how active he was in securing the loyalty of all the eastern nations, also through developing personal bonds with the reigning families. Also, the angle he provides on the whole relationship with Cleopatra, and on the interference of their *ménage* in State affairs, is extremely interesting and instructive.

Marcus Tullius Cicero's literary work would have been considerably less voluminous if the Antonii hadn't existed. The life of the lawyer and statesman from Arpinium crosses the path of the Antonii, and our Mark Antony in particular, many times. Except for a few examples of Antony's letters, we are only party to Cicero's side of the almost constant bickering, which spanned the entire lives of the two men, but we get a strong feeling of what went on with the other side from some of Cicero's phrases, which sound like comebacks and rebuttals of Mark Antony's attacks. Clearly, Cicero's importance in moulding all the negative aspects of Antony's persona is paramount. Overall, it seems that the Philippics and his other comments on Antony are so impregnated with bitter bile that all impartiality is lost, and so are the benchmarks for the behaviour of all leaders of this era. These accusatory speeches frequently present a distorted image of the facts, and the invectives contained in his works have been used as hooks on which to hang sinister or derisory portraits of the Triumvir, which would be used again by the Augustan historiography. The enmity between the two men was inevitable. Cicero was one of the most influential leaders of the conservative senatorial wing, an elitist group which never truly accepted him, but which certainly welcomed the use they could make of his literary, oratory, and lawyerly skills. Antony, on the other hand, was the major menace left for the establishment to face after Julius Caesar's demise, and therefore the natural target to deprive the *populares* movement of the only leader they had who could go past empty demagogy, and bring about true sustainable change.

This work would not be complete without a close look at Julius Caesar's work on the Gallic and Civil Wars, for the role that Antony played in both. Antony is a rather marginal player in the Gallic campaign; in fact his only participation in the military action was during the siege of Alesia, and this is the only mention he earns from his illustrious uncle in the first seven chapters. He gets a lot more of the limelight in the eighth book, which was not written by Caesar, but by his general Hirtius, and which deals with the mop-up of residual resistance and the securing of prior accomplishments. While Caesar was essentially writing a diary for the benefit of the Senate in Rome, and in order to maintain favourable consensus on his actions, Hirtius writes later, and in a different context, and he shines the spotlight more in the direction of his friend Antony.[9]

The De Bello Civile, on the other hand, is the systematic and beautifully structured destruction of his opponents' remaining legitimacy, including Pompey and all the representatives of the "ancien régime". The aim was not the destruction of the ideologies, the legislation, or the political agenda behind them. The attacks were instead aimed at the vices of the professional politicians of the senatorial clique, which undermined the leadership's legitimacy. In other words,

> "if in the nomenclature adopted to mark these men, among the criticism applied to the personalities found in Rome, one can find the intolerable *adrogantia* (arrogance) to the irritating *iactantia* (boasting), to the annoying *obstentatio* (ostentation), to the needless *pertinacia* (obstinacy), to the regrettable *temeritas* (rashness), besides the dangerous *invidia* (envy), Caesar demonstrates how it had been those vices to prejudice the relationship with a group of people not only unable to understand the situation, but also responsible for having misled Pompey into error."[10]

Antony could not have put it better. Many of his choices were dictated solely by his distaste for, and lack of trust in, individuals that did not meet his moral and ethical standards, or that he simply could not respect as adversaries in a virile sense.

Among the various drawbacks for Antony of not having achieved absolute rule over Rome, we can list the fact he did not get a full mini-biography from Suetonius. But the gossip columnist of the classic world covers some critical parts of his career in the biography he wrote about Octavian. Plus, he gives some very interesting sketches of the latter's character, often in a way that exposes his many personality flaws, beginning with his duplicity and cruelness, which make the case for Antony's animosity towards him. It is quite clear that Suetonius' aim is to make the vices and the weaknesses of the First Augustus emerge. But, as he does this, time and again Antony becomes the yardstick for favourable comparison. On other occasions, some anecdotes which cast a bad light on the Princeps implicitly revalue the other Triumvir; while Suetonius has a taste for the spectacular, his contributions are always robust and credible, often grounded on other commonly accepted sources, so that his careful reading is very helpful for the biographer.

In the course of this work, and with a careful and critical review of the sources, hopefully several commonplaces will be addressed and clarified, thereby restoring a more dignified image to Mark Antony.

The first of the misconceptions to be addressed is that Mark Antony, while maybe brave on an individual basis, lacked any chief executive skills to the point of being incapable of laying out an army for battle, or exerting the kind of leadership that was so crucial for victory in antiquity, and that he obtained more through his lieutenants than his own individual capabilities.

His military leadership skill-set was extremely well rounded, and had no match in the western world. We will follow his accomplishments from the deserts of the Near East to the forests of Gaul, from the guerrilla warfare on the German border to the biggest battlefields of antiquity, Pharsalus and Philippi, from siege warfare to the massive logistic challenges of managing a force of thirty to forty thousand men: a long list of brilliant accomplishments which built up his virtually unrivalled experience as a top notch military leader. We must not underestimate the extent to which, during his campaigns, he had to endure extreme hardship, in Epyrum for example, in the nerve-wrecking months which preceded the battle of Pharsalus, when the Caesarean army was feeding on roots, and when Antony was in all likelihood, and as was his style, living a tough existence alongside his legionaries in order to build that bond of steel that would make the difference on the battlefield. The two large scale campaigns under Caesar were clearly fundamental for his development as a field general, but he gave his best when he was chief in command. In Mutina he lost, it is true, but throughout most of the engagement he was ahead of a much more numerous opponent, and he gave up when he found himself facing too many enemies simultaneously arriving from different directions. The Macedonian campaign ending at Philippi was his masterpiece: impeccable timing, clockwork logistics, and the right amount of risk taking, coupled with the masterly use of psychological warfare, which in those days was crucial for large scale success, as we shall see. Of course he had his setbacks, which come under the names of Media and Actium. But on neither of these occasions was defeat the result of poor generalship, as will be shown. The first of the two adverse outcomes was the result of miscalculation in terms of logistical choices. Actium was a real field defeat, but it resulted from a series of political choices, which forced Antony's hand, all the way to the disaster in the naval battle. At any rate, the comment from Plutarch that he, like Octavian, obtained more victories through others than by himself is easy to confute. Partly from his natural inclination as a show off, even at the high point of his career as a Triumvir, he would always lead from the front. Much of his personal success derived from this brand of very present leadership.

The second is that due to his inherently weak character he was prone to being dominated by his women.

The profiles of the women of his life (Octavia, Fulvia, and Cleopatra) have a common denominator: they were strong and not lacking in character. Some historians have tried to describe Antony as putty in the hands of strong willed wenches, and Plutarch gives credit to Fulvia for having broken him to passive obedience. But a more realistic reading gives us a man that was seeking his match among women, looking for a woman with a rich and stimulating personality, and with whom a love affair carried a component of challenge and ongoing stimulus. Oscar Wilde wrote than men are interesting when they have a future, and women are interesting when they have a past. That certainly goes for Fulvia and Cleopatra, who most definitely had stories to tell, and in a different way for Octavia, who in a different political context, i.e. in a marriage not dictated by political opportunity, could have been a successful spouse.

All three women had enough credibility to position themselves as powerful partners for Antony, women that could credibly represent him in the conduct of State affairs. Fulvia would become a shadow Consul in 40 BC, and even before the beginning of the Second Triumvirate would be targeted by Cicero for the weight she carried in the conduct of the business of the Republic. Cleopatra was at the same time a lover, and the partner who was to enable him to realize a grand scale political project for the reorganization of the east. Had she been unable to carry her weight with the oriental kings and satraps, the political vision hinged on Egypt would have been on much shakier grounds. Octavia possessed the moral and intellectual stamina to sustain the weight of Antonian politics and to incarnate his interest in Rome in his absence, and even when he had effectively already declared against her brother Octavian. All three are independent, free spirited and highly intelligent women. The reality was that Antony was attracted by these traits which we, of course, associate with the modern world, but which were extremely rare in the classical world, where the majority of female characters were subdued and quiet.

Such a characterization is probably more befitting of his enemy Octavian. When he married Livia, in 36 BC, he was the most eligible bachelor in the western world. Still, he went to the trouble of making this not especially attractive woman, a mother of two,[11] divorce her prestigious husband T. Claudius Nero, so he could marry her, thereby securing for himself a scheming and dominating woman, who was to control the palace all the way to her death at the wake of Caligula's accession to the purple.

The third regards his alleged arrogance, which supposedly attracted criticism and caused him to be detested by the people.

Antony was, first and foremost, a hugely passionate and uncompromising man. At critical times in his life he had to deploy political tactics, and he did it, as we will see, remarkably well. This cannot be interpreted as his natural disposition. He loathed the political establishment, and was probably happy when he could inflict a humiliation on, or settle a score with, a professional politician linked to a certain type of senatorial circle.

The fourth was that he abandoned Rome and its values to embrace the ways of an oriental king, and pursued interests which were contrary to those of the republic, which he had undertaken to reform. Once again for political convenience, his posturing has been interpreted as an intention to betray Rome, and its values and culture, preferring instead to adopt the ways of an eastern king or Satrap with rebellious purposes. While it is evident that Antony had many reasons for disenchantment, if not right out disgust, with the goings-on in Rome, with its corrupt politicians and with the devious ways of the privileged few, he never betrayed his origins and his primary allegiance was always to the Republic. We shall endeavour to show that his posing as an eastern monarch, and, more specifically, as a Ptolemaic king, was a necessary step in his political strategy to dispel the negative connotations of Roman rule in the eyes of the Egyptians, and win full and popular adherence to his political project.

The fifth is that he was essentially lazy, and thrived in the *far niente*, or worse, in orgiastic feasts, every time he had the resources and the authority to do so, regardless of his duties as a leader of Rome. The Antony of the after hours, be it in the house of Pompey he had seized in Rome, in the country estate that belonged to the scholar Varo (where – per Cicero in the Philippics – "girls from good families had to be mixed up with scummy whores"), in his Athenian residence, or in the royal palace of Alexandria, the door was closed to those coming to do business but was always open to actresses and musicians, at least according to the official version. This cliché, which we find widely in Plutarch, must be dispelled. While Antony was probably not a workaholic, and was certainly a *bon viveur*, he certainly knew how to get business done. The Second Triumvirate had a very specific agenda to carry out, and Antony was, by a long shot, the dominating figure at the time, so the burden of the vast majority of the decision making must have fallen to him. In Greece and the Middle East, the amplitude of the reforms and changes brought was such that it must have required a frenetic pace for the entire length of his stay. The fact remains, as we shall see, that the measures he enacted and the organization he laid out largely outlived him, under Augustus and after.

The sixth is that he was cruel and bloodthirsty, and that he enjoyed inflicting death. While in general Antony, by unanimous consensus, was of solar disposition, and was always ready for laughter and enjoyment (and such people are never cruel or sadistic), this accusation derives from few specific episodes or contextual situations, which we shall later put into their relevant context. The most important is, of course, the period of the proscriptions, which will be reviewed in detail, in order to ascertain the relative importance of the Triumvirs, and the objectivity of the sources. As one would expect, the execution of Cicero resonated hugely, and was, indeed, a gory episode. There are, in addition, a few examples of cruel punishments inflicted on mutinous troops, sloppy soldier-ship, and merciless killings of some of his enemies which have also been stigmatized. These too need to be revised in a more objective and contextual light to be able to formulate a fair appraisal.

The seventh is that he was morally fragile, quick to lose spirit and courage, and prone to depression in the face of adversity. Everyone can relate to the image of Mark

Antony deserting the Actium waters in the pursuit of the fleeing Cleopatra, and abandoning his battleships to the systematic annihilation performed by Agrippa's fleet. By extension, servile historiography has also portrayed a depressive Antony retreating from Parthia, careless of the suffering of his men, who were decimated by malnutrition and enemy arrows for three straight weeks. In reality, Antony's life was marked by several downturns of fortune, and he proved amazingly resilient and with a real propensity to bounce back during the down cycles. He proved it in 43 BC, after Mutina, after the Parthia campaign, and he would have probably done it again, if opportunism had not deprived him of all his fair weather friends who subsequently betrayed him and his project at the end. His final lassitude and disillusionment and state of melancholy and abandonment were a consequence of this betrayal.

The eighth is that he was a warmonger at best, but that he had no political vision or statesman-like abilities. We will examine in detail two major contributions of his political activity. The first is the period after the Ides of March 44 BC and the assassination of Julius Caesar, when he steered Rome across a major turning point and avoided the dangers of anarchy, bloodshed, or regression into the old oligarchic ways. But, even more importantly, we will dwell on his mission to restructure and reorganize the Greek East, a mission which he endeavoured to complete by executing a visionary project: designing the Roman way to the Orient.

The last and most important is that he was pursuing only his personal goals in his quest for absolute rule, pushed by his monstrous ambition. As we go through all the main sources the word "ambitious" is the most frequently recurring derogatory term we find used to describe Antony. But what does "ambitious" mean in the context of the late Roman Republic?

In Rome, the "cursus honorum", which consisted in aiming for the top roles of the civil service, was the only conceivable career path for the upper class man. The stoicism that ruled the lives of the virtuous men stipulated that the service of the State and the dedication of one's life to the public good was the only dignified mission for men of standing. The Roman Warren Buffett and Bill Gates could have been of equestrian (knight) census, or even freedmen (former slaves), but not noblemen by any means, and certainly not people that could have made a mark in society, been remembered, or even accepted in the upper echelons of society. Wealth would always be welcome, but it would follow power, and not vice versa. Even Crassus, the Cresus of the Republic, gambled his family fortunes to obtain political primacy, and then obtained exponential returns once at the top.

No matter how hard one tries, very few examples of primacy on the political scenes, not supported by a good dose of "ambition", come to mind. For many decades, provided it had ever existed, the idealized character of the statesman devoted to the common good had been remarkable for its absence from Rome's political scene. For decades, Rome had fallen victim to the various radical demagogues on one side, and the conservative career politicians and leaders that were just perpetuating their own species on the other.

After the death of Julius Caesar, whatever is left of the Roman Republican institutions is wholly hollow of any factual content, to de-legitimize all those that were still standing for it. Cicero's posing as the saviour of the country is quite simply pathetic, an attempt – maybe and at best – in good faith, but myopic and utopic, to reconstruct the Republic on a class of good men (*boni vires*) that did not exist any longer, if it ever had.

In the end, two bids for power remained. One was launched by Octavian, and proved more crafty, cunning, and planned, thanks to the natural deviousness of the young man. The other, more instinctual, rough at times, but a condensation of actions coming straight from his gut, came from Mark Antony. But how many of his instinctual moves were driven by his lust for power, and how many by a rational assessment of the spaces left open by the lack of capable leaders after Caesar's death? How much of it was due to his alleged arrogance, and how much was a disdain for all the other contemporary politicians? Why was he a reliable and straightforward civil servant while the remnants of Republican institutions were still functioning, and a faithful second in command for Caesar, a man that could stand by his loyalties as long as they were pledged to a credible State, worthy cause, or a leader to whom he could look up? The simplest and most superficial review of the historical context of his youth and his upbringing will clarify the point. The profound crisis of the Roman values had been evident for over fifty years, and the murder of Julius Caesar, instead of resolving it with a return to the Republican moral values, risked making it degenerate further towards a restoration of privilege, and empty conservatism. Antony stepped up to a new challenge, with all his charisma, his decisiveness, his bluntness, to give the final push to the trembling structure, and make it collapse, but only so it could be reconstructed for the common good, and not for personal power, as Octavian would later do. Not only should the discussion of the following pages dispel these tired clichés, but it should leave the reader with a different image of Mark Antony from the traditional one we have described. Instead, this work will strive to promote an image of integrity, of respect for values, truthfulness and honourableness, even at the cost of personal and political advantage. We will try to prove that he was a visionary leader, who had understood early on that an irreversible process of change had begun, and that the ruling class had no choice but to adopt a radically different approach.

The analysis provided in this work would like to bring to the forefront his many positive traits and virtues: beginning with his personal courage, often highlighted and recognized even by his detractors, and moving on to his integrity and loyalty, to his sense of self deprecation, a gift given only to the greatest of minds, to his piety and respect for worthy opponents, to his worldliness, and understanding of different people and cultures, to the passion he put into everything he did, and to his underlying *joie de vivre*, which makes him so human and so easy to relate to.

By the end of this work the reader will maybe share a different view of Mark Antony, and can return him to the place in history where this great man of antiquity rightfully belongs. Here is the narration of his fifty-three year life.

Chapter One

The Making of a Roman Hero

Marcus Antonius (Antony or Mark Antony hereafter) was born to a distinguished yet plebeian family, on an unknown date that general consensus places in 83 BC. In Rome, at that time, the distinction between patricians (families constituting the historical nobility) and plebeians (all others) did not necessarily indicate a particular level of wealth or privilege, but rather served purpose only to demonstrate access to public offices, such as the *tribunatus plebis* or tribunate of the plebs, the magistracy in charge of defending the interests of the lower class, or other largely symbolic legacies of the old days when Republican Rome had faced class struggle.

The Antonii did not sport a *cognomen*, the given name that, if it stuck with the person, passed from generation to generation and ended up identifying a branch in a large clan's (or *gens*) family tree. With little imagination, the first born family members were mostly – or all – called by the *praenom* Mark, and their *nomen*, Antony. Whereas the *praenom* served the same purpose that it does in today's society, the *nomen* identified the clan or *gens* to which the person belonged, and the *cognomen* further distinguished lineage within a clan as it branched out, whether it was attributed by merit, anecdotes, or because it pointed to physical characteristics of a family member. Romans wore their *cognomen* with great pride, no matter how obscure its origins or how odd its meaning.

For example, the Claudii's two main branches went either as Claudius Pulcher (pretty or handsome) or, in the case of the branch that became the imperial clan, Claudius Nero (most likely "brave" although the exact translation is still not sure). The nose of Marcus Tullius Cicero (chick pea) was not marked by any wart or excrescence of sorts, but most likely that of one of his ancestors was. Caesar, a name that was to become a synonym for absolute rule, is probably a derivation from the Punic word for "elephant", since an ancestor of Gaius Julius fought at the Trasimene battle and allegedly killed or wounded one of Hannibal's pachyderms. Less originally, a long list can be made with the various "red beard", "blue eyed", "the quick", "the slow", "the farmer", "big nose", and so forth, not to mention all the *cognomen* that we cannot easily interpret because of their origins in Etruscan or some other provincial, or indeed even foreign, language.

For an especially distinguished individual, a fourth part – the *agnomen* – could be added to the name. Ultra-conservative political leader Lucius Cornelius Sulla (Sulla) thanked the Gods his way, and attributed to himself the indicative of Felix,

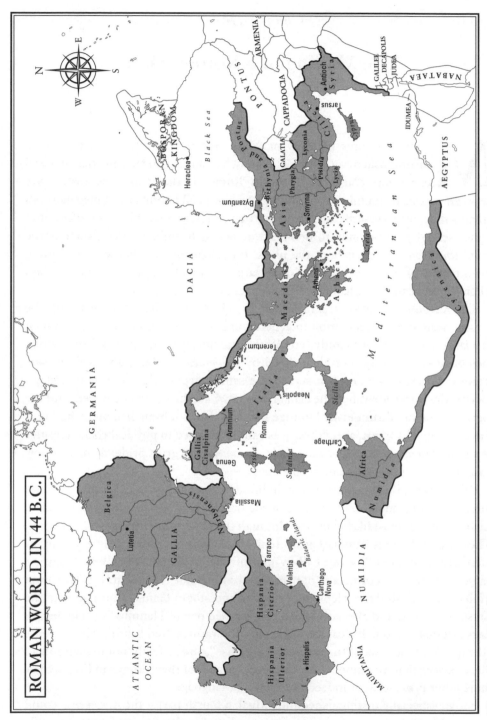

The Roman world in 44 BC

"the fortunate one" or "the one favoured by the Gods", after a life exposed to peril but crowned by great success, to indicate the Gods' favour to his cause. Later in this work there will be more examples of Roman onomatology. As the clans grew, and new branches could make their individual claim to fame, full names became longer.

The Antonii, however, in spite of their very respectable lineage, sadly never did manage to add that third name to their business card.

Nor did they ever pretend to descend from divinity, a claim which was not ridiculed in Rome, as long as it was made by senior leaders. The Julii boasted direct descent from Venus. The Pompeys asserted their origins from Hercules, which was considered to be a lesser deal, as it was well known that Hercules never did abide by the laws of Lykurgos, was somewhat of a ladies' man, with the result that his progeny was scattered all over the Earth, and so subsequently many could claim to be related to the famous hero without surprising anyone.

In a show of originality, Antony's first biographer Plutarch has them descend from Anton, a son of Hercules himself, of whom nobody else had ever heard. Neither did anybody in the clan, as far as we know, ever claim family ties with the promiscuous mythological hero. But Plutarch probably saw a good character fit in many ways and ventured the association. Rather, we know that later in his life Antony welcomed or even encouraged some association with another God, Dionysos, but we know that it was for contextual reasons and as part of a specific propaganda project, as we shall see in Chapters 6–8. The association also fitted his late lifestyle preferences, and it might have been a way to ridicule other high profile deifications, including Julius Caesar himself and its reflection upon his adoptive son Octavian. All other godlike symbolism stems only from his association with Cleopatra and Egyptian court tradition.

If the Antonii never found a true family *cognomen* that stuck with them, and the first born had invariably Marcus for a given name,[1] their contemporaries and historiography at large had to find ways to distinguish them, which is why Mark Antony's grandfather Marcus Antonius is commonly referred to as Marcus Antonius Orator (MA Orator hereafter).

MA Orator's two sons (Marcus and Gaius) both earned nicknames which they gladly would have done without. The older one was referred to as Creticus, for having suffered a tough defeat at the hands of the pirates, who backed the hostile King Mithridathes of Pontus, and who he was supposed to destroy in the waters of Crete. Giving him this name was a cruel mockery, as places or people names would be given to generals that had won a war and subjugated a nation. For example Emperor Trajan was called Dacicus and Particus when he beat the Dacians and the Parthians (modern day Rumanians and Iranians), and the Senate gave Emperor Claudius the name of Britannicus when Britannia was ably conquered and subdued.

Unfortunately for our man, "the Conqueror of Crete" did not carry the same panache, as everyone knew that he had to make a financial arrangement with the Cretese in order to take the remainder of his fleet back after being routed. Furthermore, translating literally from Latin, Creticus also can mean "man of clay" or "man of chalk", thus making the mockery double edged and even crueller.

The second born, Gaius, was called Hybrida (half-beast) behind his back, supposedly for the various atrocities that he had committed against the Greek population as he plundered the land during the Mithridatic war, when he served under Sulla as a cavalry commander. And, unluckily and maybe undeservedly for them, his two daughters, both called Antonia, found themselves referred to as Antoniae Hybridae – something that might have cooled off more than one suitor.

It is important that we resist the temptation to plunge directly into Mark Antony's life without considering the wider context around the two preceding generations of his family because, as we will see, his heritage of family allegiances and feuds played a fundamental role in the making of Antony's destiny.

So, let's take a step back to the year 99 BC, which marks the first (and only) consulship of MA Orator, grandfather of our protagonist Mark Antony.

Oratory was a big deal in ancient Rome and in the classic world at large. It was considered almost a prerogative of the upper classes, and especially cultivated in a certain intellectual *milieu*, notably the famous "Scipionic Circle", under the patronage of the prominent Scipio family, who had given Rome the conquerors of Carthage, and a tradition of leadership that had lasted for over a century.

MA Orator's rhetorical skills must have been of the highest grade. His style was that of the so called Asian school, which called for a more ornate and flamboyant delivery. At the other end of the spectrum was the so called Attic style, simple, concise, and unequivocal. It seems Julius Caesar, a powerful public speaker, was an attic speaker, which was akin to his writing style: logical, consequential, with a few sudden surges of energy and punch, but without ever getting carried away in emotional or otherwise spectacular speeches. The most famous public speaker of Roman antiquity, Marcus Tullius Cicero (Cicero), is associated with the *Rhodiensis* school, from the island of Rhodes, which was a happy compromise between the two, crisp and clear but with some changes of pace, inflammatory highs, and the introduction of more elaborate imaging. Considerations of style, however, did not get in the way of Cicero's appreciation of true excellence: his *De Oratore* is dedicated to Quintus Hortensius Hortalus (Hortensius), who was the most important representative of the Asian school at their time, and MA Orator is one of the protagonists of the essay, which follows the characteristic format of an imaginary dialogue between contemporary and non-contemporary characters.

MA Orator was not only an esteemed public speaker and admired member of Rome's cultural scene: his career led him to cover all the main Republican offices, from praetorship[2] all the way to consulship[3] and onwards to censorship.[4] He even marked some successes in naval warfare, as he fought the Mediterranean pirates. He must have fared better than his son Creticus later did, and obtained a victory of some scale, if the Senate awarded him the rare honour of a Naval Triumph. As far as more traditional campaigning is concerned, we know that he fought in the Social Wars, which, as we will see, pitted Rome to the other central Italian populations, which were seeking political status and recognition, as well as a role in Roman policymaking, in return for the human capital they had invested, as allies in Rome's foreign and domestic belligerent undertakings.

Mark Antony's illustrious grandfather reached the height of his political career in 99 BC when he was made Consul, the summit of the Roman *cursus honorum* or political and military career. The contingent political situation could hardly have been more difficult.

Without ever degenerating into full armed conflict, the class struggle was still very present in Rome, only based on census rather than patrician or plebeian birth. Traditionally the two opposing factions are referred to as *optimates* (the landowners and senatorial establishment), and *populares* (working class and the other), with a third intermediate social layer called the *equites* or equestrians (knights, so called because in the early days of the Republic upon military levy they were called to supply an armed horseman to the republican army, as opposed to a foot legionary).

The Rome of the late Republic could only be in a state of permanent turmoil. A City-State of almost one million souls, Rome had quickly expanded to control all of the Mediterranean basin, which the Romans had taken to calling "*mare nostrum*", our sea; the entire Spanish peninsula; southern France, which was referred to as Transalpine Gaul; the Tunisian tip of the Maghreb region; the Greek peninsula and the Balkans including Macedonia; most of modern day Turkey and the rest of the near east, including Syria all the way to the river Euphrates, which marked the border with the Parthian empire; and, of course, the whole of Italy. In addition, the reach of Rome's power covered most of the other regional independent states, including Egypt, which were de facto vassals of the Republic and created a natural buffer from the outside world.

Geographic expansion had outpaced the creation of infrastructure for effective governance. One of the weak points in the organization of the State was the absence of a professional and permanent body of civil servants, or bureaucrats if the reader prefers, vital to govern the overseas territories. When a Proconsul or Propraetor (Governor) was appointed to a provincial office, he would be followed by his own staff, who would support him for the short duration of the mandate. The mechanism, designed to prevent abuse, did not foster any stability or continuity, and in some cases had the reverse effect of stimulating near sighted policies.

As the military conquests had brought a huge inflow of wealth to the State, the Romans had never bothered to develop a proper fiscal policy and taxation system.

Roman citizens residing in Rome were largely exempt from taxes, while in the provinces the collection of tributes was auctioned out to independent professionals.

But other profound mutations were accentuating the mismatch between the existing institutions and the true condition of Roman society. The Rome of the early Republic had thrived on the concept of the citizen-farmer-soldier, where each and every individual was a true stakeholder in the State. Faced with a threat to the Republic, the citizen would leave his field and take up arms, to return to his property once his military duties were done. But when the scope and size of the conflicts escalated, General Gaius Marius (Marius) saw best to transform this tradition and enrol, on a permanent basis, legionaries that would be paid with cash during their service and with land at the end of their term. At the same time, the second century BC had seen the fast growth of a class of land owners who farmed the land and raised cattle and sheep on a totally different scale from the traditional family-sized enterprise, mainly with the use of the slave labour that abounded as a result of the many prisoners of war captured and brought back after one conflict or another. These two effects combined put huge pressure on traditional rural society, and many families started migrating to the city to constitute an underprivileged urban proletariat, constantly struggling to make a living in overcrowded slums, incurring substantial debt from ruthless and usury uncontrolled moneylenders, and well positioned as a reservoir for insurrectional or at least rioting hands, over the basics of land and debt. At the other end of the social spectrum, the landowners and the nobility thrived in this polarized society, and in time were able to consolidate power thanks to an elitist Senate and Tribunes of the plebs left toothless by conservative policies.

The bloodstains of the Gracchi brothers, populist leaders killed by their *optimates* opponents a few years apart from each other, during riots over the land distribution agenda, were still fresh. In the last decade of the second century BC a certain Thorius tried to introduce some form of real estate tax for the benefit of the urban masses, but the attempt fell through and the situation returned to where it had been two decades earlier. At this particular time, the agitator on duty on the side of the *populares* was an Appuleius Saturninus, who had a dubious sidekick named Glaucia. They enjoyed the backing of Marius, the populist general, who had a coarse style but an impressive military resume, and was at the end of his sixth consular mandate. The senatorial establishment and the *optimates* fielded Quintus Caecilius Metellus, a man of noble family origins and high standards. Metellus was politically outmanoeuvred and forced into exile, leaving Appuleius and Glaucia in charge. When it became clear that the second Consul elect, who was to be MA Orator's partner, was not going to be Glaucia, Appuleius armed a mob with clubs and knives and marched through town, to make the point that oratory was not the only means to move forward a political career.

They did indeed find a solution for the electoral rivalry: they sought out the other candidate, and clubbed him to death on the spot. It seems that public opinion forced Marius to react against his own political faction, given the blatancy of the illegal action. What happened next is a famous page of Roman history: after a brief siege and capture on the Capitol, rather than kill the rogues on the spot, Marius locked them in the courtyard of the Senate house. Exhausted by the constant fighting and intolerant of the prospect of more street combat, the populace took the matter into its own hands by climbing on the roof and hurling tiles onto the captives, until they were dead.

This was the situation in Rome when MA Orator was called to co-hold executive power as a Consul.[5] This is clearly a testament to his balance, wisdom, and moral strength. He received what a rugby man would call a hospital pass, and signed up for the job.

But the civil strife over land distribution was not the only source of instability with which Republican Rome had to contend. The various Italian populations which, over the decades, had helped Rome establish itself in Italy and in the Mediterranean, were increasingly vocal about their subordinate status under Roman rule, and were demanding full Roman citizenship, political rights, and more clout in Rome's political agenda in return for their past and present military allegiance. This soon led to a bloody war between the Italian League and the Romans, known as the Social War. During this period, the intestine struggle was not centre stage, but it was almost certainly an issue nonetheless. The *populares* leader, Marius, was fighting the Italian tribesmen, and then took sick for a while, while the *optimates* strongman Sulla was besieging the cities of Samnium, but the axe between the two was all but buried. And the career of MA Orator continued, this time as Censor. This was an extremely delicate role, in so much as it was the gatekeeper of the Senate in terms of extending or denying senatorial seats. Judging from the outcomes a few years later, we can only doubt that he took advantage of the position to make friends in the opposite political faction. The civil struggle was about to degenerate from city alley riots into fully-fledged war, with opposing Roman armies faced in pitched battles.

The catalyst for the outburst was the high profile ruler Mithridates VI, King of Ponthus, a small state in modern day northern Turkey. Mithridates was a decisive and ambitious man, but also cruel and ruthless, who was to become a nemesis for Rome, managing repeatedly to rise up after enduring tough defeats at the hands of the various Roman generals. He was a charismatic leader who was to inspire one of Mozart's first full scale operas.[6]

Mithridates seized the opportunity offered by the Social Wars in Italy and the resulting distraction in Rome to expand his domains in the Near East, and moved to gain control of Bythinia and Cappadocia, in today's north eastern Turkey, two kingdoms that were under Rome's sphere of influence. At the same time, he ordered the slaughter of all the Roman and Italian settlers in his domains. Estimates of the number of Italians hacked to pieces in just a few days range from 80,000 to 150,000.

Such acts could not be left unpunished by Rome. In 88 BC, Sulla, the strongman of the conservative wing, was made Consul for the first time. By the end of the Social Wars, his military prestige had equalled, if not surpassed, that of Marius. Logic and law alike dictated that he was the one to lead the inevitable Roman retaliation against the Mithridatic menace. But, following a consolidated pattern, the *popularis* Tribune Sulpicius staged anti-Sullan rioting and moved to strip him out of the eastern command, in favour of old Marius, who gladly took the bait.

This was too much for Sulla, who, in an unprecedented move, marched on Rome with his veteran legions still quartered in southern Italy, to reinforce his Consular authority against the *populares* mobsters. The first of the Sullan purges (also called proscriptions, from the lists of proscribed citizens that were posted in the Forum, so that Romans who were not impacted would not worry about the consequences) quickly followed, and political adversaries incurred the penalty reserved for traitors of Rome: they were dragged up the Gaemonian Stairs to be hurled to their deaths from the famous Tarpeian Rock. But when Sulla finally left Italy to begin his war operations in 87 BC, the Marians made their big comeback. Sulla was declared a public enemy, and the strongman Lucius Cornelius Cinna, from the same clan, seized full control of the Eternal City.

At that point, of course, the *optimates* leaders were running for shelter. Knowing the operating style of Marius and his lieutenants, there was little chance that they would have been invited to settle all their political differences in the course of a roundtable or a Senate debate. Many fled, including our MA Orator, but most were found and summarily executed by the Marian squads, their heads displayed at the *rostra*, the ramming heads of captured Carthaginian ships that adorned the speakers' platform in the Forum.

Now, if you are a leader of a political faction during a *coup* from the adverse side, and you are trying to keep a low profile in your hideout, a piece of advice: do not go overboard with room service in an attempt to relieve the stress. The whereabouts of the fleeing MA Orator were given away by an innkeeper, whose suspicions were raised by a special wine order from the incognito guest. When this information got back to Rome, Marius, in a blind rage, wanted there and then to make the journey and kill the man with his own bare hands, which must surely be an indication of how much weight MA Orator must have carried in the *optimates* ranks. Eventually, a group of assassins was dispatched for the task, but the victim, in a demonstration of his remarkable oratory skills, charmed the armed men with a long and eloquent speech, thereby distracting them from their primary responsibility for some time, hours even. The situation duly escalated and more pressing orders were issued; he was finally stabbed to death and decapitated, and his head was displayed alongside those of his party comrades.

The Antonii had paid their first dues to the Civil Wars that marked Roman history in the first century BC. At this point, Mark Antony had not yet been born, but the murder of the most prominent family member at the hands of assassins must have cast a long shadow over the upbringing of the Triumvir. Certainly, the tales of the murder related by family members, and the details of the displayed head in the Forum and of the decapitated body left to rot in the countryside must have deeply impressed the young Antony, who was to develop a quasi religious form of respect for the bodies of defeated enemies, no matter how much he had loathed them in their lifetimes. And MA Orator was not the only toll paid by his family: Lucius Julius Caesar, his maternal grandfather, and one of the Roman leaders in the Social Wars, had also fallen victim to the Marian-Cinnan proscription. The young Mark Antony had lost not one but two kin to political vendettas. Deep down inside, he must have felt that his family's account with Rome's politics had a large credit balance.

Orator's first born son, and Mark Antony's father, Marcus Antonius Creticus (Creticus) was probably 28 years old at the time of his father's death. He is traditionally associated with the villains and the inept of the late Roman Republic. We know how his military command against the Mediterranean pirates and their Cretese flankers ended. Adding further insult to injury, a shameful treaty, including substantial financial compensation, had to be signed in order to close the hostilities, and repatriate the remainder of his fleet safely.

There exists some important evidence that could suggest that his military ineptitude was coupled with avarice and avidity. The main source of this evidence is the trial documentation of a high profile corruption case brought against Gaius Verres, former Governor of Sicily. The young legal eagle Cicero was hired by the plaintiff, the exploited Sicilian provincials, to represent them against their dishonest Governor.

During those tumultuous days, fortunes were easily accumulated by those predatory types that were fast to jump on the winners' bandwagon, and whose absence of scruples allowed them to scavenge on the misfortunes of those that were on the wrong side or had fallen in disgrace.

Verres was yet another ruthless opportunist who rode on the fortunes of Sulla to establish his career and personal wealth. By the time of the events, his resume was already thick with unpunished frauds, kept in the dark through bribery. In 73 he was made Governor of the prosperous province of Sicily, an office that by law he should have held for one year.

But when the time for him to step down came, southern Italy was being ravaged by the Slave War, which saw the rebel Thracian (Bulgarian) gladiator Spartacus roam around Italy with an army of fugitive slaves for two years. Before Marcus Crassus finally cornered him in the south of the peninsula and destroyed them, he and his runaway slaves inflicted severe losses on the Roman legions and humiliated more than one Consul and General.

At the same time, to further complicate the situation, the exploits of the renegade Marian general Sertorius, in Spain, were also sharing the limelight. So, Verres decided to take advantage of the ensuing distraction to strengthen his grip on the island and milk it as much as he could. The shortage of available magistrates to replace him, and a distracted Senate, helped him elude the system of checks that ensured the frequent replacement of the Governor. And in terms of the results achieved, it seems he did a remarkably good job, and his exploitation of the provincials became infamous.

The key concept of a province in the Roman world was that the land was the property of the Roman Republic, who gave it in usufruct to the provincial inhabitants in return for tributes. Provincial administration was an extremely decentralized affair, where the discretion of the Governor went all the way to power of life and death over the population with limited right to appeal. The loose control and the large amount of discretion given in decision making were the reasons why the Governor and his aides, the provincial Praetors, were rotated so frequently.

The collection of tributes, especially on grains, was subcontracted – or even better, auctioned – to the ill-reputed order of the Publicans, of equestrian census, who, unlike the senatorial nobility, were not embarrassed to soil their hands with money. The most famous representative of this order is probably Saint Matthew the Evangelist, who upon meeting Jesus gave up the predatory profession, always qualified in the Gospels with the adjectives "sinful", "heathen", and the like, and embraced his new spiritual life.

Since he has been mentioned twice already, it is time to introduce the most important character of Cicero (chick pea, or wart). Cicero was a new man, a *homus novu*s (the Roman reference to someone from the provinces), and a stranger to the political establishment. He had come to Rome from Arpinium, a rural area half way between Rome and Naples, the same town that gave us Gaius Marius, of whom he was a very distant relative. His family, of equestrian census and Volscian tribal heritage, was part of the affluent rural gentry that would rarely emerge in national politics by embarking in the *cursus honorum*, but that would be happy to live sandwiched between the Roman nobility and the urban masses. The Ciceros were quite affluent, thanks to a successful laundry business, and owned a house in Rome, a real house, as opposed to an apartment in one of those ugly and unsanitary blocks called *insulae* (islands) where the commoners lived. But they had not sufficiently penetrated the right Roman circles to guarantee easy access to Rome's finest schools for the young Marcus Tullius, despite his superior intellect. His father Marcus started pulling on his network of patrons and sponsors (i.e. the clientships to which he belonged) to secure top notch schooling for the young prodigy student. Among his most useful contacts were the Antonii, as Cicero's great-uncle had served under MA

Orator in his Pirate War. He was also pulling on the clientele relationships, like the Crassus and Scaurus households, so that the young Cicero was able, as a teenager, to witness the most important episodes of Roman politics from a good observation point. Still a teenager, Cicero's father had served under Pompey Magnus' father in the Social Wars. He and his kin had struggled under Cinna because of their association with the Antonii and others, and his uncle had been barbarically tortured and killed under Sulla by a young nobleman called Catilina. Cicero's calling was with the *optimates* party, but throughout his life, with a few exceptions, he remained predominantly an outside supporter, an ideologist and opinion leader, but was reluctant to get into the thick of the action. It was during those eventful years that he retreated between his books and his studies, and perfecting his oratory skills. He emerged from his solitary confinement when the Sullan proscriptions were over, and the conservative reforms, aimed at reducing the power of the Tribunes of the plebs and harnessing the Provincial Governors with the aim of air-tightening the central authority of the Senate, were being carried out. He approved of the Sullan reforms, and only distanced himself from the brutal means that the gangly and albino dictator had used to enforce them. He embarked on his career as a lawyer, and then formally engaged in the *cursus honorum*, obtaining a *quaestorship* in Sicily for the year 75 BC, just prior to Verres. He behaved with great dedication and honesty, thereby securing the friendship of the Sicilians, but at the same time he must have become familiar with all the traditional corrupt ways of provincial administration.

The frequent combination of dishonest Governors and rapacious Publicans invariably had tough consequences for the provincials. If we take at face value the accusations made by the 36-year-old lawyer Cicero at the trial against the dishonest Governor, the excesses perpetrated by Verres and his entourage dwarf every Hollywood characterization of tyranny and depravation ever seen.

So powerful was the impact of the first of the two speeches, and so impressive and convincing were the witnesses brought, that the second and third speeches did not need to be delivered, as Verres fled in self-imposed exile before the sentencing was even pronounced. But now that he had centre stage and upper hand on such a high profile trial, Cicero was not going to let go so easily, and still went ahead and published a 500-page document containing the rest of his accusations. The defence attorney was none other than the superstar lawyer Hortensius, so that a victory counted for triple in terms of publicity. A slam dunk victory against one of the legal eagles in town: the man from Arpinium was not going to let go of the limelight easily.

Hortensius scored an own goal when he quoted Creticus as a benchmark for Verres. Judging by the reaction, he must have said something to the effect that whatever Verres did, Creticus had done it before, and therefore it fell within acceptable common practice. It was easy for Cicero to ridicule the move, and expose Creticus' own wrongdoing in predatory and illicit taxation practices, albeit on a smaller scale than those of Verres.

How did the scam work? The commodity markets in Rome's days were not very efficient, causing violent seasonal price fluctuations of the wheat and other cereals. Assessing taxes in the low season, when prices were sky high, as opposed to after the harvest, made a huge difference.

The complex tax legislation peculiar to Sicily provided fertile ground for the dishonest officials and conniving tax collectors to systematically defraud the farmers. To the traditional *decuma* or 10% levy, one had to add a 6% surcharge, and a hefty transportation charge. The *decuma* could be collected in cash rather than in nature, so that a discretionary price adjustment could be compounded to the tax, an adjustment that would always go against the producer and his township. On top of that, Rome, the Governor (for his own account) and other privileged categories of magistrates, could buy the grains at regulated prices. If, on the Governor's discretion, it was found that the quality of the grains was not up to standard, a reimbursement might have been made, and the amount could exceed the market price of the grain to indemnify the buyer for the prejudice suffered. Needless to say, the measures used to enforce the above were often brutal, as one can read in the reports from the witnesses in the Verres trial. The combined tax pressure at that period has been estimated at 75% of the value of the production, and had the effect of driving the farmers off the land and creating the basis for the phenomenon of the *latifondum*,[7] which was to plague Sicily for the following two millennia and create the backdrop for the birth of the Mafia organization.

This was the game Creticus was probably playing, and Verres picked up on it in a big way.

The result of all this was that the Antonii's dirtiest secrets were exposed in the legal revelations of the year, only a few months after Creticus passed away, possibly having committed suicide and certainly impoverished, in a self imposed exile, of which we do not know the exact circumstances. For the Antonii, this was really rubbing it in needlessly, especially since the trial had already been won. Mark Antony's account with Cicero was officially open, and the tally was to be delivered during the proscriptions in 42 BC, when Antony, Octavian, and Lepidus systematically eliminated all their political opponents. Funnily enough, the 70-year-old Verres was to fall victim to the same proscriptions, not so much because the old crook represented a political threat to the Second Triumvirate, but because the booty he had amassed over the years was too conspicuous to go unnoticed, and too appetizing at a time when the war had exhausted all financial resources. It seems that he took it like a man and died with dignity, possibly comforted by the news that Cicero had met his fate days earlier.

It is also interesting to put Cicero's motives in perspective, and to refrain from jumping to the conclusion that the lawyer from Arpinium was on a humanitarian mission or was some kind of *El Zorro* protecting the Sicilian farmers from exploitation. Cicero was a lawyer, and a politician on the fast track. Less than a year later, he successfully defended a certain Marcus Fronteius, and later the famous Proconsul[8] Aulus Gabinius against the exact same charges as Verres, for crimes perpetrated in the Gallic and Syrian provinces. Both men were Pompey's protégés, the former a leader of the *equites* class, the latter a first rank General. Many of his contemporaries must have looked on his legal exploits with a very cynical eye, and Mark Antony must have been one of them.

Surprisingly enough, Antony's first biographer Plutarch makes no comment on the above in Antony's biography. In fact, while he deals with MA Orator in a quite cursory manner, his paragraph on Creticus is full of praise for his kindness and generosity, but makes no mention of his greed and predatory behaviour. The presentation of the character is enriched by an anecdote, whereby he tricked his reluctant wife into donating a precious silver bowl to a needy friend, and then had to face the consequences. Now, Plutarch is not at all lenient with Antony. So it is unclear why he would omit the juicy details of the embezzlement charges against his father, his partnership with a corrupt Governor, or his goofiness as a military leader, and hand him over to posterity as a Good Samaritan. On the contrary, the profiling of Creticus is used by Plutarch as a leader to introduce Antony's own generosity, which he highlights upfront in the biography, identifying it as one of his key traits. Antony wanted to reward a friend by means of a generous payment of 250,000 dinarii, and his administrator, in an attempt to dissuade him from making the large disbursement, put the sum on display in coin. Antony sized it up and, unimpressed with what he saw, ordered the sum to be doubled. We will have to try to match these tributes from Plutarch with all the charges of embezzlement that his enemies brought against him in 44 BC after Caesar's death.

Back to the family of the Antonii, and another surprise for the reader expecting consistency and continuity when choosing their allies was the choice of Creticus' wife and future mother of Antony: Julia Antonia was a first cousin of Gaius Julius Caesar, soon to become a rising star in Rome's political firmament. This would not be surprising per se, if it wasn't for the strong allegiance of the Julii to the Marian faction.[9] Marius had married Julia Caesaris, who was Julius Caesar's aunt. When Sulla seized power again in 82 BC, and the Second Sullan proscription began, young Caesar had to escape from Rome and hide in the countryside before obtaining a pardon and returning to the city. When his mother died, Caesar defied public opinion by displaying Marius' armour in the funeral procession. Some say that Marius' entry onto the political scene was made possible by his marriage into the powerful – and patrician – Julii clan.

Julia was probably born in 104 BC, so the marriage with Creticus must have taken place in the early part of the eighth decade BC, contextually with the assassination of MA Orator by the Marian hit men.

Whatever the motives of this marriage, which linked a Sullan to a Marian clan in such a tough period, it made Mark Antony a nephew of Julius Caesar. Interestingly enough, when forty years later Antony married Octavia, sister of Octavian and daughter of Atia, a Julii on her mother's side, he closed a family tree loop and rejoined his mother's lineage.

We have seen how Creticus did not survive his military failure for very long. Three years after his humiliating defeat, in 71 BC, and aged only 44, he died in his self imposed retirement.

The 33-year-old wife made another choice that was to have an impact on her twelve-year-old son Mark, and remarried another controversial character called Publius Cornelius Lentulus Sura (Sura). It seems that Julia did not choose a beacon of integrity for a second husband and a stepfather for Antony, although he was one of the many offspring of the super-prestigious *gens* Cornelia, who had given Rome so many first rank leaders, some of which we have already met in the few preceding pages.

Sura had already been in trouble in his career. The agnomen Sura (leg) was attributed to him when, upon being accused of squandering public money while serving as a *questor*,[10] he bared and showed his leg in a gesture common to children exculpating themselves from committing a fault while playing ball. Other than for the good giggle that the Romans must have gotten out of it, and the *agnomen* that quickly ensued, the gesture did not help much, and he lost his job. But by 71 BC his career was back on track, albeit in a more junior role, and following his marriage with Julia he was made a senator. Evidently, Rome allowed wrongdoings to be sponged and officials to be given a second chance.

Ambitious Sura was not content with that. He had proclaimed to his inner circle of friends that, according to prophecy, his destiny was to be the third Cornelius to be the sole ruler of Rome – after Cornelius Cinna in 84–83 and Cornelius Sulla from 82 until the time of his death. So, in 63–62 BC we find him among the ring leaders of the famous Catilina conspiracy.

Catilina was another prototype of a nobleman turned revolutionary. A lot has been written about his motives in preparing a coup, whether he was led by a thirst for power or by a desire to defend the common good from the inept senatorial class. The fact is, yet again, his agenda was to jump on the old bandwagon of land distribution, debt forgiveness, and the dismantling of all the changes Sulla had made against the functioning of the Republican institutions once he had regained power in 82 BC. His choice of fellow conspirators, who could never have been described as a bunch of pure and uninterested souls, Sura first and foremost, suggests he was inspired by more selfish motives. The two main sources about Catilina and his attempted coup are the historian Sallust and, of course, Cicero himself. The consensus about him is that he was a bright yet ruthless man. He had blood on his hands from the proscription that Sulla had launched against the Marians, where the "factional cleansing" carried out had spiralled out of control, and most likely beyond Sulla's original design and wishes. Other ruthless men like Crassus, the Triumvir to be, went on to get rich trading in the proscribed men's estates. Famous is the remark of the rich man reading his name on the list of the newly declared enemies of the State:

"By Jove, my villa in Tusculum has sentenced me to death!"

But Catilina's wildness went way beyond greed: he had seduced one of the Vestal Virgins, the High Priestesses that watched the Sacred Fire of Vesta, which was a heinous crime in Rome, and apparently had killed his own son, either because he voiced his disapproval of his father's actions, or, as Sallust says, because his most recent mistress would not live under the same roof as his progeny.

As for Sura, other accusations made against him ranged from also seducing a Vestal Virgin, an offence which carried the death penalty for the unfortunate Priestess by being buried alive, to other scandalous behaviours with the young men of his entourage that formed an unofficial body guard, and were his partners in his nocturnal adventures and crimes.

In 63 BC Catilina formed a dangerous pair with Gaius Antonius Hybrida (uncle of Mark Antony) whom we have already met: the man that was perhaps equally ruthless but had a lot less drive, direction, and intellectual means. During the consular elections, Cicero managed to make a deal with Hybrida, who broke his alliance with Catilina. They subsequently ran for office together, and then Cicero confined Hybrida to a subordinate role in exchange for the promise of obtaining for him a Praetorship down the line. The deal worked out, and Catilina was left alone, beaten and enraged. To add insult to injury, the two prominent politicians Julius Caesar and Marcus Crassus (Crassus), who were his financial backers behind the scenes, began to gradually withdraw their support when they saw that his star was fading, and they could bet their money on other horses.

A second failure to be elected Consul for 62 BC exacerbated Catilina's frustration and prompted him to step up his game, causing his rapid descent into the realm of illegality. Rumours of the conspiracy brewing had already leaked. The ever present Cicero had taken the lead in denouncing the plot in front of the Senate.

"Quo usque tandem abutere, Catilina, patientia nostra?"

"Until when, o Catilina, you will abuse of our patience? Don't you realize that we all know what you are preparing?" The opening of the *Catilinariae*, the series of vehement speeches Cicero delivered to expose the conspirators, has become proverbial over the centuries, the first three words still used in modern day Rome when someone is testing the other's patience with a poorly hidden agenda.

Catilina had already fled when formal proof of the upcoming putsch was given by some turncoat Gallic conspirators, who got cold feet at the last minute and gave up the others. But Sura and friends were still at hand, ready to execute a plan that included the mass slaughter of senators at the hands of a 400 strong militia, which had been prepared and was awaiting orders. The conspiracy chiefs were apprehended and a heated debate followed in the Senate house between Caesar, pushing for their imprisonment, and the hardliners Cicero and Marcus Porcius Cato the Younger (Cato), who favoured the death penalty. In a borderline illegal move, Cicero pushed the Senate to vote an extraordinary measure or *consultus ultimus*, and put the six chief conspirators to death. They were immediately taken to the sinister *Tullianus* prison, a short walk away from the Forum, and strangled with the *laqueum,* the small piece of rope used – very rarely – for quick and low profile executions. Cicero announced the deed to the Senate with the lapidary comment: "Vixerunt", "They lived".

We know that Antony was shocked by this execution, and he put this one on the Cicero account, together with the Creticus story. Antony later claimed that Cicero would not return Sura's corpse to the family until his mother had gone directly to beg Cicero's own mother. The list of grudges between Antony and Cicero was building up.

As for Catilina, he wouldn't go down without one last fight, and ran to Tuscany where his army was on stand-by. It is not without surprise that we discover, leading the troops sent to face him, none other than Hybrida. But on the morning of the battle, Hybrida pretended to be sick, and left the command to his deputy, who easily defeated the insurrectional forces. Some[11] found this diplomatic move suspicious. What if Hybrida was in cahoots with the Catiline conspiracy from the beginning, and now just trying to keep his options open for all battle outcomes? If this was true, and he was playing a double game, he did so remarkably well: a few minutes after the battle was over, he rushed to decapitate the fallen Catilina's body, and deliver the severed head to the Senate. Mark Antony, and his family in general, at this time must have been in quite an embarrassing spot, as his stepfather was on the side of the conspirators, and his uncle at the head of the Republican troops, albeit rumoured to be a fifth columnist.

Let's now proceed to sum up the main events of the last twenty years in the eyes of the 23-year-old Mark Antony. The shadows of the family pride MA Orator, and of the maternal grandfather Lucius, assassinated by the Marian squads, were still present in the ancestral home. His father, who he probably considered – rightly or wrongly – to be a noble and disinterested person, had been impeached, humiliated, and forced to hide from the public only to meet with death. This would quite probably have had, in accordance with what we learn from Cicero in the Second Philippic, some severe financial consequences for the Antonii. The paternal uncle's image had been tainted as part of some of the less glorious military pages in the history of Rome. Swamped in debt, and compromised by dubious revolutionaries like Catilina and his men, Hybrida had later chosen to grasp at another chance of success by consorting with the devil, in the person of Marcus Tullius Cicero. His stepfather Sura had been executed without trial in the midst of a controversial revolutionary action. And this incident must have made an impression on him, since it seems he and Sura had somehow bonded, and that Antony regarded him highly.

Also Hybrida, like Sura, had been expelled from the Senate and had to start his career all over from much lower offices. Whatever the reasons, right or wrong, that were at the root of this, young Mark Antony concluded that his family members had been systematically prosecuted, unjustly accused, and frustrated in their careers and lives by a corrupt system and group of people that manipulated the rules of the Republic. It does not necessarily follow that Antony grew fond of Hybrida on a personal level, but the general point remains.

It is logical now to conclude that, at this point, his value system must have taken a knock, and he, like many Romans of his generation, must have struggled to retain his faith in the institutions of Rome. He almost certainly began to develop a cynical view of the world, and an even more cynical view of Rome's ruling class and professional politicians.

His family had historical Sullan loyalties, and he came from a core Republican tradition, but had connected with the Julii of Caius Julius Caesar, in which Sulla had seen many Marii hidden, and was considered a possible Catilina sympathizer. While it is virtually impossible to imagine what would have been on the young Mark Antony's good and bad list, we can be sure of one thing: the grudge he held against Marcus Tullius Cicero, whose literary output and political speeches had already affected three family members, was already growing strong.

Around 63 BC, at the time when Cicero and Hybrida were co-operating, Roman public opinion was coming to terms with the Sullan purges, and was trying to clear its conscience of the excesses perpetrated during that time, not unlike many European countries after World War II. Under the severe scrutiny of Cato, the integrist stoic Quaestor, Rome began to organize the trials of those that had taken advantage of the situation for personal enrichment. The young magistrate Gaius Julius Caesar found himself presiding over some of them.

Cato was to become one of the nemeses of Caesar during the later stages of the civil strife, but in a different way from the senatorial nobility, the "boni viri", or good men, as Cicero would refer to them. He was the grandson of Cato the Elder, the Censor, the restless instigator of the destruction of Carthage at the end of the Punic wars. His thoughts and actions were fully in accordance with the Republican tradition, but also with the true principles of stoicism in the almost religious sense of the State and not dictated by opportunism.

Despite the continuing instability, Rome's prosperity grew during those years thanks to the substantial revenues derived from the conquests in Asia carried out by military superstars Lucullus and Pompey Magnus (the Great). To a large extent, all Pompey had to do was to finish up what Lucullus had already accomplished, with a much greater deployment of resources at his disposal, which he had secured thanks to his leverage over the Senate.

In September 61 BC, when he celebrated his Asian and Spanish triumphs, Pompey Magnus, one of the main architects of the Republican expansion in the Mediterranean, could boast to having subdued over 12 million people, and could parade in the streets of Rome with over 300 sovereigns, princes, and high dignitaries of the submitted nations. In reality Pompey had returned from his campaigns in December 62 BC, shortly after the Catiline coup, and at the same time as the Bona Dea affair which will be described shortly. Clearly, being at the apex of his successes, Pompey was a leading voice in the optimates field. He wanted to consolidate his power by cementing his grip over the military through large land grants, and by piloting the law making on the annexation of the new Asian provinces.

But it would be wrong to assume that the *optimates* were a cohesive conservative gathering, sworn to a party political agenda, as nothing could be further from the truth. Cicero, the new man, obsessed with public praise and recognition, was constantly trying to increase his personal prestige, while the members of the traditional aristocracy were not acknowledging his merits. The rigorous Cato and the bitter Lucullus, the General that before Pompey Magnus had done most of the dirty work in the east, were strongly opposing the Pompeian agenda, as did the other senior leader Metellus Celer. All elections were polluted by bribery of unknown scale, mainly on the Pompeian side, to keep the counterparts at bay, and intimidation became part of the normal course of politics. Personal enmities and other motives determined political agendas. In the end, Pompey's worthy endeavours were being stalemated by their aristocratic opponents, and by the same token other prominent personalities were feeling constrained by the few that pulled the levers of the Senate's meetings. First and foremost, Crassus, who had become the main sponsor of the wealthy equestrian class, and the great puppeteer behind the main corporations of tax collectors, was seeing his interests and plans clash with the establishment as defined. He was coming to realize that many of the new provinces could not keep pace with the expectations on revenue streams, and the Publicans, or professional tax collectors, had their commitments with the State treasury at risk, and were very strongly in favour of renegotiating the arrangements made, thus provoking the vehement reaction of the inflexible Cato.

But Pompey and Crassus were not the only powerful men that had come in the line of fire of Cato and the conservative wing of the Senate: after successful campaigning in Spain, in the summer of 60 BC Gaius Julius Caesar was returning home expecting a well deserved triumph, which would open the way to a Consulship for this unpredictable but charismatic *populares* leader. Again, Cato interfered to try to impede this, his motivation being mostly personal, such as his dislike for Caesar's mannerisms and ambition, or his romantic involvement with his half sister Servilia, the mother of Marcus Brutus.

But it was to no avail. The political momentum of the 40-year-old Caesar was such that he was elected to Consul in the year 59 BC with a landslide victory. All the infuriated Cato could do was manoeuvre to have his relative Bibulus appointed as second Consul, only to be put out to pasture and relegated to a role of figurehead, in the year that went down in the annals as the Consulship of Julius *and* Caesar.

But this was not all. The dictator-to-be Caesar was relentlessly moving to broaden his support base as much as possible in order to deliver all the reforms he had planned, and further consolidate the virtuous circle of his successes. It was then that the interests of the left-wing reformist Caesar, of the superstar General Pompey, and of the plutocrat businessman Crassus, were pooled to form that alliance that went from secretive to informal, but which was never formally ratified in any way, that became known as the First Triumvirate. For seven years, the First Triumvirate had positioned itself as a power front which overwhelmed the senatorial aristocracy, and de facto controlled the Roman political scene. All that Cato obtained through his interference and obstruction tactics was to cement this alliance of leaders, which otherwise would not have been possible, thus reuniting a broad popular electoral base, the military, and the wealthy middle class. All the previous differences, including the affairs that the womanizer Caesar had had with the wives of both the other Triumvirs were put aside, and all other motives sacrificed to the commonly agreed goals. And the first of the goals on which the trio got to work was the enactment of an agrarian law that would have solved Pompey's riddle of the veterans' settlements, and regulated the difficult situation of the Italian countryside as described above.

As expected, Cato, representing the interests of the landowners, tried forcefully to obstruct the legislative path, and to boycott the Senate's proceedings. He tried to drag the discussion and to delay a vote that would have certainly been favourable thanks to the preparatory work that the triumvirs had carried out. The impatient Caesar was quickly exasperated by the obstructionism, and had Cato taken to jail. Later he tried to pre-empt the Senate's discussion, and went directly with his law project in front of a popular assembly held in the Forum. Again, Cato and the other Consul Bibulus tried to sabotage the proceedings, but at this point Pompey and Crassus weighed in with the help of a good number of muscle men who were conveniently patrolling the meeting area. Cato and Bibulus had to leave the scene in a humiliating retreat.

From then on, the road was downhill for the three men, and Caesar was able to introduce an impressive amount of innovative legislation that spanned from tax collection rules (to the joy of his ally Crassus) to the foundation of new colonies for the resettlement of the most destitute families of the urban plebs, to the rules governing provincial governorships, to – interestingly for future repercussions – the support, in exchange for money, for King Ptolemy XII's claim to the Egyptian throne, always unsecure because of the ongoing domestic struggle.

And he also got to prepare his following career move, obtaining a five year command, that was to be renewed, of a region including the whole Illyricum – the northern Balkans – and Cisalpine Gaul – i.e. the *Gallia Togata*, where the Gauls were heavily Romanized and wore the Roman dress called *toga*, which today corresponds to northern Italy – and later also taking in Transalpine Gaul after the designated Proconsul died.

This is the political scene at the time when the young Mark Antony made his formal entrance into Rome's elite circles. Certainly the errors of his father and his uncle represented a millstone around his neck in his early career steps, but at least his family connections and noble birth guaranteed him invitations to the right dinner parties. The first political heavyweight he befriended, and that had a strong direct influence on him, was Publius Scribonius Curio (Curio), a left-wing aristocrat and intellectual, only a few years his senior but already a quite prominent figure.

Curio was to become an intellectual of renown, and an opinion leader in the *populares* ranks. Some think that years later he was instrumental in convincing Caesar to pass the Rubicon and march against Pompey and the Senate, for which Dante Alighieri finds him a place in his *Inferno* amongst the fomenters of discord, with his tongue conveniently cut off to prevent him from doing it again.

"Con la lingua tagliata nella strozza / Curio, c'ha dir fu così ardito!"[12]

"With the tongue cut in the throat / Curio, who was so daring in his speech." But young Curio's influence on Antony in the mid-sixties was of a totally different level, and rather than Dante's *Inferno*, we must look for parallelism with Collodi's *Pinocchio* and his naughty friend Lucignolo: Curio led him into a prolonged period of orgiastic indulgence in wine, women and song, resulting in the accumulation of debt for the staggering sum of six million sesterces – one and a half times the personal net worth that was necessary to gain access to the senatorial rank in Rome's society. But more importantly Curio was at the time one of the very few outspoken critics of the Triumvirate; he denounced its exaggerated weight in public life. Many, of course, disapproved of the daily display of omnipotence in law-making, but nobody spoke up openly for fear of retaliation. The opposition's only recourse was to unofficial invective and libel. Cicero himself was lying quite low, and restricted himself to a few comments in letters to his friend Atticus, possibly because he could still reasonably hope to straddle between the Triumvirs and the aristocrats to obtain favour and office with whoever prevailed in the end. His indecisiveness could hardly be mistaken for balance. As a landowner, he disliked the Agrarian reform promulgated by Caesar. He privately professed appreciation for the few, like Curio, who stood up against the Triumvirs, but in public he praised Pompey and declared his allegiance to him. But at the same time he strived to gain full acceptance, and the recognition and praise that came with it, in the aristocratic circles of the Senate where Cato and his chums treated him with disdain.

Carried away by the impetus of the second Philippic as he spoke against Antony in late 44 BC, Cicero accuses him of having been involved in a homosexual relationship with Curio, even going so far as to add saucy details, such as the young Antony climbing up to Curio's balcony driven by lust, only to be booted out by Curio's angered father. Out of context, it is quite odd to see these facts exposed sixteen years later: at the time, there was a certain appreciation for Curio's political stance, yet no criticism whatsoever of his morality. It is most likely that these allegations are an expression of Cicero's pent-up anger against the Triumvir rather than based in hard facts. Such allegations were never again levelled at Antony during his lifetime; in fact there was never even any suspicion of such conduct. The same cannot be said of many other prominent Romans.

Homosexuality in the classical world was not a taboo subject between certain bounds which defined what was acceptable and what was not.[13]

In Greece, it was customary that an older man (the *erastes*) who, as a mentor, took a youth (the *eroumenos*) under his wing, obtained sexual favours in return for his guidance in life. The expression "pederasty" comes from the merger of the two Greek words *paidion* (child), and *erastes* above. What attracted criticism and was considered against nature was if these relationships were to continue after the boy turned pubescent and started growing bodily hair. But until then, it was fair game, and the practice was certainly not discouraged. Those that continued to engage in passive homosexual intercourse would be relegated in the underworld of the *pornoi*, or male prostitutes.

As for Rome, from the early days, homosexuality was not defined by intercourse between individuals of the same sex, but by holding the passive role in the act. Sodomizing a slave or a war prisoner was totally acceptable throughout most of Rome's history and did not carry any stigma for the active player, who was merely asserting his manhood over a lesser individual, but being the passive actor in a homosexual sex act was seriously frowned upon. It is difficult to see a man of Antony's integrity and arrogance acquiesce to the desires of a man from his midst, knowing that the inevitable rumours would have seriously impaired his chances of success or, at the very least, attracted some ridicule. So it is a lot more plausible to infer from Plutarch's words that the two were organizing traditional orgies and dancing the nights away, rather than to uncritically accept that two machos were deliberately jeopardizing their public image to satisfy an improbable sexual desire. If he had had homosexual inclinations, he could have easily satisfied them in more discreet ways.

At any rate, the accusation of homosexuality from Cicero never stuck, and was never confirmed or repeated by other sources, a sign that the rumours must have been unsubstantiated, as this kind of gossip found fertile ground in Rome's society, not to mention mural graffiti. For example, the same gossip stuck perfectly on Octavian, Cicero's *protégé* of the hour at the time of the Philippics. When Antony, in his later propaganda efforts, accused him of having obtained his adoption by conceding Caesar sexual favours, he must have found ample credit, and the confirmation of this by the always well-informed Suetonius established the fact as a given. The latter historian also vouched for the rumours which circulated about the future Emperor lying with the General and Consul Aulus Hirtius in exchange for the sum of 250,000 dinarii, and that he would soften the hair on his adolescent legs with hot walnut shells in order to make the contact more pleasant. The Romans thrived on such salacious gossip, which spread like brushfire. Suetonius also reports another anecdote which relates how one day, an actor in the theatre made a *double-entendre* joke about someone's homosexuality, and the crowd turned immediately towards Octavian, by that time called Caesar Augustus, and applauded as if the actor had, without any shadow of a doubt, targeted him with his line.

Nevertheless, the situation for Antony must have been quite awkward. He had closely befriended the only person in Rome that was daring enough to openly challenge the almighty Triumvirs, one of which was his maternal uncle.

And Curio's position became even more difficult with the surfacing of the mysterious Vettius affair. This shady character, Vettius, had publicly accused Bibulus of plotting to kill Caesar and Pompey, in a conspiracy that involved, among other nobles, the same Curio and the young Marcus Brutus, nephew of Cato and son of the beautiful Servilia, the best known of Caesar's lovers. There was more than one hearing for the Vettius accusations, and his version of the story kept evolving. In the end, he was held for further questioning, but was found dead the next morning in the room where he had been locked, with strangulation marks around his throat. The truth on the death of the devious denouncer and on the conspiracy was never established, with some suspecting Caesar to be the hidden orchestrator, and others pointing at the Consul's foes, maybe even at the ruthless Tribune Clodius, whom we shall shortly meet. But, whatever had really happened behind the scenes, the events are symptomatic of the fact that the tension had escalated and that the young Antony was socializing with very compromising and potentially dangerous people.

During this period, Mark Antony was probably already having a relationship with a certain Fadia, the daughter of a freedman of Middle Eastern origins, a Quintus Fadius Gallus. This relationship would also be criticized by Cicero, as usual, in the Philippics and other writings. Cicero even says the two got married. He alleged that the marriage was one of convenience to pay off the huge debt incurred while partying with Curio, and Cicero even goes as far as saying that more than one offspring resulted from this union. By now, we have learned to take some of Cicero's gossiping with a grain of salt. The marriage with the daughter of a freedman would have been unacceptable for a Roman upper-class man, no matter in what contempt he held the ways of the establishment and the crumbling values of the society.

We don't know the precise date of his first real marriage, which he contracted with one of the Antioniae Hybridae sisters, his first cousin. While this was not unusual in Rome, it is puzzling that he gave up the opportunity to make a marriage that would have helped him further his career, unless he and Julia were betting on the fortunes of Hybrida, who had some decent spells in his career in spite of his many flaws, and made it as far as Consulate and a provincial command. It is fair to assume that the marriage must have taken place before 60 BC, when Hybrida was impeached and exiled. In any case, Antonia's character does not play any role in his history, until the day Antony repudiates her, on an unfounded suspicion of infidelity, to make room for more important players.

Thanks to Curio, Antony could add another first rank political figure to his address book, in the colourful character of Publius Clodius Pulcher (Clodius). Only a few pages into this work, Clodius is already the n-th profile of aristocrat-turned-left-wing agitator to devote himself to the shakeout of the traditional institutions and the rebalancing of power from the senatorial elite to forms of more direct democracy, and, in particular, the matter of redistribution of wealth that had been at the centre of Rome's political arena since the end of the Punic wars. For all the instability they created, it must be said that these demagogues were all extremely amusing. None of them had the stamina to go the full length and drive institutional reform on a long term basis, but the pattern they followed is indicative of the profound crisis of Roman society in that period.

The difference between Clodius and his many fellow demagogues is that Clodius, throughout his career, and especially during his tribunate in the early fifties, was a true agent of change and led far-reaching legislative reforms that were to grant him huge popularity and personal success.

His early career though was marked by spectacular bravado in what was known as the Bona Dea affair which entailed significant personal risk but which left us in no doubt as to where his political agenda was heading. In December 62 BC, while serving as a Quaestor,[14] in the course of the religious festivities of the Bona Dea, whose celebrations were solely reserved for women and clergy, he sneaked into Julius Caesar's house, where the religious functions were being officiated, disguised as a woman. Later, it was commonly held that the real purpose behind this act was to meet Caesar's wife Pompeia, with whom supposedly he had an affair. But many see the bravado not as the act of a daring lover, but as a pretext to provoke and defy the senatorial order and his chief representative Cicero, by breaking the rules of Roman society and getting away with it.

As charges for his scandalous and blasphemous behaviour were brought and the trial prepared, Clodius' followers, led by Curio, staged riots and protests in the city. Cicero, who had formerly been his ally since receiving backing from him two years earlier during the Catilina conspiracy, turned against him and volunteered as a witness for the prosecution. But eventually, possibly with Caesar's and Crassus' support in the form of bribes and political pressure, Clodius was acquitted, and his acquittal, in spite of the flagrance of his crime, dealt a blow to the great momentum that Cicero was enjoying on Rome's political scene. The bitter lawyer commented to his friends that the cause had been lost because the judges were short of cash.

In any case, if ancient Rome had had tabloids, Clodius would have been a regular feature. He was rumoured to have had an ongoing incestuous affair with his beautiful sister Clodia, who was to become the object of passion of the famous poet Catullus, and was to inspire him for his sonnets of hopeless love, but also of rage and insult, under the poetic name of Lesbia. The frustrated Catullus challenges her morality in several passages in his sonnets, and somehow corroborates the gossip, or at least confirms that the scandalous allegations must have been public knowledge.

The next major step for the popular demagogue in furthering his promising career was to access the Tribunate of the Plebs.

As he was from the Patrician clan of the Claudii Pulchri, he needed to complete the *transitio in plebem*, the religious and social act by which a patrician gave up his birth status and became a plebeian, and thereby acquire the right to be invested of the Tribunician powers. When he eventually overcame the many technical hurdles and made it, with the continuing support of Caesar, his legislative reform programme got under way. Under his new name of Clodius (instead of the original Claudius), a bold move to burn the bridges with his patrician gens of the Claudii, he had several laws passed that moved the power balance in the direction of popular assemblies and away from the Senate house.

But he also found the time to further destabilize Cicero's position and free the scene of one of the most formidable opponents of the *populares* field: he conveniently dug out the Catilina affair and the execution of Sura and his men, and launched an attack on the illegality of the proceedings. Eventually he succeeded in passing a law that exiled Cicero as far as 500 miles from Rome, and confiscated his estate. Antony must have secretly – or openly for that matter – rejoiced when the statesman's mansion on the Palatine was expropriated and transformed into a place for public worship of the gods. It was to take him two years and one of his most moving orations[15] to get it back.

At any rate, the friendship with Curio and Clodius concluded the process of choice of field for Mark Antony, away from the nobility and the *optimates* forces of his family tradition, and into the ranks of the most flamboyant reformers and revolutionaries.

We must interpret this affiliation as a sign of his juvenile enthusiasm and lack of a calculated career strategy, which would have instead implied an earlier move into the ranks of the followers of Caesar, who was certainly a *populares* leader, but of a completely different breed.

The friendship with Curio and Clodius introduces another key player in Antony's life. Fulvia Flacca Bambula, who became his wife in 47 BC and a *pasionaria* in his future struggle with Octavian, had married Clodius in 62 BC, and was going to marry Curio in 52 BC after the murder of Clodius at the hands of the followers of his opponent Milo.

Well introduced into political circles, rich and ruthless, she was to form a mighty political alliance with Antony, throwing the full weight of her network behind him, including the armed urban gangs that had contributed to Clodius' good fortunes and were still loyal to her after the death of her first two husbands. She also came from a noble plebeian family, which already counted Consuls and senators in its ranks, although the last generation had been weaker. On her mother's side, she was a direct descendant of the great Scipio Africanus, conqueror of Carthage.

Fulvia has acquired a sinister reputation because of her association with Antony. Plutarch's introduction of the lady says it all, when he describes her as a woman that:

> "did not tend to spinning the wool or to the domestic chores, nor would she have settled for dominating a private citizen, but she wanted to rule over a ruler, and command to a commander. So Cleopatra was in Fulvia's debt, for teaching Antony how to be dominated by a woman, and for handing him over to her already docile and trained to obey women."[16]

According to Cicero in the Philippics, at some point, a long time before their marriage was celebrated in 47 BC, Antony and Fulvia became lovers and the tittle-tattle on the unofficial relationship spread quickly in gossipy Rome.

A narration of Antony's youth would not be complete without a mention of his Greek sojourn, where he completed his education and at the same time dedicated himself to military training.

Some have seen this departure as a desire to distance himself from the association with Clodius, who around 58 BC was pursuing politics hostile to the Caesar-Pompey-Crassus alliance, and was erring on the extremist side.[17] Others place this stay in Greece as early as 62 BC to make it more consistent with the norms of his age group in terms of the completion of his educational curriculum, and also explain it by his need to avoid his creditors, at a time when his credit lines were beginning to squeak dangerously.

Whereas the motives for the second explanation seem more robust, a later departure date in the early 50s seems nevertheless to be a better bet. The chronology makes more sense[18] to us, as some have argued, and Antony must have been itching for action. The young Antony must also have come to the conclusion that continuing the connection with extremist circles hostile to Caesar would jeopardize his possible future career ambitions under the wing of Julius Caesar. Plus, a young man of his temperament could not possibly have lasted for more than two years studying Asian rhetoric, let alone all the way from 62 BC, even if, at the same time, he was applying himself to the martial arts of fencing, javelin throwing, and archery, which might have been more congenial to his preferences and developing personality. The other angle which supports the later date is that his stay would have coincided with uncle and father-in-law Hybrida's governorship in neighbouring Macedonia. Uncle Hybrida had obtained this prestigious post as a part of his deal with Cicero, and, while in Macedonia, he had not wasted the opportunity to make a fool out of himself yet again: he had moved against the neighbouring populations of the Istrians and the Dardans, who were not exactly military powerhouses, and had been defeated and humiliated. His military ineptitude was a good match for his dishonesty, and apparently evidence of his misconduct made it to Rome. While Cicero's coverage at home was not sufficient to allow him to survive politically for another day in the face of the attacks that Caesar, his acquired cousin, unleashed on him *in absentia*, it was enough to limit his punishment to a luxury exile.

In terms of Antony's CV, it can be said that a Greek education definitely set you apart in Roman society.

"Graecia capta ferum victorem cepit, et artes intulit agresti Latio."[19]

"The conquered Greece captured the rude conqueror, and brought the Arts in rustic Latium." So wrote the poet Horace, sanctioning for eternity the inferiority complex that the Romans had with regard to Greek civilization. Greek was the language of philosophy and culture at large. Emperor Marcus Aurelius, of Spanish birth, did not think for a second to write his "Meditations" in Latin, but endeavoured to write directly in flawless Attic. All the Roman leaders knew Homer and the Tragics like the back of their hands, and took great pride in marking important moments with an erudite Greek quotation. Greek had become the language of culture in the same way that in nineteenth century Europe French was the language of diplomacy. This was not a sign of provincialism, but of true admiration and appreciation for the Greek intellect. From the standpoint of individual development, learning the Greek culture, philosophy, and civilization in Rome or in the former Magna Graecia colonies was not the same thing.

"Even if you had learned your Greek in Athens and not in Ragusa... you still wouldn't be up to the role." So Cicero mocked his opponent in the run for the role of accusator in the Verres trial. The audience must have been able to relate to this line and get a good laugh from it, signifying the importance of Hellenic style in terms of one's credibility at senior leadership levels.

The Greek sojourn served the purpose of placing Antony on par from a cultural qualifications standpoint with the top tiers of Roman society, and to give him that indispensable touch of worldliness, without which his career would have been constrained, in the fast expanding Republic.

But the outcome of his stay was not only checking the "international experience" and "Greek culture" boxes on his CV. It was then that he truly started feeling the fascination of the Greek culture and lifestyle. As his disappointment and disillusionment with the Roman scene grew over time, he started to long for his Athens days, and to feel the calling to trade his Roman ways for the Greek ones.

In wrapping up this chapter on Antony's youth, and on the historical and social context in which he grew up, we have to differ from the conclusion that Antony's upbringing was a "misspent youth".[20] In fact, he went through a whole array of traumatic yet developmental situations, which clearly had a fundamental importance in shaping the great leader he would become, his value system, and the criteria he used in picking his friends and enemies. Certainly his upbringing defined which were the aspects of Roman life and politics for which he would stand up, and which were the ones he could not respect and wanted overthrown.

It is interesting to spend some time focusing on the Roman political scene in order to give some context to Antony's background, and to understand how, from his youth, he identified Roman career officers either with phony idealists like Cato, upholding privileges under the guise of traditional values, or opportunistic demagogues à la Clodius, seeking personal advancement under the pretension of protecting the needy, or professional politicians like Cicero, straddling the agendas of the potentates of the day to remain afloat no matter what happened. And then there was the true reformist with a credible programme, the personal charisma, the personality, and the decisiveness to carry it out, and to make change happen and stay. This man was Caius Julius Caesar.

Chapter Two

East!

Mark Antony was not an especially early bloomer as a military commander or political leader. In order for him to get some real action in first person we have to wait until 57 BC when, at the age of 26, he followed the new Governor Aulus Gabinius (Gabinius) to the province of Syria. Gabinius was heading east on his new assignment with a broad mandate to patrol the troublesome Parthian border, which coincided with the Euphrates river, pacify and keep under control ebullient Judaea, and, later, ensure that the succession on Ptolemy's throne in Egypt followed Rome's desires. He had stopped over in Athens, where of course he met with all the prominent Romans in the Greek capital, including the young Mark Antony.

Gabinius was a first-rate personality of the late Republic. Throughout the 60s BC he had invested himself in supporting Pompey's rise to power, favouring him with legislation as a Tribune, as well as participating in his military expeditions to tame the Mediterranean pirates.

A shrewd politician, he could sit astride the agendas of different parties and manoeuvre across different alliances, such as when in 61 BC he backed Clodius in the motion for Cicero's exile that we have discussed earlier.

Syria had been a province for three years already, since Pompey had pushed aside the last king of the Seleucid dynasty, ending a reign which lasted for 250 consecutive years, but clearly there was significant unfinished business in the area, so Gabinius' appointment was possibly the result of a mix of gratitude for his ten year allegiance and the need for a trusted veteran on the job.

This province effectively constituted the core of the Seleucid Empire, which was established in 309 BC when the Macedonian General Seleukos I was able finally to overcome the other powerful General Antigonous and his son Demetrios, and conquered Babylon and the whole of Syria and Mesopotamia. He founded the new capital city of Seleukia, and began organizing the Seleukian Empire in just the same decentralized way the Achmenides Emperors had organized the Persian one. He had kept the traditional forms of decentralized government, the Satrapies, but had covered them with a strong personal touch, with the creation of a central administration in the Greek style, built with the contribution of a new Greek-speaking aristocracy, which he paired up with the pre-existing Aramaic-speaking one.

By the middle of the first century BC, the progressive and inexorable weakening of the Seleucid Empire had been under way for 120 years already. Rome had put a stern "halt" to their imperialistic expansion when, as we shall see later in this book, the Republic's envoys had intimated Antioch IV to back out of Egypt, and replace the Capitoline oversight to the rule of a Syrian Satrap on the banks of the Nile. At the same time, the force of the Parthians, who were progressively claiming more of what is today's Iran and Iraq, was increasing, and the coastal cities of Phoenicia were gaining more and more independence from the Empire. Last but not least, the ambitious early kings of the Hasmonean dynasty in Judaea were raising their heads, and fighting to build an independent state around their capital of Jerusalem. Indeed, the unrest in Palestine brought about a substantial dwindling of the Seleucid Empire. The traditionalist Macchabean resistance had overcome the opposite "philohellenic" Jewish faction, and the three brothers Judas, Jonathan, and Simon Machabee were able to gradually chip away at the Seleucid power, especially after the death of Antioch IV. The loss of influence of the Seleucids was so visible that the Jews were able to negotiate a separate alliance treaty with Rome, which recognized them as a political entity with special status, while in 160 BC Judaea was still formally a part of the Seleucid Empire.

The following twenty years saw continuing decadence, started, as per usual, by a dynastic struggle between the offspring of Antioch IV and his brother Seleukos IV. The real winners of this strife were, of course, those watching from the outside, namely the Parthians and the Jews. The former inflicted a harsh defeat on the Seleucids, made even tougher by the capture of King Demetrios. The latter freed up Jerusalem and got a first taste of independence.

Antioch VII deluded his subjects to be able to restore his dynastic splendour and reassert his power on both fronts, but before he could complete his restoration he was killed during a Parthian attack, and effectively left the status quo unchanged: Hasmonaean rule in Jerusalem, and Babylon steady in Parthian hands. From 129 BC onwards, the history of the Seleucid Kingdom is limited to that of Syria alone, and of its small time succession struggles, but on a scale that did not make it onto the Roman Senate's radar screen. Of course, there would have been discussion on the appetite for an eventual annexation. While the following thirty years of Syrian history are highly entertaining because of the fast pace of fighting, ruthless treasons and assassinations and merciless family feuds, their narration would not add much to our main story. It will suffice to say that the events resemble closely the history of the Ptolemies, which will be concisely exposed in Chapter 8.

By the late 90s the dynasty was so exhausted that a late Regent invited King Tigranes of Armenia to take over power in Antioch.[1] Tigranes was the son-in-law of our old acquaintance Mithridates VI, King of Ponthus, who was currently, as per his custom, at war against Rome. While this intervention could have been interpreted as some form of regency, invited for the sake of internal order, the surviving Seleucids did not give up their hopes to be reinstated, and applied for the support and recognition of the Senate of Rome. While the Romans recognized the legitimacy of the request, they did not intervene right away. The intervention followed shortly though: General Lucullus was at war with Mithridates VI, and Tigranes was a natural extension to the list of the hostiles.

The Roman intervention proved to be decisive, and Lucullus disposed quickly of Tigranes, who had to retreat into Armenia. We are now in 68 BC, with the entrance of King Antiochus XIII in Antioch, claiming the throne with full Roman backing. The predatory instinct and the desire for personal supremacy were very deeply rooted in the DNA of the descendants of Seleukos, and old habits die hard. For the following four years Antioch XIII lost and re-gained the crown to and from other family members, until 64 BC, when Pompey Magnus decided he had seen enough. The strategic importance of Syria was such that the country could not be abandoned to a state of perennial chaos, and in the hands of such unreliable sovereigns as well, while the Parthians were pushing at the Euphrates borders, the Armenians were not entirely tamed in the north east, and other populations in the south were equally unstable. Therefore Pompey decided that annexation of Syria as a Roman province represented a better insurance policy for the Roman world than leaving it as a vassal kingdom. The Seleucid kings were progressively sidelined, and the last possible heir to the throne, for good measure, was murdered upon Pompey's request by an Arab warlord. Syria was then formally ordained as a province, thus guaranteeing another steady flow of tax revenues for Rome, thanks to its flourishing agriculture, and to the trade revenues of the Phoenician harbours of Sydon and Tyre, and of the inland cities of Damascus and Hyerapolis. In a form of respect for its great tradition, only the city of Antioch was exonerated from taxation.

In sum, when Antony and Gabinius arrived at their destination, the Hellenistic kingdom of the Seleucids had ended a few years earlier, when Pompey had deposed the last king. Pompey had been campaigning in the Middle East to get rid of the evergreen Mithridates VI for good, who finally died in 63 BC. The old lion, a major element of disruption in the Hellenistic order since he had seized power killing his mother fifty years earlier, did not go down without a fight, and he would have survived another day if it hadn't been for his son's treason. In the end he died after an attempt at self-poisoning partly frustrated by years of antidote-taking, and after killing his surviving wife and young children.

Five years later, in 57 BC, the situation did not quite conform to the Roman standards for a pacified province. Neither did it three years later, because we learn that there was some work left for Crassus in 54 BC when he took over from Gabinius.

The rest of the Asian provinces had undergone a similar process of disaggregation of the rule, since the death of Alexander the Great 270 years earlier. While in the beginning, the power in the Eastern Mediterranean had been a private affair between the four heirs of Alexander, Ptolemy, Seleukos, Lysimachos, and Antigonous Monophtalmos, fragmentation had followed. For example, the end of the kingdom of Cappadocia had given rise to the independent states of Ponthus and Bythinia. In turn, these states had been lurching from one succession crisis to another, vacillating between fluctuating levels of diplomatic relations with Rome, dominated by financial interest in a similar manner to the Egyptian situation, and perennial instability with the stronger player trying to impose puppet kings on the neighbouring thrones.

As a general feeling, the comment below, referring to the situation of neighbouring Cappadocia, can be extended to cover the broader area:

> "the Roman Senate was in no way being treated as the government of an omnipotent superpower, whose wishes were commands, but merely as a distant, and therefore relatively powerless, interference in the power play of the Eastern monarchies".[2]

The military interventions of the past two decades of course reinforced the liaison with Roman government, but it is clear that the situation which presented itself to Gabinius and the young Antony was that of an area where the concept of Rome remained extremely close, and where consolidation had barely begun. The events to come during the Civil Wars would not improve the status quo, so Antony was to retain an image of the situation which would have influenced his vision twenty years later.

The area that went under the name of Roman Syria was larger than today's Syria, and also covered most of modern day Lebanon, Jordan, Israel and Palestine, all the way east to the river Euphrates, and west to the Egyptian border.

The challenges in this vast province came not only from the organization of former Seleucid Syria, recently annexed, but from the threat presented by the neighbouring Parthian empire, the dynastic struggle and continuing unrest in Judaea, and the shock waves that could have come from the independent kingdom of Egypt.

Plutarch makes us understand that Mark Antony must have had some bargaining power with Gabinius in order to be able to negotiate a command when the latter offered him to join his mission to the east as a simple aide. It is easy to imagine that the extensive network he had built was put to fruition, or that Gabinius was really eager to have in his team some well connected, high breed youths which could make his achievements resonate better back at home, and build consensus to help his future advancement.

One can wonder why Gabinius would give a field command to a 26–year–old man from a well to do family, and with a well connected mother, but whose military pedigree did not go past theory and gym training, as opposed to an easier and less risky staff job. There are two thoughts that come naturally to the mind.

First, in 57 BC the Pompey-Caesar relationship was especially good, so we cannot rule out that Uncle Julius could have played a role in this sudden career advancement. Alternatively, albeit from a different and maybe opposing field, the

Clodius connection might have contributed. The two were going to have a falling out, or at least a violent altercation, but it would not have been for some time, and when Antony left Rome he could still have pulled some strings.[3] Both paths could have been followed if he had needed sponsorship.

Second, Antony's clock must have been ticking, and he must have been an especially eager young man with something to prove, exuding motivation and willpower, and transmitting this feeling extremely well thanks to his remarkable physical appearance and athletic build.

Were Antony's accomplishments at this point in line with what one would have expected from a young man with his family background? Let's briefly benchmark with what we can call his peer group, being some of the most noteworthy names of the late Republic, and see where they were in their respective careers at age 26.

Julius Caesar had a late start because of his Marian affiliation, and due to this well known connection he had to lay low until Sulla's death. He had also been to Greece to study oratory, and in the course of his travels he had been kidnapped by the Adriatic pirates, which he later captured and executed. Upon his return to Rome, at 26 and well within the average age, he was made a military Tribune. This and the following successes did not keep him from self commiserating for being an underachiever and shedding some bitter tears another eleven years later in Portugal, in front of a statue of Heracles.[4] So at the age of 26 he was not very much ahead of Antony at the same age.

Pompey had been the prodigy child: at 23 he had raised three legions, funded out of his family wealth, to support Sulla in his reclaim of power. At 24 he conquered Sicily from the Marians, and he arranged for the brutal execution of the most prominent opponents, thus earning the nickname of *adolescens carnifex*, the adolescent butcher or executioner. At 25 he was campaigning in the Roman province of Africa (Tunisia), where he defeated Gnaeus Domitius Aenobarbus (Emperor Nero's great-grandfather) and the Numidian King Hiarbas, a Marian sympathizer, after a hard-fought battle.

Sulla, on the contrary, at 26 had been busy just making ends meet and squandering whatever modest financial resources he had, in the company of a crew of actors, mimes, prostitutes and drunks. A marriage with a rich widow was to give him a lift, but his career did not really start until 106 BC, when he was 32 years old, and he took part in the Jugurthine war in Numidia under Gaius Marius.

Crassus was another example of how the Civil War could be a career accelerator: at 26 he had to flee to Spain to escape the Cinnan purges, which we have discussed on the occasion of the death of MA Orator. But when Sulla's tall and gangly outline showed at the horizon, he quickly reached for the family safe and armed a legion out of his own pocket, just like Pompey, to help him conquer Rome. Three years later he had the prestigious command of one wing of the Sullan army at the decisive battle of the Colline Gate against the Marians. His fortunes were made, and the return on his investment was thousands fold, to the point that he became proverbial for his wealth, with the name of *dives Crassus*, the rich Crassus.

Brutus, the famous Republican leader, and the head of the conspiracy that was going to eliminate Caesar, at 26 went to Cyprus with his uncle Cato Minor (the Younger), to occupy the island that had just been handed over by King Ptolemy XII, and control the anti-Roman factions. The future leader of the opposition to the Triumvirate was still acting in the shade of a more senior officer, and on a relatively low profile mission for that matter. His real political career did not truly start until his return.

Cassius Longinus, the other leader of the conspiracy of the Ides of March, also had a slow start, and no significant achievement can be found on his record until he left for Parthia as a staff officer under Crassus, when he was already 33 or 34 years of age.

In sum, we cannot really conclude that Antony's youth had been misspent,[5] or that the wine, women, and song had seriously derailed his career, even if we benchmark to Rome's best and brightest.

It would also appear, looking at the careers of the most prominent personalities in the first century BC, that the pace of the events and the instability of the political scene did not lend themselves to the pursuit of the stereotypical *cursus honorum*, but rather favoured risk taking, ruthlessness, and personal edge in order to guarantee advancement.

To conclude, the Syrian mission constituted a great opportunity for Antony to cut his teeth and catch up with his career ambitions, which were entirely justified given his family background. The timing was perfectly in line with the benchmarks of the time for promising young men of illustrious birth, as we have seen.

The Parthian front was meant to be a central area of focus in Gabinius' mission, but the succession of political events in Rome did not give him a chance to make progress towards a full invasion of the country. Crassus wanted to keep the privilege of leading the aggression himself, with the results that we shall see.

It is now time to introduce the Partian nation, who represented Rome's main threat and nemesis on the eastern border for 400 years. We will meet the Parthians again later in Mark Antony's life when he campaigned deep into Mesopotamia, all the way to setting siege to the city of Ctesiphon.

The Romans locked horns with the Parthians several times in their history, until the Parthian kingdom and the Arsacid kings gave way to the Sassanid dynasty in the mid-third century AD, and we start calling the people more appropriately Persians. The conflicts had very different outcomes, depending on the relative strength of the two belligerent superpowers, and the pressure that they were facing on other fronts. For the Parthians the eastern tribesmen represented what the Germanic barbarians were going to be for the Romans. At times, the axe was buried and diplomacy between the two prevailed. Augustus in 20 BC ensured the return of Crassus' eagles, the silver emblems of his legions destroyed at Carrhae, and some of the surviving captives, just by threatening military aggression. He then proceeded[6] to celebrate as if he had obtained a military victory. Diplomacy went as far as providing a slave girl, Thea Musa, as a wife to the Parthic King Phraates, who did not know or did not care about her previous status.

Surprisingly, even the inept Nero scored some diplomatic points in AD 63: he had dispatched the star general Corbulo to settle the latest dispute over Armenia, and this seasoned soldier had won some decisive battles. But Nero, for once in his lifetime conscious of budgetary constraints, obtained huge success at home when he concluded a favourable peace treaty with the Parthian King Thiridates, who came all the way to Rome, and formally accepted a subordinate status. They paraded in Rome together, the Parthian accepting secondary status to the Roman, and the military budget for the year could be significantly reduced.

It was only a temporary solution of course, and forty years later Trajan re-launched a full war against them, imitated by some of the Severan Emperors, albeit on a smaller scale.

The Parthian kingdom originated sometime around 250 BC, when a chieftain of mysterious and almost mythical origins, named Arsaces, took advantage of weakness and internal struggle within the Seleucid Empire to conquer the land between modern Turkmenistan and Mesopotamia, inclusive of them. The Arsacid rulers were certainly not ethnic Persians, but probably came from the plains east of Iran or were of Scythian or Bactrian origins.

The following 100 years of Parthian history are marked by the ongoing struggle with the Seleucid kings to consolidate the independence obtained. Again, the ongoing tussle had alternating outcomes, depending on the relative health of the two nations, and on the strength of the leaders. Early in the second century BC, in a moment of relative peace on the eastern front, they tried to raid Greece, then under Roman protection, got a first taste of the Roman military expertise, and quickly retreated to their territories. On the eastern border, the Parthian kingdom had its fair share of challenges, mainly to keep in check local belligerent tribes. Over the centuries, the main source of conflict was the control of Armenia, a vast territory that represented a buffer between the two superpowers, and its control through a puppet king aligned to the respective interests. In the first century BC Armenia was – albeit intermittently – still a regional power in its own right, and its allegiance could have significant impact on the political equilibrium. It was not before the campaigns of Lucullus and Pompey that Armenia would regress to a vassal state condition and a target for successive land grabs.

Already at this time the presence of this aggressive and potentially formidable neighbour was unsettling for Rome, and dealing with it was only a matter of time. We don't have to come to think that the Parthian campaign was solely an aggressive move dictated by imperialistic goals, or worse, by the short term desire for booty.

The decision making process must have been influenced by a necessity to stabilize the border and pre-empt the Parthian desires to expand across the Euphrates, which had become manifest in the preceding years.

We can pick up our narration in the year 57 BC, when the weak King Phraates III was deposed by his two sons, Mithridates III and Orodes II. Clearly, "The Parthian Book of Beautiful Baby Names" must have been extremely short, and many of the names of the eastern rulers are seemingly endlessly repeated, creating some confusion at times. A struggle to prevail quickly followed between the two brothers, with Orodes imposing himself as the new king, with the support of the nobility led by the prestigious Surenas, while Mithridates was relegated to a role of provincial Governor in the south. When they saw the situation and understood the potential consequences, the Romans would not sit on the fence. While it was under the weak leadership of Phraates III, Pompey and Lucullus had had an easy play in keeping Parthia in check, so the perspective to uphold and support Mithridates, perceived to be more manageable than his rambunctious brother, was considered be more advantageous for Rome. Orodes could have meant bad news for the Roman east.

So Gabinius did not limit himself to border patrol, but he started a programme of interference in Parthia's internal affairs, and armed intervention, which led him to cross the river Euphrates, on the border between Syria and Parthia. There was too much to gain for Rome in making Parthia a subordinate state, led by puppet King Mithridates or by a defeated Orodes: the most important consequence would have been the direct access to the Persian Gulf, and the wealth coming from the control over the eastern trade. But the mission was aborted, as we have said, due to the decisions of the three strongmen, Caesar, Pompey, and Crassus, who had made different plans as a consequence of their allocation of power: Crassus, his mouth probably watering at the huge opportunity to plunder on a vast, wealthy, and weakened kingdom, was looking forward to taking over from Gabinius directly.

There is no specific account of Antony's direct intervention in Parthian Mesopotamia, but it is logical to assume that the star young officer was part of the expedition corps, and gained some first-hand expertise on the territory and the enemies.

The Parthian campaign led by Crassus was a major event in the history of Rome, and it is especially relevant for this narration because the desire for revenge and the healing of bruised honour in the public opinion became an important agenda item for Julius Caesar and, later, for Mark Antony. Caesar amassed large armies and prepared in detail for a punitive expedition, which was called off when already on its starting blocks when Caesar was assassinated. Years later Antony took over the task, and his unsuccessful expedition was to have serious repercussions on his relative strength with Octavian. It is thus well worth spending a few more words on what happened to Crassus.

Marcus Licinius Crassus was aged 60 when he set sail to cross the Mediterranean and attack Parthia. Some say that, as he approached the twilight of his career, he wanted to achieve something as spectacular as emulating Alexander the Great and storming across the Middle East, possibly all the way to India. But initially he had to take over where Gabinius had left. His first idea was to utilize Mithridates, Orodes' brother, to destabilize the enemy.

The public opinion in Rome was not favourable to this war, which was generally considered needless, and just one more unpleasant reminder that the First Triumvirate controlled Rome's foreign policy as much as the domestic one. When Crassus left Rome, in November 55 BC, he did so among the curses of his many opponents.

A law passed by the Tribune Gaius Trebonius gave Crassus the authority to recruit seven legions and wage war against a rival power that, at least for the near term, did not present a specific threat. Surrounded by threatening omens, he decided to move into Parthia eastwards from Syria, as opposed to crossing Turkey and Armenia, and then head south-east.

Initially he fared quite well, and all the cities in the region of the western banks of the river Euphrates, which had strong Hellenistic heritage as a consequence of their Seleucid reminiscences, gladly surrendered to Rome, which was seen as a good alternative to the unpleasant rule of a Parthian Satrap. But then Crassus wasted most of 54 BC waiting for more reinforcements, letting his inexperienced troops plunder Mesopotamia, and even going to dip his greedy hands in the treasure of the Temple of Jerusalem and the Temple of Venus in Hyerapolis. Inevitably he lost all the momentum he had built, and he camped for the winter west of the Euphrates. He also failed to secure the help of Artavasdes, King of Armenia, which could have much furthered his cause. Early in 53 BC he marched east full steam ahead, guided by some treacherous Arab scouts, until he made contact with the enemy troops led by Surenas, who had already defeated, captured, and led to his destiny Mithridates III in southern Mesopotamia. At the same time, Orodes attacked Armenia, and Artavasdes immediately turned coat to avoid worse consequences, and sided with the Parthians.

The Parthians needed some more time to organize their defence, and in all likelihood they had left behind Surenas with an army made largely of mounted archers only to slow down the Roman legions, but with no real ambitions of defeating them.

Rather than playing the role of the designated victim, Surenas came up with a brilliant stratagem. The Roman legions had been partly successful in the past against the Parthian mounted archers by enduring the volleys of arrows in their typical *testudo* (turtle) formation, where they would lock their heavy shields together in an impenetrable fortress, and then close up on them rapidly when the Parthians had run out of arrows and were reloading their quivers. But Surenas arranged for a large column of camels to guarantee a continuing supply of arrows for a bombardment that lasted for hours, and that turned into a complete slaughter, where over 20,000 Romans lost their lives.

Crassus was then lured into yet another trap by the Parthians, when they asked him to exit the secure walls of the city of Carrhae, where he had found shelter, to negotiate terms of withdrawal. They killed him, decapitated him, and poured melted gold into his mouth to deride his proverbial greed.

It was left for Crassus' second in command Cassius Longinius, one of Caesar's future assassins who was then serving under Crassus and had managed to escape the carnage, to secure the Syrian border from greater damage, and avoid Parthian raids into the Roman provinces.

At the time of the Carrhae disaster, as we will see, Antony was in transit between Gaul, where he had joined his uncle, Caesar, and Rome, where he was formally beginning his political career. But the border patrol missions he had conducted with Gabinius were to be of great importance to him when he undertook his own Parthian expedition, and the learning very important to limit the damage under the same circumstance.

The other two major fronts which saw young Mark Antony getting a taste of the action were the Egyptian front and of course the Judaean situation. What was going on in the Promised Land in 57 BC?

It had taken 250 years for the Jews to shake off the Seleucid domination, thanks to the leadership of Simon Machabeus and his son John Hyrcanus, who managed to take the war deep into Syrian territory. Hyrcanus' son Aristobulos had decimated his own family to be the first Jew to wear the regal diadem since the Babylonian captivity, establishing the rule of the Hasmonean dynasty. Aristobulos' brother Alexander, who reigned after him, was not second to him in cruelty, and suppressed successive rebellions in true bloodbaths and mass exiles. When he died, his wife named the first born Hyrcanus High Priest, and sidelined the second born Aristobulos as she had spotted very early the distinctive traits of a troublemaker.

It was not long before Aristobulos had seized power through the armed conquer of the Citadel of Jerusalem, and forced Hyrcanus to step aside. The partisans of Hyrcanus stepped in, and helped him raise an army of 50,000 Nabatean warriors that defeated Aristobulos, who was soon kept under siege in Jerusalem. The Romans did not like to see this kind of commotion perturbing their protectorates. A strong peacekeeping force arrived soon, and the Proconsul Scaurus who was in the lead decided to side with Aristobulos, helped in the decision by the 300 silver talents that were paid to him. We are now in 63 BC.

One important fact must be highlighted, because of the future repercussions it would have: the main ally of Hyrcanus was Antipater, whose son was that Herod that would reign over Judaea and become known as Herod the Great. Antipater did not have the pure Jewish lineage of the Hasmonaeans, but had also some Idumenean blood (from Lebanon more or less). This would create some followership issues for him in the immediate term, and different degrees of disowning in official Jewish historiography.

Pompey Magnus did not like the deal Scaurus had cut, and upheld Hyrcanus' rights. Aristobulos locked himself in the fortress of Alexandreion and engaged in lengthy negotiations with Pompey. In the meantime, in Jerusalem a full Civil War had broken out between the two opposing factions, which were also rallying points for opposing Jewish religious sects. According to Josephus the body count of street violence quickly went as high as 12,000. In the end, strong off the help of Pompey, Hyrcanus had the upper hand and was restored to his post of High Priest and *de facto* ruler, some say because he was considered a more reliable ally for Rome than his flamboyant brother.

It was not over: his son Alexander was able to escape from Roman hands, reorganize, and wage guerrilla warfare against his uncle Hyrcanus and the official government, from his fortresses of Alexandreion, Hyrcania, and Macheruntes. On this prolonged volatile scenario, and after decades of uninterrupted bloodshed, we have now arrived at 57 BC, with the beginning of the governorship of Gabinius, called to stabilize a situation that could spread out to the broader region, or create significant annoyance for Rome. Mark Antony's early military exploits served the purpose of resolving an intestine struggle with the potential to escalate to fully fledged rebellion.

As the campaigning began, the young and itchy Antony was the one chosen to draw first blood. Paired with the local allied troops supplied by Antipater, he pressed Alexander closely. At the first pitched battle, Alexander lost 3,000 men, and another 3,000 were taken prisoners, out of a total force of 12,000. The Jewish historian Josephus spends words of flattery to describe Antony's bravery and military skills.

> "In this battle the Commander Mark Antony distinguished himself. He had always and everywhere given proof of his courage, but never as on this occasion."

Soon after, all the strongholds of Alexander fell to Gabinius, who formally dismantled the monarchy and appointed once more Hyrcanus as High Priest, with a prominent role in the leadership of the nation with a formula based on the support of the religious establishment and the aristocracy. It is important to consider the importance of affiliation to the different sects in which the Jewish society of the first century was divided.

The Pharisees were in essence the representatives of the traditionalist clergy, and were to take an increasingly pro-Roman posture over time. The other groups attributed to them a certain intellectual arrogance, as they considered themselves as the repositories of the true interpretation of the scripture, which the Christian reader will recall in their disputes with Jesus Christ in the Temple of Jerusalem in the Gospel of Mark. They were the backbone of the Hyrcanus rule in the Gabinius organization. Our main source on this period, Josephus, was declaredly one of them.

The Sadducees were their opponents. A more radical wing, they were in favour of a more literal interpretation of the scripture, and they maintained a very intransigent attitude against the Roman presence in the Holy Land. Die hard fighters, they were annihilated during the siege of Jerusalem by Titus in AD 70.

The third largest sect was composed by the Essenes, also anti-Roman, but of more mystical and ascetic inclinations.

The other famous sect, the Zealots, that was to give Rome so much grief over the next 120 years, had not truly emerged as a powerful constituency yet. Their creed was in the mainstream Pharisee doctrine, but topped up with the strongest anti-Roman feelings.

The Sadducees clearly provided the fertile grounds for Aristobulos' and Alexander's party recruitment in preparation for the second round. This saw the evasion of Aristobulos from captivity in Rome, and his staging of one more bid for power, which was quickly rebutted by Antony and the other Generals, who inflicted on him 5,000 casualties. He was sent back to Rome in chains on the next ship out.

But the move of the old father had given Alexander some breathing space, and the time to organize a large scale insurrection, raise an army, and massacre a large number of Romans. As far as Gabinius went, the measure was full at this point, and the ensuing battle of Mount Thabor was the final showdown and saw a crushing defeat for the Jewish rebel army. Aristobulos was apprehended and spent more time in captivity in Rome, until five years later in 49 BC Caesar freed him up and tried to use him as a pawn in his struggle against Pompey. In order to avoid trouble, the Pompeians soon had him captured and poisoned. Using his traditional respect for dead enemies, Antony used all his influence to have the body properly preserved in honey, until it could be returned to his followers for royal burial. Soon after Alexander was apprehended and beheaded in Antioch at the command of Pompey. Alexander was not the last of the Hasmonean dynasty to give Rome some grief, because his brother Antigonus was to organize yet another rebellion, which would keep Mark Antony and his Generals busy in the years 40–37 BC.

The internal situation in Judaea was not the only challenge that Gabinius and Antony had to face, as trouble had been brewing under the pyramids. The Egyptian front opened for them in the spring of 55 BC, and in fact the campaign took place in between the battles against Aristobulos and the battle of Mount Thabor.

Technically, the Egyptian state of affairs was outside the scope of Gabinius, whose charter ended at the Egyptian border. Egypt at that time was still an independent State, with a legitimate king, albeit well aligned with Roman interests, and enjoying Rome's benevolence and protection, as we will see in more detail in Chapter 8.

In reality, stability on the Nile was paramount to ensure a steady flow of grains to Rome, as Egypt was progressively replacing Sicily and Greece as the main supplier of wheat for Rome. Since bread was a cornerstone more than a staple in the common Roman diet, it is clear that this was a subject of fundamental importance. So when the Pharaoh Ptolemy XII Auletes (i.e. the oboe player, a hobby much frowned upon by his courtesans, in the stiff and quasi-religious Pharaonic Court ceremonial) was ousted by a rebellion led by his sister Berenice and her husband the General Archelaus, the Romans were hesitating on the opportunity of a military intervention.

In reality, Ptolemy had been the cause of his own troubles: he had contracted huge debt with the intent to bribe some Roman senators and extract even more lucrative deals, and then he had imposed heavy taxation on his subjects to replenish the safe. The angry and rebellious Alexandrines had left him little choice but to escape to Rome, possibly accompanied by the young Princess Cleopatra, and so the beautiful but inept Princess Berenice had taken over. When the Egyptians had sent envoys to Rome to explain the situation and obtain justice, he had them intercepted and killed so his version of the facts would remain the official and prevailing one.

As for the Roman intervention, discouraged also by the prophecies of the Sybilline books, Ptolemy helped resolve the stalemate, and offered a 10,000 talents bounty, an enormous sum of money, as a reward to help him return to the throne of his fathers. In essence, Ptolemy XII kept borrowing from the Romans to strengthen his throne, and was pledging his kingdom as a security. We will later see how throughout the Civil War, Rome knocked at the Egyptian door to collect in full. According to Plutarch, Antony was decisive in convincing Gabinius to take the mission, and equally fundamental in leading the march through the Sinai, conquering the fortified town of Pelagium, and finally in the successful capture of Alexandria from the usurpers' troops.

This time it was Plutarch who let us know how he distinguished himself for bravery in battle.

"In all the great and frequent skirmishes and battles, he gave continual proof of his personal valour and military conduct; and once in particular, by wheeling about and attacking the rear of the enemy, he gave the victory to the assailants in front, and received for this service mark of distinction."[7]

In victory, he proved generous and magnanimous. We learn again from Plutarch that he rendered honours to the dead Archelaus' body. Archelaus was a respected professional soldier from Ponthus, son of one of Mithridathes' generals, and was well known in the Roman circles, where he had gained some consideration from Pompey Magnus, and according to Plutarch, Antony may have befriended him at some point. We have already seen how funeral honours for defeated enemies were one of his trademarks. As for the rebellious Alexandrians, he protected them from retaliation from Ptolemy and his troops, thus gaining huge personal prestige and reconnaissance. The grateful citizens of the capital of Egypt would not forget this, and, upon his return almost two decades later, he was still remembered. The love story between Antony and the splendid capital of Hellenistic Egypt had begun, fourteen years before his famous meeting with Cleopatra.

As for Ptolemy, he did not pretend to be a match for Antony's mercifulness, and he had his sister Berenice executed, alongside, as we learn from Cassius Dio:

"many of the most illustrious and rich citizens, as he needed much money."[8]

We have to assume that he was not planning to pay the 10,000 talents promised to Gabinius out of his own pocket, which was permanently empty, but that he was counting on his rebellious subjects to foot the bill, albeit unwillingly.

The reader should not feel too bad for Berenice. As she was preparing for her coup, she had married the strongman Seleucus (one of the Macedonian courtesans that populated the Ptolemaic Court, unrelated to the royal dynasty of the Seleucids) to help her reign, but she had him killed and married Archelaus when she saw that this latter was likely to do a better job. We can easily spot in her some of the traits of ruthless opportunism that were running in the DNA of the last dynasty of Pharaohs, and to which we will return at a later stage.

In the end, Gabinius run into legal trouble when he went back to Rome, in what seemed to be an unfortunately common consequence of governorships at the time. The Egypt campaign had been highly unpopular in Rome, from a legal as much as a superstitious angle: there was no legal foundation for a provincial Governor to invade an allied kingdom to take part in a succession war, and the expedition had been strongly discouraged from the Sybilline prophecies; since he had acted largely on his own initiative, he was the man to take the blame. A flood of the Tiber had been interpreted as a divine punishment for the unlawful expedition, and upon his return to Rome Gabinius was chased by an angry mob and had to lock himself in his house. When he stood trial, it took all of his patron Pompey's wealth and influence and Cicero's (again!) oratory skills to get him off the hook. But nothing could save him from the other accusation of having enriched himself with 100 million sesterces from the Syrians' tax money, following, as we have seen, a well consolidated tradition. He had to wait until Caesar's dictatorship six years later to be pardoned and recalled to Rome.

Antony, who has been identified as the chief fomenter and persuader for the campaign, was not associated in the blame. Evidently, he was still too junior to be considered a heavyweight influencer, no matter what the underlying reality was. Or maybe a big veteran like Gabinius would not admit having acted under the advice of a 28-year-old whippersnapper on his first military campaign, no matter his lineage or bravery in battle.

In Alexandria, in the course of the celebrations that must have followed, Antony could also have met two of the younger Ptolemy family members. The first Ptolemy XIII, an 8-year-old boy, was to die tragically a few years later during Caesar's brief Egyptian adventure, drowning in the Nile while escaping from the battlefield. And, more importantly, he might have met his 13-year-old sister, Cleopatra VII Thea Philopatrix (Cleopatra), Aulete's daughter and Berenice's niece. It is left for us to imagine if the two noticed each other, or if the 29-year-old Antony could have fathomed that twenty years later he would have been at the summit of the sophisticated court ceremonial he was admiring. The two were divided by an abyss in terms of the royal protocol, and it is impossible that they got to socialize at all. But word of the young and handsome soldier that had been so gallant in battle and so generous in victory must have reached the ear of the young princess.

The three year mark was near, Gabinius' mandate was almost over, and for Antony the time to move on was quickly approaching. By the time he left the Middle East, Mark Antony had added a string of achievements to his resume, and he had acquired or developed invaluable skills. He had road tested his warrior self, and demonstrated his bravery in battle. He had proven himself as a military leader, and probably defined his style, based on that no-nonsense camaraderie that the troops love: soldier between soldiers, eating the legionaries' meals standing by a camp fire, and, why not, sharing some vulgar jokes and a good laugh. He had savoured success, popularity, recognition. He had gained personal exposure to kings, military chiefs, and religious leaders. He had permeated himself with knowledge of Greater Syria and Egypt, Hellenistic culture, and everything that went with the eastern ways of life and rule. He had seen a Roman provincial government at work, and understood the many reasons why the model adopted did not lend itself to the multicultural, historically complex reality of the Greek East. And, most importantly, he had earned himself a strong reputation and visibility back at home.

A new page of his life opened. Antony did not go back to Rome, but waited for the good season and sailed straight to Massilia (modern day Marseilles) to offer his services to his uncle Julius Caesar, who was on his sixth year of campaign in Gaul.

The Gallic campaign had begun almost by chance, with one of those Iron Age (starting late for the Alpine populations) migrations of Helvetian tribes from today's Switzerland and Western Austria, crossing over into the territories of the Aedui and the Sequani, long time allies and tributaries of Rome. Caesar dealt quickly with them, beating them time and again on their way from Lyon to (roughly) Toulouse.

But continuing support for the interests of the Aedui was a perfect excuse to conquer the Celtic tribes led by Ariovistus, who had a history of prevarications versus the Aedui. Caesar went to great lengths to humiliate and provoke them, and finally crush them in battle. Since then, the Gallic wars were a sequel of small police operations directed at small coalitions of Gallic nations, bringing the challenge of a diversified warfare in different geographic contexts, for example the naval warfare on the sandy shores of western Normandy with the Veneti, siege warfare against the Treviri, and the ambush guerrilla of the Belgians under Ambiorix. Overall, with the exception of a few occasional minor setbacks, the success of the Roman expedition was never in question, thanks to the display of discipline, military might, and siege engineering skills.

Antony's arrival in Gaul coincides with an escalation in the violence of the war, and in the resolve of most Celtic tribesmen to stand up against the Roman rule at all cost. It is at the beginning of 52 BC that Caesar made his first trip home in a long time, with the pretext of attending to activities pertaining to his Magistracy, in reality to walk a scene that was getting more turbulent by the day, and which was by this time clearly heading towards a full on Civil War. The murder of Clodius at the end of 53 BC had been the loudest alarm bell of all, and had been quickly followed by increased enrolment of troops. The rumours of this explosive situation fast made it to Cisalpine Gaul, one of the traditional reservoirs for the recruitment of legionaries, and the echoes had spread out to Transalpine Gaul.

The last episode before the escalation of the violence in the conflict had been the conquest of the city of Avaricus, a gem of the Gallic culture, and capital of the Bythurigii in the Loire Valley area. The rape of the city by the exasperated legionaries, with mass slaughter of the population, and the enslavement of 46,000 of its inhabitants was probably the trigger that ignited the most violent stages of the revolt.

The year 52 clearly marks the advent to supremacy of Advernian Prince Vercingetorix, and the adoption of his resolute methods by the broad coalition he managed to assemble. Caesar stresses repeatedly how this young leader, following a consolidated family tradition, was motivated by pursuit of personal rule, rather than desire of independence from Rome for the Gallic people, against a tradition that portrays him as a freedom fighter against the yoke of the Roman imperialism. Accordingly, he was challenged repeatedly by his countrymen on the grounds that he would have accepted supremacy over the Gauls even if it had been offered to him by Caesar.

Vercingetorix made the war theatre more difficult for the Romans in two ways: first, he used the iron fist to control his allies, demanding large hostage contingents from each tribe, and staging mass executions and torture at the first signs of treason or just faltering in motivation to combat. Secondly, he enacted a scorched earth campaign around the Roman chain of supply, devastating the farmland to disrupt the logistics of the 40,000 men that Caesar had to feed.

The botched attack to the city of Gergovia in this period, and the resulting loss of 600 men and considerable pride for Caesar, was nothing more than an incentive for the latter to pick up the pace on his turn, and try to expedite the end of the conflict. This was badly needed, as for every point that the rebel coalition scored more Gauls would betray their Roman loyalties and defect to Vercingetorix. The latest to change their loyalties had been the Aedui, Rome's traditional allies, whose defence had originated Caesar's first entry in Transalpine Gaul.

To keep momentum on his side, Vercingetorix launched a large scale cavalry manoeuvre. When he was defeated, he had no better option than to haste for the fortified citadel of Alesia, roughly 120 km south of Paris, and barricade inside. Caesar followed closely, and encircled Alesia with a system of moats, palisades, and forts, thus locking 80,000 people in a ring of spikes and traps. The topic moment came as the Gallic coalition quickly assembled a large army and moved to the help of the besieged. For over three days the Romans fought the much more numerous enemy. On the first day, Caesar soundly defeated the newly arrived troops, and for the two following days he kept chasing back the besieged into the fortress with huge losses, as they attempted to escape to freedom.

The first appearance of Mark Antony in Caesar's writing is at this point, on the last grand scene of the Gaul campaign. He was charged with the critical mission, shared with Gaius Trebonius, who will have some relevance in this narration later, of defending the pressure points of the ring around Alesia from the desperate attempts of Vercingetorix's men to make a break for safety, and that mission was perfectly accomplished.

Throughout Caesar's Commentaries, the memoirs he was writing to give the Senate full visibility on his accomplishments, there is very little room for the co-protagonists of the story on the Roman side. The whole intent of the narration was to keep a log of the main events as a means to keep the Senate and the people posted, and testify his continuing accountability for resources and accomplishments. Accordingly, the few references are for his closest aides, such as the veteran Labienus, or the other young legates, mainly from prominent families, as one would expect. In this group we find the relations of Cicero, Brutus, Crassus, and more akin to the nobility and intelligentsia of the capital city.

But after Alesia, Caesar dropped the pen, so that the final book (VIII) of the commentary was finished by his general and Consul to be Aulus Hirtius, who happened to be Antony's close friend at the time. As a consequence, Antony takes centre stage in Book VIII, and we have very close visibility on his involvement and direct impact on the concluding stages of the campaign, directed at the clean-up of the remaining pockets of resistance and at the reorganization of the provinces, ravaged by eight years of war.

Antony did not serve in the late stages of the Gallic War on a continuative basis. When in Alesia, he was a Legatus, or Lieutenant General. After Alesia, as we have seen, he made a brief return to Rome, where he was made a Quaestor, and, as such, was appointed by Caesar to manage the winter quartering of the bulk of the Roman army in Gaul, while Caesar himself planned on blitzing the remainder of the insurrectional forces.

It is interesting to see how the brief career of a Roman magistrate could take him in a short time to cover such a vast array of diversified experiences. In a brief spell Antony was able to participate in a guerrilla theatre, in one of the most complex sieges of antiquity, in the largest pitched battle since the Punic wars, and now in the organizational and logistic challenge linked with managing a force of over 30,000 veterans and support troops. Antony had the possibility to graduate at a totally different level from his early accomplishments in the Near East.

His early performance must have been very impressive, if only months later we find him at a higher level of empowerment and responsibility, i.e. the management of the winter quartering for the whole army.

After Alesia, and specifically at the mark of the New Year, Caesar changed his strategy again, and transitioned to a new approach to the war. As he did not expect any more large concentration of enemy troops seeking a large pitched battle, he decentralized the Roman forces and dispatched some large contingents to peripheral provinces, in order to secure these settlements against possible further rebellions. At the same time, he kept blitzing on the populations that could still represent a threat. The first and most obvious targets were the Belgian tribes that could still rally around Ambiorix, who had managed to vanish, but was reported to be still alive and capable to strike.

Close second were the proud Bellovacii, Carnutes, and Treviri, who still had some fight left in them. This time he kept Mark Antony near him, in charge of the XII legion. As he kept storming around the north eastern border, Antony followed him closely, patrolled and secured the Bellovacian territory after they had been vanquished, and proceeded to the capture of the last Gallic leader worthy of note, a certain Commius, putting the word "end" to the De Bello Gallico.

The closing remarks by Hirtius are on Antony's return to Rome to receive his appointment to Augur, and make way for Caesar's upcoming arrival. The faithful Hirtius confirms the extreme tension of the political situation in Rome, where the anti-Caesarean faction, which, as we will see, was by then led by Pompey, was busy scheming on all the possible destabilizing moves.

Antony travelled back and forth between Gaul and Rome before finally settling down, in preparation for the next stage of his career. His military preparation was now complete, and he was about to measure himself with a totally different set of challenges. On the horizon, the backdrop for his political career was going to be made up by some of the most virulent pages of the Civil War, and the final showdown between Caesar and the Pompeians.

The period between 50 BC, his return to Rome as an Augur first and as a Tribune next, and the re-organization of the State after the battle of Pharsalus, was going to represent his definitive consecration as a senior leader, as one of the most important and dependable field lieutenants for Caesar, and as one of the cornerstones of his reconstruction. Less than ten years had elapsed from his wild days with Curio and Clodius, and only seven from his Athens sojourn where he had perfected his grammar and oratory skills, and Antony had emerged as one of the men from Caesar's inner circle on whom the future dictator counted for his political programme. Here was a man who could be safely relied upon to conduct military affairs, but who was also bright enough to manage delicate assignments and responsibilities in the minefield that was the Roman political scene in 50 BC. Caesar knew perfectly well that the credibility of the team he was fielding was going to determine the ultimate success of his programme.

Chapter Three

The Civil War

In order to better understand the first career steps of Mark Antony upon his return from war in the east and in Gaul, it will be helpful to briefly rewind the clock on the political situation in Rome and see how it had evolved since the beginning of the First Triumvirate in 60 BC.

We have seen how, unlike the Second Triumvirate, which was to be formalized by the Senate as a legal vehicle to introduce reforms, the First had been just a power sharing deal made by the three strongest personalities of the time, Caesar, Pompey, and Crassus. The Triumvirate had extended its term in 55 BC, and some attempts by others, such as the noble Domitius Ahenobarbus (copper bearded) to capture some of the power and make room for themselves at the table that counted, had been easily repelled. The coalition was airtight, and did not need to expand its exclusive membership.

Caesar, who before his departure to Gaul had engaged in pushing his own demagogical agenda, had scored major publicity points with his land distribution legislation and all the other reforms he was able to conduct during his consulship, and with the support of the two other Triumvirs. He was at the apogee of his career, but at the same time he had attracted considerable resentment and envy from the opposition, those *optimates* who had much to lose from all the reforms introduced in the rural world.

For several years the arrangement between the Triumvirs worked extremely well. Caesar had his new father-in-law appointed as Consul for the year 58 BC, and had his mandate in Gaul renewed for another five years. Pompey kept managing his favourite province of Spain through his subordinates, while he was comfortably residing in Rome. He and Crassus held a joint consulship for the year 55 BC, and the two continued to make the good and the bad weather in Rome.

The death of Crassus in Parthia in 53 BC, described in Chapter 2, was the first big blow that shook up the First Triumvirate and the alliance between Pompey and Caesar, and would be fatal for it shortly thereafter.

The Triumvirs were the most prominent figures of public life, but not the only ones. One level down, the various demagogues were still struggling to make a name for themselves. The most famous casualty of this violent struggle, as we have seen, had been that of Clodius, at the hands of the muscle men of his opponent Milo, in the course of an apparently random confrontation in a tavern in Bovillae, outside the southern gates of Rome.

The commotion that followed, when his associates were organizing a funeral pyre in the middle of the Forum, and launched a vengeful manhunt around the city, was more than the Romans were ready to accept.[1] Things were degenerating once again into a situation of near-anarchy, with groups of armed thugs roaming the streets and holding hostage the civilian population.

In the meantime, during Caesar's absence from 59 BC to 50 BC, Pompey had gradually drifted away from his alliance with him, and increasingly embraced the positions of the Senate's right wing. In turn, the same elitist conservative clique that snubbed Cicero by denying him a membership card, had begun to consider Magnus (who, upon his return from Asia, was distrusted as a man only devoted to his personal agenda) as a good alternative to the continuing unrest brought by the radical *populares* and Clodius' gangsters. So in a short space of time, the conqueror of the east became the person the Romans relied on to restore order in the Eternal City, but was also suddenly considered to be an *optimates* leader. This faction clearly wanted to take advantage of the civil strife to re-conquer some of the lost grounds on the institutional concessions that had been made to the *populares*, and move back to the old ways of oligarchic rule.

At the same time, in 54 BC, destiny played another trick on history as Julia, Caesar's daughter and Pompey's wife, died in childbirth. Apparently Pompey deeply and genuinely grieved for the loss. It had been a rare example of a political marriage which was also a union based on true love. The loss of Julia pushed the two pivotal figures of this period, Caesar and Pompey, another big step apart. While Pompey suffered from his loss, he went on to find consolation in his marriage to the daughter of Scipio Nasica (Big Nose), one of the *boni vires*, grandson of the senator who had murdered the second of the Gracchi brothers.[2] This marriage was a political statement and an explicit sign of a turn in his political attitude, as well as the birth of a new alliance, to replace the Triumviral one. Despite the new deal, the appointment of the new strong man of the right wing as sole Consul for the year 52 BC, an unprecedented appointment, raised many eyebrows, including that of the political purist Cato, who did not like or trust Pompey any more than when he was a political opponent.

In 51 BC, the Senatorial right wing decided that the Caesar-Pompey alliance had sufficiently lost cohesiveness to make a political attack on Caesar viable.

The envy for his political power and prestige, and the fear of a mighty leader in the reformist line-up was past the danger zone, and many thought that the direction it had taken needed to be reversed quickly.

The first to strike was Marcus Claudius Marcellus (Marcellus), an aristocrat who was elected Consul for 51 BC. Marcellus started arguing that, after the final victory against the Gallic rebels in Alesia, there was no point in continuing to extend the duration of Caesar's extraordinary – and very lucrative – Gallic command. The same Marcellus went on challenging Caesar's right to run for Consul for the second time upon his impending return, an office that he could have easily won, based on a legal technicality. And then, the political plays took the form of pushing the Senate to make Caesar reduce the military force under his command, by returning to Pompey a Spanish legion the Magnus had loaned to him to tame the Vercingetorix insurrection. All these moves fit into a long term design progressively to reduce the Proconsul's influence, and eventually to destroy him politically with a trial for abuses committed in Gaul. Although Marcellus did not succeed in carrying out his entire plan during the term of his Consulship, it was clear that the winds in Rome had changed, and that more intestine fighting was on the horizon. No matter all the fine juridical points on the expiry of Caesar's proconsular mandate, for the exact term of the 55 BC renewal might have been imprecise, the year 50 BC was to see some grand scale settlement of scores, beginning, according to Pompey's point of view, from the Kalends (the 1st) of March, when he would lay down his *imperium*, his military command. A Tribunician decision came to further precipitate the events: Caesar was allowed to run for Consul without returning from Gaul. This meant that in theory he could have been in office – from Proconsul to Consul again – without interruption, and gone from one *imperium* to the next without ever disarming. The venomous Marcellus, the still resentful Bibulus, the jealous Domitius Ahenobarbus, the vengeful Cato, were actively co-operating to lay their trap.

Unexpected help came from Curio, the young senator, who, as we have already seen, had been a fierce critic of the First Triumvirate ten years earlier, at the time of his dissolute nights with Mark Antony.[3] His support might have been prompted by financial help he had almost certainly received from Caesar, given the young politician's propensity to incur debt to finance his flamboyant lifestyle. Curio was very argumentative and in the beginning straddled between the two political men: why would Caesar step down from his extraordinary Proconsulate while Pompey could have kept his position, when both the appointments had been voted by the Senate and the people at the same time? His following interventions in the debate were tantamount to publicly accusing Pompey of aiming for absolute rule. In the senatorial debate that followed, the only decision that was taken was that both Caesar and Pompey would surrender one legion, which would be sent to reinforce the Parthian border. This decision was to be only a temporary victory for Caesar. In December of that same year, 50 BC, the Senate voted that Caesar was to lay down his *imperium* and in a separate ruling allowed Pompey to keep his. Practically speaking, Pompey was given full power to silence Caesar. Marcellus succeeded in forcing his wishes on the Senate, and Pompey was feeling stronger than ever in his position. He was, after all, a man of the establishment, while Caesar was nothing but a populist threat, which had been instrumental in securing for Pompey the loyalty of the armies, but that in the future could only harm his agenda.

It was at the wake of these events, in 50 BC, that Antony, by now back in Rome for three or four months already, was made Tribune of the Plebs, together with a Quintus Cassius, a distant relative of the conspirator to be, Cassius Longinius. Significantly, the election of Antony to this delicate role was chosen as the starting point for Caesar's own narration of the Civil War (De Bello Civile).

The *Tribunatus Plebis* had been one of the cornerstones of Rome's political system since the beginning of the fifth century BC, when the Plebeians obtained the appointment of a small number of magistrates, protected by a sacred and inviolable status, to represent them, protect them against abuses from the Patricians, and veto any law issued by the Senate that in their opinion was damaging the interests of the Plebs. When Rome turned to imperial rule, this role and its powers did not disappear, but were officially taken over by the Emperor or Princeps, that simply cumulated them with the *Imperium*, or military and provincial command, with religious primacy, and with, at times, Consulate. Sulla, in his body of political reforms promulgated during his dictatorship, had aggressively reduced the scope and prerogatives of these Tribunes, until their only power was the *ius auxiliandi*, the right to help, or the power to suspend any action undertaken by a patrician magistrate against a Plebeian. But in the following years the role was restored to its former status, encompassing its full powers as initially designed, and especially the *intercessio*, or veto power, that could suspend the Senate's deliberations. In this specific situation, a Tribune could have stopped the Senate from acting against Caesar, a move that could have been prejudicial to the interests of the Plebeians.

So, this role at such a delicate time was a stringent test for Antony's political sense and judgment. Caesar was the man of the masses and the new rallying flag for the *populares*. During his prolonged absence, the Tribunes, protected by their sacred status, were on the watch to protect the *populares* agenda while the Senate was shifting increasingly to the defensive mode and towards the *optimates* agenda.

Antony had been made an Augur before stepping up to the post of Tribune, and he kept this religious role for many years, even well into his years as a Triumvir. Augurs were religious magistrates derived from Etruscan traditions, charged with divination of future events from the observation of bird flight and song, lightning during storms, and the like. In Rome's superstitious society, this role was considered important and prestigious, as omens could impact decision making and public opinion on major events like military expeditions, appointment of magistrates, and senatorial sessions. Suffice to say, the role had been open because the last occupant of the vacant seat was Crassus Junior, who had met his fate in Parthia only days before his father, on the first day of combat against Surenas and his archers. Plutarch makes the two appointments sound as if they had been almost simultaneous. Probably, as he was watching the body language of the *optimates* stiffen, Caesar pressed to move a resolute and reliable man such as Antony into a more operating role, rather than a prestigious but largely symbolic one. Antony took the job seriously, and upheld Caesar's agenda while he was away. According to Plutarch[4] he managed to have his letters from Gaul publicly read, against the wishes of many senators, thus winning some hearts to Caesar's cause. Plutarch even gets a little carried away in his narration, attributing to Antony the motion for simultaneous disarmament of Caesar and Pompey, which is otherwise commonly attributed to Curio. Antony was not yet at the point in his career where he could have had the gravitas to be a proponent of such major motions, while Curio had been a political heavyweight for years already.

In addition to his religious post, prior to making it to Tribune, Antony had had a brief spell as a Quaestor, and in fact his trip to Rome during the Gaul adventure had been motivated by his accepting the office. Of course, his appointment had been favoured by Julius Caesar, who had pushed even Cicero to support him, as he later admitted in the Philippics. But in his race to Augur, Antony had beaten a young Domitius, from one of Rome's most ancient and prestigious clans, who, additionally, was supported by Cato himself. Regardless of all the horse trading that must have been happening on the side, given the importance of the role, Antony must have had substantial personal credibility. Once again, suffice to say that the post had been left vacant by the death of old Hortentius, the famous lawyer and speaker, himself.

We know how, even if for a while he had not fully manifested his intentions, by the end of 50 BC Pompey had fully come out into the open. Everyone thought that, when this would happen, it would be the tie breaker in the factional struggle. The debate on the course of action to follow heated up and the anti-Caesarean sentiment became more manifest. As the Consuls moved for decisive action for Caesar's disarmament and impeachment, Antony used the Tribune's veto power (*intercessio*) to stop this arbitrary decision. But in an unprecedented pronouncement, the Tribunes were invited to leave the Senate's assembly, and the Veto issued by Antony was simply disregarded.

This was, undoubtedly, an illegal course of action. The role of the Tribune of the Plebs was vested with a sacred status, exactly to protect this key control point from abuse by the senatorial class. Excluding the Tribunes from the debate and preventing them from using their Veto privilege was equivalent to denying to the whole *populares* class any input in the motion against Caesar. It was really like stripping the people of Rome of the most basic form of control over the Senate's decision making.

Caesar, as one would expect, dwelled on this in the opener of his book on the Civil War. Upon reading the same pages, we get a reminder of how small the world is. The Senate's spokesperson for the anti-Caesarean motion was a Cornelius Lentulus, thus related to Mark Antony's stepfather, executed in the course of the repression of Catiline's putsch! His motives, according to Caesar, included his desire for primacy, and he was possibly staging a plot involving foreign princes, who saw their agenda better represented by the Pompeian side.

Antony, and his colleague in the Tribunate, Quintus Cassius, lashed out at the scandalous move, but then realized that the situation could take a turn for the worse still, and that, at this point, the Pompeian faction could have taken even more dramatic steps than a simple silencing and expulsion from a meeting. Fearing for his own safety, Antony disguised himself as a slave and escaped at night, running north to meet Caesar at Ravenna where he had set up camp, and where he had met Curio, who by now had openly declared his support for Caesar. It is also probable that, when the two met, Caesar had already rolled his famous dice and crossed the fatal Rubicon with a few cohorts of the veteran XIII Legion, with the intention of marching to Rome and straightening all the accounts with the Pompeians. This would mean the meeting took place in Ariminium, modern Rimini, 50 km to the south of the famous stream.

It is easy to infer from the events that the expulsion of Antony from the senatorial debate was due to his perceived loyalty to Caesar: we have discussed how his ascension to the Tribunate had been largely due to Caesar's political manoeuvring. But a different interpretation is also plausible and legitimate: the expulsion of the Tribunes could also have been independent of the individuals in the role, and was rather one more attempt by the Senate to escape from the constitutional controls and acquire more power, as it had during the Sulla dictatorship.

Over the years, Antony had already proven to be his own man, a free and independent spirit, with all the strength of character and personality necessary to use his own judgment to make decisions. The episode with Clodius in the Forum is very telling. So it is reasonable to think that the injustice suffered may well have been the decisive blow to Antony's confidence in the Republican institutions, already shaky after being tested by all the facts narrated so far. There is more to the escape to Ariminium than just a young subordinate on his way to join his chief after a setback; what we are seeing is a young leader, disgusted by Rome's corruption, making the final choice to side with the man that represented a clean break with the crumbling institutions and the decadence of the costumes. In fact, while many kept identifying Antony's motives with a thirst for primacy and greatness, his behaviour during this phase points to a uncompromising man, a career man for sure, but whose standards made him stand tall among the majority of his contemporaries who we have met so far, and who made his choices based on a solid value system, distrust in the decaying powers, and his instinctual temperament. He had taken the Tribunate seriously, and was going to do his job conscientiously. It also happened that Caesar's political agenda coincided more closely with what he was institutionally asked to uphold. As far as the senatorial gang, which was making up the rules as it went along, were concerned, he saw them for the devious and conniving bunch that they were, subservient to the strong man of the moment, and sworn to the conservation of class privileges.

This parallelism finds more grounds in Caesar's very own narration of the events in the early pages of the De Bello Civile: while describing the expulsion of Antony and Q. Cassius from the Senate, Caesar refers to them as "the Tribunes". It is evident that this was a deliberate choice, and not an expedient to keep the focus of the narration on events rather than on the protagonists. The purpose was to emphasize that the offence had been made against the sacred representatives of the most venerable institution, rather than to the emissaries of the Caesarean faction. The subtle distinction made the offence all the more heinous, and the perpetrators look even less worthy of respect.

Antony was for sure at the very centre of Caesar's attention, and his name comes up explicitly only a few lines later in the narration, when Caesar's invasion of Italy had begun, and the young Tribune is reported leading a 500 men vanguard to the conquest of the city of Aretium (Arezzo) in Etruria, and days later that of Sulmona in Brutium, another 180 km south, where he was welcomed by the inhabitants as a liberator.

Later Cicero lashed out again at Antony over his escape, saying he had been the cause of the Civil War, making a comparison to Helen and the Trojan War, but this comment is little more than a theatrical outburst in the heat of the delivery of the Philippics. Antony and Caesar did not connect until after the "dice had been cast", and as we pointed out, Antony had started in his official role with the best intentions to play by the book. The scene and the casting for the beginning of the Civil War had been ready for at least two years, and the events would have followed the same course no matter who had been vested with the Tribunician powers at that particular time.

The facts are of course well known, with Caesar crossing the Rubicon and storming south with 5,000 veterans of the formidable XIII Legion, a former Pompeian unit that had been road tested in Gaul for the whole eight years. Pompey managed to make it from Capua, where he was based, to Brundusium in Puglia, the heel of the Italian boot, and make a *rocambolesque* departure to Epyrum where he established his basecamp, and started pulling on all the relationships he had built over the years to build a powerful army with the aim of restoring to power the *optimates* and senatorial side. The most compromised *boni viri* followed him across the Adriatic, fearing Caesar's retaliation.

This important part of the Civil Wars was to be fought over a vast area which stretched from Spain to Northern Turkey, so that it became critical for Caesar to carefully place his pawns on the most important cells of the chessboard.

Illyria (or the northern Balkans) technically would have been Caesar's governorship before Gaul, and fallen within his sphere of influence in the spirit of the first Triumvirate. It went to Gaius Antonius, not Hybrida this time, but Mark

Antony's younger brother. At this point, he had achieved little to deserve such a prestigious position, so we have to assume that family ties, the brother's growing reputation, and the overall scarcity of experienced leaders in the Caesarean camp must have played a role in the appointment. Gaius unfortunately proved as bad a commander as his father and his uncle. He was defeated in the island of Curicta (modern day Krk, in Croatia), was forced to hand over fifteen *cohortes* to the enemy, and was taken prisoner. It would not be the last time for him, as we shall see.

Sicily was traditionally one of the strategic hubs in the Mediterranean, both for its central location and for its importance as a source of grain and other provisions. It went to Curio, because of his seniority in Caesar's ranks. The legitimate Governor was Cato, who, when Pompey escaped to Epyrum, made a run for Corfu, and thus abandoned the island without a fight.

Unfortunately for Curio, the Sicilian responsibility carried some oversight on the African front, where King Juba of Numidia, a Pompeian loyalist, was up in arms. Curio was defeated, and perished in battle, leaving Fulvia a widow for the second time. And, what is worse, Juba slaughtered all the (many) prisoners taken. The Romans would certainly have taken good note of this, and payback was to be delivered at the battle of Thapsos less than three years later, when the legionaries of the Fifth Legion were to crush him and his elephant-mounted troops, leaving him with ritual suicide as the only option.

Caesar did not cross the Adriatic right away, but played his hand very rationally. In the *Commentarii* on the Civil War he clarifies the reason for this, as he questions the opportunity of embarking in a naval expedition with scant preparation and scarcity of appropriate vessels. Pompey had sailed across the Adriatic taking most of the transport ships available in Brundusium, but only the inexperienced troops that had followed him to Southern Italy. On the other hand, his most experienced legions were still stationed in Spain, which was governed by Varo, scholar and gentleman of Pompeian loyalties. So before Pompey could have feasibly rebuilt a credible army, and crossed back to Italy to counterattack, it would have taken considerable time, maybe one year or more. But had he been reunited with his best troops, he would have represented a more serious and immediate threat. Hence Caesar took the decision to attack Spain first. The phrase that symbolized his intentions was that he wanted to deal "first with the Army without a General, and then with the General without an Army". At the same time Antony could have consolidated the Caesarean grip over Italy, where there was no sign of resistance left, after all the walled cities had surrendered, and all the magistrates had either fled to Greece with Pompey, or joined Caesar's side. This short term necessity was not at all an easy task, in a country that had already been ravaged by civil war many times, and where the people could have legitimately expected mass retaliation from the new victors on a scale carried out by Marius, Cinna, and Sulla.

Antony, still legally a Tribune of the Plebs, called the Council of the Plebs to assembly, and Caesar, who of course had great influence over the *populares*, reassured the people on peace, forgiveness, prosperity ahead, and distributions of grain and money to follow shortly. His only controversial move was the seizure of the public Treasury funds, threatening the magistrate that was guarding them. That gave his exhausted finances some relief, along with other money he had confiscated during his march towards Rome, but not enough to support his entire military force, and he had to borrow from his officers and Centurions to pay the soldiers.

On the way to Spain, he set siege to the town of Massilia (Marseilles), which had turned to Pompey's side. Interestingly, the confrontation in Massilia saw, on the lead for the Caesareans, none other than Decimus Brutus, one of Caesar's lieutenants in Gaul, and future assassin, and Domitius Ahenobarbus, the prominent patrician whose offspring we shall meet again soon, who had just been abandoned by Pompey to defend some Italian strongholds, captured by Caesar, then immediately pardoned and released.

When Caesar's legions arrived in the area of the city of Llerda, on the banks of the river Ebro, in southern Spain, they found a large army waiting for them, at the orders of the experienced legates Petreius and Afranius. This brief Spanish "blitz" was not marked by any large battle, but consisted mainly of a series of skirmishes and small engagements, in a chess game where the two sides kept trying to outsmart each other to gain a position of advantage. As Caesar kept increasing the odds in his favour, the enemy's morale crumbled, and the large scale defection of the Pompeian soldiers began. Petreius tried to put a halt to it, but so discouraged were his soldiers that he failed. Within days, the capitulation was complete, and the loyalist legions were either disbanded or absorbed. As for their leaders, they were pardoned, as usual, as long as they ceased hostilities. The mercy shown was gratefully accepted, but, one more time, the promise to stay out of the conflict was broken.

After dealing with the potential reinforcement for Pompey, Caesar crossed over the Adriatic Sea in pursuit of Pompey and the majority of the senatorial loyalists on New Year's Day, 48 BC. He sailed with a small contingent and not with the bulk of his army; as per usual he preferred speed to scale, and wanted to press Pompey closely without giving him the time to organize. But he prepared the next move, and sent envoys with specific instructions.[5]

They were to see Gabinius first, and tell him to cross the Adriatic Sea to meet in Epyrum. Antony was to be the second choice if Gabinius had refused or failed to cross over. Evidently, Caesar's moves had been so sudden that his forces had not had the time to fully coordinate yet, and were still led fairly independently.

For the 34-year-old Mark Antony, playing second fiddle to his old General and mentor Gabinius was not a bad start. But Gabinius did not have the courage to sail in the middle of winter, and took the land route, coasting both the Adriatic shores. That did not work out as he had hoped: he was soon blocked by hostile troops in Dalmatia, and could not make progress southwards.

It was now down to Antony to save the day: with his cargo ships he braved the Adriatic waves and the Pompeian warships that were guarding the coast. According to the sources, Antony was actually extremely afraid of the naval blockade operated by Bibulus, the former Consular colleague of Caesar with a vengeful tooth, which would have made him reluctant to sail. But, all of a sudden, Bibulus took sick and died, and was replaced by Libo, a man that Antony held in much lower esteem.[6]

When Pompey made it to Brundusium before Caesar, he was able to requisition all or most of the warships available on site, and those were the ships still in his possession and available for the blockade. Warships of the time were the powerful Roman galleys *triremes* and *quadriremes*, powered by rowers and therefore able to manoeuvre in any wind condition. On the contrary, the cargo ships left for Antony and the Caesareans to cross the Adriatic were powered by the traditional square Latin sails, and were thus at a strong disadvantage unless the wind was blowing in the right direction.

It was only thanks to suddenly raising favourable winds that he avoided the rams of the Pompeians' assault vessels with his heavier form of transport, and managed to land in a place called Nimphaeum, thus supplying Caesar with fresh troops and partly compensating the numerical unbalance between the two armies. He had managed to break a perfectly organized naval blockade, and he rushed to conquer the fortified city of Lissus on the Albanian coast. After this brilliant and daring intervention, which had saved the destiny of the expedition and changed the fate of the war, he was no longer Number Two in Caesar's pecking order.

Despite Antony's arrival, the early rounds of the fight went to Pompey. For a prolonged period of time both armies kept each other in check by building two opposing fortified lines, for a staggering total length of nearly 50 km. When finally the fighting started, the better fed and equipped Pompeians won the first two bouts. It would seem the losses could have been even higher without the personal engagement of Antony in the fighting. Like in Judaea and Egypt, he led from the front, on occasion turning back towards the enemy fleeing Caesarean troops.

Antony dealt very well with the psychological difficulty of leading an army of Romans against an army of Romans. So far he had fought Jewish militias, rebel Egyptians, and Celtic barbarians, but these were the first field engagements in a civil war in a very long time, since the defeat of Catilina or the second entry of Sulla in Rome. This effect may have amplified the difficulty of turning around a battle situation where the own troops are being defeated and need to come back, a task which it seems Antony accomplished perfectly.

In any case, this part of the Civil War was turning into a conflict in the style of the Great War, with the two armies entrenched behind their fortifications trying to erode the other's confidence, launching sporadic small scale attacks. Caesar could not get Pompey to accept a large pitched battle, as the latter was slowly prevailing thanks to his better logistics, and was not entirely confident in the quality of the troops he had rallied.

Pompey ended up yielding to the pressure of his own generals and conceded to go into battle, but this was against his better judgment. He was too sly an old fox not to realize that his army was not of the highest grade. True, all his debtors around the Middle East had sent troops to reinforce his legions. Even Cleopatra had sent him some ships with her Marines. But even if he could line up 40,000 soldiers against Caesar's 22,000,[7] and 7,000 cavalry against Caesar's 1,500, he would have much preferred to play a game of attrition, so weary was he of the inferior quality of his patchwork army. He had had months to prepare and had better food and water supplies, while his enemies were struggling to find grasses and roots to put meals together, and he believed this would give him a distinct advantage. Was he taken by the general enthusiasm that was reigning in his camp? Did he feel a sense of unease over all the vassal kings who had brought him troops and that were itching for battle? Probably all of the above, and so on 9 July, 49 BC, Pompey left camp and lined up the army for battle.

The general scheme of a pitched battle often followed a well established pattern. The Romans would lay out the army following a scheme called the *triplex acies*, or with the platoons arranged on three orders, the last one, made up by the veterans, being a fall back or reserve contingent. The early phases typically saw the intervention of light allied infantry, called *velites*, who were involved in some skirmishes with the launch of light javelins, but were helped by specialized contingents of slingers, archers, and stone throwers. Typically, the heavy infantry would endure this using their testudo (turtle) formation, by locking their large rectangular shields together. At this stage the casualties would still be very light, but many shields would have been damaged by the missiles, or would have arrows and pieces of javelins stuck in them, thus making them cumbersome to use at close range. The Roman javelin or *pilum* featured two pegs which joined the iron spear to the wooden shaft: the first was really an iron nail that could not be dislodged. The second was a wooden peg that was designed to give way upon impact, so that the javelin would bend around the nail, thereby making it impossible to return to the sender, but also so that extraction from a shield would be more difficult, and the shield would become more cumbersome and at some point would have been discarded, making the soldier vulnerable during the fight at close range.

Then the real battle would start, with the heavy infantry fighting at close quarters, shield to shield, the soldiers using the short Spanish sword, the *gladium*, thrusting and slashing at whatever target would open between the shields. This was a long, nerve-wrecking exercise, which would push the legionaries' physical and mental resources to their limits. Victory could come in two ways: a legion would break through the centre of enemy lines and then quickly turn around to sandwich them, or alternatively swivel around the enemy lines and flank them.

The breaking or the flanking would always generate panic in the enemy lines, as the soldiers would have to face attacks coming from two directions. And as soon as one of the two contestants panicked, slaughter would quickly follow. Those that turned their shoulders to the enemy and tried to run or retreat were doomed. This is why every *centuria*, or platoon, of a legion, had two leaders: the Centurion or captain, leading from the front, and the *optio*, or sergeant major, at the back, ready to cut down those that would be tempted to escape. The question arises whether the modern word "option" derives from the choice that roman legionaries had to make on which blade to face if the battle turned sour.

According to the sources, few were the battles of antiquity where victory was achieved by a small margin of casualties: more often, the body count was very dramatically skewed in favour of the winner, and probably not just by post war propaganda, but also by the battle dynamics described. This was also the reason why generals at the head of navigated legionaries who would not panic and would stand their ground in moments of difficulty tended to have the upper hand on larger armies formed by less experienced recruits. As we will see, Pharsalus was not to be an exception to this rule.

Back to the flanking, as the soldiers held the shield in the left hand and the *gladium* in the right, an attack had more chances to succeed if it was carried out from the right side, forcing the soldiers engaged frontally to turn to cover their weak side. This is why generals preferred to launch an attack on their left wing, and at the same time fielded their most loyal or experienced troops on the right wing, which invariably would come under pressure from the enemy; if it had yielded it would have put the whole army in jeopardy of being totally destroyed. The centre could be thickened and reinforced with more rows of infantrymen, or by positioning reserve troops at the back, or supported by other contingents of allied troops, but the wings, and especially the right wing, were too crucial to take chances.

Caesar took the right wing for himself with his favourite Tenth Legion of Gallic War veterans from southern Spain, with their red bull symbol painted on their shields, gave the centre and the left to Sulla (grandson of the dictator!) and Domitius, while Antony led the equally prestigious left wing.

Pompey played a variation on the flanking theme, trying to perform the manoeuvre with a cavalry column. Caesar anticipated the move, and successfully countered it by hiding 3,000 foot soldiers carrying lances. When the riders approached, they were tackled by the 3,000 men, suffered heavy losses, and fell back towards their Pompeian comrades, creating havoc in their own lines. That was all the Caesarean forces were waiting for to counterattack. By nightfall, Mark Antony and his soldiers were sitting in the Pompeian camp, in the tents that the early occupants had adorned with ivy and laurel anticipating an easy victory, feasting on the delicacies that their over-confident enemies had ordered for their celebrations.

We learn from Cicero[8] who, in all likelihood, wanted to underline his cruelty rather than his courage, that Antony fought sword in hand at the front of his troops, and killed the Pompeian General Lucius Domitius Ahenobarbus. It is the only reference to this fact; Caesar does not mention it in the De Bello Civile. Destiny was to play a trick on the families of the two. Lucius' son Gnaeus was to continue the tradition of his father and fight against the Caesarean cause, and later the Second Triumvirate. But subsequently he would make peace with Antony, who would give his daughter Antonia, born from his marriage with Octavia, to Gnaeus' son, also called Lucius. The son of Antonia and Lucius, Gnaeus, would marry into the Julio-Claudian clan, with Agrippinilla, daughter of Germanicus and Agrippina, and sister, among others, to the Emperor to be, Gaius (Caligula). Their first and only offspring, reuniting the chromosomes of the Julii (from Antony's side), the Claudii (from Germanicus), the Antonii, and adding the volatile personality traits of the Domitii, was also called Lucius Domitius Ahenobarbus, after his noble ancestor killed at the hands of the other great-grandfather Antony. But when his mother Agrippinilla married Emperor Claudius, and he was formally adopted into the Claudian clan, he changed his given name to the one with which he rose to immortal fame, albeit for the wrong reasons: Nero Caesar.

All of Pompey's key leadership escaped the pursuit of the Caesareans, and scattered around the Mediterranean looking for support and fresh forces from traditional allies: Cassius Longinius headed to the east to Ponthus-Bythinia, at the court of King Pharnaces. Sextus and Gnaeus, Pompey's older sons, went to Spain to recruit more legionaries. Cato and Scipio hastened to Africa, to meet King Juba. As for Pompey himself, he thought he would find shelter in Egypt, at the court of the Ptolemys, who were in debt to Rome for a huge sum. Probably Pompey was counting on the collection of the money to sustain the re-launch of hostilities. Instead, he was killed upon landing by the devious eunuch Pothinus and the General Achillas, advisors of the child King Ptolemy XIII, who thought the treacherous act would win them Caesar's sympathy.

Caesar was immediately on Pompey's tracks, per his habit of tracking his enemies closely, and, in this specific case, to deny him the time to organize fund raising and re-arm. As a matter of fact, when Pompey was assassinated, he was hoping to collect on Ptolemy's XII Auletes debt to Rome, and use it to raise another army.

When Julius Caesar landed in Alexandria, with a reduced force of 4,000 men, of which 800 were on horseback, just days after the murder of his former son-in-law and enemy, he was presented with his signet ring and severed head by the Egyptian courtesans. The Egyptian events that followed are material for the continuity of the narration and for Antony's life.

Caesar might have received a warmer welcome in Alexandria if he had not walked straight into the hornets' nest that was the latest dynastic struggle of the Ptolemies. After the Gabinius mission, of which Antony was a protagonist, the popularity of Ptolemy XII among his subjects had not improved significantly, and the periodic rioting of the Alexandrians against his rule never ceased. When he finally passed away, those he had named for his succession as co-rulers, his 17-year-old daughter Cleopatra VII, and his 10-year-old son Ptolemy XIII, followed a Ptolemaic tradition, dictated by the intention of excluding the other noble families from succession claims and promptly married. The two regents, the sly eunuch Pothinius and the strongman General Achillas, supported the young Ptolemy XIII over his sister, who had to flee to Egypt, only to return at the head of an army, which on Caesar's arrival was stationed on the banks of the Nile opposite the regular troops.

When Caesar's soldiers entered the streets of Alexandria, they were made the object of attacks by the local population, who did not like to see Roman uniforms in the city, and the hostility further escalated when Caesar made it clear that he wanted to collect on the huge amount of money that the late Pharaoh owed to the Roman *aerarium*, the public Treasury. Soon full urban guerrilla warfare erupted between Caesar's 4,000 men, and the 20,000 deployed by Achillas, and the Roman dictator had to set fire to some buildings, damaging Alexandria's world famous library, in order to extricate himself from a dangerous situation. The edge of Caesar's legionaries over the local troops was very thin, as many of Achillas' men were none other than the Roman troops left behind by Gabinius that had gone native and, after marrying local women, had re-enlisted in the Egyptian armed forces. He remained in the end besieged in the royal palace, but with the Ptolemaic princes and Pothinus in his custody.

It is at this point that Cleopatra staged her famous *coup de théâtre* and managed to be smuggled across the Egyptian lines wrapped in a carpet, and delivered to Caesar. The Roman leader being the ladies' man that he was, it was not difficult for the fascinating queen to seduce him with her known charms, and have him endorse officially her claim to the throne. In a short period of time, many events followed at a frantic pace. Cleopatra's sister Arsinoe, this far in Caesar's hands, escaped and took control of the Egyptian army, was proclaimed Queen, had Achillas killed and replaced him with another courtesan named Ganymedes, probably an eunuch in his turn. Pothinius was found plotting from within the palace with the besiegers and was put to death by the Romans.

The fighting at land and at sea continued for many days, with alternate outcomes. Caesar had a close call with death during an engagement at sea, when he had to jump from a boat and swim to shore. But over time he received reinforcements from Rome, as well as from the King of Pergamum and from Hyrcanus of Jerusalem. The arrival of these contingents turned the course of the events, and the Egyptians were definitively routed in a final battle. The young Ptolemy XIII died tragically as his boat capsized in the Nile and he drowned. That left Cleopatra co-ruler with her younger brother Ptolemy XIV, who she had to marry, but de facto uncontested queen of the Roman protectorate. She and 55-year-old Caesar left for a luxurious cruise, which lasted over three months, sailing down the Nile in the glamorous royal barge, enjoying the pleasures of life and each other's stimulating company, just like she had, allegedly, done with Pompey's son four years earlier, so that when six years later it was Antony's turn, she had fully perfected her entertainment act.

Caesar had followed his instinct, and chased after Pompey immediately after Pharsalus. But after he was done with Egypt, he had to attend to Middle Eastern matters, as Cassius' mission to Ponthus and Bythinia had probably been successful and King Pharnaces, the son of Mithridates, had taken arms against Rome, and killed Roman settlers, just like his father had done forty years before. So Caesar landed on the Turkish coast and dealt with Pharnaces in one quick battle near the town of Zela. For some reason the general public think that the famous "Veni, Vidi, Vici"[9] is a quotation on the Gallic campaign, which, as we know, had lasted eight years, so "I came, I saw, I conquered" would have been an inappropriate comment to make. In reality, the comment is a dismissive remark, which came to us via the Greek historians and Suetonius, and not from Caesar first hand, to underline what scarce opponents the Pharnaces' forces had proven to be. For the first time recorded, Caesar dropped his traditional aplomb and let out some borderline derogatory remarks at the address of Pompey. He said something along the lines of "Did Pompey and his Generals really earn a reputation of great warriors by vanquishing mediocre fighters like these?"

Before leaving for Egypt, Caesar had appointed Antony Magister Equitum, or Master of Horse, and Lepidus *Quaestor* for the city of Rome. As we have seen, the latter role was more or less a role of a mayor. The former role on the other hand had nothing to do with commanding cavalry, but was the official title of the deputy of a dictator. While Caesar was gone, in Turkey or Egypt, Antony was the sole ruler of Italy and commander in chief of all the armies stationed in the peninsula.

This period has been especially targeted by Antony's detractors to stigmatize some examples of obnoxious behaviour on his part. Most of the juicy anecdotes reported by Cicero in the Philippics belong to this relatively brief spell. Allegedly he engaged in a shameless display of wealth, as he paraded his chariot loaded with golden vases and other riches. He spent time in the company of mimes and actresses (which was considered incompatible with his role and status), the most famous of them being a Citheris, who might have been his lover for a prolonged period of time. His arrogance went as far as helping himself fondly to the favours bestowed by many prominent citizens' wives – the new strong man in town apparently became a matron hunter. Antony was certainly a ladies' man. Plutarch says that he "had an ill name for familiarity with other people's wives". This fame would continue to follow him throughout his life and travels around the world. In promiscuous and libertine Rome, this cannot have been a source of scandal *per se*, but we suppose the disapproval must have stemmed from Antony's abuse of his position of power, and he was accused of taking advantage of his status for womanizing. But most importantly we read that his attitude became increasingly arrogant and intolerant towards the Senate, and citizens pleading their cases. It is hard to say how many of these allegations are grounded in reality, and how much is slander. For sure, we have learned to take Cicero with more than a grain of salt, and Plutarch himself is very bipolar in all his value judgments. Was the rude and arrogant Magister Equitum the same man that the preceding year he had praised for being so accessible to the common legionaries, soldier among the soldiers, sharing their meals by the campfires, and thus obtaining general sympathy and long lasting personal loyalties? While a touch of general arrogance might have surfaced in the Antony persona while he was holding the reins of command in his hands, his overall temperament was probably not inclined to power trips, but rather to target vengefully some layers of the Roman society that he held in disdain and contempt.

We also need to put some perspective around the situation in Italy in 48 BC and onwards. The last time Antony had been in Rome, he had to escape at night in disguise, forced by that same senatorial class and their associates that now were trying to obtain favours from him in his new capacity. Clearly, if we think of what Antony had to witness and endure over time from his fellow citizens, and in what regard he must have held their overwhelming majority, expecting univocal fairness and tolerance for all would be a very tall order.

As for the *nouveau riche* attitude, it would appear that Mark Antony's finances had improved significantly during his brief stay in Gaul, no doubt thanks to the slave trade, which was the most important fallout of a military victory in the classical world. According to estimates during the eight years of Caesar's campaigning in Gaul, up to a million people were enslaved and sold. Considering that, at the high end of the market, a slave could trade as high as one thousand dinarii, if we try to adjust for purchasing power, the amount of capital that would have been raised at retail prices was close to fifteen billion US dollars in today's money.

Increasingly, we have to consider that the factional break remained very real, and the potential for more sedition remained very high, and needed to be managed with an iron fist, with little indulgence to politeness and form.

To make things all the more dangerous, the legions stationed in Italy that did not follow Caesar were composed of veterans close to or at the end of their term, and to whom the Republic owed their back ended bonuses, which it did not have funds sufficient to pay. Retirement bonuses were of the utmost importance in the life of a legionary. The basic daily salary was very low, enough to rent a modest apartment in Rome, a loaf of bread, and the services of a slave prostitute. The real economic returns for a soldier came from the plunder of conquered cities and the enslavement of civilian populations, as we have seen, or from retirement bonuses, which could amount to the same amount of coined cash – or land in lieu – received in the full eighteen years of service.

So the delay in collecting on their bonuses was making the legionaries mutinous, to the point of pushing them to rob and plunder the Campania farmland, and mainly the estates of wealthy senators and knights. Antony certainly dealt with the problem and bought some time, but upon Caesar's return the situation was still ebullient.

When Caesar came back to Rome from the east to organize for the pursuit in Africa of the last standing Republican contingent (Cato, Scipio, Cicero), and their allied Juba, the situation had degenerated into a complete mutiny. The way he handled it, according to the sources,[10] is one of the most impressive displays of personal and situational leadership in history. In front of the yelling legionaries demanding to be discharged and paid, while he still needed them to sail to Tunisia and end the remaining resistance, he silenced them with one word.

"Quirites!"

"Citizens!" For the legionaries, who were used to being called "Milites" or "Soldiers", being addressed as "Citizens" must have represented a huge burn in their pride. The shift in attitude was instantaneous, and suddenly all the rioters were asking for reintegration and participation in the African campaign, even volunteering for self-decimation or at least clamouring for punishment by death for the ring leaders. The great gambler Caesar was forgiving with them, and sailed to Africa with his reinstated veteran troops, but left behind his favourite Tenth Legion, his disappointment with them being too profound.

Back to all the allegations of extravagant and censorable behaviour: there must have been some truth amongst all the propaganda, because it is in this period that Mark Antony had a falling out with Caesar and fell from his graces and the position of privilege that he had so far enjoyed.

As far as his tenure as Magister Equitum goes, it has to be remarked that deputizing for Caesar and maintaining peace and order in an electrified situation were not the only mandates that Antony had to fulfil. This view would be seriously minimalistic. There were at least two more major facets requiring his attention.

One was to hermetically seal Rome's gates and keep Pompeian sympathizers from quitting the city and swelling the enemy ranks in Macedonia or, even worse, bringing financial means to sustain the enemy army.

The other one was to use his personal presence and dialectics to win more leading personalities to the Caesarean cause, to secure increased followership once the military victory had been completed, and re-organization of the State had begun.

For example, Cicero was perceived as a weak link in the *optimates* line-up. Never fully accepted as a peer by the Pompeys and the Catos, still a *homus novus*, a newcomer to the club, despite his many political victories, and fundamentally a frightful man, he had been flirting at times with Julius Caesar. Like him, others could be aligned to Caesar's politics if the party line was represented by a powerful and inspirational figure, who could have worked ahead in this sense in the absence of the dictator.

One reason frequently mentioned for this falling out between Caesar and Antony could have been the widespread gossip about the fact that Antony had occupied the late Pompey's mansion, and considered it war spoils, i.e. did not want to pay for an asset that lawfully could have been given to the *Res Publica* or returned to the family.

Another one was certainly all the disturbance and the commotion that followed the entrance on the political scene of Publius Cornelius Lentulus Dolabella (Dolabella).

The *gens Cornelia* in all its different branches was huge. Already in the days of Lucius Cornelius Sulla, it has been estimated[11] that 40 % of the senators in office were related to this clan. It will suffice to remark that Dolabella is already the third member of the Cornelii Lentuli branch that we have met in these few pages.

As for Dolabella's background and agenda, if the reader lists the main characteristics of all the patricians-turned-demagogues that we have met this far, he certainly checks all the boxes. The year before the facts in 47 BC, he had also completed the transition *in plebem*, like Clodius before him, and he was starting his Tribunate on the n-th debt forgiveness campaign. He and Mark Antony went way back, and possibly had met in the Clodius circle in their respective youths. Somehow, in the early days following Caesar's return, Dolabella had earned his sympathy and trust, as he was appointed admiral together with Hortensius (the son of the lawyer and orator that had befriended and opposed Cicero) with the mandate to rebuild the depleted Caesarean fleet, which the dictator needed badly to secure his grip on the Italian peninsula.

Several things about Dolabella did not go down well at all with Mark Antony.

The first was that, following the examples of the many demagogues that we have seen at work in Rome for the past 100 years, Dolabella and his men staged a forceful occupation of the Forum, a demonstration which we might call an armed sit-in, to force the approval of the debt legislation. It has been pointed out how Dolabella, heavily indebted himself, was to be the first beneficiary of his law.[12] Of course, a forceful adoption of a political programme was hardly a novelty for the Romans, used to the rule of violence in politics on a much grander scale. But in the context of the new Caesarean order, still in search of stable footing, there was no room for disturbances or abuse. The populace had to be reassured that the days of instability were over, and law and order were there to stay. Whenever he had an opportunity, Caesar, in the Commentaries to the Civil War, insisted on the many displays of illegality and disrespect of the Republican laws that had characterized the period preceding the crossing of the Rubicon, at the hands of the Pompeian and senatorial faction. Now the pressure was on to make it apparent that a new era had begun, and that during Caesar's dictatorship the streets were safe. Mark Antony, the man in charge of upholding the laws and supposedly a beacon of the new order, was way too proud to have such a challenge delivered on his watch, and right in the centre of Rome as well. His hands were itching: Dolabella and his men had been on the short irons with their political opponent Trebellius for a while, causing all sorts of intramural turbulence, just like Clodius' partisans had fought Milo's, and hence weakening Antony's position as the man in charge of peacekeeping.

When Dolabella's men barricaded in the Forum, he stormed with armed troops from the Capitol, stomped the sedition down, and for good measure hurled a few rioters from the Tarpeian Rock. The armed urban gangs that Fulvia managed, and that she had inherited from her first husband Clodius, might have come in handy for the purpose.

The second reason for enmity was that Dolabella was suspected of having a relationship with Antonia Hybrida, Antony's cousin and first wife. True or not, similarly to what Caesar had chosen to do with his former wife Pompeia at the time of the Bona Dea affair starring Clodius, the suspicion was bad enough to call for immediate action, and Antonia was sent back to Uncle Hybrida without hesitation, thus ending an insignificant relationship and making room for the more influential women in his life.

To add insult to injury, two years earlier Dolabella had married Cicero's daughter Tullia. It is difficult to understand why Cicero had decided to establish family links with a left-wing extremist, and a man whose early political demeanour was very similar to that of the radical leaders Cicero had always fought. It is entirely probable that he was truly appreciative of the man's qualities, which distinguished him among the group of demagogues. We know that he must have had some charisma and some personal *atouts*, as he certainly attracted the sympathy and the esteem of Caesar, who was a good judge of character and men. Here we choose to consider this union of the Devil and Holy Water as one more oddity in the maze of Rome's political marriages and alliances, but to Antony it must have sounded like the humiliating suspicion of conjugal infidelity and it was coming from the enemy field. Or, perhaps, he was just looking for an excuse to get rid of Antonia Hybrida.

But let us now put some further context around this unique character. Antony was reportedly very athletic and handsome, so one would expect that the man his wife preferred would be equally attractive by Roman standards. But Dolabella was apparently a very diminutive fellow, of insignificant build, so small that one day

Cicero, seeing him sporting a large sabre by his side, could not refrain from asking the bystanders: "Who has tied up my son-in-law to a sword?"

Was he making up for his lack of physical prowess with the *charme* of the mature and influential statesman, albeit of radical inclinations? Truth is, Dolabella was born in 70 BC, which made him 23 years of age at the time of events. When he married Tullia, daughter of Cicero, he was 21, and he had just repudiated and divorced his first wife Fabia, herself from a prime Patrician family, and made his entrance in public life by participating in some high profile trials.

The union between Mark Antony and his cousin Antonia had yielded a daughter called – alas – Antonia. She will play a small part in this narration, as she had been betrothed to the third Triumvir Lepidus. The engagement was broken for unclear reasons, and years later she was re-routed by her father towards a rich Anatolian Greek man named Phithodorus, on whom Antony was counting for financial backing for his Parthian campaign. This fact was strongly censored by the usual suspects in Rome's upper class echelons, but by now it is clear to all that the righteousness of the Roman elite was not a variable in Antony's value system.

The third reason for personal resentment was that, arguably, the population had come to like Dolabella more than Mark Antony, and the latter was becoming envious of the growing popularity of the *enfant prodige* of Roman politics.[13] Antony was a man endeared to the legions, his opponent to the masses, also as a consequence of his extremist populist political programme.

Plutarch goes as far as saying that Caesar did not especially like either one of the two men[14] on a personal basis. But in those days, he probably was especially lenient towards Dolabella, maybe remembering the days long gone when he himself had been a political maverick and a secret backer of Catilina, at least for a period.

Whatever the nuances of the context described, our Triumvir to be did not handle the various situations in a way that met with Caesar's expectations. It is difficult to ascertain what annoyed Caesar the most. The first easy inference is that Caesar needed to show that under his rule the Romans could look forward to urban peace and quiet, so that it was of paramount importance to keep a display of harmony and order. Also, his executive staff was going to be a big part of extending his legitimacy in the eyes of the people, so that Caesar must have been especially intolerant of any character weaknesses. So even if Antony's alleged displays of arrogance were quite superficial in nature, they clashed with the style and the image that he had in mind for his personal brand of power. Probably the last thing Caesar wanted was for his right hand man to be the object of salacious and common gossip because of his womanizing, his unpleasant attitude to the upper classes, his divorce over a pretext, and his lavish lifestyle. All of this of course was compounded with the most damaging publicity of all, the Pompey house affair.

But if we want to accept a more extreme reading of Antony's overall posture, or at least how some might have interpreted it, we can take these few lines from Dio:[15]

> "With the toga ornate by a purple stripe, with the six *lictors* that accompanied him, and the regular Senate sessions, he gave an appearance of democracy, but with that sword hanging on his side, all the soldiers that followed him, and his overall demeanour, he announced very clearly the arrival of monarchy."

For some or all of the reasons discussed, it is a fact that Caesar was really annoyed with Mark Antony, and he gave him the cold shoulder for a while, until at least mid-45 BC, and upon his return chose Lepidus over him to be his co-consul.

Who was Lepidus, and how did he enter the political scene and make it into Caesar's close circle?

In spite of his age – he was probably class of '89 and therefore six years older than Antony – Marcus Aemilius Lepidus ("the Humorous") was a Patrician who had not yet made a big splash on the Roman political scene. While the Aemilii lineage had a long tradition in the Republic senior leadership, having given Rome many Consuls and generals, their most recent claim to fame had been a half-aborted rebellion led by Lepidus' father right after Sulla's death in 77, promptly suppressed by the regular Republican troops, and which ended with the death of Lepidus Senior in his hideout in Sardinia shortly after the defeat.

At the onset of the Civil War in 49 BC, and at the tender age of 40, he was an Urban Praetor, so still a junior role to Antony, and he certainly had no significant military achievement on his record. So it is somehow puzzling that this Mr Nobody, without even having played a role in the pursuit of Pompey in Greece or any other Civil War theatre, suddenly leapfrogged Caesar's nephew and two-year sidekick in the race for Consulship in 46 BC. Two further years down the line he was eventually deputized to the role of Master of Horse in 44 BC, when Caesar was made dictator for life shortly before his assassination at the Ides of March.

Probably, Lepidus had made a good move at the right time and stably endeared himself to Caesar: as a Praetor, in the period preceding Caesar's departure to the pursuit of Pompey, he was the first to call for his appointment as a dictator: this was not to be forgotten by Caesar, who, without any doubt, had a weak spot for flattery. Probably the compliment paved the way for his future career progress. A little over one year later, we find him named Governor of Hispania Citerior, and even allowed to celebrate a totally undeserved triumph upon his return, as no real war had been fought against a foreign enemy.

It has to be concluded that probably, between the casualties in the war and the shaky loyalties, the candidates available for roles of responsibility were few and far between, leaving plenty of opportunity for upward mobility for those that had entered the *cursus honorum* and looked reliable enough from an allegiance standpoint.

It was during this period of cold shoulder treatment from Caesar that Antony, in 47 BC, decided to remarry, this time with the high profile, populist *pasionaria* Fulvia Flacca Bambula (Fulvia), survivor of two marriages with celebrities Clodius and Curio. Some have construed that the choice was aimed at reinforcing his personal network to try to make up for lost ground in his political career.

We have grown to consider Antony as a non-conformist man, more prone to follow his own instincts than to bend to the rules of the society in which he lived but whose rules he never fully embraced. For once, and for very different reasons from the source, we can tend to believe Cicero in the Second Philippic[16] when he says that Fulvia had been his lover for quite some time, and that the circumstances simply gave them the opportunity to formalize a relationship based on real emotions and affinities, not to say true love. Over the years, she was to become Antony's closest associate, aide, and, undisputedly, advisor on the most important political and military affairs.

The war with the remnants of the Pompeian faction, at this time, was all but over. The Spanish campaign from the winter of 46 BC to the spring of 45 BC that culminated with the battle of Munda was the last large scale war episode during Antony's political eclipse, and one of the few in those belligerent times that did not see his personal involvement. Spain had gradually become a rallying point for Pompeian survivors after the major battles of Pharsalus and Thapsos. Caesar had made a mistake by assigning the province of Further Spain to Quintus Cassius Longinius, cousin of the more famous Gaius, the murderer of Caesar, who proved incompetent and cruel, so that he was soon facing mutiny by his local allies and his troops alike. His accidental death, falling in a ditch, did not change the course of events, as Caesar was already planning to replace him, but by that time Cneus and Sextus Pompey, the sons of Pompey Magnus, had already seized the opportunity created by his weak governorship, and built a strong Spanish pole of anti-Caesarean resistance, also leveraging the strong local allegiance to the name of Pompey. Titus Labienus, the brilliant General and companion of Julius Caesar throughout the Gallic campaign, who had defected to the opposite camp, quickly joined them from North Africa with all the able men he could find, and in the end the Pompey brothers could count on a force of thirteen legions, many of which were well broken into fighting and eager to take revenge for the defeats suffered.

On 17 March, 45 BC, Cneus Pompey accepted the pitched battle that Caesar was offering outside the city of Munda in southern Spain, strong of a larger army and a favourable position, so that Caesar's troops had to charge uphill, under a shower of arrows and javelins. Caesar is said to have advanced personally as close as ten steps from the enemy lines, and to have received many arrows on his shield. The Pompeian lines broke first under the impetus of the Spaniards of the veteran

Tenth Legion, and the usual butchery followed, with enemy losses reported at, a possibly inflated, thirty times the Caesarean side casualty count of 1,000. The winners piled up the severed heads of the corpses in front of the walls of Munda, where the surviving Pompeians had retreated. Labienus had died in the battle, and Cneus was apprehended and decapitated by sword a few days later. He had ensured victory, and Caesar could now head back home. Antony went to meet Caesar at the foot of the Alps, and rode with him in his wagon, while his nephew Octavian, who had been accompanying the expedition, followed in a different cart. It is generally thought that it was at this point that Caesar formally pardoned Antony, and any differences between the two were put aside.

So by mid-45 BC, as we said earlier, Antony was no longer on the receiving end of Caesar's cold shoulder treatment, and he was restored to his role in Caesar's most inner circle, with a position of prominence equal to or even greater than the one he had before. He was named as his co-Consul for the following year (44 BC), possibly in an alternate scheme that was to see Lepidus succeed him in 43.[17]

By that time, Caesar had dropped a substantial part of his moralistic and rigorous façade: he himself had yielded to the temptation of showing off some of the signs of his uncontested power. The dictatorship for life and the title of Imperator already amounted to monarchy, a parliamentary monarchy maybe, but a monarchy nevertheless. Caesar was an impatient man and he was in a hurry; he did not have the time or the patience for long Senate debates, so that these became predominantly informative in their nature, while the substance was never in question. Superficially, albeit not pushing his ostentation to the extremes of harnessed lions, as Antony did, he would sport all his triumphal insignia, laurel wreath included, on a daily basis. Yet if we compare the behaviour of the two, we find that Antony's, while more flamboyant, was more superficial, whereas Caesar's probably struck inner cords in a deeper and stronger manner with the Roman people. The difference is, of course, that Caesar had been the object of disproportionate flattery by the senators, with one more sign of worship coming up every day, while Mark Antony's exterior displays were the fruits of his own inclination and of the mood of the day.

Caesar was not only becoming ostentatious, he was becoming defiant. He had become open and upfront in saying how stupid Sulla had been thirty years earlier when he had laid down his dictatorship and retired. He had gotten to the point of saying in public that all that there was left of the Republic was the name, which was largely true in a situation of lifetime dictatorship, but still sounded shocking when it was voiced by him.

On a more substantial basis, he was repaying all his allies, to whom he was in debt, by proliferating the number of magistrates and senators (50% up to 900) and appointing them to the newly created offices.

Criticism for his autocratic style was found mostly at the guard level, alongside the mumbling in the streets of Rome on where his quest for primacy was heading. Progressively the discontent became more visible and the desire for a shakeout began to crystallize. An attempt to depose him or murder him was only a matter of time. Progressively, rumours of one or more conspiracies began to spread out. It was thus an excess of confidence that brought him down. The plot must have had some scale, and no matter how secretive Brutus and friends were the inevitable leaks must have occurred. Around the core group of the Liberators, a term frequently used to describe Caesar's murderers, revolved a support group of about sixty prominent citizens mostly of senatorial rank. The fact that Cicero was in the know says much about his position on the public scene. He was deemed good to talk the talk, but he was not considered reliable enough when it came to the deeds.

The famous episode of the Lupercalia took place in the middle of this increasingly visible display of despotism. It was the last of a series of alarm bells, only one month before the fatal Ides of March, 44 BC.

During a public appearance in front of a large crowd gathered for religious festivities, for three consecutive times a naked – per religious protocol – Mark Antony tried to crown Caesar with a diadem, in a gesture that unequivocally brought royalty to mind. The diadem was a gold embroidered white linen headband, which had first been introduced by Alexander the Great as a chic alternative to the huge ornate tiaras worn by eastern monarchs. Taken in the context of the public relations minefield where the two were treading, just a small step in that direction could have had explosive consequences. Three times Caesar refused the diadem, to the satisfaction of the cheering crowd, and on the third time he uncovered his neck, as if he was offering it to the knife of anyone that suspected him of harbouring designs of monarchic rule.

Meanwhile, someone, possibly political opponents trying to be provocative, had crowned some statues of Caesar. As the Tribunes Flavus and Marcellus removed the crowns, Caesar bit the bait, if bait it was, by getting remarkably upset, and had the two Tribunes punished by banishment.

We are now in 44 BC: the conspiracy being prepared had gained visibility even outside political inner circles. According to Plutarch, there had even been a very clumsy attempt by Gaius Trebonius, who we have seen at Caesar's side in Gaul and at the siege of Marseilles before he defected to the opposite side, to associate Antony to the plot.

This time, Plutarch is not the sole source to report this matter, which sounds rather unlikely not to say impossible: even if the relationship between Caesar and Antony had known better days, an open attempt to win one of the top three men of the regime to a conspiracy involving the dictator's assassination would have been a suicidal move with the potential to compromise the whole plot. We find echoes of the attempt by Cicero,[18] who sarcastically thanks him for not stepping in and reporting the plot, thus allowing the assassination to go on, but then he forces the hand by saying this happened not out of wisdom but cowardice.

The possibility remains that the source for Plutarch has been Cicero's malevolence alone – and this eventuality would restore the overall logic of the events.

Cicero, always trying to add more notes of colour to the Philippics[19] by tainting Mark Antony with stupidity, wrote that it was the aborted Lupercalia crowning that sentenced Caesar to death. While this assertion clashes with the logic of a well thought out counter revolutionary attempt, here we lean strongly towards a reading of the episode as a staged performance of the dictator and the Consul, in order to signify strongly that the former rejected any royal insignia that the latter, incarnating popular demand, was offering to him.

But there is another quite fascinating and insightful version of the episode that is transmitted to us by Cassius Dio, as he gives us an extensive extract from a speech by Fufius Calenus, an Antonian supporter, arguing with Cicero in Antony's defence in January 43 BC, at the time of the Third Philippic oration. Per Calenus, Antony had seen how Caesar was getting carried away in his exterior manifestations of supreme power and monarchic poses, and was attracting resentment, and he wanted to save him from the popular hostility. To this end, he orchestrated the offering in such a way that he had no alternative but to publicly refuse the diadem, which he really secretly coveted. This would be a symbolic wake-up call for Caesar, so that in future he could mitigate the display of his ambitions. In essence, the suggestion is that the gesture was staged, but by Antony alone, while Caesar was not aware of his intentions. And the way Calenus phrased the argument suggests that his interpretation was widespread and commonly accepted knowledge.[20]

But there is at least another famous reported episode which points to some suspicion of treason lingering over Antony: in the continuing widespread rumours of plotting against Caesar, someone apparently revealed their suspicion of Antony to him. Caesar then responded that he was not afraid of those that were well-built and thick-haired (i.e. Antony and Dolabella), but rather of those that were slight and getting bald (i.e. Brutus and Cassius).

There has been another, somewhat original, analysis of Mark Antony's behaviour since his much criticized days as Master of Horse.[21] Antony had realized that the Republican model had reached its limits, and that in order to continue expansion and dominance, a more effective rule mechanism had to be enforced. It was time for the Romans to get used to more autocratic ways. His parading around and despotic ways, ignoring the resulting disapproval, were meant to give the Romans a taste of the times that would inevitably come with the new order. His foresight would prove very accurate.

As discussed, Antony had returned to the good graces of Julius Caesar, and his outspoken personality and lack of inhibition was a perfect match for the theatrical gesture at the Lupercalia. Also, he was probably one of the few in Caesar's entourage, and possibly the one with enough credibility, whom the dictator could ask to perform such an act while appearing credible to the masses.

The attempted crowning during the religious function is undeniably a gesture that conveys to us a sense of intimacy restored, and it is all the more certain that he had fully resumed his position of primacy and his career track, after absorbing the criticism for his flashy appearances and arrogant behaviour of 47 BC.

Whatever the motives we choose to accept, the fact that Antony had climbed back to the top of the pecking order was there for all to see. Dio[22] gives us an idea of how closely Mark Antony had been assimilated to Caesar's triumphal ways, and to the adulation that a part of the senatorial class was attributing to the dictator when he says that the Roman senators:

> "wanted to have a Temple dedicated to him (i.e. Caesar) and his clemency, and to make Antony a Priest of both (i.e. of Caesar and his clemency) as if he had been a *Flamen Dialis* (i.e. a priest of the Jove cult)."

This passage is very important for the events to follow, and not only for the near term consequences as far as Caesar is concerned. Dio is not speaking in metaphor, but is referring to the actual deification by senatorial order, a concept that will become central in the 30s BC, in the propaganda war that will oppose Antony to Caesar's adoptive son and heir Octavian.

As for Antony, what this new consideration proves is that he had learned his lesson regarding public behaviour, and had graduated to the next level. He was ready to offer Caesar the same level of decisive service in the establishment of the new order, which he had already provided on many battlefields.

Chapter Four

Enemy of the State

F inally, the fatal Ides of March (15 March in the Roman calendar) came. In spite of all the omens, ignored by the usually superstitious Caesar, and the growing evidence of the conspiracy being prepared, Caesar went as a sacrificial lamb to meet the daggers of Brutus, Cassius, Casca, and the others. He fell at the foot of Pompey's statue before a meeting of the Senate, while the muscular Mark Antony, whose reaction had been anticipated and carefully pre-empted, was being held on a pretext by Gaius Trebonius in the lobby.[1]

Mayhem quickly spread across the city. Clearly, for quite some time, neither side – Caesar's friends and foes – had a full appreciation of how much support they could rally around their respective causes, nor how the balance of power could shift in the decapitated Republic.

Clearly both factions tried to ride on the emotions of the Roman population: the Republican or Pompeian side paraded a skullcap, symbol of the freed slaves, on a pike, to represent the end of the rule of an illegitimate tyrant. The anti-Caesarean triumphant marches saw some unlikely participants. For example, none other than Publius Cornelius Dolabella, until then a Caesarean supporter and populist agitator, in spite of his family ties with Cicero, was seen celebrating in the streets with the mobs.

The most astounding part was that Dolabella had just been appointed by Caesar to Consulship in his stead, as Caesar was beginning to prepare his Parthian military campaign for later in the year. He was not yet formally in the role because Antony had initially been vehemently opposed to Dolabella's appointment to co-consul during the Senate meeting, prompting Caesar to leave the hall visibly annoyed, and the formalization had to be postponed. However, Antony subsequently, for the sake of avoiding yet more agitation, made necessity a virtue and accepted his arch-enemy as a partner in the Consulate.

Dolabella's reaction played beautifully into the hands of Brutus and his associates, at least in the immediate aftermath, because a Consul in charge, applauding the assassination of the dictator, added a whole new dimension of legitimacy to the plot. The other player that may have brought some institutional weight and military force to the cause was Decimus Brutus, named by Caesar Governor of Cisalpine Gaul, and as such entrusted with legions that could have been mobilized quickly and that could have marched to Rome in just over a week if things had degenerated.

As for the main actors on the Caesarean side, quite surprisingly, in the beginning they were taken off guard, as if an assassination attempt had not been in the air for months. Antony barricaded himself into his own house, after sneaking away from the scene in disguise, certainly fearing that he could be next on the hit list.

And the idea apparently had been discussed by the conspiracy team, instigated mainly by Cassius, who apparently also wanted Lepidus killed to pre-empt any problem with him, but the idea met with strong opposition in Brutus' integrity: they wanted to execute a wrongdoer and a tyrant, not stage a political *coup d'Etat* by murdering a legitimate Consul and another important magistrate in office.

Lepidus made haste for the Tiberine island, less than a mile away on the Tiber, where he had troops quartered, and then, under military escort, moved to Campus Martius, again a relatively short walk away along the banks of the river.

According to Appian,[2] the reason for this move was to put the troops under Antony's command, as,

"he was closer to Caesar and he was also Consul."

Master of Horse or not, Lepidus must have thought that it was a perfectly good time to leave the driver's seat to a stronger leader with better military command experience than his own, which was indeed quite scarce, so he was happy to make way for Mark Antony. At any rate, a clear pecking order was established for all to see. Even during the period when he had been temporarily ostracized from power, nobody had forgotten who Antony was and where he belonged on the public scene.

But regardless of such solid military support, all the sources are in agreement that Antony took a very cautious stance as he approached the conspirators and initiated talks. Per Appian,[3] his opening move at the negotiations table was to propose to remit the whole matter to the hands of the Senate for judgment and deliberation on the course of action to follow.

The same Appian reports that Brutus and Cassius rejoiced at the news: what music to their ears to hear their adversary giving up the home turf advantage, and proposing to play a decisive match in the Senate, which, rightly or wrongly, they still considered a powerful ally to their cause. If we stop to think about it, however, we cannot but realize that the largely rejuvenated senatorial body, beefed up with tens of new entrants from Caesar's clientele, some even "new men" from distant provinces, quite probably did not ensure the same predictable behaviour as it would have in the years 50–49 BC, and the most conservative wing could well have lost some of its traditional power. The conspirators must have realized that Antony's generous offer could have been a Trojan horse, and that our 39-year-old Consul might have been ambushing them in an uncharacteristically subtle way.

As we will see, his generosity was sharply double-edged, and was part of a broader strategy.

The forty-eight hours following the murder were confusing for everyone. What was legal and what was illegal had become open to subjective interpretations. Were the conspirators criminals or liberators? Had Caesar been a tyrant whose aim had been absolute rule? And if a tyrant and a despot had been killed, were all his acts null and void, at least until his legitimacy had been established? Antony put paid to these interrogations at the first Senate meeting which he called for 17 March in the Temple of the minor Goddess Tellus – the earth, conveniently located far enough from the Capitol, where Brutus & co had barricaded themselves in under the protection of a contingent of gladiators.

The Senate meeting, as one would have expected, was extremely tense. Many diverse points of view were expressed, from Cicero's speech in favour of peace and concord, to the full endorsement of the assassination and calls to cancel all of the dictator's legislation and acts.

Finally Mark Antony resorted to a brilliant diplomatic strategy. He questioned the audience: who was in charge of the Republic? The legitimacy of everything Caesar had put in place during the period of his rule was hanging by a thread, were the assassination to be recognized as tyrannicide. But Antony knew that those who were to deliberate on the nullity of Caesar's acts had been named to their posts in the main by Caesar himself. Were they to step down from their Senate seats, from Practorships, Tribunates, governorships, as a consequence? And those that were not in office, they had a stake in the game too, because they had been named in the five year succession plan prepared in view of the Parthian campaign. With this and the pragmatism of the Romans in mind, we can easily understand why that issue was resolved on the spot, and all of Caesar's resolutions were upheld. Consequently, of course, the issue of Caesar's legitimacy as a ruler was also settled.

Antony had resolved to step into Caesar's shoes also from the standpoint of adopting his style and his disposition towards clemency and forgiveness. In the same Senate meeting of 17 March, the murderers were granted full amnesty, and encouraged to fill the different posts in the Republican administration where they were due to take office at the earliest opportunity. At this point, not only had Antony been Caesar's closest advisor and partner, when he was alive, but he was also the most experienced military leader, the recipient of the legacy of command, and was invested with the moral heritage of the man who had pardoned his adversary at Pharsalum and at other cruel battles. His moves in this extremely volatile situation were impeccable.

His proposal, immediately endorsed by the Senate, to abolish permanently dictatorship from Rome's legislation, played along the same tune. Whether or not this was really just propaganda or rather the fruit of a genuine desire to clearly distinguish himself from the late Caesar is arguable. This is a key to deciphering Antony's personality. Was he an impulsive idealist, an instinctual political animal, or a complex combination of the two? His approach was clearly a continuation of the conciliatory approach and the senior statesman demeanour that he had so well interpreted after the Ides of March. But there must have been an inner struggle between the man who at the Lupercalia festival had raised the alert about Caesar posing as a monarch, and the forward looking leader that had understood that the self perpetuating oligarchic system was suitable to run a city-state, but was not suitable for the scale and the complexity that the Roman world had reached by the second half of the first century BC.

One of the main achievements of Antony's diplomacy was to keep the Senate from spinning all the way in favour of the Liberators. That would have meant full endorsement of their role as tyrannicides, and consequently doomsday for the whole Caesarean Party. And the risk would have been all the more real if Antony had played the avenger card right away, as opposed to taking the more balanced route. Instinctual as he was, Antony had made the right decision in an extremely uncertain and volatile situation, and his reflex proved decisive in ensuring the continuation of the change process.

While he chose to handle the initial talks with the opposition as diplomatically as he could, Antony quickly grew more secure and powerful in his position: he was the man of the hour and the main remaining reference point on the Caesarean side, after Lepidus had stepped aside and handed over the command of the troops to him. An additional diplomatic overture was the double dinner meeting arranged for the night after the Senate's meeting, with Lepidus to dine with Brutus, and Antony with Cassius. In order to provide the now besieged plotters some reassurance, and make them come to the negotiation table, the sons of Lepidus and Antony (the toddler Marcus Antonius aka Anthillus, whom he had had with Fulvia) were given as hostages. Reportedly, even when walking on the blade of a razor, Cassius did not lose his resolve: asked by Antony if he still carried his dagger under his clothes, he confirmed and offered to show him how long the blade was, in case he also was thinking of running for kingship.

In any case, it is in the state of mind of a man playing with a strong hand that Mark Antony approached the moment of the funeral oration that he delivered in the Forum. This moment marks an important turning point in events, and a strong shift of popular sentiment away from the anti-Caesarean camp.

From the classical sources, to Shakespeare, and to the silver screen, this critical episode has been the subject of several interpretations around a common theme consisting of a sober and measured start, moderate and conciliatory towards the conspirators, evolving in a Rossinian crescendo to more inflammatory tones, and openly trying to stir the emotions of the masses to ignite fury and a desire for vengeance. The convergence on this view is complete, whereas there is more divergence on the content of the actual speech.

Shakespeare accentuates the soft, almost subdued start of the speech, as if Antony, fearful of an attempt on his life by Brutus and Cassius, wanted to conceal his real intentions until he had taken the stage and gauged the vibrations he received from the assembly of the mourners and bystanders. This is probably because in his play, Brutus and Cassius were in a stronger position than they had been in reality. In the play Antony takes the stand not in his own right, as a Consul and relative of Caesar, but because Brutus asks him to do so. While he broadly follows Plutarch, ending his speech wielding the bloodied toga on a pole, he is, for most of the speech, surprisingly moderate, to the extent that he could almost be accused of sarcasm, with the continuing refrain "But Brutus says he was ambitious, and Brutus is an honourable man". In fact, Shakespeare's Antony delivers one of the most masterly pieces of rhetoric in literature, in which he utilizes the expedient of refuting Brutus' accusation and condemns the motives without ever explicitly accusing him of lying, and in fact continues to praise him, thereby obtaining the same result by triangulating evidence against the allegation in a brilliant rhetorical trick. The logical approach scheme followed is almost sophistic, and the elaborate style of the Asian school of rhetoric comes certainly to mind.

This version of the funerary oration is beautiful and is certainly believable, and it is thought that Antony had all the skills, intellectual calibre, and cold blood to conceive and deliver it. The fact is, this overly sophisticated approach was not needed. Mark Antony was under military protection from the first hour thanks to Lepidus' troops, had a bodyguard of *lictors*,[4] and, first and foremost, he was the senior Consul in charge. He was the heir apparent and guardian of the will of an undisputed populist leader, who had won a huge new province for the prosperity of the Republic, and had left an inheritance of a nice sum of money to every free citizen of Rome (three hundred sesterces), which was now entrusted to Antony to distribute. Brutus was hardly in the position to instil fear into him, but in reality could only ride the one horse of Caesar's alleged royal ambitions. So there was no compelling case for the future Triumvir to circle around the issue and avoid a more direct confrontation, which would have seen him easily taking the upper hand. The case for him to be so tactful was to position himself as the man incarnating the institutions, rising above the factions, and, vested with all the *gravitas* of a senior statesman, never attacking directly and openly Brutus and his associates, whom he had officially pardoned, but leaving justice and vengeance for the hands of the popular indignation.

Cassius Dio's reading is that, since the conspirators had barricaded on the Capitol, and the Caesareans had occupied the Forum, Mark Antony had become a political arbitrager to avoid any of the factions having the upper hand too easily, and, we may add, giving events too sharp a turn at a time of uncertainty.[5]

Other transcripts or summaries have survived to our days. In Cassius Dio's long version of the speech, the cause and effect relationship between a mild commemorative speech and the violent reaction of the population is not evident. The long panegyric that he transmitted to us is not the kind that fuels vehement reactions and outbursts of rage and passion, rather a eulogy and list of achievements for the good of Rome, and the envy that these could have raised in the conspirators. Clearly there must have been a good dose of this, but the centrepiece must have been a lot more ornate.

For sure the impact of the speech was the desired one, and the stirred up mob ran to avenge Caesar, by setting fire to the houses of the main conspirators, using the burning charcoals of the funeral pyre that had been improvised right in the Forum, just like for Clodius eight years earlier.

To characterize the pervasive frenzy that animated Rome in the immediate aftermath, suffice to say that the angry mob also did summary justice to the Tribune (hence sacred and inviolable!) Elvius Cinna. He was a Caesarean supporter, but was unfortunately mistaken for his almost homonymous Praetor Cornelius Cinna, conspirator, by the ignited Romans returning from Caesar's funeral. In the same way, the Tribune Gaius Casca feared for his life due to his homonymy with the other Tribune Servilius Casca, the man that had dealt the first stab wound to Caesar. The Roman *gens* system did not lend itself for situations of rioting and sedition.

For Antony, this surge of popular wrath was the pressure gauge he had to read his grip on the masses, and the needle was clearly pointing in an encouraging direction.

The fact that the Senate, with Antony's consensus, had voted an amnesty for the murderers did not seem to make much of a difference, and many wanted to take matters into their own hands.

A certain Amatius made the most serious attempt with a determined group of avengers. A radical member of the *populares* party, this man claimed a spurious relation with Gaius Marius himself. But Antony (and Dolabella, Tribune at the time, as it seems) stamped down hard on him and his followers, with many thrown down, in the traditional fashion, from the Tarpeian rock. Even Cicero celebrates the accomplishment, and in the First Philippic grins at the ghastly image of the corpses dragged with a meat hook to be thrown in the river Tiber. Regardless of Antony's claims of impartiality and protection, the conspirators were getting more edgy by the day. After the funeral oration, their popularity with the urban plebeians and with the veterans was falling day after day, and all they had to do was quickly leave for the provincial offices which Caesar had planned for them in his succession.

And by way of generosity, and as originally intended, all the top brass of the conspiracy was meant to get all the premium destinations. As we shall see, this was to be carefully reconsidered, in an opportunistic turn of events. The two that made it to their initial seats of Asia (Turkey) and Cisalpine Gaul (Northern Italy) were Trebonius and Decimus Brutus. Brutus and Cassius also had good spots ahead of them, Macedonia and Syria, but events were to take a different turn.

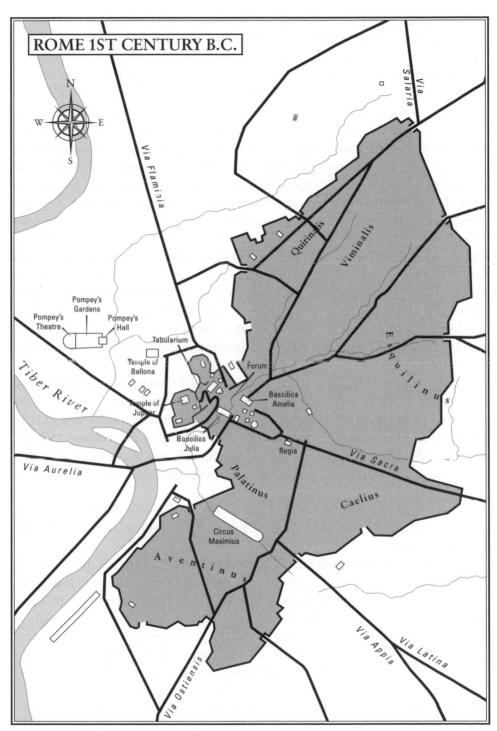

Map of Republican Rome (*Courtesy of Patrick Parrelli*)

By incarnating law and order, defending Brutus' and Cassius' personal safety, and even by recalling young Sextus Pompeius from Spain, and the payment to him of a gargantuan indemnity (fifty million dinarii), Antony was also trying to endear himself to the Senate. Appian[6] goes as far as saying that he was even in Cicero's good graces for a period of time. And we find this echoed in the First Philippic, when Cicero, partly in good faith, says he had built high hopes on Mark Antony as the guarantor of law and order. It was also wise not to overplay his hand and obtain too crushing a victory. Offering the defeated conspirators a way out of the uncomfortable position where he had them cornered, Antony also maintained in existence the appearance of a counter-power, and did not present himself too blatantly as a new absolute ruler. But, at the same time, Antony's stance was generating bad will between himself and that portion of the Roman population that wanted to be avenged of the loss of their benefactor. Maybe conscious of this potential backlash, and in any case for good measure, he started accumulating a huge bodyguard of veterans and Centurions, which was to total six thousand at its high point, all handpicked amongst the best and bravest. Of course, he would not let go of his signature regiment of Itureian archers, lethal marksmen from Lebanon's mountains, that were his true personal bodyguard, and that most likely had been following him since his first mission in the Middle East under Gabinius.

By the summertime, only three months after the assassination, Antony had made great strides to consolidate his power. According to Appian, hours after the murder, Caesar's third wife, Calpurnia, had gone to his house, and entrusted to him his personal fortune amounting to the astronomical sum of four thousand talents, his will and testament, and, most importantly, blank letters of appointment, which Antony could modify at will, preparing to distribute public offices according to his inclinations.

Antony had also quickly secured the loyalty of Caesar's personal secretary, Faberius, who could lead him through all the voluminous paperwork the dictator had left behind.

Clearly, he made very good use of Caesar's blank orders and letters that Calpurnia had committed to him. Both his brothers Lucius and Gaius moved up the ladder, so that we find them now in posts of Praetor and Tribune respectively, probably undeservedly if we think that Gaius' early exploits had been modest. All his manoeuvring was increasing his power, and the possession and free interpretation of Caesar's "in progress" deliberations further enhanced it. Within three months he was able to have legislation "for the enforcement of Caesar's will" issued, under the supervision of a senatorial committee. The new power broker Fulvia must have helped to interpret even better and implement the wishes of the deceased leader.

Foreign policy was certainly well in focus during this period. Many of the alliances with foreign tributary states had lost their referent in a short period of time, whether it was Pompey, Caesar, or one of the many other senior deceased statesmen. Maintenance was badly needed. Antony struck a much criticized deal with Deiotarus, King of Galatia, with some likely immediate economic benefits for Rome's treasury, possibly with input and some supervision from the shrewd Fulvia. The cries of scandal were pathetic. These sponsorships were extremely common in Rome; indeed suffice to flip back a few pages to the Ptolemy / Gabinius deal.

The deal reinstated Deiotarus as king of the whole Galatian territory, after a long string of events that saw this monarch initially side with Pompey, be pardoned by Caesar after Pharsalus, be saved by Caesar's intervention during the Pharnaces campaign (veni, vidi, vici), and finally be dragged through a series of local disputes with other princes over control over provinces that had seen his dominions shrink considerably.

According to Suetonius, a large part of Antony's focus was on managing senatorial and other appointments, in order to strengthen his supporter base. He went at increasing the number of senators even more aggressively than Caesar himself. The Senate, six hundred strong only thirty years before, was now at 1,000 seats, and a large group of officeholders were mockingly referred to as *orcini* in Latin, or *Caronites* in Greek, from the word *orcus*, a synonym of Ade or the world of the dead, or from the mythological Caron, who ferried the souls of the deceased across the river Acheron that marked the boundary with the world of the dead. To the sarcastic Romans, Caesar had sent the letters of appointment to them from the afterlife.

Of course, Antony could not have figured it all out by himself or with Fulvia, without resorting to the help of Caesar's old secretary Faberius, who easily led him through all the files he had received in safekeeping. He quickly secured his loyalty, and started exploring the voluminous paperwork the dictator had left behind. Once he got the hang of it, he did not stop at senatorial appointments, but went on to name different magistrates, and moved on to the touchy subjects of releasing political prisoners and recalling exiles.

Other initiatives from this period are very telling about Antony's intentions to bring the political system more in line with the people and their needs. Antony had opened the doors to magistracy for Centurions, and to the deserving soldiers from the Legio V Alaudae, the skylarks, so called because they wore the crest on their helmets frontally as opposed to sideways.[7] This sounded like blasphemy to the elitist Cicero, who cried scandal in the First and Second Philippic, and possibly in other circles earlier on. Again, how much of this was due to the populist desire to please the veterans, and how much was a more carefully studied move aimed at dealing a blow to the senatorial club that had made the ladder to power almost inaccessible to the new men is debatable. This is probably the rationale behind another measure he enacted, which allowed those tried for crimes *de vi et de maiestate*, or for brutality and sedition against the State to appeal. The latter is possibly the weakest of the initiatives, and reeks strongly of populism, if not demagogy.

The issue of land distribution and settlement of the veterans, central as it had been in Rome's life, could not be avoided by Antony in these critical months when he held the State on his shoulders. His agrarian laws tackled this urgent issue, by creating some new colonies. Many of Caesar's veterans were due to retire, and we have already underlined how paramount these retirement grants were, and how impatient soldiers could get.

Provincial governorship assignments were of course on top of his list of action items. We know how Antony coveted a big provincial assignment, and at the same time he had two important conditions to see fulfilled. The first was to take two large provinces such as Macedonia and Syria from the undeserving hands of Brutus and Cassius. Those were the places where the legions meant to fight the Parthians and avenge Crassus had been amassed. The second was to obtain his next command without forcing the hand of the Senate, and thus become too big a target for accusations of pursuing personal rule.

Once again, he played it very smartly, and used a twofold strategy.

Power in Rome, as we have seen, was a sword with two equally sharp edges, as everyone had recently learned from the fate of Julius Caesar, and senatorial disapproval was where gossip began, and bad ideas began to circulate. So Antony had to play it in such a way that nobody could point fingers at him. His first move was to campaign to get the Syria assignment to the star rookie Dolabella, at the expense of Cassius, who had to settle for the much smaller Cyrenaica job. After all, Caesar had meant to give Cassius the governorship, but had he lived he would have kept the Parthian military command to himself. And since the Parthian game plan was somehow still unresolved, one could argue that all the bets were off and Syria was also up for grabs.

Not that Antony was comfortable placing the same military strike force in the hands of Dolabella; that did not give him any sense of reassurance at all. He later managed to keep the troops in Macedonia, needlessly, but supposedly for protection from neighbouring populations.

Once the Senate had bought this idea, and one could think that Dolabella's family ties to opinion leader Cicero did play a role, it was much easier for him to get Macedonia at the expense of Brutus. The senators could not possibly treat him worse than Dolabella, and it was quite obvious that the new pecking order must be respected: the principle that Caesar's decisions could be modified had been accepted.

All these moves were ratified sometime in April of 44 BC, while the new appointments for Brutus and Cassius were not decided until well after the summer. The problem of the two being sitting ducks in the streets of Rome was still present, and they had to be taken away from the reach of all the potential Amatiuses until the daggers had been sheathed.

In reality, this was a great opportunity for them to become less and less conspicuous, organize their fundraising, and re-establish their ties with outside potential allies, as well as with those parts of the Senate that still harboured nostalgic feelings.

As for Lepidus, it would be naive to think that in a matter of days, after three years of prominence at Caesar's side, he could accept an entirely subordinate role, passively aligned to Antony's desires. He remained a strong constituency, and commanded great loyalty from a large group of supporters, which, in tradition with Roman custom, he had built while he was the second powerhouse in the Republic. Mark Antony did not underestimate him by any means, and on the contrary he took several steps in the following months to find favour with him. First of all, he managed to arrange his engagement with his daughter Antonia – an engagement that was to be broken later when the political circumstances changed. Secondly, he procured to have him elected *Pontifex Maximus*, the highest religious charge in Rome, formerly occupied by Caesar in person. Down the road, he was to go out to pasture in rich and prestigious Cisalpine Gaul.

But by this time, Lepidus was no longer the main worry that kept Antony awake at night. Four days after the death of Caesar, the reading of the testament in Antony's (and Pompey's!) very home had introduced a small yet formidable newcomer on the scene: Gaius Octavianus (Octavian hereafter), his nephew, who upon his post mortem adoption by the deceased dictator sported the name of Caesar.

Octavian was born of Gaius Octavianus, and Atia, Caesar's niece, born of the marriage of his sister Julia and an Actius Balbus. So Octavian and Antony were distantly related to each other because both their mothers had the Julii blood in their veins. The relationship between Antony and Octavian started to deteriorate as soon as they met for the first time, the first never short of a nasty comment for his younger distant relative, scorning him for being the Velletri born offspring of a moneylender and a baker girl from Ariccia. Modern day Romans draw a very strong boundary between birth *intra moenia* and in the surrounding rural countryside. For the past two centuries Ariccia's claim to fame has been the roast suckling pig used by modern day Romans for Sunday picnic sandwiches, and Velletri's vineyards have yielded a product suitable for the same occasions, but nothing more from an oenological standpoint. But evidently, two thousand years ago, the characterization and the stigma it carried were pretty much the same. Romans have always had and will always have a binary view of the world. Mankind is divided into Romans, i.e. born within the *pomerium*, the sacred city limits, and burinis, from the Latin *butyrum,* or butter, being the lesser forms of life whose mission is to bring daily dairy products and fresh produce to the city for the use of the true Romans. So Antony did frequently rub this alleged rural heritage in Octavian's face.

But even the historian Suetonius, who we have previously defined as the gossip columnist of historiography, rejects the notion that Octavian had stemmed from a lineage of country bumpkins. He tells us that the Octavii were of patrician origins and senatorial census, and Atia herself came from respectable loins on her father's side also. Plus both Atia and Antony's mothers were mainstream Juliis, so Antony ought to have shown more restraint than firing away at a distant relation. These comments did not fail to strike other chords, since at the end of the year, in the heat of the Third Philippic, Cicero, who was a "burino" from Arpinium himself, felt he had to intervene and defend provincial pride, but also because he was actively trying to captivate Octavian's benevolence.

Cicero was familiar with name calling provoked by his obscure provincial origins, and had developed a repertoire of witty comebacks. Once a senator had told Cicero that he probably did not even know his own genealogy as far as his father, to which the Arpinas answered that the same question would have put the senator's mother in a tight spot.

But the one that had given him a really hard time about his provincial origins had been the late Catilina(!), who in the Senate used to call him a "tenant in the City of Rome",[8] meaning that his arrival was so recent that he did not even own his house. He lashed back at Antony:

"You criticize Atia, but your wife is from Tusculum, daughter of an idiot who left her the cognomen of Stutter (Bambulio), and granddaughter of that crazy Tuditanus who used to throw money from the window." Little it mattered to him that Fulvia descended directly from Cornelia, mother of the Gracchi, one of the most celebrated beacons of Roman matronly motherhood and virtues.

Born in 63, and thus twenty years younger than Antony, Octavian was too young to have taken part in the Civil War. Nevertheless, aged only 16, he had followed Caesar to Spain, and, though he did not take part in any of the actual fighting, he had cut his teeth on the hardship of the journey, and the other inconveniences of military campaigns in inhospitable territories. He made such an impression on Caesar that he let him participate – undeservedly according to protocol – in his African triumph.

The opening of Caesar's will revealed that he was the heir to four fifths of Caesar's fortune, as well as the important matter of the formal adoption, which opened gateways for him to much bigger claims. Soon Octavian came back to Rome from Illyria (modern day Albania) where he was learning his Greek letters in the city of Apollonia, and confronted Antony to collect on his heritage, that, it can be recalled, Calpurnia had entrusted to Antony for safekeeping.

In Apollonia he was studying with the famous Apollodorus of Pergamum, but that was not all, otherwise he could have gone to the much more stimulating environment provided by Athens. Caesar, who had been grooming him for quite some time, had sent him to this location, where a large military contingent was stationed, so that he could also receive basic military instruction on the side. With him were his lifetime friends Agrippa and Mecenas, who were to play a decisive role in consolidating his supremacy. The troops stationed in Macedonia would have protected him from danger, and he may have commanded allegiance from the troops and the officers as extensions of their overall loyalty to Caesar. Formally, these legions depended on Antony, but, as Octavian had been co-located with them for a prolonged period of time, he might have won the loyalty of the legates and Centurions by exploiting his relationship with Caesar. It remains to be proven if he could have leveraged this traction to the point of putting himself at the head of these soldiers, and thus making way for Rome to settle the scores with the assassins of his adoptive father. But this seems a very remote possibility.

From his first encounter with Mark Antony, it was clear that their relationship was not going to be a harmonious one.

Appian, Antony's biggest fan among the historians of the era, because of his Alexandrine upbringing and because of the legacy that the Triumvir had left in Egypt, gives us an articulate and detailed account of the first meeting between the two men. Be it apocryphal or not, the content seems like a plausible transcript of what they actually said to each other. Octavian started out with the ritualistic approach dictated by ceremony, calling Antony "father", and praising his behaviour in the early days after the Ides. But that opener hid a punch line that soon followed, when he qualified the starting statement with "and then there were other instances in which you did not behave just as appropriately". The reference was to Antony letting the conspirators go unpunished, believing it would have been a much better course of action if he had them executed on the spot. Their mannerisms and attitudes are described by Appian. Octavian was arrogant and condescending, wielding his name and newly acquired paternity – to which he owed everything – while Antony was supposedly cut and dry, irritated by the very fact that the discussion was even taking place, seeing his masterly political play challenged by a mere boy. So he put Octavian swiftly back in his place, and that first encounter was to set the tone for all future dealings, at least in the initial stages.

Appian also raises the point of the widespread concerns over whether the two could have reconciled their differences quickly, and that Antony could have associated Octavian to his cause as a junior member, still leveraging the clout that came with the name of Caesar. The point was a fair one. If they had found common ground right away, instead of waiting until the summer of the following year, some bloody episodes of the Civil Wars could have been avoided. The Liberators could have been annihilated swiftly, as they would not have had the time to regroup and reorganize, and the Mutina and Philippi would have been leapfrogged by history. But Antony either underestimated the amount of trouble Octavian could have generated associating with the senatorial clique, or, purely and simply, was not ready to be dragged into power plays, and chose to stand by his principles rather than consorting with someone he did not quite respect. Of course, he later would do this, but the circumstances had changed and the landscape had become a lot clearer. In mid-44 there was no pressing case for compromising his principles.

The entry on the scene of young Octavian was a very destabilizing event for Mark Antony. As sneaky and oblique as Antony was bold and direct, the young man proved to be a master, even from an early age, in political deceit.

An early clash centred on the inheritance of course. It is not entirely clear what was the state of the finances Julius Caesar had left behind for posterity, and really how much was available for Octavian to collect. Mark Antony had held[9] that many hands had reached into the money until finally it made it into his safekeeping. What is established is that the border between Caesar's personal finances and the public purse had been blurred for a period of time, and that made the whole heritage issue somewhat less than clean cut. By the end of the process, Octavian was in a cash raising frenzy, in order to be able to start distributing it, and that took him to selling at slashed down prices some of the real estate that had come with the inheritance, thus giving the impression that he was subsidizing the Roman people well beyond the cash legate received. But nobody really knows for sure where the funds Octavian eventually raised had come from. Had he laid hands on the Parthian war chest left by Caesar? Could he have counted on grants and donations from wealthy Caesarean supporters? Or maybe he had intercepted another form of public funds? This was the big advantage in being the winner and the survivor of the struggle: once he had power, Octavian had all the time and the means to clean up after him and make all the evidence of possibly embarrassing events disappear. The fact is, nobody knows exactly how Caesar's fortunes had been amassed, and we have seen how the borderline between State and personal finances had been confused at best, with some escapades well into the realm of the illicit. At some point, gossiping, discontent, and possible litigation over unduly appropriated properties was bound to surface. The heirs of the expropriated families would show up to recover their assets once the dust had settled on the tumultuous times. So cashing in the real estate piece and paying the money out in order to build personal equity with the populace was a smart move and a very good hedge on the bet, with the added byproduct of making Antony look like the one imposing hardship on Octavian after tampering with the inheritance.

On the contrary, many think that the accusations of embezzlement thrown at Mark Antony are totally unfair. He was the one left with the burden of running the show in Rome after the Ides. Most importantly, Antony had to deal with the veterans who were waiting to be paid after all the Civil War campaigns. No matter how he juggled the finances he was clearly in a situation shaped by *force majeure*. We must not forget that Antony had Caesar's will in his hands and at his complete disposal for a prolonged period of time. If he had desired to enrich himself unduly, he could have directly tampered with the testament also, and done so on a grand scale.

So far, Cleopatra has been deliberately kept on the margins of this narration, so as to focus attention on Antony's behaviour and the motives of his every move. But at the opening of Julius Caesar's will and testament, both the Queen of Egypt and her son Cesarion Ptolemy XV were noticeable by their absence.

This should not come as a surprise. During her whole stay in Rome at the side of Caesar, Cleopatra had done nothing to ingratiate herself with the Romans. A spirited and independent woman, raised in an atmosphere of semi-religious worship by the Egyptian Court protocol, and now linked to a man that was posing as a totalitarian ruler over Rome, she almost certainly did not behave graciously towards the locals, but rather, she displayed breathtaking arrogance.

In spite of her amazing beauty, her seductive ways, and her obvious intelligence and culture, the consensus she was able to generate against herself was complete.

From the usual suspect Cicero, to Horace, to Catullus, nobody could refrain from calling her a whore and an obnoxious wench in prose or verses, and in more or less elegant terms. Cicero was the most livid of all. He had approached her to obtain access to some rare books kept in the legendary library of Alexandria, partly destroyed by the fire Caesar had started during the Alexandrine war. Her courtesans had informed him that per protocol he would have to bow for the entire time it took to make his plea. The studious man reluctantly obeyed, for the sake of culture – only to see his request briskly denied in the end.

The position of Cesarion was even more difficult. Conceived in October 48 BC, he came into the world on 23 June 47 BC, right at the time Caesar was disposing of Gnaeus Pompey in Munda, Spain. But Caesar did not hesitate to announce the news to the incredulous and disconcerted Senate, and we can imagine that the comments in the capital must have been more cries of scandal than congratulatory.

So Caesar, shrewd man that he was, understood that the two had no future whatsoever in the Roman world once he had passed away. If he had included them in his will, be it in financial terms or for the eventual adoption of Cesarion under Roman law, he would have just made them a more visible target for hatred or resentment. Oblivion of their whole story would have served them better.

Cicero, who until that day had written to his friends on a daily basis to say how much he hated that Queen, limited himself to commenting with much relief that Cleopatra would soon be forgotten.

So she set sail towards Alexandria to re-consolidate her dynastic power against possible new challenges, the first mitigating measure being the killing off of her brother/husband Ptolemy XIV. She had recent memories of the succession struggle that had her sidelined only two years before with the claim to the throne of her brother Ptolemy XIII, which had been resolved only with Caesar's intervention. Her sister Arsinoe, whom Caesar had dragged in chains in his Egyptian triumph thus attracting the compassion of the Romans, was going to follow along the same destiny, less than three years later, in the Temple of Apollon at Ephesus where she was living in exile.

The fourteen year long political battle between Antony and Octavian could now begin.

Octavian, with his innate political sense, quickly occupied all the spaces on the political scene that Antony had left unattended or undefended, and identified and attacked all the pressure points in his relative's political citadel.

Antony had alienated a part of the political elite with his alleged displays of arrogance and Octavian went to great lengths to befriend those clusters of senators that held grudges towards Antony.

Antony had granted immunity to Caesar's murderers and Octavian rode, at least initially, on the anger of those that wanted the conspirators brought to justice and executed.

Antony had laid his hands on Caesar's money so Octavian fought tenaciously to recover the inheritance in full, except for the part that Antony had already spent, and then proceeded to pay out the part Caesar had promised to the citizens of Rome and obtain credit for it.[10]

Antony treated Octavian with scorn and disdain, made crude remarks at his expense, and refused to meet him openly to discuss the main themes of interest. The sentence he used regularly when he was addressing him or referring to him was the proverbial:

"O puer, qui omnia nomini debes."

"Oh child, you who owe everything to a name." Octavian simulated openness and peacefulness, and made public steps to approach Antony and sort out their disagreements.

In order to reinforce his political stature and increase his credibility, Octavian applied for the post of Tribune of the Plebs, and Antony used all his influence to interfere, on the grounds of the youth and patrician status of his new young nemesis.

Also on the use of Caesar's moral legacy, Antony was being extremely cautious and understated, while Octavian was trying to score propaganda points. At the Ludii Ceriales ceremonies planned for May 44, Octavian wanted to display Caesar's golden chair, and Antony had to make the unpopular move to block the initiative, probably perceiving it as politically incorrect in the context. Later Octavian was to promote and finance the Ludii Victoriae Caesaris (Games of Caesar's Victory) to celebrate the memory of his deceased adoptive father.

It would be wrong to think that the young Octavian was a stranger to the Roman political circles, where many senior men had already had a chance to take a good look at him at close range, particularly as he was being chaperoned around by Julius Caesar. Aulus Hirtius the General and Consul, for example, was rumoured to have taken an especially close look as his eroumenos, maybe under the supervision of Caesar who was himself no stranger to this type of situation, to the point that many think that he had initiated him to this peculiar form of homosexual mentoring himself. When Hirtius died from battle wounds, the gossip went around that Octavian had facilitated his death, maybe embarrassed by this past relationship and eager to silence the inevitable rumours that would have embarrassed him as a *princeps*.

Little by little, the sly young fox was chipping away at the position of dominance that Antony had achieved, and forcing him to react in order to reaffirm his grip on power.

This gradual erosion led Antony to a pragmatic idea which he implemented immediately: why leave to a political opponent such as Decimus Brutus, the prized possession of Cisalpine Gaul, the fertile plain of the river Padum (Po), "The flower of Italy … the ornament of the dignity of the Roman people",[11] as well as the control of substantial military power? He immediately endeavoured to trade the post of Governor of Macedonia, where he was destined, with the governorship of Cisalpine Gaul. At the same time, he appointed his brother Gaius Antonius to Macedonia, thus becoming the second man with the same name, after his old uncle Hybrida, to the job. Macedonia, although lacking the allure of Cisalpine Gaul, remained an important province as it was Rome's springboard to the eastern provinces.

As for the other brother, Lucius, he was to close the power circle by managing the Pontine land assignment, which was to allocate land to the veterans. This represented another huge power brokerage exercise, as these were the highly desirable plains just thirty miles south of Rome, on the way to Campania.

At this point, Antony was visibly under pressure from many directions, and his temper was getting shorter. The bid for power from young Octavian was out for everyone to see, and a final confrontation was beginning to look inevitable.

The troops that Caesar had amassed for the aborted Parthian expedition had been recalled to Italy, and the soldiers once landed in Brundisium confronted Antony for a bonus in lieu of the opportunity for Parthian booty foregone. When they rejected Antony's best monetary offer and the situation heated up and gave signs of degenerating into mutiny, he did not call them "Quirites!" or give them a speech in order to placate them, but more simply offered his wife Fulvia the spectacle of three hundred of them being executed on the spot.

Inflicting death on rebellious troops was hardly a novelty in Rome, where the institution of the decimation, by which lots were drawn and one soldier out of ten was clubbed to death by his comrades, was deeply rooted in military life and discipline.

Nevertheless, this act of cruelty, possibly stemming from frustration with the events, was a blow for Antony's public image and popularity with the legionaries. Only five years had passed since he was standing by the campfires near Pharsalus, encouraging them with his example and sharing their scarce rations and crude jokes. What had happened to that Mark Antony? At the same time Octavian, with his strong financial resources and carefully studied public image, was becoming the pet of the masses, and was rallying troops around his flag, from Apulia, to Capua, to Tuscany, while Antony had a tough time counting the defections from his ranks. It has to be assumed that Octavian, now called Caesar, after his acceptance of the formal adoption that came with the inheritance package, played on an unwritten sense of dynastic loyalty that the legionaries possessed in spades, and that they displayed to him as he stepped in the dead dictator's shoes as his lawful son. Plus, he was probably orchestrating a large scale propaganda campaign, even to the point of spreading leaflets among Antony's troops.

At the climax of this cold war, two entire legions, the Fourth and the Martia, quit the Antonian camp. Cicero, in the Fourth Philippic, praises the courage and civic sense of the legionaries, and asks for special recognition for them. We will see these legions fighting and defeating Antony in Mutina less than six months later.

The detonator for the crisis, and the opener of a new chapter in Rome's Civil Wars, was the Cisalpine Gaul situation, and how it was managed within the tricky triangle of Decimus Brutus – Antony – Octavian. For Antony, trading rocky and dry Macedonia for this rich province was easier said than done, as we will see. Pressed to release control of the Po plain to our Triumvir to be, was Decimus Brutus going to yield to him, or was he to endorse the young Octavian's cause and resist the Republic's strongman? It must have been a very puzzling choice to make.

Antony had helped him to obtain immunity for the death of Caesar, while Octavian had started out positioning himself as an avenger. But now Antony was the one requesting him to step down, while in the immediate term Octavian could not present any risk. Octavian played one of his masterly strokes of opportunism, and decided that revenge could wait for better days. He approached Decimus Brutus, implicitly pledged to bury the axe, and offered him his support if he resisted Antony and sided with his cause.

What great news for the senators and other politicians hostile to Antony, who now had a new, legitimate, and popular champion to uphold, and who were now paying back, with interest, all that they had had to endure while Antony's star was at its zenith. Cicero could not hide his joy, and was now publicly adulating Octavian to stir him up, even if this was surplus to requirements.

What exactly had happened in a few months? How do we explain such a sudden swing in the political equilibrium?

Cassius Dio hints that the Romans would always support the underdog no matter what, in order to maintain the balance of power, thereby perpetuating the Republican institutions against monarchic ambition. For all the power he had accumulated before and after Caesar's death, and all the careful PR game he had staged for months in the attempt to hide his cards, Antony had become an easy target for public resentment, which had always been there and always would be. Roman public opinion would always hedge its bets between the leader of the day, and the upcoming underdog, to make sure nobody got too powerful, thus perpetuating the Republican institutions, and safeguarding the appearance of liberty and democracy, even though their substance was long lost. Success was the way to glory and deification, but a mortal sin at the same time.

An apparent attempt on Antony's life was reported in early autumn 44 BC, carried out by traitors in his own camp, who were soon apprehended and neutralized. Neither of the Greek historians, maybe influenced by the Augustan propaganda, put forward a firm viewpoint on the subject, while the well-informed Suetonius had no doubt about the identity of the orchestrator of the assassination attempt, and points his finger straight at Octavian. While there remains an element of doubt for us, Antony must have had none, as he had the assassins in his hands and must have found ways to extract a full confession from them, and he was way too proud and cocky to conceive of making slander one of his weapons against his enemies.

While Antony was struggling to stay on top of things, Cicero was preparing for the next significant moment of his public life – the last one, as we shall see. He had been sitting on the fence, relegated to a marginal role for far too long.

During the initial spell of Antony's service as Master of Horse, Cicero had been stuck in Brundusium. Caesar was in Egypt, and Mark Antony barely tolerated him – probably just to abide by Caesar's will to forgive all his opponents who had put down their arms and given themselves up. Caesar and Cicero also had a mutual respect and a cold appreciation for each other, but probably little more. In 47 BC, Cicero had gone to meet Caesar on his return journey from the Pharnaces expedition and the dictator had been particularly cordial to him, dismounting from his horse to walk and converse with the lawyer and statesman for a good while.

But at the Ides, Cicero was among those who had publicly rejoiced. He even expressed regret for:

"having missed the party… "

Much has been said on the way he had "missed the party". Maybe his personal regrets were directed at his own lack of courage to engage directly, and limit his participation to ex post endorsement. His resolve to provoke and attack Mark Antony can also be seen as a desire to catch up with the events, take a courageous position, and avoid the possibility of his memory being tainted with cowardice. An aim, if such it was, that he did not entirely accomplish.

To set the stage, discussing the role of Mark Antony, he added that, "the tree (of tyranny) had been cut down but not eradicated yet" pointing out the fact that Antony was picking up where Caesar had left off. But when, in the spring of 44, the stars had started to align with Antony's wishes, Cicero had left town and retreated to his villa in Tusculum. In reality, Cicero was edgy because of the overall instability of the situation. He was a politician, yes, but of the kind that does well when he can operate:

"in negotio sine periculo et in otio cum dignitate."

That is, to be in business without risk, and in peaceful meditation with dignity, as he would explain to his friends. It was so that he applied for a *legatio libera*, a sort of diplomatic mission without a clear purpose, to his former son-in-law Dolabella. The idea was to visit Syria, and make a stop in Athens to see his son Marcus, studying philosophy. He intended to stay away until the New Year, when Antony would step down from the Consulship and the moderate Caesareans Hirtius and Pansa would take over, and another season for the Senate would open. His travel plans came to nothing due to bad weather, and his ship was pushed back to the Italian shores twice, at which point he gave up on the idea of a trip and went back to his senatorial duties in Rome. But he did not do it right away. He had taken his sweet time, and made a stopover in Velia, to meet Brutus and discuss the political agenda. When he finally arrived in Rome, he further delayed his appearance in the Senate, giving the excuse of poor health.

In the meantime Antony was becoming increasingly impatient. On the Senate's agenda for those days was the attribution of divine honours to the late Julius Caesar, an item of great political significance. Cicero still carried significant weight in the Senate, and his absence would lessen the value of any deliberation. Antony instructed him in no uncertain terms to fulfil his duties, and threatened to have his house demolished if he continued to neglect them.

Cicero took a diplomatic break, excusing himself due to tiredness from travelling. When he reappeared in public, he was brandishing the first of the fourteen Philippics: the speeches he pronounced against Antony and his politics. The Philippics have a special significance for the biographer. These speeches not only provide the backdrop for the developments that took place in those fast-moving and eventful months, and are an attempt to give purpose and momentum to a political faction, but they are also, beginning with the Second, dominated by venomous invective, and as such they are a collection of those calumnies and denigrations that Augustan propaganda would come to rely on to tarnish Antony's image. When Renaissance scholars would unearth the texts, the authoritativeness of the author sufficed to corroborate the validity of their content, and contribute to Antony's historical vilification.

The first Philippic is still on the surface rather mellow in tone and content, somewhat conciliatory, and seemingly shows confidence that peace was still possible and civil strife could be avoided. It remains critical of Antony's manipulation of Caesar's will and papers, crisp in the intent of opposing his designs, but still manifesting, on the surface at least, openness to dialogue and appeasement. But if one breaks through the thin ice of appeasement, the sarcasm directly underneath is freezing cold. The rhetorical technique used to express his naive deception and that of the *boni viri* is exquisite in its form. Commenting on Antony's demeanour during the month of March:

"One had the impression that a new light of salvation had raised before our eyes. Not only tyranny was gone, but also the fear of a new tyranny..."

The last statement was a reference to the motion from Antony – later approved – to prohibit dictatorship as an institution from the Roman legislative body.

Not only did he not take his distance from the intellectual paternity of the conspiracy, but on the contrary he drew a parallel between Lucius Brutus, who 500 years before had chased the Tarquinii kings from Rome, and Marcus Brutus, who in killing Caesar had honoured his lineage by a matching act of heroism. He stood his ground on the financial issues, and hinted at doubts about the fate of the huge amounts of money, confiscated to the Pompeians, that Caesar had left behind in the Temple of the Goddess Opi. He did not withhold his criticism on the use Antony had made of Caesar's paperwork on magistracies appointments, as well as on ongoing legislation. This criticism only centres on the technicalities of jurisprudence, and does not cry scandal, which anyway would not have overly impressed the Roman audience, who had seen worse in the past fifty years.

The careful reader will find that Cicero condemns many of Antony's deeds as demagogical, or useless, or both, using irony and sarcasm, and never outright attack, in the same way that the future Triumvir would deal with the conspirator in March. The commentary on all the legislation passed on Antony's initiative earlier in the year is dismissive, especially with respect to the aspects of it which were closer to the *populares* agenda, such as the magistrate appointment for the military, and the right to popular appeal. The criticism, while it stems from political creed, can be considered partly legitimate, but the tone is derisory, and inappropriate if one thinks that the senatorial debates on the issues in question had already been successfully concluded.

The way Cicero leaves the door open for Antony to repent and change his ways is nothing but patronizing:

"I think that noblemen of great aspirations like the two of you are (i.e. Antony and Dolabella, consuls in 44 BC), aim, not as credulous people imagine, to money, which is always despised by the great and illustrious, not to power based on violence, which the Roman people would never tolerate, but to the love of the citizens and to the glory."

Furthermore, Cicero makes use of a deliberately disrespectful rhetorical device, by at times using the plural, as if addressing both Consuls, but then referring only to "Dolabella", as if he had been the only one worth his time. But the poison from the Arpinium lawyer was in the tail. Oh Antony, he said, from the Senate meeting on 17 March to the funeral speech, to the actions on the following days, your behaviour was so exemplary, and raised the highest hopes. But then a change came, and now you seem to covet money and personal power. Where did this change originate? Often, continued Cicero, these kinds of changes find their roots from within the domestic walls. The reference to the manipulative Fulvia was not subtle, and criticism of this sort fuelled Plutarch's allegations that Mark Antony was really putty in the hands of strong willed women.

It can be exceedingly irritating when someone who is held in low esteem, or even openly despised, acts in a magnanimous and reconciliatory manner, willing to wipe the slate clean. Mark Antony was clearly annoyed by such high handedness.

Or maybe, the innuendo that at the house of the Antonii it was Fulvia Flacca Bambula that actually wore the trousers, or the toga if the reader prefers, was the part that struck a nerve with Antony. It was clear that the attempt to reconcile their differences was only a façade, and that, knowing Antony as he did, he could only expect a violent reaction. At any rate, the comeback from Antony, which he delivered in mid–September, and the transcripts of which have not survived to our day, but the content of which we can largely deduce from the successive responses, was clearly not subtly ironic like Cicero's. It must have been a particularly harsh speech, which, however, Cicero did not hear directly in the Senate hall because his friends kept him out of trouble and away from Antony while it was being delivered. Antony's anger had been building up for a long time, and he wanted to pull out his laundry list, and settle all the scores that dated back to his father and his stepfather's days, not to mention all the other blows Cicero had dealt to him over time. The gloves had to come off.

And his speech must indeed have hit home hard, judging by Cicero's hardened reaction in the form of his vehement and vitriolic speech on 15 November, known as the Second Philippic. A large part of the speech is a point–per–point rebuttal of what Antony must have said, with space left for the invective, which we know Cicero could take to an art form.

And, between the situation brewing in Cisalpine Gaul, Antony's sudden loss of popularity and the bond he was creating with the rising star Octavian, Cicero must have felt secure and comfortable enough to have seized the opportunity to deal a strong blow back. By the time he was done, things had reached the point of no return.

The opener is already quite personal. It is without doubt a declaration of war, and takes him on a road from which he could not come back.

> "For what destiny, o Senators, for the past twenty years there has not been an enemy of the Republic that did not also declare war on me personally at the same time?"

Three lines and maybe fifteen seconds into the speech, and Antony had already been compared to Catilina, Clodius, and the other troublemakers of the first century BC. One page later, and the tone and pace of the oration had already been established. The tempo had started with a spiteful reference to Antony's liaisons with Q. Fadius, father of that Fadia, a freedman, "infimo ordini", "from the lowest social class". And from then onwards, the speech crescendoed, from his friendship with Curio and Clodius, to the abominable liaison between the three represented by the evil woman that had shared their respective beds, Fulvia, which was all the three rogues deserved.

The Second Philippic jumps straight into the invective, without following the traditional scheme of the oration, with an opener, or *exordium*, a *narratio*, or exposition of events, a *partitio*, or exposure of the remainder of the arguments to follow, a *confirmatio*, or the exposure of the logical case for the thesis exposed, a *refutatio*, or countering of the opponent's arguments, and finally the *peroratio*, or the final appeal to the audience. It dives into a nitty-gritty point per point rebuttal of all the accusations which Antony had fired at him, with pages and pages of insults, and delivered in the high handed tones of someone who is stating the obvious for all to see. But the reader has to go through many pages before he finds something more factual than the accusations that Antony was a bad speaker, that only his sidekicks could appreciate his oratory, that he had divorced Antonia, a virtuous woman, on a mere pretext, that in 49 BC he had to peddle an office because he was mired in debt, and that his manners were poor because he had once given a public reading of a private letter. Coming to more substantive matters, after a long opening with no other purpose than to weaken the credibility of his counterpart through unproven accusations, Cicero moved to a full panegyric of his own past activity as a statesman or a Consul. As we don't have the text of Antony's speech, we cannot confirm if the old Latin adagio: "excusatio non petita, accusatio manifesta", " an excuse not requested is a clear accusation", would have been relevant here, but we could have certainly been spared the list of the personalities of the time that Cicero calls as witnesses to vouch for the goodness of his own actions. It is quite clear that Antony had put Cicero on the defensive, himself bringing up some embarrassing anecdotes from the past, before calling him on his involvement in the murder of Julius Caesar, whether it was real or not. Antony had started by pointing to the lawyer as the instigator of Clodius' murder (he had later defended Milo in court) and as a stoker of the enmity between Caesar and Pompey Magnus. By doing so, Antony was preparing the stage for his *plat de resistance*. Cicero's counter argument is weak, and, for sure, does not do him honour. All the Liberators, he argued, are such noble idealists, that they did not need my encouragement to rid Rome of the tyrant. As for me, I was not part of it, hence I am innocent, but I approve of the killing like many others, practically everyone, except for the few who enjoyed seeing Caesar enthroned. We are all guilty and hence nobody is guilty: "some did not have a precise plan, others did not have the courage, others yet the opportunity: but nobody lacked the desire."

You, Antony, continued Cicero, accuse me of the crime, but still have a position which is unclear yet respectful towards Brutus, Cassius, Domitius – why do you come after me and not them?

This sophism, because a sophism it is, deliberately ignores the importance of the work Antony had done in keeping the situation under control after the Ides, and in avoiding more bloodshed and potential anarchy.

But the mudslinging was only at the beginning: the conjugal infidelity was soon brought out to the light, with a reference to Citheris, actress and former slave, aka Volumnia, from the name of her former master and lover, of whose existence Fulvia was probably aware, so the reference would have been a public insult to her too.

The speech continued to spiral with the discussion of Cicero's role in Caesar's murder. You Antony, accuse me of having flanked the murderers? Cicero's argument here turns a twisted sophism, in too subtle a distinction between approval and participation, into an obtuse interpretation of Antony's actions. "You helped them by sending them away from Rome to safety, and keeping office, so you were in it too", missing the political content of Antony's posture which has been discussed earlier, or, more likely, ignoring it on purpose. And then the real burn, commenting on how Trebonius had tried to recruit him in the plot, and he allegedly declined but did not disclose.

> "For what you thought on that occasion, I praise you; for what you did not report, I thank you; for what you did not do, I forgive you. Such actions would have called for a real man."[12]

The vast majority of Cicero's accusations in the Second philippic were either unfounded or embellished for rhetorical purposes, and the charges brought on serious political matters were liberally intercalated with other accusations that were tabloid material at the very best, and that serve no other purpose than to denigrate Antony as a man, and cast a sinister shadow around him and his alleged moral corruption and stupidity. If anything, the success obtained by this oration to taint indelibly Antony's image for posterity is proof that a glossy packaging of false information can be an effective vehicle for slander. But this does nothing to uphold Cicero's honour.

For example, in accusing Antony of having manoeuvred to be included in the will and testaments of complete strangers in return for political favours, Cicero remarks spitefully that Antony did not even receive his inheritance from his own father. The inference we can glean from this is that either Creticus had died in poverty, or that he had disinherited Mark Antony, with a preference for the first possibility, because Cicero would not have missed the opportunity to give us the gory detail on the second if it had been the case. Either way, the reference to a sad page of family history could have been avoided, and it is another example of Cicero taking cheap shots at points of little importance for lack of more substantial criticism.

So shameless is Cicero in his mud slinging, that he criticizes Antony for having been bankrupt before wearing the toga practexta, i.e. before the age of 16. This is in line with another comment Cicero makes in another passage of the Philippics, when he says that Antony had inherited from many, but not from his own father, the exiled Creticus, but Cicero magnanimously concedes that this was not the fault of the teenage boy. But Antony, hear me! hear me!, had the audacity to still sit in the first fourteen rows of seats at the theatre, which the Lex Roscia had prohibited to the members of bankrupt families! Anathema and eternal shame!

Spent and obnubilated by the impetus of his own speech, or better said, of his own writing, Cicero then attacked Antony for his participation in the Gabinius mission (which was a regular Proconsular mission, until the Egypt spell!), for the years in Gaul under Caesar, which had brought Rome huge financial prosperity, and then, for the *gran finale*, he attacked him for his audacity and arrogance for using the Tribunician veto power in January 49 BC to block the illegal motions against Julius Caesar by Marcellus. This comment alone, in the eyes of every Roman, should have destroyed any credibility the Philippics had there and then, and buried Cicero in the shame of his lies and eloquent fabrications.

The fabrication of the love affair with Curio is another perfectly good example. Antony is portrayed as the passive lover in the duo, climbing up to his balcony in the middle of the night to avoid being caught by Curio's father, in order to satisfy his insatiable lust and womanly needs. If this had been true, with all the precautions taken, it remains to be explained how the evidence made it to Cicero.

Another continuing mystery of the Second Philippic is Cicero's fondness for Dolabella, and the overall criteria he used to separate the good from the bad, which we can only find questionable at the very least. He stresses Antony's cowardice (!) for not following Caesar to Spain, Africa, and Asia, while Dolabella went, and was even wounded in combat. One of the most villainous deeds that Antony carried out was his interference with Dolabella's Consular election. But then, when it comes to challenging Antony for the freeing of the political prisoners and the recalling of the political exiles, the big fault exposed is not having recalled that noble spirit of his uncle Hybrida, who, after a long career as a scoundrel, had finally managed to get himself kicked out of the city, but with whom Cicero had cut a political deal as the reader will remember. The reader will recall the exploits of Uncle Hybrida in his Catilina days and earlier, has already had a glimpse of what kind of troublemaker Dolabella was, and will see more of him in action just a few pages on. There are plenty of reasons to cast more than a shadow of suspicion on the whole construction.

The fact is that, carried away by his oratorical fire, Cicero lost the ability to distinguish between fact and fiction, and between political invective and pure personal insult. The Second Philippic may indeed be a powerful response to Antony's own attacks and a point-by-point rebuttal of Antony's accusations, but it fails to be positive in that it provides no solution to the crisis, other than very generic appeals to the wisdom of the Fathers and to the civic sense of the new generations of the Roman leaders, and the theatrical offer of his own blood for the peace and the prosperity of Rome. In the mish mash of facts, speculations, lies, inaccuracies, sophisms, invectives and insults, and the exposure of some – quite common – power brokerage plays, the possibility of objective judgment is compromised.

On one aspect though, Cicero saw right: the diagnostic of the hatred Antony had developed towards Rome: not a hatred of Rome as a concept, but of a form of rule in the hands of a political class which ranged from obsolete to inept to corrupt, and of which Cicero remained the main upholder.

Finally, after all the appeals for courage and civic values, and the accusations of cowardice of Antony, it must be pointed out that the Second Philippic was never pronounced or read out in the Senate or in public at large, contrary to Antony's speech, to which it was a response. Rather, it was shared with a small circle of friends of unswerving loyalties. It was, however, probably the grapevine which transmitted its contents to Antony.

On 20 December, the Senate meeting was buzzing with the important decisions to be taken. Most importantly, it was announced that Decimus Brutus would not quit Cisalpine, and would stand up against Antony's demands. His position, which had Octavian's support, was endorsed by the Senate.

Secondly, Dolabella was to leave shortly for Syria to assume governorship and military command. This was a big reminder that Antony's Consulate had only eleven days left – the new Consul elects were moderate pro-Caesareans Hirtius (the one that had written the Eighth book of the De Bello Gallico, Antony's old time friend) and Pansa.

Antony had already marched north in late November with four legions; three of these were those he had repatriated from Macedonia and the fourth was made up of Caesar's veterans. All of them had been weakened by the many defections as discussed, but they were backed up by his 6,000-strong bodyguard, and a powerful cavalry squadron. Deep inside, he knew he could count on nine more legions, if he could mobilize at some stage his potential allies Lepidus, A. Pollio, and M. Plancus from Gaul and Spain. He marched north towards Decimus Brutus, while Octavian was preparing to oppose him with the veteran troops he had recruited with the money from his inheritance. Soon Decimus Brutus was besieged in the city of Mutina, today's Modena, fifty kilometres west of Bologna.

Antony, coming from the south, had made a quick stopover in Rome. He had stopped at Tivoli, at the gates of the city, where one day Emperor Hadrian would establish his residence, and had met with a delegation of senators and knights who had reassured him of their backing. Antony was at the head of maybe 30,000 men, and the thought of making a forceful entry into Rome and seizing power *manu militari* might have crossed his mind, frustrated and irritated by the events as he was. We will never know if it was the discussion with the delegation of Romans that dissuaded him from doing so, or if, on the contrary, his supporters were encouraging him. But if he entered the *pomerium* at all, he did it with a few bodyguards. It was in this way that he continued on his way towards the north east.

The Third Philippic was pronounced in these days, in front of a broader auditorium, and was an attempt to crystallize the anti-Antonian momentum of the masses, and to force the hand of the Senate to military intervention.

The central point of the Third Philippic, which relies less on personal insult, was to rally support around the only two bastions left for the defence of the good men.

"The immortal Gods gave us two defences: Octavian for Rome, and Brutus (Decimus) for Gaul."[13]

It was the first real call for action. Two veteran legions, the Fourth and the Martia, had defected from Antony's camp after the facts of Brundusium. In ten days there were going to be two new Consuls, who were to take the most opportune measures. Young Octavian, under Cicero's wing, was to be the defendant of the Republic. With all the irony of fate, Cicero was really leading a fox into the henhouse.

Antony, at this point, was on the borderline of being declared an enemy of the State, much to Cicero's delight. The bond between Octavian and Cicero was strengthening, at least on the surface, the latter having taken on the informal role of defender of the Republic, and *consiglieri* of the young man who one day was to obliterate it forever.

It is no wonder, though, that the opening of the Third Philippic pronounced on that day is a panegyric to the young Caesar, who had been the true deterrent to Antony's return to Rome in arms, after the killing of his mutinous soldiers in Burundusium, which had rendered him more ruthless and bloodthirsty than usual, and praise for the heroic behaviour of the Legions Fourth and Martia, and the equally heroic behaviour of Decimus Brutus, who had made it clear that he was not going to quit Cisalpine Gaul, in spite of a very specific law passed by the Senate. If the reader is still wondering exactly how Antony's reputation and image have been so damaged – and this for millennia – the Third Philippic is worth reading. In the speech, Decimus Brutus is a true hero, a descendant of that Brutus who chased Tarquinius the Proud, the last king and real tyrant, out of Rome. Antony, on the other hand, was just as despicable as the Etruscan king, although his greedy deeds had been conceived amongst knitting baskets, as he was merely a puppet in the hands of his wife, rather than the occupants of a royal palace. Or, Antony was possibly even worse, as Tarquinius was just a despot, but not a bloodthirsty criminal. The Fourth Philippic was pronounced immediately afterwards, as it is a follow up on the Third for the benefit of a popular assembly just outside the Senate House, with no addition of substance, except for an unlikely comment about Antony bragging about being a second Catiline.

On that day, Cicero also showed that Antony had hit a sensitive spot with his continuous references to Octavian's provincial origins, and he gave proof that he felt offended, personally, as a fellow municipal citizen, as discussed previously. But the personal aspects of the invective were not over. Antony had evidently targeted Cicero's nephew, Quintus, formerly a Caesarean and an Antonian, but who had recently changed sides and joined Octavian's camp. His remarks on the young man had been very hard, and he had gone as far as saying that he was plotting to kill his own father. Hence the irate return from Cicero: what temerity on the part of Antony to accuse an upstanding young man of such base thoughts. How sordid of that rascal Antony to utter such lies, to defame one of the young family members of the Tullii Cicero! The fact is, in private Cicero acknowledged that Antony was right, as proven by his comments in letters to his friend Atticus six years earlier:

> "in reality one of the two (Dolabella) makes me suffer more not because he is my son, but because he has a more pronounced devotion, the other (Quintus), – helas! What a disgrace! Nothing more painful has ever happened to me in life! – spoiled by our tolerance, went to extents which I am ashamed to say. I am waiting for your letter as you promised me more detail after seeing him."[14]

And again, in the same period:

> "I confronted the young Quintus very harshly. All is due to his greed and the hope of a large inheritance. This is no small trouble, but I hope that what we feared will never be perpetrated."[15]

With these words in mind, and after having caught Cicero red handed, let's go back to the vehement close of the Third Philippic, and think how his invectives might have sounded to the congregation of Romans:

> "You know well Antony's insolence, and you also know well his friends and his household (i.e. Fulvia and the two brothers). The greatest disgrace and dishonour would be to become servants of such dissolute, vicious, shameless, gambling addicted, drunken people."

If nothing else, during that December meeting, Cicero obtained the confirmation of Decimus Brutus' governorship, and praise for Octavian's intervention and for the position taken by the Legions Fourth and Martia, which were important tokens from the Senate.

Still, Mark Antony's friends in Rome were still working on a diplomatic solution, and striving to avoid bloodshed. The day of 1 January 43 BC saw the opening of the new Senate's session with two important interventions. Antony's partisan Fufius Calenus spoke in the Senate in favour of appeasement, and Cicero pronounced the Fifth of his Philippics.

Cicero, as we have seen, had bet all he had on war, and had everything to lose from a peaceful solution, and the return of Antony onto the Roman scene. He had taken Antony's pulse with the First Philippic, obtained a clear appraisal of the man's anger, lashed back personally and venomously with the Second, tried to stir the masses with the Third and the Fourth, and then he continued with a formal motion to make him an enemy of the State with the Fifth. He was perfectly conscious of how far he had exposed himself while posing as the leader of the "good men" and the saviour of the institutions. In reality, he had pushed too far. Many saw merit in the motion from Calenus, and considered it more opportune to hear from Antony, sending him ambassadors before legionaries.

He decided to force his hand in the four day Senate meeting that ensued. He made a formal war proposal, and he might have gotten his way on 2 January, if it had not been for a Tribunician veto. On the next day, things had calmed down, and the idea of sending ambassadors was gaining the upper hand over more belligerent intentions. The only points for the anti-Antonian faction were scored by his maternal uncle Lucius Caesar, who had his agrarian laws on the constitution of new colonies abrogated – a symbolic concession at the very best from the Senate.

The question remains as to why Cicero was so psycho–rigid and uncompromising in his views against Mark Antony. His positions went beyond political factions, and they are hard to reconcile with the fact that Cicero was a consummate political animal, and he had proven prone to compromise when the situation called for it – to the point of consorting with the likes of Antonius Hybrida in order to make it to consul. It is probable that by this time both his and Mark Antony's tolerance for each other had hit an all time low, and for anybody else that stood in their way, and both were prone to picking fights for no particular reason or to overreacting when provoked, beyond what political savvy would have called for.

They shared the distaste for the Roman political scene: Antony as a consequence of his experiences since boyhood and Cicero due to the *tedium vitae*, or tiredness of life, that had pervaded him progressively since Pharsalum and Thapsos.

Antony had not won. But Cicero had clearly lost, and he was no longer the man making the good and the bad weather in the Senate. His return as an opinion leader had failed. But for once, after years of straddling between his flirtatious behaviour towards Caesar, and his loyalty to the old establishment of the Catos, the Pompeys, the Scipios, he would not stand down. He kept lashing out his Philippics, the Third one being an appeal to Lepidus in the Forum and an open cry for war. A substantial part of the energy for this effort was due to his instinct for self preservation, knowing perfectly well that an improvement in Antony's fortunes would have marked the hour of his violent death.

Destiny bought him some time in that respect. But his early January production is a symptom of narrow mindedness and short sightedness that must have cost him significant credibility even at the time of the facts. He kept praising Dolabella, who only weeks later was to be declared enemy of the State, in a much less controversial manner than Mark Antony. In the heat of the invective, he even advocated the repeal of all the laws initiated by Mark Antony, and wanted to submit them again to the approval *iter*, the establishment of the new colonies in Campania he had criticized before. But the most important one, the law abrogating the institute of dictatorship, he had praised in the First Philippic, calling it the "wake of a new era of hope". Now, less than two months later, he was dubbing it a "law imposed with violence and procedural flaw".

The ambassadors were finally sent to meet Antony, and took off on 5 January with a mandate to be back before three weeks had passed. The Senate chose a heavyweight trio, made up of Lucius Caesar, Antony's maternal uncle and fierce opponent, Sulpicius Rufus, prominent senator and intellectual, and L. Calpurnius Piso. The terms proposed were quite strict. Antony was encouraged to let the ambassadors see Decimus Brutus immediately, to submit to the Senate's authority, abandon his claim on the "*Gallia Togata*", enter Italy (i.e. pass the river Rubicon that marked the border with Cisalpine Gaul) and establish camp not less than 200 miles from Rome. Later he was to head back for his original destination of Macedonia.

While the Embassy was gone, the struggle in Rome between the Antonians, trying to depict Cicero and the conservative wing as warmongers, and their adversaries, pushing the concept that Antony was an enemy of the State and that the levy of new armies should be accelerated, continued relentlessly. Depicting

Cicero as a warmonger, judging from the words of the Seventh Philippic, was not the most difficult thing to accomplish.

> "I have always been in favour of peace … but peace with Antony I do refute, because it is shameful, because it is dangerous, because it is impossible."

The rhythm of Cicero's speeches continued to stir up public opinion, with the pledge for war embellished by rallying cries for the senators to carry out the sacred mission with which they had been entrusted, and the bond of their mandate with the values of the tradition. But, *in fine*, they were still belligerent calls. The references to Antony in the January Philippic still included gratuitous insults, and yet more references to how his decision making took place in the ladies' quarters of the house amidst knitting baskets. These were, of course, references to Fulvia's advisory role, which did not go unnoticed.

On whom could Antony count in this tough situation? How did his closest associates compare to the opposite party? His brothers seem to have inherited the bad genes of the Antonii DNA. Gaius was in Macedonia, continuing the tradition of Hybrida in terms of ruthless rule and poor soldier's work. Lucius was the most volatile and violent of the three brothers, and, according to Cicero, Antony's black soul, and the inspiring force behind his worst choices. During an Asian sojourn, he had participated in gladiatorial games as a *mirmillio*, the gladiator with a conch-shaped helmet, and slain a friend dressed as a Thracian, with a long and curved sword. Cicero picked on this episode three times in the Philippics, to show what thugs the Antonii really were. Allegedly he was the one responsible for orchestrating the disappearance of the confiscated monies, and his savagery had even included physical threats to Antony when he saw his determination falter. But in the political arena there were some noteworthy characters that stood by Antony. In Rome, Fufius Calenus was the most important. Cicero argued with him but did not dare deride him as he would typically do with others. The two went way back. When Clodius had been killed, Calenus, a member of the *populares*, had set up the accusation charter against Milo, so he was a long time foe of the lawyer from Arpinum. Cicero contradicted him openly but treated him with great respect. Trebellius, who was Dolabella's historical enemy, but nonetheless could count on vast popular support, was also a declared Antonian. The old popular adagio, whereby the enemies of my enemies are my friends, was common practice in the Rome of the late Republic.

Munatius Plancus was a strong flanker at this time too. He was to acquire more prominence later on and would take office as a Consul for the following year. One day, one of his claims to fame was to be the originator of the name Augustus to salute Rome's first Emperor, and those to follow in the centuries. During the January negotiations, as we will recall, Antony had offered to trade Cisalpine with

Transalpine Gaul, perhaps knowing that he could count on Plancus to do the trade. Later in life, though, this character will attract criticism for his political opportunism.

Asinius Pollio was also a strong backer of the Antonian camp at this stage. An encyclopaedic intellectual, he commanded huge respect at the time, and had also already distinguished himself as a military man in many of Caesar's campaigns and in the African war against Juba. Later, as Antony's situation became unsustainable, he would politely refuse to fight against Antony at Actium on account of their friendship, but he would be absorbed in the Augustan effort to organize Rome's cultural life, and he protected poets like Vergil and Horace.

Lucius Calpurnius Piso was another prominent personality, at least partly in the Antonian camp, or at least preserving independence of judgment and objectivity. Issued from a prominent gens – who would go on to have more claims to fame, with the alleged murder of Germanicus on behalf of Emperor Tiberius, and the origin of a plot to overthrow Nero, brutally repressed – he commanded huge respect in the Senate. Cassius Dio gives us the full transcripts of his wholehearted support of Antony in the Senate and of his stern comebacks at Cicero, which were similar in style to the speeches of Fufius Calenus that we get from Appian. Piso was one of the ambassadors that were sent to Mutina, which proves that at least there was some balance in public opinion, and that the diplomatic expedition was not a symbolic gesture.

Publius Ventidius Basso (Ventidius) was a brilliant General and a self made man. He could not have started out in life any lower: as a child, he had marched among the prisoners taken from the rebels of the Social Wars. From then, he had worked his way up in the armies, but had not come in through the privileged door of the Cursus Honorum. He had progressed until he had been noticed and handpicked by Julius Caesar in Gaul. He would become one of Antony's closest lieutenants and later win some key battles against the Parthians in the east.

We mustn't forget Trebellius, Dolabella's old enemy from the riots in 48 BC, who had evolved into a fervent Antonian, and could still count on a strong followership in Rome.

So all things considered, the Antonian line-up was not a crew to be sneered at or dismissed as a group of low level adventurers: it included intellectuals, generals, distinguished statesmen. Cicero's tone in the Philippics would have us believe that Antony was alone with his companions in drunken orgies and his dissipate brothers, and does not acknowledge that in Rome and in other important posts there were high profile personalities that saw in him the continuity of Caesar's roadmap, and leadership towards change and reform.

We can safely say, therefore, that Antony's supporters in Rome were numerous, authoritative, and vocal. The voices that were raised in his support during those turbulent days were strong, loud, and clear. Cicero got a strong taste of his own medicine, from F. Calenus, as we have seen, and from L. Calpurnius Piso, and we also have some excerpts from Appian and Cassius Dio respectively. These speeches are an important bellwether to avoid falling into the misunderstanding that univocal anti-Antonian consensus had built up in Rome to the non return point. Certainly, the comments from Cicero, who assimilated the whole Antonian clan to a bunch of drunken thugs, hired assassins, and vulgar thieves, were utterly out of place.

The Calenus Speech, in the tradition of Cassius Dio, was the deepest and most systematic destruction of the content of the Philippics that had been pronounced to that date, and also exposed Cicero's bad faith in mixing personal motives with political invective, thus rendering poor service to the citizenship. But, to belittle him in front of everyone, he also stooped to criticism on a personal level. Cicero had started it, so now his own dirty laundry was to be dragged out in public.

Cicero had questioned Antony's women and morality? What about the fact that Cicero himself had just sidelined his wife Terentia, to pick up a relationship with Publilia, forty years younger than him? When he had found out that he could not cope with such a young tigress, he wanted out of this new relationship, and sought comfort in the arms of the 60-year-old Cerellia, a better match for the old man that he was. If we didn't know better, we would think he was actively trying to make himself look ridiculous.

Cicero was criticizing Antony for his rowdy parties, and for his occasional public drunkenness? What about his own son Marcus, a known drunk, who had frequently been caught in embarrassing situations?

After a few blows to his ego, he went on with more substantive matters.

The ridiculousness of the accusation of having caused Caesar's death, beginning with the Lupercalia incident[16] was quickly countered by the argument we have already reported. But wasn't Cicero himself one of the moral murderers of Julius Caesar? The same Cicero who had armed the hand of Milo against Clodius, and had stirred Caesar and Pompey against each other? The same Cicero, who was indebted to both his benefactors, Caesar, who had pardoned him many times, and welcomed him back to the political life, and even Antony, who had saved him from trouble in Brundusium, on his way back from Pharsalum? It was not Antony that was a coward, but Cicero, who used the excuse of his visit to Greece to stay away from Rome at a time when leadership was most needed, and he had been exposed by Antony for this. And here we have Cicero demanding that Antony's acts be condemned and repealed. But what we are seeing here is a self accusation of the Senate, since all his deeds, including the law on the assignment of the provinces, were approved by the Senate, in the presence of Cicero. Where was Cicero then? Those were not acts of coercion, as Antony was unarmed. And while he was heading to Mutina, to enact a senatorial decision, he wanted to wage war upon him?

According to Dio, Cicero did not take this speech at all well; clearly he could dish out the criticism but was a lot less able to take it.

The Piso speech pronounced in the same period was in the same vein. How absurd it was of Cicero to accuse him of stealing public money! Brutus himself had said publicly that the public treasury was empty after the murder. Moreover, it had been Antony who had requested an investigation, to which Cicero had agreed.

The move against Decimus Brutus was legal, and it was Brutus that was not respecting the "Lex de Imperium Provinciarum". The people had wanted that law to be passed; it was for the people and not for Cicero to decide who was a friend and who was a foe. Did Antony ever put anyone to death without trial (a clear reference to the execution of the Catilina associates)? Didn't he secure an amnesty for the conspirators instead? And why make restitution to young Sextus Pompey instead of embezzling those funds also?

And if he was to stage a putsch, because he wanted to be the ruler of Rome, why did he not do it on the way from Brundusium, when he was at the head of his legions and Rome was defenceless, and instead come by with a few soldiers only? And now, going to Mutina to take his office assigned by law, he was leaving behind his family, held hostage outside the Senate's doors.

Piso concluded that Rome should not act based on private hatred or vendettas, and he stigmatized Cicero's motives and behaviour. These strong and passionate defences did not come from second rated Antonian clients or partisans, but from highly respected, almost venerable public figures. And these speeches must have sent chills up the spines of the conspiracy sympathizers, who knew that the more time elapsed, the bigger were the odds that a Caesarean avenger front could build momentum soon.

Not that at this point the letter of the law mattered all that much, but, in his correspondence with the Senate, Antony was holding on to his legal right to occupy Cisalpine Gaul, and to the "Lex de Imperium Provinciarum". But also, according to Appian, he had made it clear somehow that he meant to punish Decimus Brutus to begin Caesar's vengeance – and this is a statement that, if accurate, could have been the detonator of the hostilities.[17] But for once, it seems that this comment from Appian is an illation that does not find an easy justification in the context.

As far as the outcome of the diplomatic mission, Antony did not refuse the offer right away, but sent back the emissaries with a counterproposal, which can be considered extremely reasonable in the context.

His counterproposal was the following. First of all, he declared himself willing to put down his arms, if land grants for his men could be made immediately. This was maybe a long shot, but it was a necessary opener for him to secure or strengthen the loyalty of his troops, and establish a platform for all the horse trading to come. Secondly, the benefits for his associates (which we can take to mean his brothers) were to be maintained. But, most importantly, he announced that he was ready to quit the Gallia Togata (i.e. Cisalpine, where the Gauls wore the toga, the Roman way) if he was given the Gallia Comata (i.e. across the Alps, where the Gauls wore long hair, or comae) with six legions, and was able to keep it as long as Brutus and Cassius kept their provinces or were in office as Consuls or Proconsuls. Antony needed a provincial command to retain some military force, or he would have been easy prey for his enemies. While he harboured some hope of having his brother Gaius running for Consul for 41 BC, the consensus was that Brutus and Cassius were going to get it. So he was looking at a prolonged period of time where they would have military forces and he wouldn't, and he needed to hedge his bet over the medium term. From an historical perspective, if he had abided by the senatorial intimation, the restoration of the old rule could have continued uninterruptedly to completion. Brutus would have swept away with Antony the only credible change agent remaining, and the inertia would have taken the Republic political scene back to where it was in the 50s. So it is important to stress how critical Antony's distrust for his counterparts was in shaping the destiny of Rome differently. Dio[18] interpreted Antony's thinking differently, i.e. Antony actively wanted Brutus and Cassius to become Consuls, so that they could have kept the pressure on Octavian and limited his ambitions. This line of thought is perfectly compatible with the points discussed above. In essence, Antony had taken good notes from the experience of Julius Caesar in 49 BC, as he negotiated next steps prior to crossing the Rubicon: it was paramount for him to hang on to an *imperium*, a military command, and to the financial means to satisfy his troops and his followers.

Not only were the requests reasonable and legitimate, but we must also consider the fact that the attempt to remove from a prestigious and important office one of the slayers of Caesar was in good faith, and that there was merit in the attempt to avoid the bloodshed that would have arisen from a pitched battle opposing two armies of fellow citizens, something that Cicero wanted at all cost. And his arguments must have resonated with many, both among his followers and with the broader audience of those who had kept some impartiality of judgment. And Antony probably had some oratorical skills of his own, and a sharp and witty tongue: in the Thirteenth Philippic Cicero protests at having been called a *lanista*, or a trainer of gladiators, with reference to his continuing pressure to wage war. As has been pointed out, that must have hit home hard, because Antony was far from alone in holding this view.[19]

Antony's counterproposal was brought by one of his main men, Lucius Varus Cotyla (Cotyla, i.e. drinking bowl or mug), who travelled back to the capital with the remainder of the Embassy (Sulpicius Rufus died during the journey). Unfortunately, the proposal was rejected in its entirety, and on 2 February the Senate declared the state of *tumultus* – which was a state of emergency, but not as grave as *bellum* (war). Cicero did not like this lexical and juridical subtlety, but, after much arguing, had to make necessity a virtue and live with it. In the Eighth Philippic, he launched into a vehement protest, arguing on how one cannot really go without the other, and, looking carefully, the criteria used in the old days to define a state of *tumultus* were even tougher and more stringent than those for a *bellum*. He poured out his remaining bile by saying that Antony had treated the ambassadors arrogantly, had not suspended the siege pending the negotiations, and had kept them from seeing Decimus Brutus. In frustration, he continued like a broken record on Cotyla, the bodyguards, and the Greeks appointed to magistracies. It should be noted that, in those days, one of Cicero's most vocal partisans was Lucius Caesar, Antony's uncle and enemy, who also had been instrumental in the execution of Sura and the other Catilinians.

The beginning of 43 BC was not done with bringing new developments and *coups de theatre*, which kept shifting the power balance around. It was only two days later that messengers brought a letter from Marcus Brutus, who had been below periscope depth for a while, communicating that Greece and Macedonia were under his military control, and no longer under that of Gaius Antonius. What had happened? The influential Brutus had intercepted the tributes coming from Asia, probably with the consensus of Trebonius, the Proconsul, himself a Caesaricide. All of a sudden, his pockets filled, it was much easier for Brutus to command loyalty. Other garrisons, and even a large cavalry force, meant to join Dolabella, declared in his favour, and so did the Proconsul of Macedonia Hortensius Hortalus, due to step down in favour of Gaius Antonius. When Gaius arrived, Brutus' forces easily defeated him without much bloodshed, convinced his cohorts to defect to Brutus, and imprisoned Gaius. Attempts to rescue him by his partisans failed. At the climax of the excitement and blinded by hatred for the Antonii clan, Cicero went as far as advocating the execution of Gaius.

This was tough news for the Antonian cause, as their territorial grip was halved, but a thrill for the Senate. The senators must have been delighted to listen to Cicero and Pansa, and give Brutus the same kind of *imperium pro praetor*, or temporary command, they would later give Octavian, in order to give a legal justification to his armed presence in the provinces. But the main significance of this event was that it had the full potential to give new decisive impetus to the conservative party, which was proving half hearted in dealing with Mark Antony, and gave more credibility and purpose to everything Cicero had been preaching for the past four months. Furthermore, this development gave the Caesaricide front a geographical continuum in the east. Brutus' dominance in the Greek and Balkan region would stand shoulder to shoulder with that of Trebonius in Asia (western Turkey), and would be connected with that of Cassius in Cyrenaica. And then there would be the random variable of Dolabella, maybe a sympathizer but of the unpredictable kind. He would prove to be even more unpredictable than the others might have thought only three weeks later.

The diminutive but fierce Tribune, Consul, and commander, after having taken part in the celebrations of the murder of Caesar ("the Party" to use Cicero's words) was now the sole representative of the *populares*/Caesarean alliance in the east,[20] dominated by Brutus and Cassius, the same way Decimus Brutus was the only "Liberator" in the west, sandwiched between Antony, Lepidus, Octavian, and the diehard Caesareans in the other provinces. As Dolabella was crossing through Asia on the way to Syria, Trebonius denied him access to the cities of Smirne and Pergamum, maybe to slow him down and favour Cassius who had his eyes on the same provinces. He swiftly besieged and quickly captured him with the accusation of having given the tax proceeds to Brutus to finance his Greek takeover. When the soldiers came to apprehend him, Trebonius told them proudly that he was off to see Dolabella in person, to which the Centurion in charge responded that he was free to go where he pleased, but his head was staying right there. And he meant it literally, so the first of the conspirators met his violent death that night.[21]

Before the winter began to thaw out, both Consuls Pansa and Hirtius were sent to the rescue of the besieged Decimus Brutus, and Octavian joined the hostilities with his army of veterans, for which he was paying from his personal resources. He was a *Dux Privatus*, or private leader, and without political coverage he would have been in an illegal position. Technically Octavian was leading a private army in a province of the Republic. This is why he had begun to correspond with Cicero, paid him a visit in his villa at Puteoli, and overall tried his best to look as genuine and truthful as possible. The *escamotage* to legalize the presence of the troops was quickly found, and Cicero managed – without much difficulty it seems – to obtain for his protégé the *imperium pro praetore*, or the military command in place of a *Praetor*, the title with which Rome invested citizens for emergency situations where a new magistrate could not be immediately dispatched so that he could participate in the hostilities.

Facing three armies at the same time, Antony was heavily outnumbered. Still, he could count on two veteran legions, a strong cohort of praetorian elite troops, and a large ala, a cavalry contingent, on top of the usual light support infantries. During the siege of Mutina and the subsequent battles, the loyalty of the legionaries and of the allied troops was put to serious test, and there were several defections both ways. The most spectacular were of course that of the Legions Fourth and Martia, but Antony also welcomed an important Gallic ala, or cavalry squadron, among his ranks. But it is clear that the outcome of the situation was far from certain and that the tension among the soldiers was palpable, and it took huge presence to keep control. The word "mutiny" has since been adopted to describe a chaotic situation with change of fields and rebellion, such as in those days of the spring of 43 BC.

Consul Pansa Caetronianus could field a larger army, but made largely of raw recruits. We have already discussed how in those days a smaller but more experienced force could easily defeat a more numerous, but less experienced one.

The beginning of the battle of Forum Gallorum, modern Castelfranco Emilia, on 15 April 43 BC was no exception to that rule.

After some hard fighting, Pansa's troops eventually yielded to the impetus of the veterans, who then took to inflicting the usual tough punishment upon their ranks. But when Antony was in the process of preparing for the celebrations, he was astounded to see the cohorts of the other Consul, Hirtius, appearing on the battlefield, and charging his exhausted troops. There were more men than he could handle, and a close victory turned into a sour defeat, made all the more bitter by the loss of many standards of the cohorts, and, ultimate insult for Roman soldiers, the silver eagles that were the legions' emblems.

In order to secure victory, the Senate had also summoned Lepidus, who could have dispatched troops from Gallia Narboniensis in a short time. But Lepidus apparently was secretly sending reinforcements to Mark Antony,[22] and certainly he was not stepping into the fight like he had been asked. There are several possible interpretations for this behaviour. Part of it might have been opportunism and keeping his options open for different outcomes. Antony was outnumbered, but was still a formidable fighter, and, as we have amply demonstrated, a very smart and experienced General. Or maybe, the courtesies Antony had paid to him at the apogees of his power were beginning to bear fruit. Dio goes as far as to say that they were related – this was not quite true yet, but Lepidus' engagement with Antony's daughter Antonia was still in good standing. Plus the reader will remember how Antony had endeavoured to have him elected to *Pontifex Maximus*, the head of the Roman clergy in the role left open by the death of Julius Caesar.

The mistake that cost him the Mutina war had probably occurred in the field of military intelligence. Antony had underestimated the proximity of the reinforcements from the other Consul Hirtius, and was counting on facing the different enemies separately, and overcoming them thanks to the quality and experience of his troops.

Real life went differently, and worsened six days later in Mutina, when he had to face Hirtius again (Pansa had been gravely wounded in Forum Gallorum and would die a few days later), only this time paired up with Octavian and his veteran troops.

This time the match was really unbalanced, and, notwithstanding the gallantry of Mark Antony and his men, the coalition troops obtained a large victory. One important blow was dealt to the Republican cause though: while storming the Antonian camp, Hirtius himself was mortally wounded. The Republic had lost both Consuls and was temporarily without executive power and military lead.

The fight had been fierce. Suetonius gives us a snapshot of Octavian getting his boots dirty on the battlefield, in uncharacteristic fashion, picking up an eagle from a wounded standard bearer, and engaging in first person to recover the body of the fallen Hirtius. Maybe Suetonius embellished the story, or maybe Octavian was so thrilled by the victory that he could not stop himself. Others minimize his intervention in the actual fighting. He knew that after Mutina he was no longer the challenger on the scene, and he was now looking upon Mark Antony as an equal, over whom, to say the least, he had a strong temporary advantage.

Antony was beaten for the moment, but he proved to be remarkably resilient under the circumstances. He reformed his battered ranks and marched west on the Via Aemilia, the Consular road which still crosses the Plain of the Po in its entire length, towards Placentia (Piacenza), and then he turned south at Tortona to cross the Maritime Alps not far from the Ligurian coast, meet the Via Aurelia near Savona, and enter Gaul making way for the town of Forum Julii (Frejus) in what is, in modern France, the beautiful Department of the Var.

He needed to rally quickly all the Caesarean leaders still in positions of authority and military command, such as Lepidus, Pollio, Plancus. These men had not thrown their weight into the fight in Mutina, still weighing the political implications of the possible move. But now, they could hear the cheers coming from Rome, which welcomed the old political establishment back to power, celebrated the tyrannicide, Decimus Brutus, welcomed the news of the exploits of Brutus and Cassius in Greece and in the east, and, in sum, announced the beginning of what would inevitably end up in a full restoration of the old order. An intervention from Antony was needed to materialize their worries in a resolute stance against the return of the old oligarchy to power, and the annihilation of all Caesar had achieved during his meteoric career. The first and decisive stop for Antony was thus necessarily the military camp which served as Lepidus' headquarters in Forum Julii.

Chapter Five

Triumvir

It is of no doubt that, during his strategic retreat, Antony had to reach deep into his soul to find his best leadership capabilities and skills in order to make it to safety. Plutarch gives him again the tribute of his admiration, on how he led the demoralized survivors, shared their meagre rations and enduring hardship, just as we had seen him do in Egypt, Gaul, and Epyrum.

Perhaps Plutarch, for poetic reasons, exaggerates what the Antonians had to suffer on their way to Liguria, and then across the Alps: drinking rotten water and, on the verge of starvation, eating animals never eaten by man before. It is certainly hard to imagine how a march across the most fertile plains of Italy can turn into such an ordeal, especially in the beautiful Italian spring. The Po is the largest river in southern Europe, and Antony followed it for most of its length. The Via Aemilia, which follows the river almost all the way, and which Antony must have taken, is still one of the key traffic arteries for those that want to cross the Po plain from the North Adriatic to the Ligurian Sea, crossing over 300 km of flat lands, until the southern extension of the Maritime Alps appears on the horizon, announced by the green rolling hills of southern Piedmont. At that point the traveller has to make a slight detour from his straight line itinerary, and descend in the deep valleys which divide the Maritime Alps from the Northern Tuscan Apennines.

Even as we try to imagine the conditions of their journey once Antony had turned south-west, and headed directly towards the coast, we have to reject any images of frostbitten legionaries dipping their *caligae* (military boots) in the snow of inaccessible alpine peaks.

They would have crossed the Langhe, already at that time the premium wine producer in Italy, in the first century BC.

"Et de Murra ad nostrae Romae metropolim perduximus vina."

"And from La Morra we took to Rome, our City, some wine." So wrote Caesar when he set camp in La Morra, home to some of the fine Barolos, Barbarescos, and Barbera wines, on the way home from Gaul. Back from barbaric lands where these fine drinks are unknown, finally to Italy to enjoy good wines, and while we are here let's take a few bottles back to Rome to appreciate them.

The overall comment that comes to mind is, crossing lovely pre-alpine rolling hills covered with vineyards cannot have been a huge undertaking for hardened veterans, nor would have been the clearing of a few – low – mountain passes, crossing over on the way to Provence, which certainly was not the most undesirable destination at the end of the journey. There are no indications of the enemy armies having engaged in a pursuit: they too had suffered heavy losses in Mutina, and, more importantly, both the Consuls were dead and there was a leadership vacuum which needed to be refilled in accordance with procedure.

It would be unfair to say that the difficulties for the legionaries as far as drinking was concerned could have been too much Barolo, or too cold spring water from the mountain streams thawing after the winter. As for the "animals that men had never eaten before", nothing too exotic comes to mind in southern Piedmont, as that region to this day pullulates with deer, wild boar, hare, and all sorts of game that endanger the motorway traffic. All of this, after crossing "the flower of Italy", to put it in Cicero's words, in the month of May, as the crops ripen in one of Europe's most fertile lands. But Plutarch wants to give this retreat an epic twist, to further emphasize what kind of leadership it takes to guide men through defeat and humiliating retreat, after having fought against all odds and against a much larger opponent, and to break a lance for Antony's exemplary conduct, after several pages of sharp criticism. Historiography then has signed off on the heroic representation of the events.

With this, we do not want to downplay the difficulties of this retreat, and the extent of Antony's achievement, as well as its importance as an experience which, seven years later and in a more hostile territory, he would have to repeat. For Antony, what needs to be emphasized is that this was his first setback, and his first taste of defeat. We are in the spring of 43, so only nine months after the highest point of his political career. It is not easy to digest a setback of this size, especially when it is the first fiasco in one's life and it happens at the age of 40. It must have hurt even more, because the taste of victory had been just inches away, and much of the punishment suffered could have been avoided with a little more attention to tactics and a little more prudence. Also, against all the odds, Antony's decisive success in Mutina had been well within reach, and a victory would have definitely changed the course of history.

We have to conclude that the praise from Plutarch was well deserved, as finding the stamina and moral resources for an instant rebound must have been quite an accomplishment, especially because he had to put up a display of leadership in order to sustain and encourage his defeated and humiliated legionaries. He must also have been worried for his own family, and for Fulvia in particular, since now that he was a defeated enemy of the State, she could well have suffered the backlash at the hands of his enemies. In reality, Fulvia had found shelter at the house of Atticus, Cicero's best friend, a free thinker and intellectual who had never taken political sides from the days of Marius and Sulla when he had been questioned in the factional struggles as a frequenter of the houses of the people in question.

Whatever the circumstances of the march, we find Antony, unshaven as a sign of mourning, and covered in a dirty dark cloak, with which he had replaced the scarlet General's cape, at the doorstep of Lepidus' camp in Forum Julii, calling to be received. Apparently, at first Lepidus was not sure how to react and left Antony waiting for a while. Lepidus himself was in a very difficult situation: he had been trying to hedge his bets, and to keep his relationship with Antony on good terms, possibly sending him some reinforcements or at least logistic support, but at the same time he could not shrug off his aversion to risk. While he was a smart opportunist, and knew perfectly well how to navigate the political system, Lepidus was certainly not the man to take gambles without being reasonably certain of a successful outcome. Sneaking a little support to the Antonian side was one thing, but formally receiving an enemy of the State in his territory and in his camp for everyone to see was a different matter. The Senate and Decimus could still have had the final victory, and Lepidus hesitated for a long time before making a final decision and showing his hand.

When he crossed into Gaul to meet Lepidus, Antony was accompanied by more than just his Mutina veterans: his old comrade Ventidius Bassus (Ventidius) had brought him three legions. Ventidius was a man with very humble origins, which made him all the more loved and respected by the common soldiers. In his youth, he had been a prisoner of war in the Social Wars, and he had worked his way up in the Roman army from a very low entry point, trading pack mules. In 43 BC this old soldier had canvassed central Italy searching for retired Antonian soldiers who still had some fight left in them – maybe the same legionaries whose unswerving loyalty he had commanded since devoting himself to finding the funds to pay their end of service bonuses.

During the siege of Mutina, Ventidius had witnessed the daily propaganda bombardment from Cicero and his weekly Philippics, and at one point he had gotten so irritated that he had been tempted to march towards Rome and settle the score with the whole conservative senatorial lobby. Being a hugely respected veteran and General, he had an easy time rallying many retired soldiers from the different colonies around his own and Antony's flag, so he was very quickly at the head of a strong contingent, fully capable of threatening the city. Many panicked, and Cicero, since old habits die hard, went into hiding as he waited for the situation to play itself out. At that point Ventidius changed his mind and resumed his progress northbound. He made it safely across the Po plain – the Consuls were dead, and Octavian did not have the capacity, or possibly the desire, to obstruct his progress in view of his mercenary troops and his formidable opponent. Or, maybe, the young Caesar's thoughts were already running along the lines of leaving Antony some breathing space to recuperate him later as an ally, which was, in fact, the case. It was so that Ventidius and his three legions, along with further reinforcements brought by his brother Lucius, joined Antony on 3 May 43 BC.

In Mutina, Antony had also salvaged a very numerous and powerful Gallic ala, or cavalry squadron. So when he went to knock at the door of Lepidus, he must have been able to count on a force that, while maybe not made up of top notch fighters, and which may have included many wounded or exhausted soldiers, could count somewhere in the vicinity of 20,000 experienced men, of proven combat skills.

During this hectic period, Lepidus had had to practise diplomatic acrobatics when making excuses to the Senate for not taking a more active role in the campaign against Antony. The Senate had done whatever was in their power to keep Lepidus and Plancus from joining Antony's cause, as soon as they had begun to expect this eventuality. They tried to organize a diversion and ask the two to found a new colony (and this is how the city of Lugdunum, today's Lyon, was founded), but this proved to be insufficient as a distraction. While Lepidus tried to sit on the fence as long as he could, probably torn on what strategy to follow, Cicero was doing whatever was in his power to make the vacillating Proconsul swing to the Senate's side and not yield to Antony's lure. He flattered him to the point of having the Senate vote to erect a golden statue in his honour in the Forum, as a reward for the role he had played in negotiating the peace with Sextus Pompey and securing his recall to Rome. But, despite all the attempts made to win him over, Lepidus stopped hesitating, and formally embraced Antony's cause. In a theatrical gesture, his lieutenant committed suicide with his sword in front of the soldiers, to condemn the betrayal perpetrated by his leader. Velleius Paterculus, one of the most prolific authors in the Augustan disinformation campaign, will ignore most of the aspects of the Antonian comeback in the second part of 43 BC, but emphasizes this otherwise insignificant episode.

As the Senate learned that Lepidus was flying Antony's colours, the former quickly joined the latter on the list of enemies of the State. In the troubled Senate session where the decision was taken, the most vocal of the proponents was his brother. Soon enough, it became clear to everyone that Antony and his new partner Lepidus could count on A. Pollio and M. Plancus too: adding the provincial armies to the Mutina survivors and the Ventidius recruits, the Antonian alliance could count on over 50,000 men, against the 20,000 that Decimus could line up against them. Of course, Octavian's private force could still have evened out the odds in the struggle if he had sided with the Senate. All of a sudden, uncertainty was prevailing again.

In the meantime, in Rome, the celebrations for the victory over Antony had begun. Only, contrary to what he coveted, it was not Octavian who was getting centre stage, but Decimus Brutus. Antony had been formally declared a *hostis*, an enemy of the State, to Cicero's utmost satisfaction, so that the winners Decimus and Octavian, instead of the late Hirtius and Pansa, could lawfully be awarded a full triumph. But the right to celebrate a triumph was granted to Decimus alone, while

Octavian was given the right to celebrate an ovation, a smaller ceremony in which the victorious leader paraded in the city on horseback (and not on a chariot), and at the end of the procession slew a sheep (*ovis*) instead of the traditional sacrificial bull which concluded the triumphal procession.

This lesser form of tribute might have been decided on account of his young age, and on the deliberate choice of the Senate not to feed his pride too much. But it may also be representative of the fact that he had played a much smaller role in the victory than the others. Cassius Dio tells us that his soldiers had watched the fighting "from the walls" of Mutina, and hints that his money and his political skills were worth more than his leadership. There must have been a visible twist in his personality that made him suspicious to those that had the opportunity to watch him in action at close range. The fact alone that gossip was rife that he had played a role in the deaths of Hirtius and Pansa – in order to make Consul sooner – gives us a feel for how uninspiring he might have been. Roman historians actually report it to us as a concrete possibility, rather than unfounded rumour, that a physician sent by Octavian treacherously poisoned both Consuls' wounds. If it was only according to the scandal hunter Suetonius[1] we could take the comment with a pinch of salt, but we also find the same allegation in Tacitus,[2] who carries a completely different weight in terms of reliability. Maybe, if we are inclined towards generosity and extend Octavian the benefit of the doubt, we could say that he was already falling victim to that defence mechanism that hit all the high flyers of Rome whose star shone too bright, and for whom a replacement was being sought, in line with the wishes of the common people.

Had Octavian already begun to descend from the high point of his meteoric career? Or maybe he had never really got there in the first place. He had skilfully been used by Cicero for a while, but in the weeks after Mutina he realized that he was an instrument in the hands of the Senate, and he had maybe represented little more than just another string in the bow of the Philippics, and a good rallying point for disgruntled and nostalgic troops. The reward received was falling hugely short of expectations.

So Octavian was clearly disappointed with the level of honours he received, and with the fact that he was not appointed Consul on the spot. Whatever the most important reason, the Romans and especially the Senate were not yet ready to take a risk as big as swinging all the way in his favour, just like had happened to Caesar and Antony before, and were getting ready to play another hand of their favourite game of *divide et impera*, or "divide and conquer". While Antony had been declared an enemy of the State, his property confiscated and his allies outlawed, Octavian was not yet a clear winner. The distribution of the different awards and recognitions was tailored to foster the right degree of envy and competitiveness to make everybody feel sufficiently uncomfortable so that the Senate could retain ultimate control. Even among his loyal ranks, some of his backers had been rewarded to different degrees for the same reason, some above and some below their merits. There is no better way to loosen the cohesiveness of a group than to single out a few for reward, thereby arousing feelings of jealousy. Aware of the danger of gaps opening in his ranks, Octavian did not fall into this political trap, and managed to keep a solid grasp on his force.

Even if there was probably no need for an explanation, Consul Pansa had opened his heart to him on his death bed after the Mutina battle, and his last words must have sounded something like this:

> "My son, Hirtius and I loved your father, but there is no way we could have taken a different course from what we did after he was killed. We came here to fight Antony only with the intent to bring him back to reason, and then reconcile him with you. But this reconciliation will have to happen before all those Pompeians in Rome take the whole Caesarean legacy and men to pieces, and return Rome to where it was before. And we should not let this happen."

Whether he went to see Pansa carrying a jar of poison or not, Octavian could not have agreed more with the concept, except for the different little twist he was to give to the plan, which was the quest for personal supremacy he was going to pursue, when the time was right.

As we have seen, in the meantime the Caesaricides had stolen the show after Mutina, and were quickly returning to power, carried along by the enthusiasm of the conservative wing of the Senate, which was finding an increasingly solid footing. Their grip on the eastern front was complete with the appointment of Cassius to the Praetorship of Syria, and with the mission to conquer and punish Dolabella – who had also been declared enemy of the State – for the attack and killing of Trebonius. In the XI Philippic, Cicero passionately supported Cassius' appointment in Dolabella's place, we believe with great personal embarrassment or conveniently selective memory. Dolabella had shown that his only loyalty was to his ambition for personal power, just weeks after Cicero had publicly made a role model of him. Cassius, empowered by the Senate in this sense, made his move on Syria, defeated and captured the young Proconsul, and then ended his turbulent career at the age of 27.

Cassius had arrived in Syria before Dolabella. He had a larger army and was a smarter and more experienced General. Cleopatra had sent Dolabella some reinforcements, as he represented the Caesarean party in the east: four legions, albeit probably largely incomplete, still made up not of Egyptian soldiers, but of real Roman legionaries. These were the same troops that Caesar had left behind to secure the stability of Egypt. But Cassius intercepted them in Palestine, and they decided to defect to him rather than fighting. It was so that Crassus had gone after Dolabella at the head of twelve legions, and he had an easy play at defeating him, besieging him in the city of Laodicea, and driving him to suicide to avoid bigger trouble.

To make the family reunion of the conservative Republicans all the more complete, Sextus Pompey was named supreme commander of the Roman fleet. After suffering defeats at the hands of Julius Caesar, Sextus had stuck around Cordoba in southern Spain, enjoying the protection of the local population.[3] The Antonian sympathizer, nobleman and intellectual Asinius Pollio had pressed him closely, and eventually forced him to accept battle. So it happened that Pollio lost his cloak during the battle, and as Sextus paraded it around the battle front, the rumour spread that he had died, and his soldiers lost heart and eventually withdrew, leaving Sextus in charge of the region. Lepidus had had to cut a deal with him, which Antony later had to ratify and top up with a huge monetary indemnity to make up for all the riches that the Pompeiis had lost. And here, after a spectacular rebound, we find him returned to a huge Republican command. He would be the last to surrender to the Triumvirs, and would remain as a thorn in their side for much longer.

The complex double crossing between Octavian on one side, and Cicero and the Senate on the other, was close to its end, and both parties were ready to come out in the open. In his naivety Cicero thought he could manipulate one of the most conniving manipulators of the classical age, and was soon to find out that he had been riding on the back of a tiger, and that dismounting and just sweeping him out to the side was not a viable option. Octavian thought he had the street paved in front of him, and that he was entitled to primacy in the Republic, supported by popular sentiment thanks to his role as the official heir of Julius Caesar. His first request was to be made a Consul, replacing one of the deceased Hirtius and Pansa. His talk and body language must have betrayed his arrogance and certainty, and this must have acted as a wake-up call for Cicero, who, in his private correspondence, came out with the famous sentence:

"Laudandum adulescens, ornandum, tollendum."

"The young man must be praised, honoured, elevated." Which would have been fine, except that in Latin the verb "tollendum" has the double meaning of "raised" as in "elevated to higher places" and almost "deified", but also of "removed" and maybe even "eliminated".

Cicero's deliberate use of this word was to signify that things were going down a slippery slope, and to acknowledge that maybe his enthusiasm for the young man had been premature, and that now it was time to carefully reconsider. This witty remark was eventually leaked, and made it to the ears of Octavian, who, of course, objected to the double meaning of the comment, and, when the time came, did not forgive or forget.

Octavian's body language did not fool anybody any longer. The temporary alliance with the Senate was a decoy that he no longer needed in order to pursue his ambition. He was not yet ready to take on Mark Antony and his allies now that they had regrouped, but he did not need to be the weapon or the flag of the *ancient regime*. Furthermore, if we consider a more romanticized view of events, Octavian may no longer have wished to consort within the circles where the assassination of his father Julius Caesar had been conceived and organized. For both reasons, he knew exactly what he wanted as he made his way south towards Rome at the head of almost 40,000 men.

When the Senate attributed higher recognition to D. Brutus than to himself, Octavian's anger had been largely simulated, as in reality things were going down the expected path and in accordance with his desires. Had the Senate decided to please him at all costs, he would have had a more difficult time from a public image standpoint in flexing his muscles, taking a more decisive stance against Brutus and his men, and patching back together the relationship with Mark Antony, thus following the advice he had received from the dying Pansa.

The winking and signalling to Antony took the form of releasing war prisoners, and sending more explicit messaging to A. Pollio and Lepidus. When the formal embrace between Antony and Lepidus finally took place, the worst nightmare of the *optimates* league suddenly became a terrible reality, and they all began to brace themselves for a very rough landing. The investigations into Antony's wrongdoings during his Consulate, launched at Cicero's instigation, instantly became a lower priority and were subsequently dropped. Many in Rome were confused by this sudden change in scenario, and reached out to Brutus for guidance, and coordination on future strategies, in view of a sudden return of the Caesarean Party.

Octavian had an easy time securing the loyalty of Caesar's veterans through this period of uncertainty, on the grounds of common interests and agenda on top of the dynastic allegiance that has been described earlier.

"Why would you trust Caesar's murderers to maintain and respect what Caesar awarded to you in terms of bonuses and benefits, and that I have endeavoured to deliver? To me personally, come what may. But you have all to lose from a Pompeian revival. The best would be, if I could make it to Consul and control the events for whatever time needed."

What he meant to say is that he was the best guarantor for the payment of bonuses and indemnities as they came due.

And it was so that, like his adoptive father, Octavian crossed the fatal Rubicon, followed by his armies. The Eagles of his legions had not yet been seen from the walls of Rome, yet the candidacy of Octavian for Consul had already been approved, and sufficient funds to make the veterans happy had miraculously appeared. For a while, some pressed for an armed resistance to him, to the point of encouraging the fearful Cicero to emerge from hiding, but in the end common sense prevailed and the young Octavian was greeted at the city gates with a display of phony enthusiasm. Cicero insisted on delivering the Consular appointment first hand, but was received very coldly by the new Consul. We do not know if Octavian came up with any "tollendum" type sarcastic jokes, but in the context this might have been totally unnecessary as Cicero would have already been entirely humble and subdued in his demeanour.

When Octavian obtained the election to the vacant Consul position, paired with an unusually quiet Cicero, some must have thought that this was a relatively small request under the circumstances, almost a symbolic reward for someone that had at his disposal a military force of the size of Octavian's. But he had a very precise agenda behind his request, as he wanted to keep his ascent to power within some strict legal boundaries. He therefore proceeded to introduce some legislation which translated immediately into two major political victories.

The first was to pass a law (*Lex Curiata*) on adoptions to give stronger footing to his own adoption by Julius Caesar. While adoptions were extremely common in Rome, they were normally contracts between two living parties, one offering and the other accepting the adoption. But adoption as part of a will and testament was unheard of, and Antony must have raised the point and exposed the irregularity in his early dealings with Octavian, and he would do it again ten years later in the middle of the propaganda war that opposed the two before the battle of Actium. Now the matter was sanitized and grandfathered. Absolute regularity of the adoption was of paramount importance. Also when Caesar was formally deified, or assimilated to divinity by senatorial order, the process made Octavian "filius divi Julii" or "Son of the Divine Julius", and therefore, by assimilation, of divine nature himself. Later this feature would become important in the Augustan propaganda efforts, when Octavian was asserting himself as he criticized Antony for posing as the New Dionysos during his Egyptian years. While for Antony the Dionysian comparison, as we will see, was purely superficial and part of a local court ceremonial, and in all the earlier examples of claiming divine descent the protagonists themselves probably smiled at it, in this case the association was of a much more serious nature.

The second was the formal outlawing of the conspirators (Lex Pedia), and the constitution of a tribunal to try them, *in absentia* in the majority of cases, of course. Naturally, there were too many unsheathed swords around for the trials to be anything more than a farce, and all the defendants were found guilty as charged by the judges. Only one voice sung out of the choir, and it was that of a Silicius Corona, who was much praised by his fellow magistrates for his free spirit and independent thinking. We don't know if he was truly a brave man of unyielding principles, or if he had misread Octavian and his potential for retaliation. He got away with his opposition unharmed, but he made a very early entry in the proscription lists only weeks later.

The passing of the Lex Pedia, from the name of Octavian relative and Consular colleague Pedius, was a crucial accomplishment. As he was tried for murder and outlawed, all of a sudden the extreme precariousness of the position of Decimus Brutus became apparent.

The law was issued at the end of August, 43 BC. It had been less than three months since Decimus Brutus had been awarded a Triumph, and less than four since he and Octavian had fought side by side against Antony, and since Brutus, Cassius, and Sextus Pompey had been appointed to all the top jobs in the Republic. Now Decimus was facing the federation of the three powerhouses Antony, Octavian, and Lepidus, with escape an unlikely prospect.

His only option, as his demoralized troops began to defect to the opposing field, was to make a difficult run for the east and join his comrades Brutus and Cassius, which he attempted to do, shamelessly disguised in a Gallic cloak, which was a real curse for a Roman. In the end, instead of crossing the Adriatic or descending the Balkans, he had to take the long way around and go as far as modern Hungary, planning then to head south into Turkey, before he was intercepted by a local warlord, who identified him in spite of his masquerade and turned him over to Antony's men. Antony must have savoured the moment and thought about the mutability of destiny, before having him put to death. While he had no specific grudges against Decimus Brutus, another act of mercy would have been out of place. Too many lessons had been learned in the past eighteen months, over and above the legacy of Caesar's experience, on the consequences of repeatedly pardoning one's enemies. The second of the Liberators to fall after Trebonius, Decimus, met his fate in a humiliating and undignified way, protesting and sobbing to his last minute, contrary to typical Roman stoicism and courage in the face of death.

As soon as Octavian had filed away the two issues of the Lex Curiata and the Lex Pedia, his next priority was to move to the north Adriatic shores of Italy, supposedly to meet Antony and Lepidus in his Consular capacity, and reconcile them with the Senate and the people of Rome, but in reality it was to seal his alliance with them, and put together a military force that could match what Brutus and Cassius had at their disposal in the east, and deal with them for good at the earliest possible moment.

While Octavian was marching north, the faithful Pedius took care of repealing the decisions that had made Antony and Lepidus public enemies, and formally reinstated them in their original posts. The reunion of the three could now lawfully take place, whereas it would have been inappropriate before the formal pardon and reconciliation with the Senate.

The meeting that shaped the destinies of the world for the next thirteen years at least was carefully prepared, and took place at the end of November 43 BC. While an understanding on the general principles had already been concluded through the various intermediaries, and the interest in striking a deal was common to all parties, mistrust still initially prevailed. As pointed out, the "winking" from Octavian had been going on for a while, but Antony was still fresh from the consequences of the hostile propaganda attacks against him from the Mutina days, and possibly from the assassination attempt in the summer of 44 BC; it mattered little if it had been organized by Octavian himself, or, as others have conjectured, by Brutus and Cassius. The times still called for extreme prudence on all sides.

Lepidus acted as a facilitator and as a guarantor for the meeting at the same time. Both Octavian and Antony advanced with their legions to the opposite banks of the river Lanuvium, the stream today called Reno, near the city of Bononia (Bologna), where an island was conveniently situated halfway between the banks in the shallow waters. After briefly inspecting the site, Lepidus took off his red cloak and waved it to signal to both parties that everything was clear, and both leaders advanced to the island with 300 armed horsemen each. Then the three proceeded to a tent that had been placed in the middle of the island, and got down to their discussions. They were to emerge three days later, with a general understanding on the steps to be taken, and a list of action points.

While the First Triumvirate had been a secret, or rather, an unofficial agreement to balance the power of two political leaders that were also representing two political factions, with the third wheel Crassus providing an element of equilibrium and avoiding a dangerous dualism between two dominating personalities, the meeting which took place in Bononia gave birth to something entirely different by all accounts. The Romans could have very specific expectations on how the new Republic was going to function, in accordance with a full law that was promulgated on 27 November of that year, the Lex Titia. The Triumvirs were given – or gave themselves – the mandate to run the Republic for a period of five years, and re-write the rules that governed public life, with the title of "Triumviri Rei Publicae Constiutuendae", or The Three Men Founders of a New Republic. In theory, they had the same attributions as the Consuls, while they did not replace them. The powers they had attributed themselves with the Lex Titia were endless. They kept for themselves the prerogative to appoint all the key magistrates, including the Consuls, and they attributed to their mandate an initial term of five years, which was then punctually renewed when it came due.

For the entire term of the Second Triumvirate, the Consuls remained nominally in charge of the executive. In theory, they were on par with the Triumvirs. This paradox is perfectly in line with one of the most deeply rooted Roman traditions, that is, to keep stacking up institutions without ever obliterating the pre-existing ones. For example, the Consuls remained in effect throughout the Principate or

Empire, and frequently the Emperor himself, i.e. an absolute monarch, would also serve as Consul just like a private citizen of distinction during the Republic.

The Triumvirs also had control over the provinces, and immediately took a first cut at dividing them among themselves.

Antony, of course, was the senior member of the Triumvirate, and took the lion's share. He got the whole of Gaul, the wealthiest piece by far, with the exception of the southwest, the Gallia Narboniensis, the region which ended with the Pyrenees, which went to Lepidus along with Spain. As for Octavian, he got the three large Mediterranean islands of Sicily, Sardinia, and Corsica, plus the province of Africa, which consisted of modern day Tunisia, part of Libya, and some other parts of the Maghreb. It is not necessary here to dwell too long on this division, as it was clearly a placeholder for the final configuration that would be defined after the defeat of Brutus and Cassius and the re-conquering of Greece and the east.

The usual string of omens[4] announced the destinies of the three Triumvirs, i.e. the upcoming supremacy of Octavian over those that at the time were the two senior members of the alliance.

> "For what concerns Lepidus, a snake had coiled around the sword of a Centurion, and a stray wolf had entered his camp and run into his tent and his table as he was eating, announcing his power and at the same time his decline to come. For Antony, milk running in the (camp) moat, and singing heard at night announced the future joys (i.e. Cleopatra) and the ruin that would have followed. Such prodigies took place for the two men before they entered Italy (passed the Rubicon). For Octavian instead, an eagle had landed on his tent, and had killed two crows that were trying to rip off the decorative plumes, thus announcing his victory over the two rivals."

The Romans had a special ability to record these types of events and to interpret them, and they did so especially well after the predicted events had already taken place. So Dio could easily show how the upcoming proscriptions had been announced by events which could only imply the presence of a poltergeist:

> "The standards of the legions based in Rome became covered with spider webs, weapons floated from the ground and raised to the sky with great clanging noise, many bees gathered at the top of the Temple of Asclepius, and a flock of vultures landed on the Temple of the Genius of the Roman People and on the Temple of Concord."

The enactment of the proscriptions, or the process of physical elimination of all real and potential enemies of the Triumvirate, was one of the most immediate undertakings of the trio. They got around the task methodically and systematically, following the old Latin adagio for which "it is better to abound than to fall short". The first day a list of seventeen citizens who were condemned to death was posted, but it was merely the opener for more lists which contained hundreds of names. The process was uncompromising, and all the Triumvirs had to sacrifice friends and relatives to the desires of the other two.

Plutarch is scandalized by Antony sacrificing his maternal uncle Lucius Caesar, but we know that he was no friend of his, and in fact he had been one of the fiercest Ciceronian supporters early the same year, when Antony was under pressure in Mutina. Lepidus' brother Lucius Aemilius Paullus also made it on the lists and barely escaped execution; apparently his proscription was not on the initiative of Antony or Octavian, but retribution from his own brother, as he had been at the core of the decision to have Lepidus declared public enemy after he had joined Antony.

Writes Appian:

> "They marked down not only the powerful men they mistrusted, but also their personal foes. In exchange, they surrendered their own relations and friends to each other, both then and later. Extra names were constantly added to the list, some from enmity, others only because they had been a nuisance, or were friends of enemies, or enemies of friends, or were notably wealthy. They needed, you understand, a great deal of money for the war. Brutus and Cassius were profiting from the taxes of Asia ... and from the support of Kings and Satraps, while they themselves ... were short of resources."[5]

The sad days of the Sullan proscriptions were back, and the ownership of a valuable property coupled with an uncertain political allegiance could be tantamount to a death sentence. The total tally of the victims of the proscription process is uncertain, and ranges from a high estimate of 2,300 lives, of which 300 were of senatorial census, down to a few hundred. So, clearly the proscriptions served the dual purpose of cleansing the Roman political scene of those elements that represented a potential threat to the new order, and supplying financial resources for the military campaign in the Hellenic East.

Plutarch is extremely tough in his analysis, making the whole deed appear more exaggeratedly barbaric and wild, motivated by cruelty and the thirst for blood rather than by cold political calculation.

> "I believe nothing ever happened that was crueller than this barter: trading death for death, they killed those they handed over just like those that they were given, but they were more evil towards their friends, that they made die without even hating them."[6]

Romans always found a way to see the humorous side of the most tragic events and situations. This is a special ability that they (or we, if the reader will allow) have developed and perfected throughout the past three eventful millennia that their (our) hometown has witnessed. The proscriptions were too juicy an opportunity to pass. It was in this way that an anonymous wise tongue spread a witty verse to comment on the actions of the two Consuls of that year, Lepidus and Plancus:

"De Germanis non de Gallibus duo triumphant Consules."

"The two Consuls have triumphed over the Germanii, not the Gauls." In Latin, the word Germanus has the double meaning of German and brother. Clearly, since neither of the two Consuls had ever been to Germania, the verse was a cruel joke at the fact that they had prevailed over their closest relatives, as opposed to over some barbaric population.[7]

While clearly the cold blooded elimination of the upper echelons of a political faction is a reproachable act, the accusations of savagery and gruesome enjoyment are out of place. This operation was carried out in a carefully calculated and surgical way to the maximum extent possible. None of the historians for example point to the existence of the professional *delatores* or informants that accused and doomed many innocents, and turned other proscriptions into witch hunts, such as under Emperor Domitian, or to the people attempting to benefit personally by trading in the estates of the condemned, such as happened under Sulla, who apparently was not even entirely aware of how many were being killed. On the contrary, the passionate and temperamental Antony, the scheming and cold Octavian, and the prudent and careful Lepidus knew exactly who had to be eliminated, and they may even have erred a little on the safe side.

There were, of course, bounties for those that would capture and kill a proscribed man: 25,000 *dinari* for a free man, and 10,000 plus his freedom for a slave.

And in this freshly created equilibrium, it makes no sense, as Velleius Paterculus or Livy did, to try to divide the blame unequally, giving Octavian a lighter load and partially letting him off the hook. In fact, Velleius is the historian that spends the least time on the major historical events that were the Triumviral proscriptions. He limits his testimony to a few commentaries, which are mostly of an emotional nature and meant to provoke disapproval for Antony, more than provide an account of the events or offer historical analysis. He argues that, in the first place, the proscriptions were an initiative taken by Antony and Lepidus alone, to which Octavian was obliged to comply against his will, since he was alone against the other two. This is clearly incompatible with everything we have learned about the personality of the first Augustus, and with many other observations of his *Modus Operandi*. At the very most, Suetonius would have agreed that he was maybe not the most vocal in initiating the proscriptions, but once they got under way he became the most zealous and cruel in carrying them out.[8]

The second point on which the sycophantic historian is most insistent is a sappy commemoration of Cicero and his ruthless execution, a "crime" committed by Antony, which "truncated the voice of the people" and "silenced that divine voice", which on more than one occasion had "saved the State", and so on and so forth with a long tirade on the lessons for posterity, and on the curse that will haunt the vile murderers.[9] Let us listen for a moment to the voices of the most submissive and accommodating intellectuals:

> "These crimes were committed mainly by Antony and Lepidus. It appears that also Octavian had committed some, due to the sharing of the power, since he had no reasons to commit them for personal motives. He was of mild disposition (!), and he had been raised by his father (i.e. Caesar). Furthermore, as he was still a boy, and had just entered the political arena, he had no reason to hate anybody and preferred to be loved."[10]

In view of the facts exposed so far, statements like this are irreconcilable with reality. According to Dio, who had fallen victim to the Augustan propaganda, Octavian tried to save many men, while Antony:

> "instead, had cruelly and mercilessly killed not only those that had been listed, but also those that were trying to save a proscribed. Even if he was dining, he would watch carefully the severed heads, and would enjoy greatly that nasty and miserable sight."

Suetonius, better placed than anyone else in terms of physical and temporal proximity to the sources, and also extremely impartial and objective in his narration, gives another, totally different reading of the events, based on logic. He tells us that, while hesitant at the beginning, maybe already evaluating the propaganda implications, Octavian then gave his backing to the enforcement of the proscriptions with great enthusiasm. And when Lepidus asked for a moratorium, he adhered to stopping the issuance of the lists, only on condition that he could carry on at his sole discretion. On the outcome, no grey area:

> "Under the Triumvirate, many of Augustus' acts won him the hatred of the people."

And then he gives us some flashes of Octavian's arbitrary cruelty at the expense of innocent men. The historian, Emperor Trajan's long time personal secretary, prefers giving his readers many snapshot episodes that stick in the memory,

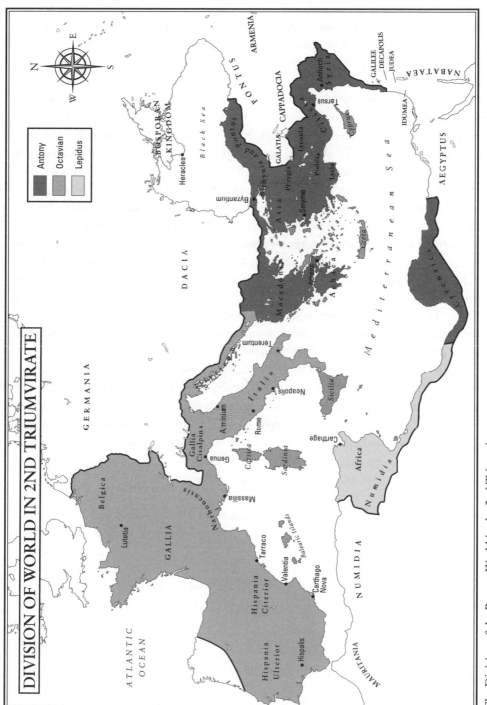

DIVISION OF WORLD IN 2ND TRIUMVIRATE

Antony
Octavian
Lepidus

ATLANTIC OCEAN

GERMANIA

GALLIA

Belgica

Lutetia

Narbonensis

Gallia Cisalpina

Ariminum

Genua

Massilia

Corsica

Sardinia

Tarraco

Valentia

Balearic Islands

Hispania Citerior

Carthago Nova

Hispania Ulterior

Hispalis

MAURITANIA

NUMIDIA

Numidia

Africa

Carthage

Rome

Neapolis

Italia

Terentum

Sicilia

Mediterranean Sea

DACIA

BOSPORAN KINGDOM

Heraclea

Black Sea

Byzantium

PONTUS

ARMENIA

Paphlagonia and Pontus

GALATIA

CAPPADOCIA

Lycaonia

CILICIA

Tarsus

Antioch

Syria

GALILEE

DECAPOLIS

JUDEA

NABATAEA

IDUMEA

Cyprus

AEGYPTUS

Asia

Phrygia

Pisidia

Smyrna

Lydia

Macedonia

Athens

Achea

Creta

Cyrenaica

Mediterranean Sea

The Division of the Roman World in the 2nd Triumvirate

rather than passing value judgment. But the impartiality is guaranteed by the balance of positive and negative that he always keeps, maybe to stress the inherent contradiction of good and evil in the human soul.

As indicated, the proscriptions were carried out in an orderly manner. Upon their armed entrance in Rome, the first seventeen names were made public, and it is easy to imagine that the first on the list was that of Marcus Tullius Cicero. The Centurion sent to carry out the assassination, a certain Laenas, had to bluff and pretend he had reinforcements on the way in order to route the many servants defending the lawyer. To Antony, he brought back the head of the orator, and his right hand, the hand that had written the Philippics. Plutarch stresses how much Mark Antony rejoiced at the sight, and gave in to laughter and other visible manifestations, and topped up generously from his own pocket the bounty for the killer. Fulvia took a hairpin from her head, and pierced the dead orator's tongue, that tongue that had spread so much malevolence on herself, on Antony, and also on her two previous husbands Clodius and Curio. She had been targeted personally in the Philippics: even in the first one, where the possibility of reconciliation with Antony was still on the table, she had been singled out as the one to blame for his errors. The desire for revenge had been building in her throughout most of her adult life, and the satisfaction must have been endless. The head and hand were finally displayed at the *rostra* in the Forum.

The desecration of Cicero's body is a unique episode in Antony's life. We have already seen how time and again he had displayed great respect for the remains of dead enemies. But for Cicero he made an exception. He represented everything the Triumvir dreaded: the lawyer from Arpinium was the symbol of the corrupt professional political class he hated, of that Rome from which he had to escape in humiliation more than once while carrying out his duties. He was the symbol of that duplicity that would be used to manipulate people and events for the self preservation of the mummified world which he detested. But first and foremost he was the man who had put his gift as a speaker and a writer to bend and misrepresent the truth, and insult Antony with an eloquent and formally elegant construction of lies.

The measure had been full for a while, and the tally had been steadily building since the days of Creticus and Sura. Antony had no time for that. Even when enmity came to the final showdown with Brutus and Cassius, it was business. With Cicero, it had become personal. So we have to believe in the reported enthusiasm that led Antony to grant the Centurion Laenas a bonus of the enormous sum of 250,000 *dinarii*. If Antony one day had been asked to take full responsibility and paternity for the execution of Cicero, he would have gladly done it without hesitation. But there are no records of the other two Triumvirs trying to save the life of the Arpinas. At this point he was one of the main threats of disturbance to the new order being built. It does not have to be forgotten how effective he had been at tearing apart the delicate political construction that Antony had built after the Ides of March. And by that time he and his ramblings about Republican *patres* and values had become a nuisance to most, let alone the fact that he had said one "tollendum" more than necessary. While there is no doubt he rejoiced in Cicero's death, the only reason that might have led an impartial historian to apportion more blame to Antony for the killings overall was the fact that Antony was the dominant personality in the trio.

Octavian was very young, he had ridden on the chariot of the *optimates* for a while, and his entourage was quite small, albeit made up of top notch human material, especially with the likes of M. Vipsanius Agrippa, a polyhedral young genius, and the bright Etruscan nobleman Mecenas. He did not have a broad base of supporters and clients other than those which had come with the Caesarean inheritance, and those he had were probably recent and therefore could not be counted on to pledge a strong allegiance. Also he had no military record of sorts: the fact that even his role in Mutina had been marginal must have been known to all.

Lepidus was a man that had played his cards well over his career, but as one of the three rulers of the western world he might have been punching above his weight. He had a power base, but it was made of long time *clientes* or people indebted to him and to his family because of favours traded in the past, rather than of true followers that he could rely on and with whom he was linked by a close bond.

Antony was another story. He was a man who had gained the open admiration of many. Even in his darkest hours, he never ceased to be a rallying point and a credible and inspirational pennant for senior people, who took the superficial excesses in which he indulged from time to time for what they were, and recognized him for his integrity, bravery, leadership, and military genius.

The inevitable excesses of course occurred at times, and Appian reports some examples of killings dictated by the opportunity to prey on large estates.[11] Still, it seems that the speculation that had been so rampant during Sulla's proscriptions, and had made the fortunes of the likes of Verres and Crassus, was somewhat limited. As the hunt for money was raging, those that had the liquidity to invest preferred to lay low and to avoid attracting too much undue attention to their assets, and thus become targets themselves. This phenomenon depressed the prices at the auctions and the expected yield of the manoeuvre, leaving the Triumvirs very short, by 200 million *dinarii* or so, of their expected financial target.

The means to cover the gap were quickly identified in a special tax to be levied on the estates of 1,400 wealthy women. It probably sounded like a speedy and expedient method to target a weaker group, which would not have put up much political resistance to the proposal, women still finding themselves on a lower tier of political rights in Roman society. Still, in an unprecedented move, these rich matrons formed a coalition, and stood up against the initiative. Their unofficial leader Hortentia went as far as addressing the mothers and the spouses of the Triumvirs, appealing to their sense of feminine solidarity in the face of unfair abuse, and later she confronted the magistrates in the Forum. Hortentia, the only voice to speak against the Triumvirate, must have been a very brave woman. Her brother, as we shall see, was serving under Brutus in Greece, and had Antony's brother Gaius in custody, pending an execution, which he would carry out soon before the battle of Philippi. She must have been in a difficult position already, and certainly most others would have opted to keep the lowest possible profile instead of taking the *junta* heads on.

Eventually the women gained sufficient popular support to have the taxation base reduced to a subset of the richest 400, and we do not know if Hortentia was one of them. The missing proceeds were obtained by an extra tax on the land revenues of the equestrian class, that is, those with fortunes in excess of 400,000 *dinarii*.

The fiscal policies described above were not the only unpopular measures that the three had to promulgate. Having silenced the opposition through the proscriptions, the only major threat that they were facing, other than Brutus in the east, was the issue of discontent among the legionaries, which, as we have seen, was not a rarity in those days, especially when the soldiers were due for retirement. So the Triumvirate selected eighteen municipalities where they were to make the land grants to the veterans. Some of the land was to be forcibly taken from the previous occupants, and this, as we shall see, was going to cause very significant problems. Land distributions per se were not a novelty in the Roman world, or in the Mediterranean basin for that matter. What made this a real issue, one more time, was the sheer magnitude of the initiative. The race to armaments in this period of intestine wars had been such that there was an unprecedented number of legions on the payroll. Once Octavian achieved uncontested power and became the first Augustus, one of his first reforms was to dramatically reduce their number. The problem of the veterans / settlers had already been a tough one at the time of the Social Wars, but now it had grown many fold, and the land confiscations threatened to disrupt the whole Italian rural world, completely change the face of the eighteen municipalities concerned – Capua, Mantua, Rimini, Rhegium among others – and create a dangerous precedent for more similar actions to come. These were times of continuous struggle after all, and nothing would have energized the troops better than the promise of a piece of land in a premium location at the end of the war. In the immediate term, protests against all these unpopular measures remained at a minimum level. There were too many drawn swords around Rome, and it was not time for open dissent, but the issue would resurface later on, when Octavian was looking for support in the deep south of Italy when facing Sextus Pompey, or when Lucius Antonius and Fulvia decided to use the discontentment for political purposes.

As we look at the final tally of the casualties, we find out that not all the proscriptions ended up in the death of the listed men. Mark Antony's maternal uncle Lucius Caesar, for example, was saved by the intercession of his sister, who told the hit men that they would have had to kill her first if they wanted to execute Lucius. Antony in the end was moved by her resolve, and acquiesced, agreeing to spare Lucius Caesar's life.

> "You are a good sister, but also you are not such a good mother. Where were
> you when he was voting to make me an enemy of the State?"

We shall now resume the narration of the developments of the war waged to the Liberators on its many fronts, culminating with the final defeat at Philippi. The viability of everything that the Second Triumvirate was building was subordinate to obtaining a military victory and to extending their rule in the Greek East, in Africa, and on the seas where Sextus Pompey was still the undisputed master. Short of that, the sheer existence of these bases of alternative power was a sufficient condition to have continuing instability at home. Plus, without Sicily and the east, the reservoir of financial means and the main outlet for the formation of new colonies and settlement of veterans for the Republic were irreparably gone.

Sextus controlling the waters of the Mediterranean was a primary concern, and it went beyond the financial considerations and the logistics of grain traffic: in order to bring the war to Macedonia and later the Asian provinces, they would have had to cross the Adriatic, thus exposing their transports to the attack of his warships, trained in years devoted to piracy. Sextus had been canvassing the Mediterranean, adding to his initially small naval force all the ships he could find, and all the anti-Caesarean sympathizers and later proscribed men he could enrol. Over the years, Caesarean generals had tried to corner and neutralize him, and he had always proven too slippery and elusive for them. So he had continued to practise his brigandage tactics, until after the Ides, when he had been pardoned, had his family wealth returned to him, and eventually, after Mutina, had received his formal naval command.

He had consolidated his control of Sicily, the best naval base in the middle of the Mediterranean, and once the Triumvirate had swung into motion, he had started assembling a small land army, enlisting the townsmen of those territories in the south which were being expropriated for the benefits of the veterans.

Octavian conducted a powerful attack onto him in 42 BC, sending a large fleet of big, high stern ships under Admiral Rufus Salvidienus, but the naval battle of the Straits, fought in very rough waters, did not produce a decisive outcome. The two sides suffered matching losses, leaving the situation unchanged.

Part of the logic of this attack was to keep Sextus busy so he could not interfere with the crossing over of the Triumviral army to Greece. But the mission against

Sextus also left the Triumvirs short on oar powered Triremes, so that the ferrying of the legions had to be organized on sail-powered commercial cargo ships, thus taking a chance with the strength and the direction of the winds, very much in the same way Antony was forced to cross the Adriatic before Pharsalus.

Some help could have come from Cleopatra herself, in the form of a fleet of warships which were going to help transport the Triumvir's army over the Adriatic. It was the second time that the Lagid Queen contributed to the Caesarean camp, the first time she had sent troops to the rescue of Dolabella against Cassius; now she was sending ships to Antony and Octavian to go in pursuit of the Liberators. Some of this goodwill must have been motivated by loyalty to the heirs of her lover Julius Caesar, and some from the cold assessment that for herself and her son Cesarion, the post-war odds for successful continuation of independent rule in the land of the Nile were certainly worse off if the Liberators were to be in charge of the Roman world. As a matter of fact, it is entirely possible that Cassius was already planning a full scale invasion of Egypt: the last kingdom that preserved a certain degree of independence in the near world, a kingdom of huge wealth, and with the enviable feature of being Rome's main source of grain. Cassius had twelve legions at his orders, and Cleopatra had tried to help Dolabella, enemy of the State. The opportunity must have been regarded as unique. But Cassius had to give up the idea, if ever he really had it, to implement the defensive moves made necessary by the visible preparations for war by the Triumvirs. As for Cleopatra's ships, they never made it to Italy, as they were wrecked by a storm as they were crossing the Mediterranean, and the mission had to be aborted. The Liberators had sent a large fleet under Admiral Murcus to intercept them, but this proved to be a needless measure.

Eventually the crossover of the Adriatic could begin, and favourable winds expedited the early conveyance of troops. All that Cassius could accomplish was to try to establish a blockade that was going to harass the reinforcements following behind, and disturb the shipment of supplies. He was hoping to disrupt the logistic of a 100,000 strong force, exactly like Pompey had done with Caesar before Pharsalus.

And just like Caesar had done, and for the very same reasons, Antony had to move fast. He knew from the experience of 49 BC the difficulties of hunting a better supplied and better organized enemy, which could afford the luxury of fighting a war of erosion, holding on to their strong positions and well organized chains of supply. It was in these circumstances that eight legions under Decidius Saxa (Stones) and Norbanus Flaccus (Floppy Ears) marched as a large *avant guarde* across mountainous Macedonia and into Thrace. Their approach was very swift and effective, and did not give Cassius and Brutus a chance to take full advantage of the mountainous nature of the land, and to lay ambushes, or otherwise obstruct their progress.

Cassius knew that the rocky land crossed by the via Egnatia, the only suitable path east, which did not provide opportunities to source provisions appropriately for a large army, and the need to reach fertile plains to find food was as much of a motive for Antony to make it to Thrace swiftly as his eagerness to fight. He and Brutus were looking at a re-enactment of the Epyrum campaign of 49 BC, and just like Antony they had treasured the experience, and were determined to play their cards better than Pompey had done.

The morale of their troops must have been high, or at least higher than their scarcely paid counterparts on Antony's side: they had enacted a campaign for forced collection of funds from the Asian city-states, which had given them a solid financial base to pay good cash bonuses, and a promise of more for the end of the war.

Immediately following the death of Dolabella, Crassus had started to increase the pressure on the cities of the Asian provinces in order to stockpile the funds he needed to pay his soldiers. The people of the beautiful city of Tarsus, soon to see the birth of Saint Paul, saw many of their young sold into slavery, after witnessing several heavy plunders of their public and private treasures. To the locals, it mattered little whether the rape of the city had happened at the hands of the Triumvirs or the Liberators. To them, they were all just Romans, and once the hostilities ceased it was Antony's job to right many wrongs, and restore justice and the credibility of the Roman administration.

After Tarsus and the region of Cylicia, it was the turn of the island of Rhodes and the region of Lycia-Pamphilia. Both were lands of sailors, and both could have helped the crossover of the Triumviral Legions. The Rhodians tried to negotiate their way out of the corner where they were stuck: Cassius, like Cicero and many others, had been educated in Greek letters on the island. The fact did not help the Rhodians significantly. After the negotiations had failed, their superior seamanship was overpowered by the heavier Roman triremes and quinquiremes, large battleships with three or five orders of oars, in a series of naval battles. Finally the alumni Cassius got to reduce the city to obedience after a brief siege. All that their pleas for mercy were worth to their cause was an orderly and systematic pillage, much preferable of course to a reckless and unruly one, and a limited number of executions, as opposed to mass slaughter, as a punishment for the resistance offered.

Xanthius, Patara, Myra, all the Lycian cities suffered the same fate at the hands of Brutus. The Xanthians, after a brutal siege, opted for mass suicide and jumped into the flames of an improvised pyre, leaving very few behind for the inevitable captivity and slavery. The other cities, educated by the destiny of the Xanthians, chose to cow-tow and cooperate, and enjoyed more lenient treatment from the Liberators after handing over the money they had been requested to contribute to the Caesaricide cause.

So, when it was all said and done, the safe of Brutus and Cassius was in excellent shape, to the detriment of the local populations, but their brutality was to leave many scars which would take substantial time and effort to heal.

The situation of Antony and Octavian, in turn, was shakier, in view of the criticism they had to take in Rome, as we have seen, over their fiscal policy. So it is with high spirits that Brutus and Cassius marched north, around the Black Gulf and towards Thrace, to meet the enemy.

Antony's *avant guarde* had made enough progress in Thracian territory to block the two mountain passes on the main road, called the Sapaei and the Corpili, so that outflanking them to attack them from two sides would have taken too much time. The first tactical diversion from the Liberators was to send Tillius Cimber with a sea born legion to land further west on the coast, to simulate a naval flanking. The decoy initially worked, and Decidius, who was guarding Corpili, moved south to join forces with his partner in Sapaei, leaving one of the passes open. But eventually the two understood the stratagem, and made quick corrective adjustments.

Then their Thracian allied King Rhoscupolis showed Cassius an alternative itinerary around the block, towards the plain of Philippi, a daring march through mountain and forests, without water or suitable camp sites, and completed the encirclement in four days' time.

In the end the risky march was completed with full success, so that the bulk of the army could reunite with Tillius' legion in Philippi. But the forces at the orders of Mark Antony ware made aware of enemy progress by their counterintelligence, as the brother and rival of Rhoscuopolis, Rhoscus, was siding with them, so that they had a chance to retreat west to Amphipolis before being caught in the trap. The Liberators' attack had the outcome of bringing the armies nearer to each other in a short time, and now they were just a few miles apart, divided only by the open terrain in front of the town of Philippi.

This vast plain sloped in the direction of the Triumviral army, so making their way towards the enemy was a slight uphill climb. The configuration of the site was ideal for Brutus and Cassius, who also were able to strike their respective camps on two hills facing each other, in proximity of water springs, and with easy access to the harbour of Neapolis a few miles south east, so that they could transfer more troops and supplies whenever they needed them. The two hills dominated the via Egnatia underneath, so that when the fortifications of the Liberators' camp were completed, with their defensive walls and towers, Brutus and Cassius had effectively shut down the way to the east. The only drawback of this otherwise ideal position was that the camps of the two leaders were quite far from each other and that would have made mutual support problematic.

Certainly they were planning on getting more military support for their cause and they sent Quintus Labienus to seek help from the unlikely source of Orodes, King of Parthia.

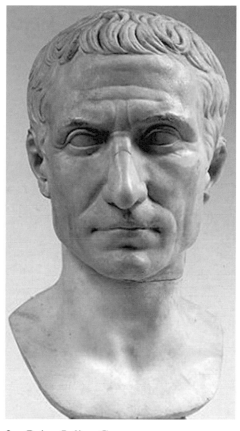

1. Lucius Cornelius Sulla, Glyphotech, Munich

2. Gaius Julius Caesar

3. Marcus Tullius Cicero

4. Ptolemy XII Auletes smashing enemies with a mace. Relief from the first pylon in the Temple at Edfu

5. The Forum today (Photo Tavares)

6. Octavian Augustus (statue known as the "Augustus of Prima Porta") Rome, Museo Chiaramonti. (Photo Nierman)

7. Mark Antony

8. Marcus Iunius Brutus, Palazzo Massimo alle Terme, Rome

9. Dionysos
and Satyrs, Paris,
Bibliotheque
Nationale

10. Cleopatra VII Théa Philopator,
Berlin, Altes Museum

11. Coinage of Fulvia Flacca Bambula (Photo Classical Numismatics Group Inc)

12. Silver Denarius by Sextus Pompey (Classical Numismatics Group Inc)

13. Herod the Great conquers Jerusalem, Jean Fouquet 1470–75 (Paris, Bibliotheque Nationale)

14. A Parthian mounted archer, Turin, Palazzo Madama (Photo Chadrin)

15. Coin of Phraates, King of Parthia (Photo PHGCOM)

16. Octavia the Younger, Rome, Ara Pacis (Photo Dell'Orto)

17. The Apis Bull, Indianapolis Museum of Art, Indianapolis

18. The battle of Actium by Lorenzo Castro, 1672

19. The death of Cleopatra by Guercino (Genova, Galleria di Palazzo Roso)

Quintus Labienus was the son of Titus Labienus, one of Caesar's lieutenants in Gaul, who had turned coat and joined Pompey at Pharsalus, and who later had died at the battle of Munda in 47 BC causing the young man to harbour feelings of hatred and revenge towards the Triumvirs. It is true that it was well known that an invasion of Parthia was well on the Caesarean agenda, so the same could reasonably be expected from those who wanted to pursue his plans and policies. But Cassius Longinus had been Crassus' second in command during the disastrous campaign that ended tragically in Carrhae, and in fact he had been the one that had mitigated the damage for the Romans from the Parthian counteroffensive. It is therefore difficult to see how he could have fared well in the field of Parthian diplomacy. At any rate it is clear that Labienus left too late to accomplish anything on time, or bring reinforcements to the Philippi battlefield. So he decided to hang around Parthia, and serve as a military advisor to King Orodes. We will meet him again before the end of this story.

In those critical days, Octavian had fallen ill and was bed ridden in Epyrum. He was subject to sudden crises that left him totally exhausted and incapable of moving, possibly due to malaria or some other disease and possibly exacerbated by stress. Antony hastened to join his forces in Amphipolis, and must have been delighted to shrug Octavian from his back, and exercise his command without the young man in his hair. Even if Octavian had been at his best, he would have added no value, or may even have been a nuisance: his military skills were paper thin, and we know that he had watched his only war from the walls of Mutina. On the other hand, he could not afford to leave all the credit and the glory for defeating the murderers of his father for Antony alone, so he would have done everything he could to play an active role in the command of operations. Therefore, Octavian had himself transported through Macedonia in a litter, while Antony was taking control of the site, building the best fortifications possible around his less desirable position, and engaging the enemy in the usual skirmishes to keep the pressure on them.

Everything was now ready for an escalation of the hostilities, with the armies, both nineteen legions strong, plus cavalry, auxiliaries, and allied troops, solidly entrenched in their camps, facing each other from a little over one mile away.

Changing the names of the places and the protagonists, the pages from Appian that describe the scene at Philippi can be exchanged with those preceding Pharsalus, without otherwise altering the narration. Antony, with challenging logistics and worse campgrounds, had to force Brutus and Cassius to come down and accept a pitched battle, or over time his position would deteriorate and become unsustainable. There was, however, one major difference with Pharsalus, and that was the sheer size of the forces in play. Both armies could count on at least 80,000 legionaries and 15,000 cavalry, Brutus maybe 20,000, and the allied *velites* were in the tens of thousands also. Only the initial expedition corps that Antony sent to Thrace was larger than Caesar's entire army in Epyrum. The challenge of managing this huge operation, probably the largest of antiquity at that time, rested entirely on Antony's shoulders, while at least Brutus and Cassius could share the burden among the two of them. As for the quality of the fighters, the balance leaned in favour of the Triumvirs. Just like Pompey's army at Pharsalus, the force of the Liberators was markedly more heterogeneous than that of their opponents, as it was made up of some of the legions that Caesar had set aside for his Parthian project, two legions of Macedonian recruits, some platoons from Pompey's Pharsalus survivors, some of those formerly with Dolabella, the Gabinians, who had surrendered to Cassius, and more besides. It was a multinational and polyglot assembly, and quite difficult to command.

It is true that Julius Caesar had once written that a bad general is more effective than two good ones sharing the command between them. Antony must have felt under a great deal of pressure as he teed up his powerful army for the final act of a struggle which had been ongoing for over 120 years, and he must have spent many sleepless nights because of the frantic preparations and the stress levels. But, regardless of his fatigue, he can only have rolled his eyes and spread his arms in despair upon seeing Octavian's adorned litter advancing in the distance towards his camp.

While on paper they had the best position and the favour of the odds, Brutus had had warning signs of his impending end. He had dreamed of a monstrous and terrifying figure, who qualified him as his evil genius, and who had given him an appointment at Philippi. And now at Philippi they were. The reassuring scepticism of Cassius, dismissive of these supernatural manifestations, could not succeed in calming the rattled Brutus.

As we have seen, it was now for Antony and Octavian to lure their enemies outside their fortifications and fight. While Brutus and Cassius had open roads to the east to get supplies for men and horse, the road westwards went into rocky Macedonia, and then into the Adriatic patrolled by Sextus Pompey and, more recently, by Gneus Domitius Ahenobarbus. So Brutus and Cassius were not at all surprised when they saw Antony lining up his legion in the plain of Philippi, in full battle gear, the silver Eagles of his legions shining in the sun, javelins beating rhythmically on their large rectangular shields, chanting insults addressed at the enemy soldiers, and offering battle almost every day. They were probably smiling from the safety of their camps, and calculating how much longer Antony could have held on with the scarce supplies he had on hand.

But little did they know that the daily offer of battle was merely a decoy, and that Antony's men were clearing a path in the marshland south of Cassius' camp, building a causeway to protect it from the launch of missiles, and throwing bridges to cross the points where the water was deep, with the intent of eventually surrounding the camp. When this pathway was nearly completed, he sent in some

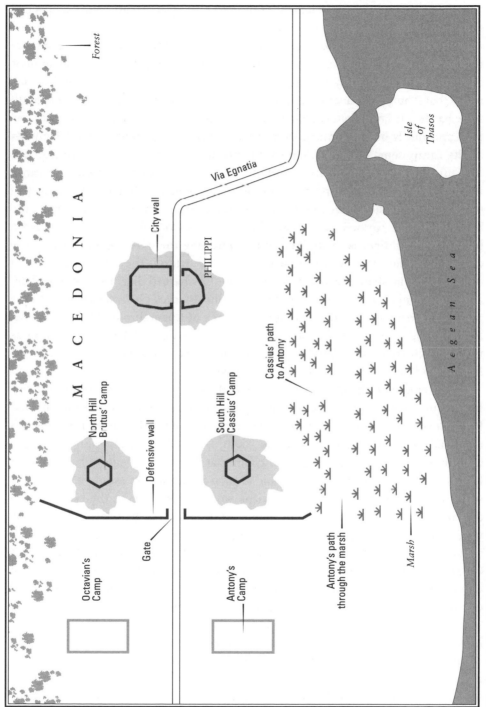

The Battlefield at Philippi Day 1 (*Courtesy of Patrick Parrelli*)

cohorts to attempt the encirclement of the two hills where Brutus and Cassius had set up camp.

Eventually Cassius realized what was happening and reacted, fortifying in haste the space between the causeway and his camp, and trying, with a certain amount of success, to cut Antony's strike force from the rest of his troops. It was at this point that Antony saw a window of opportunity to attract his opponents into a full scale battle. He immediately launched his troops across the plain to attack Cassius' men and newly built counter-fortifications. To the amazement of the defendants of the camp, some of Antony's men directly attacked the powerful fortifications. The audacity of the manoeuvre paid off. The strategic position of Cassius' camp was so strong and reassuring that there were few men guarding the ramparts, and they could be easily overcome by the powerful assault. It was so that, while the bulk of Cassius' legions were facing the Antonians frontally, they saw their camp being stormed. Brutus' men, who were witnessing the developments from their camp, about one mile away, were wounded in the pride as they saw Antony's bold offensive taking shape. Instinctively they counter charged diagonally on the plain, and on the impetus they continued their run and attacked Octavian's troops. In the confusion that ensued, and also due to the lack of leadership on Octavian's side, the left wing of the young Caesar gave up and was outflanked. Octavian's camp was taken, its Spartan defendants wiped out, and, when it was all done, three of his legions had been battered and almost destroyed.

In the end, both the charges were crowned by success, but neither was decisive for the final outcome of the battle. Antony had stormed Cassius' camp and inflicted heavy losses. But Brutus had done the same on the north side of the field and captured Octavian's camp, where the young Caesar had barely escaped capture by hiding in a ditch. He would later claim that divine premonition had been the key to his survival, so that he was able to turn a humiliating escape into a source of religious legitimacy. Servile historians would widely report the event. Given the magnitude of the engagement, one episode could not have possibly won the war, and eventually neither side was able to hold on to their gains and both had to withdraw. But the main consequence of that day of late October 42 BC was that Cassius, seeing his camp raided by the Antonians, assumed the worst had happened and panicked, without knowing that Brutus had the upper hand at the other end of the battlefield. In fact, the conjecture put forward by Appian is that Octavian had actually lost more troops than Cassius, so that the tally was favourable to the Liberators. Discouraged, Cassius quickly opted for suicide to avoid capture, but it seems that it was a pure fatality that allowed him to go through with his desperate gesture, helped by his Greek aide Pindaros: in all the accounts of the event he missed the good news of Brutus' victory by minutes, or he received them at the fatal instant and dismissed them as not worthy of faith.

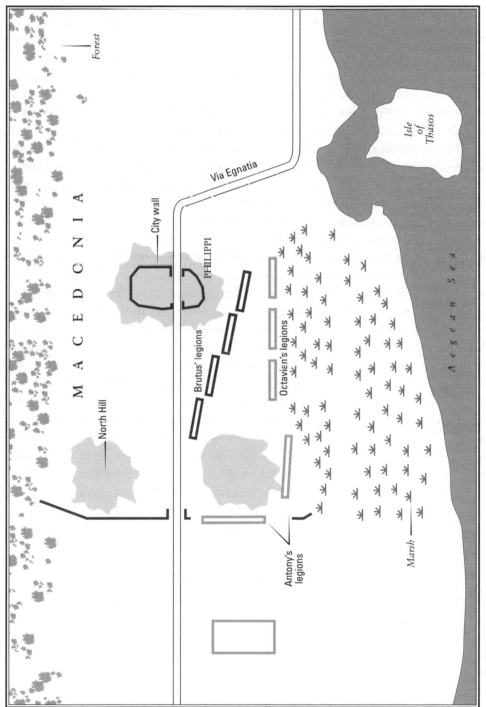

The Battlefield at Philippi Day 2 (*Courtesy of Patrick Parrelli*)

When the first round of fighting was over, it must have become clear for Brutus that the outcome had been a draw, if not in his favour, and that the pacing strategy adopted so far, and the reliance on the more solid supply lines, remained the best bet for final victory. He must have received the intelligence that the naval blockade by Mucius and Ahenobarbus had intercepted and wrecked the ships carrying two more legions to the Triumvir's camp, including the famous and formidable Martia Legion. Many soldiers had perished drowning in the Adriatic.

This might very well have been the end of it, as the army led by Antony and Octavian was really scrambling for food. Troops had already been diverted from their fighting posts to raid Achaia, 300 km to the south, to gather whatever food they could find, and the outflanking of Brutus on the south side was becoming a logistic necessity as much as a military objective.

Brutus had been deeply affected by the loss of his partner Cassius. He had taken his body for the funeral service to the Island of Taros, just off the coast, so that the troops would not suffer emotionally from having to witness the sad ceremony, and to try and avoid them dwelling too long on the consequences of having lost the most experienced military leader on their side. He also lined up all the prisoners he had taken during his raid on Octavian's camp, and killed all the slaves, so they would not be in his way and he wouldn't have to feed them, but he freed all the Roman citizens, in order to create a precedent of mercy, which might have come in handy if his side lost. Lastly, he paid another bonus to his troops, and promised them he would allow the sack of two Greek cities in case of victory, another strong sign of his financial ingenuity. Brutus, not the best field commander, but a man of strong intellectual means, knew that the initial strategy of playing a war of attrition, based on better logistics, was still a viable option. Soon the Triumvirs would run out of food again, and the wells Antony had dug for water would be polluted or insufficient. After the first battle, the rainy season had begun, and rain and mud flowed downhill towards the lower grounds of the Triumviral camp. The tents were drenched with the rain, and they suffered during the cold nights. Brutus added to the damage by deviating the course of a stream and partly flooding the enemy camp.

All of a sudden, the imponderable happened, and one morning of early November 42 BC, Brutus accepted the battle that Antony was offering. The reasons for which a smart, experienced, and balanced leader like Brutus would forfeit his advantage, and fall into the trap that Antony had laid out remain shrouded in mystery. The version from Appian is that he yielded to the plea of his troops, tired of waiting, exasperated by the daily provocation of the enemy, and eager to fight and prove their value and bravery. Brutus had been at Pharsalus, and was conscious of how history could repeat itself.

"I seem to be conducting my campaign like Pompey Magnus, no longer giving the orders but receiving them."[12]

The difference was, of course, that he was yielding to his own soldiers, and not to a shaky coalition of eastern princes, those very soldiers that he had treated extremely well, and rewarded handsomely with the money he and Cassius had looted in Asia Minor. Another interpretation points to the particular way in which Antony, that morning, had organized his army for battle. Instead of presenting his legions in the typical triple order formation in the plain between the two camps, he had, overnight, advanced four legions to occupy a small hillock on the border of the marshes, opposite Cassius' old camp, left unguarded by Brutus. At dawn he had moved the bulk of his forces eastwards through the marshes, with the clear intention to complete the encirclement of the enemy camp, thus cutting off their supplies, and threatening to reverse the situation in terms of the logistic advantage. Brutus would have found himself with his back to the mountains, and no clear way of escape. Of course, by committing most of his legions to this encircling manoeuvre, Antony had weakened the defence of his own camp, and thus taken a big risk. Brutus' decision to give battle was probably spurred by the pressure his men felt as a result of the provocations and this bold offensive move. The defection to the Triumvirs of a certain Camulatus, a soldier close to Brutus, also played a role in creating the emotional conditions which made Brutus yield to the pressure. On the morning of 23 October, when the fighting began, it was Brutus that drew first blood. Two opposing legions locked shields, skipped the skirmishing and went at it with their short Spanish *gladia* drawn.

The battlefield at Philippi was extremely narrow, because of the marshes right behind the Triumviral army, so the two lines made contact immediately, skipping all the usual skirmishes and hurling of javelins and projectiles. When the melee began to form a configuration, it was Brutus' troops that made the first breakthrough, getting the better of the enemy at the far end of the front, and attempting a flanking on the right side of the enemy lines. But this time Octavian's men, sorely defeated just a few days earlier, held strong, and forced back the enemy. Gradually the Triumviral legions gained ground inch by inch, the centre of the Republican army started to crumble and the usual panic in their ranks began to take over as they were now pressed closely against each other, and finding it difficult to move. Some, like Cato's son Marcus, tried to stand their ground and fought heroically. The vast majority, like the poet Horace, fled for their lives or perished in the stampede.

And it was at this time that Antony launched his powerful and decisive counter-attack, sweeping all the resistance away and giving the battle an irreversible momentum. When the route of the enemy was complete, he made coldly sure that Brutus and his generals could be apprehended. As his men were closing up on him, one of Brutus' aides posed as his commander, let the Antonians have him in custody, and then demanded to be taken to Antony, in order to buy the last Republican leader the time to make a dignified exit. Which Brutus did, on the following morning, looking from a hilltop to the battlefield ridden with the bodies of his legionaries, with the customary help of one of his friends who drove a sword through his rib cage.

The battle of Philippi, the battle that delivered the western world to a new era, was over, and it was Mark Antony who had won it.

The role of Octavian had been negligible. Practically inept, unskilled in the military arts, bed ridden for the entire campaign, overwhelmed at the first adversity having ended the first day of fighting shamefully hiding in a bog, he could hardly go down in history as the avenger of his father Julius Caesar.

Antony on the other hand had played it masterfully. Starting from a position of disadvantage, he had organized his camp and fortification lines to his best advantage. He had shrewdly organized several encirclement attempts, making sure that the enemy was always on his toes and on the defensive. One of his attempts had been a daring gamble, which had ended with a strong blow to the enemy's morale and pride, with the temporary conquest of their camp, and the suicide, in despair, of their senior leader.

He had played psychological warfare with his daily provocation, knowing well from field experience that it would have generated intolerable frustration in the enemy ranks. He knew all too well they would have felt humiliated at having to refuse to fight day after day, while the Antonians were taunting and mocking them, and in the long run the pressure that was building would have mounted to Brutus, which would almost certainly have happened on a regular basis. He knew his enemy, Brutus, who was a stoic intellectual and a brave man, but incapable of taking unpopular decisions and withstanding the pressure from his soldiers. Antony had used his intuition to his advantage in what can only be described as a surgical and perfectly targeted manner. Then Antony had forced the decision by driving another risky attack, which had left Brutus with no choice.

Finally, Antony had read in real time the developments of the melee, and seized the moment for the all-in attack with laser-like precision, thus bringing the final victory home. At Philippi, Antony took to full accomplishment his historical mission as a change agent, which he had undertaken after the Ides of March, transitioning Rome out of chaos, surviving the many adversities which crossed his path, and finally using all his unmatched skills as a military commander to obtain the final victory against the remnants and the legacies of an old world which had outlived its times.

As for Octavian, he had been impalpable in the fighting, but he made his presence heavily felt in the aftermath, during the cruel retaliation against the Caesaricides.

He had asked for Brutus' body to be decapitated, while Antony wanted to use his usual *pietas* and respect for the dead enemy, a respect from which he would only depart when he did not deem the opponent worthy of it. He took off his General's purple cloak, his *paludamentum*, and covered Brutus' body. Later he had a funeral pyre built for him, and he sent the ashes in an urn to his mother Servilia,

Caesar's alleged old lover, to the point that Brutus had long been rumoured to be the illegitimate fruit of the love between the two. We know that the ship which was carrying Brutus' severed head to Rome to be shown to the city sank in the Adriatic on its way home. Upon learning of her husband's death, his wife Porcia, Cato's daughter, committed suicide by swallowing burning coals. One wonders why she chose such a horrible death, when in the comfort of their home she could have conceived of a quicker and more painless ending.

We know that Antony took revenge over the officer that had executed his brother Gaius, that Hortensius, son of Hortensius Orator that we have met at the time of the Verres trial, and brother of Rome tax Lisistratha, Hortensia. He was merciful in his vengeance though, and he limited his retaliation to having him executed by sword on Gaius' grave. Octavian, on the other side, presided over the slaughter of many of the prisoners, yielding to his worst instincts. The way he dealt with the captives puts into very precise perspective the role he played during the proscriptions, and ridicules the contemporary historians' attempts to have him acquitted from the blame of the killings. Suetonius is impartial and credible when he frowns in disgust at the image of father and son, after Philippi, forced to roll dices for who would survive, and then at Octavian giggling at the suicide of the survivor in front of the body of the deceased. Let's read his comments:

> "His conduct so disgusted the remainder of the prisoners, including Marcus Favonius, a well known imitator of Cato's, that while being led off in chains they courteously saluted Antony as Imperator, but abused Augustus (i.e. Octavian) to his face with the most obscene epithets."[13]

Antony's excesses were always limited to a good party with actresses and mimes, to an occasional night devoted to womanizing, to an outburst of rage, to a cocky attitude in the face of professional politicians. But when it came to deeper human values, compassion, and piety, he had all the gravitas one would expect from a first level figure of the classical world.

On the other hand, when we read the pages on Octavian from Suetonius and Appian, and compare them with Dio or Velleius, the question that comes up is if they even refer to the same person. It is difficult to gauge the official propaganda image of mercifulness during the proscriptions when then we have to face a sadistic monster, who confronts one by one all the prisoners taken after the siege of Perusia two years later, to repeat to them obsessively: "You are going to die!". Or, for that matter, the bloodthirsty despot that sent 300 Perusian prisoners to be slaughtered on the memorial of the Ides of March that he had built.

Those few that managed to escape from Philippi alive or survived Octavian's vengeance did not have many alternatives. Most of them made it to sea and went to seek asylum either with Sextus Pompey, or with Domitius Ahenobarbus, who also was at the head of a fleet, and had decided to pursue his own course. The Triumvirs at this point were still relatively weak at sea, and we have seen how Sextus had largely proven this by repelling all the attempts by Octavian to attack him in Sicily.

There were a few more major episodes to come to ferry Rome, and the western world with it, out of the Civil Wars, and more large scale tributes in human life would be needed before the foundations for a new Golden Age could be made ready.

But Mark Antony had given the course of history an irreversible turn. Rome was not drowning any more in the current of a raging river, but was beginning to see the shore approaching, and to feel the sand under its feet again.

Still, the precariousness of the equilibrium thus reached was still evident. The massive war effort had depleted and impoverished the resources of Italy and of the west in general, and exacerbated all the problems inherited from the old Republic. The east, equally ravaged by years of war, and more recently by the passage of the Liberators, was also in urgent need of finding a stable order to prosper again. The fundamental advantage reached after Philippi is that now the Triumvirs had the power needed to make the necessary change happen, unconstrained by the lingering menace of Brutus and Cassius, and unobstructed by the inertia of the senatorial class.

After the destruction, the reconstruction could finally start.

Chapter Six

Prince of the East

With the exception of ending the struggle with Sextus Pompey, and eliminating a few leftover pockets of rebellion after the decisive battle at Philippi, even this long tail end of the Civil War could be considered to be over. The Triumvirs, if we want to consider also Lepidus, by now relegated to a subordinate role, could focus on what was, at least in theory, their main mission: the reconstruction of the State and its provinces, torn by decades of civil strife, and still in search of a viable political and economic organization.

Octavian made it back to Rome but in such poor health that his life seemed to be in danger. He was exhausted by the hardship and the stress of the military campaign. He had a big agenda ahead of him, and first and foremost the ongoing riddle of the settlement of the war veterans, which was still, for the most part, unsolved.

After his lacklustre participation in the Philippi campaign, which had been won thanks to Antony, to whom everyone rightfully attributed the credit for the victory, Octavian needed to find a solution for this question of the heritage of the Roman Republic, in order to gain some credibility in the eyes of the nation. All his propaganda efforts were going towards trying to embellish the role he had played in the war: for example, in his blatant servility to Octavian, Velleius chooses to ignore completely the fact that Philippi had been won thanks to Antony's leadership alone. Shying away from compromising disclosures, he limits himself to saying that the young Caesar, despite his infirmity, was carrying out his commander's duties on the field. Then, Velleius leapfrogs months of brilliant generalship from Antony, which even a master of bad faith such as he could not have denied, and skips to the suicide of Brutus and Cassius at the end of the battle. But this type of exercise was meant for posterity, whereas the public at the time, and those with a military background in particular, with all the fresh evidence available to them, would not be fooled.

Even during the relatively peaceful time immediately following Philippi, Octavian's leadership skills were not much better than his operating military skills. Pulling no punches as usual, Suetonius underlines how, yet again, he failed to deal effectively with the situation:

> "He failed to satisfy either the landowners, who were complaining that they were being evicted from their lands; or the veterans, who felt entitled to better rewards for their services."[1]

Antony, on the other hand, remained in the eastern provinces, which had not only been ravaged by the fighting, but were also deeply exploited and milked of much of their wealth by Brutus and Cassius. Plutarch[2] presents the facts as if Mark Antony's primary mission in the east was not healing and reconstructing after the passage of the Tyrannicides, or consolidating a form of provincial government still undefined, but extorting more tributes to pay bonuses to his victorious legions. It is out of doubt that his first move after Philippi was to descend into Greece to begin collecting, accompanied by a large army to secure the success of his fund raising mission.

With the division of responsibilities after Philippi, Lepidus took the first of a series of backwards steps, and, under suspicion of having been too soft on, or even having connived with, Sextus Pompey, he was subject to political attack to the point that he had to relinquish Spain and Narboniensis Gaul to Octavian and Antony respectively. As for Cisalpine Gaul, its status and that of its citizens was raised from that of a province to full Roman citizenship, in respect to a promise made by Caesar to its inhabitants in the distant past. While this territory would have normally been destined to Antony, he gave it to Octavian in exchange for goodwill alone in their alliance.

While fund raising was of paramount importance, it cannot have been the only reason for the long term permanence of Antony in the east. It would have been a natural thought that the Triumvirs after Philippi would have laid hands on the safe of the Liberators, or what was left of it. One would have expected the spoils of war of such a large scale confrontation and crushing victory to be consequent, but there is no certainty of how much money made it safely all the way into the hands of the Triumvirs. Clearly Brutus and Cassius must have liberally distributed bonuses to their forces, and in all likelihood what was left helped, but did not suffice to resolve the financial riddle. But, equally importantly as far as Antony's prolonged permanence in the east went, many of the Asian territories, annexed very recently, just before the beginning of the intestine hostilities, never had a chance of being properly integrated in the Roman world, and still had many internal problems to resolve, and external threats to eliminate.

The most pressing of these was the periodic resurgence of the Parthian menace, and everything it implied for control over Syria and Judaea. Certainly Antony shared with Octavian the burden of raising the funds needed to satisfy the expectations of their army, so the unfortunate Greeks had to share some of the pain. Antony had to break to them the news that, while a friend of their people and an admirer of their civilization, he was absolutely duty bound to collect taxes, and he did so in unequivocal terms, in the reconstruction of his speech made by Appian, quoting the size (170,000 men) of the army waiting to be rewarded.

"You can see the scale of our needs from the scale of those figures. Octavian will depart for Italy to distribute the land and the towns to them, and he will, to be blunt, evict the Italian population. We have counted on you for money, so that you will not be evicted from your land, your towns, your homes, your shrines, your tombs."[3]

Antony's request was a one-off, and consisted of giving in one year the same amount of money they had given to Brutus and Cassius in two, which represented a sum equivalent to ten years' worth of taxes. But after the pleading of the Greeks the amount was magnanimously reduced to nine years' worth, to be paid in two instalments. A prominent rhetorician and intellectual of the time, Ibrea, came out with an ironic remark about the request:

"O Antony, if you can levy tax twice a year (as the Liberators had recently already collected), you can doubtless give us a couple of summers, and a double harvest time!"

He also remarked that some of the monies previously paid by the Asian provinces (to the Liberators?) amounting to the astronomical sum of 200 million silver talents, might have been embezzled by the Roman administration:

"If you haven't received them, ask your collectors for them. If you have received them, and you don't have them any longer, in this case we are ruined!"[4]

The implication here is that, just as had been the case when similar suspicions surfaced in Rome in 44 BC, embezzlers had been at work, and Antony had been naive and slow at detecting dishonest behaviour, as opposed to being dishonest himself.

As predatory as such actions may seem, they have to be put in the context of the situation in Rome, which was already desperate prior to Antony's departure to Greece, and so another wave of extraordinary taxation was practically unavoidable. But Appian also tells us how Antony applied measure, sound judgment and piety in "consoling" the city-state that had suffered the most under Cassius' yoke,[5] such as the cities of Lycia that had been burned to the ground, or the island of Rhodes, whose proud inhabitants had strenuously defended themselves but been overcome, or Laodicea, the theatre of the siege of Dolabella, or Tarsus, where Antony freed all those that Cassius had sold into slavery to fill his pockets.

It is not easy to fully appreciate the feelings of gratitude that the cities of the Near East would have felt towards Antony. At the head of eight veteran legions and a large cavalry force, undisputed vanquisher of Brutus and Cassius, he could have systematically raped and pillaged the whole region, reducing thousands of inhabitants to slavery and profiting accordingly, largely for his own pocket, expropriating all the best plots of land for his veterans and winning their eternal gratitude and loyalty, and forcing the people to contribute all their gold and jewels to Rome's *aerarium* or public treasury. Such behaviour would have been his universally accepted and God-given right in his capacity as conquering hero of the time, and his just revenge on the backers – willing or unwilling – of his enemies. Nobody in those days would have frowned on such action, which would have fallen largely within the norm.

Mark Antony's Greek sojourn was uneventful other than a faux pas with the citizens of Megara upon discussing the beauties of their town, which he found unimpressive, and so he naively told them for their amazement. On the other hand, his overall philhellenic posture in Athens won him some sympathy, whether he was there for taxation purposes or not. Antony spent the winter of 42–41 BC in Athens, his old stomping grounds from his student days. After years of back to back travel, adventures, wars, treasons, and ruthless politics, he must have enjoyed those months which would have been almost a vacation. He took to dressing the Greek way, replacing the Roman toga with the square Greek dress, and attended theatre representations, cultural debates and lectures, all activities which, as a Roman aristocrat, he had been trained to appreciate, but which he had neglected due to his frenetic activity since he had sailed abroad with Gabinius sixteen years before. Away from the daily hustle and bustle of Rome, he was able to enjoy life in grand style, with Athens at his full disposal, not as a student, but as an absolute master, with an entire subcontinent at his feet. He would have been able to alternate his cultural interests with some night time partying maybe more akin to his habits, but without the scrutiny and the criticism he would have been subject to in gossip-filled Rome.

The unforgiving Plutarch does report some excesses during this period, and attributes them to his weakness for adulation and his naive acceptance of the lies which came from the members of his *entourage*. These character traits surface on more than one occasion in Antony's life, and not just via Plutarch, but also through Appian, to the point that it must be considered a distinctive trait. Mark Antony had recreated in the east the same type of following he had had in Rome in his days as Master of Horse, that is, a large group of *comites* or friends, among which he held court, where brilliant officers like Decidius Saxa, Ventidius, and Dellius, were mingled with a crowd of mimes, musicians, actresses, and other entertainers, with whom they shared some pleasure and extravagance in the "after hours". This did not mean he was distracted from his most important undertakings in the Mediterranean basin, but it proves that he could not resist the temptation of a little daily indulgence in wine, women, and song, surrounded by luxury. And probably this indulgence sometimes turned into overindulgence too. In this context Antony, while not gullible, was vulnerable to adulation and susceptible to making errors of judgment, which is exactly what he had done in Rome seven years earlier. While he had grown and matured, it is clear that some of the members of his unofficial court ware capable of influencing him to obtain advantages, or even embezzle public funds on a large scale. Listen to Plutarch comment:

> "He never imagined that those who used so much liberty in their mirth would flatter or deceive him in any business of consequence, not knowing how common it is with parasites to mix their flattery with boldness, as confectioncrs do their sweetmeats with something biting, to prevent the sense of satiety. Their freedom and impertinence at table were designed expressly to give to their obsequiousness in council the air of being not complaisance, but conviction."[6]

Plutarch, in order to ground his accusations of extravagance, tells us of the scandal Antony had caused when he had expropriated the home of a rich Greek and given it to a cook who had especially pleased him with an extraordinary banquet. But the same chronicler explains how he was capable of repenting as soon as he realized the mistakes he had made. He granted some islands in the Aegean to thc Athenians, and, in his attempt to endear the locals by display of piety, he attended personally to the restoration of the Temple of Apollon in Delphi.

After spending the winter in Athens, in the February that followed, Antony moved to Asia, beginning his journey from the city of Ephesus on the Turkish coast, where today lies the city of Izmir. Ephcsus was one of the main cities in the Mediterranean basin, a very important centre of trade and worship alike, which had prospered around the well known Temple of Apollon. The unlucky Princess Arsinoe, the sister of Cleopatra that Caesar had dragged in chains in his Egyptian triumph, was held captive in this temple.

And it is at this Ephesian appearance that we have our first report of Antony being saluted as a Dionysos by the cheering population. We must now provide some background for this association, because it will become a *leit-motif* throughout the late part of Antony's life, and it will be widely used for the final rounds of Augustan propaganda. Why would the Ephesian salute the rough and tough Roman warrior as Dionysos, the God of wine and libations?

In the Greco–Asian Hellenistic culture, the assimilation of absolute rulers to Gods was the norm, as would become customary in imperial Rome, where Emperors would be "deified" posthumously, typically by senatorial decree. Take, for example, Vespasian's famously witty remark made on his death bed:

> "I feel that I am about to become a God!"

Instigated by Nero, the philosopher Seneca wrote a sarcastic booklet to the effect that Emperor Claudius had been transformed into a pumpkin instead of a God.

In the Greco-Roman religious syncretism Dionysos became Bacchus, God of wine and libations, the God portrayed in classical mythology as carrying a thyrsus, or giant fennel staff, with which he could make the earth fertile, mainly in vineyards. His cult, both in Athens and in the Roman version, culminated in the Dionisiads or Bacchanalia, which were without doubt episodes characterized by sexual and alcoholic excesses. For the modern reader, the image of this cult has been partly distorted by the work of many of the Renaissance masters, from Titian to Veronese and from Rubens to Velasquez, who have overemphasized the traits of this deity's ludic behaviour and drunkenness, and ignored his main heritage of a God of war and conquest, no doubt endorsing the watered-down version of the God over the traditional oriental one.

Dionysos, or Bacchus in Latin, the God of wine and ecstasy, made it to Greece and to the west quite late in the classical era. The myth had maybe originated from Thrace or Asia Minor, where the controversial cult had to overcome considerable opposition and resistance in order to impose itself, although some have suggested a Mycenean origin.

In the Greek myth, Dionysos was the offspring of Zeus, as his name suggests, (*Dios* being the genitive of *Zeus* in Greek) and Semele, who is a Goddess in the Thraco-Phrigian tradition and a common mortal for the Greeks. In the mainstream tradition, Semele became Zeus' lover and asked him to manifest himself to her in his true resemblance, showing himself in all his might, just like he would normally have done with his legitimate spouse Hera. He accepted the request, with the consequence that what she saw was not bearable, and she died of fright before being burnt to ashes. As she was already with child, Zeus recovered the foetus and sewed him into his thigh to take the gestation to term. After birth, the child God Dionysos was then committed to the Nymphs of Nysa who raised him. As Ovid tells us, Dionysos would later repay the kind nymphs by endlessly renewing their youth as they grew old.

There are several accounts and variations on the theme of Dionysos eluding the prosecution of Hera, Zeus' legitimate and very jealous wife, who was extremely hostile towards the illegitimate offspring of her husband. And just like his Olympian career had started amidst many difficulties, many of the tales relating to his maturity deal with how his controversial cult had to overcome many protests from those that wanted to suppress his unusual rites.

In the myth, the first mortal to pose a serious challenge to Dionysos was a certain Lykourgos, son of Dyras, in some accounts a king of Thrace, who attacked the God, kidnapped his Bacchantes and Satyrs, and forced him to hide under the sea. But the reaction was forceful, and the daring Lykourgos was driven to madness, blinded by lightning, imprisoned, or all of the above in the various versions of the story.

In Euripides' tragedy *Bacchae*, Dionysos goes to Thebes to avenge himself of his maternal aunts who had denied his divinity, and as a punishment he drives them to madness along with all the city's female population, which he then proceeds to enlist among his Bacchants (Bacchae), celebrating his cult. Pentheus, King of Thebes, also opposed the Dionysiac rites, until the God went to the city, in disguise, to see for himself, and, still incognito, he was imprisoned in the stables. He easily escaped, provoked a powerful earthquake, and attracted the king to the mountain, where he had him torn to pieces by his infatuated women.

These and other myths iterate on the main idea of a controversial cult, often rejected and attacked by men. Inevitably, divine retribution was administered by inflicting madness or death brought by women, who were obsessed or prey to a temporary mystical fury. Just like the women that accompanied Dionysos, who were known as Bacchantes, Menads, or Thiades, in ecstatic madness, the Dionysos worshippers inebriated themselves with wine and dance, and allegedly made human sacrifices to their god. Its influence grew in the Mediterranean basin, but if the Romans had allowed other daring cults to enter their traditions, this was clearly a God that, in the original, non tempered version, was difficult to accept in the Roman Pantheon, as it clashed with the official value system of the Republic.

Dionysos did not limit himself to the enforcement and defence of his cult: the God of wine and fertility was fabled to have conquered Asia all the way to India, thus creating a very convenient precedent for Alexander the Great, himself no stranger to drunken furore and all the excesses that eventually led him to a premature death in Babylon in 323 BC. Hellenistic syncretism will have him identified in Egypt with Osiris, and this symbolism will be of great significance for the years which Antony spent in Alexandria with Cleopatra, as well as to Octavian's propaganda, to which we shall return in the course of Chapter 8.

Having put Plutarch's narration of the Ephesians saluting Antony as a new Dionysos into a greater perspective, we understand that they were saluting in him a God of conquest, unforgiving and vengeful with his foes, as he had been towards the Liberators, and certainly a God of excess and beautiful furore, intimately connected to the womb of nature. But first and foremost they saluted in him a God who had been closely connected with several Hellenistic sovereigns, making the connection sound like a sign of great flattery towards Antony. As a matter of fact, besides Alexander the Great himself, who had followed in the God's footprints to India, our old acquaintance Mithridates VI Eupator, Rome's powerful enemy and Asia's legend, had been closely associated with Dionysos. At two different times, one century apart, Seleucid rulers had been identified with the idealized God. Among the most important in the exclusive club of the Dionysiac rulers, we can cite Antigonous Monophtalmos (the One-Eyed) and his son Demetrios Polyorketes (the Besieger).

Antigonous had held Asia Minor after the death of Alexander and the breakout of his empire, and had attempted, in vain, to impose his supremacy over his colleagues Seleukos and Ptolemy I, who would eventually defeat him and his son Demetrios, and conquer most of Asia from them. But the father and son would bounce back from defeat a few years later, and conquer Greece from Ptolemy after Demetrios had inflicted on him a severe naval defeat. It is not a case that Plutarch, in his "Parallel Lives", pairs up Demetrios with Mark Antony for comparison: brilliant in battle, gifted with visionary and inspirational leadership, he would attract in life strong criticism for his licentiousness and extravagance, and, after having risen at the climax of his power on the throne of Macedonia, he would lose it in a last daring attempt to overcome his enemies in a risky overseas campaign. It is of no doubt that the comparison between Antony and the other rulers cited highlighted some striking resemblances, and that some of the Godly attributes were made to measure for him.

It has been argued[7] that Ptolemy I Soter (founder of the last Egyptian dynasty), deliberately added the Dionysiac spin to his divine attributes to appropriate beyond doubt his ideal continuity of rule with Alexander.

This would imply that the connection with Alexander was plain for all to see, and stemmed from the conquering by the Macedonian king of the land all the way to the Hindu Kush and Pakistan. Lastly, among the kings that posed as Dionysos reincarnate, we cannot forget Ptolemy XII Auletes, albeit in the Osiriac version of the myth. We will return to this aspect later.

Even though Antony had not actively sought the comparison with Dionysos, which was the result of popular spontaneity and not a deliberate act of propaganda, he thrived on it nevertheless. He played along with the idea, beginning from the day of his triumphal entrance in Ephesos between scores of licentious Bacchants, and young Pans and Satyrs cheering and chanting. But while it was normal for the Ephesines to salute the handsome warrior Antony, friend of Caesar and conqueror of the mighty Brutus and Cassius, as one of the most powerful deities of Asian origin, Antony did not overplay his hand. For example, there is no evidence of any deliberate attempt to use coinage as a means to widen the circulation of this impression, except perhaps the dinarii bearing his image adorned in ivy wreaths in 39 BC, with a dubious and possibly spurious Dionysiac connection. At this particular point, at the very beginning of the Greek period, his coinage brought only solar motives, establishing a link with Hellenistic tradition, and, according to numismatics experts, his crest with lion, sword, and star rather suggests a Herculean – Alexandrian connection. All the symbolism adopted was pointing at the "philellene" theme, representing Antony as a friend to the local population embracing the local traditions and culture, rather than just a Roman ruler trying to extract tributes from the eastern kingdoms, as Brutus and Cassius had done until a few months earlier.

But it was not all roses, Bacchants, Pans, wine, and dance. The philellene Antony, Dionysos bringer of Joy, and Dionysos the Placid, was only one side of the coin. Plutarch stresses how it was clear to everyone that on the flipside there was Dionysos the Savage and Dionysos the Eater of Raw Meat, as if the Greek world was already fully aware of the two indissoluble natures, joyful and embracing the first, hard and merciless the other, that made up the soul of the Triumvir. The reverence paid was also due to the fact that he was the strongest warrior that they had seen in a long time.

Antony was tactful, intellectually flexible and long-sighted when dealing with the situation he had inherited from Brutus and Cassius. Even with the brief glimpses that we have had of the troubled history of the eastern provinces since the breakdown of the Empire of Alexander the Great, we can appreciate the complexity of the multi-faceted world that Pompey had conquered for Rome, and that the Liberators had prostrated in their brutal ways. So, while there are not many detailed accounts of what Antony accomplished in terms of clean-up and reorganization, the evidence says that he did not force his conqueror's hand on any of the local States, dispossess any local potentate, impose any rough punishment on those that had sympathized with the Liberators, but acted always in the balanced, compassionate, and dignified way that one would have expected from the representative of the people and the Senate of Rome.

Also, he had a vested interest in gaining acceptance from the local rulers and populations, making them his personal friends and clients, and introducing some elements of personal and moral indebtedness. Such a relationship would have been hugely preferable to a cold and distant diplomatic relationship, with a Government without a face. Pompey had amply demonstrated how important this was in the eastern world, when, before Pharsalus, he had been able to draw down substantially from the network he had built, and that, regardless of the final outcome of the fighting, had enabled him to rebound and quickly wage war after his precipitous escape from Italy in 50 BC.

It was so that the first period of Antony's travels throughout the Near East was marked by a furious pace. While the collection of taxes was paramount in the short term, the reinstatement of Roman rule on solid foundations was just as important over the longer term, to guarantee those financial streams on which Rome had become increasingly dependent.

He knew exactly what needed to be done:

"Antony also sent letters to all the chief cities of the region, including Tyre, Antioch, and Sidone, and to the regional leaders in Arabia. He ordered them to free every person that had been enslaved by Cassius."

And the tone of his communication was the right one.

> "Since we have overcome his (Cassius') madness by arms, we now correct by our decrees and judicial ruling what he has laid waste."[8]

It was in Ephesus that he first met the envoys sent by John Hyrcanus, reporting maybe on the tensions building in Judaea, a theatre populated by characters that Antony knew extremely well, and which was going to keep him busy for the decade to come.

As for the individual countries, the ones close to the Parthian border, of course, presented the most delicate situation. Galatia was perhaps the easiest one to control: King Deiotarus had already been in Antony's pocket for some time, since he and Fulvia had upheld his rule in 44 BC in return for a large sum of money, attracting the unjustified criticism of Cicero in the Third Philippic.

He would certainly not go down in history with the nickname of Philoromaios, lover of the Romans! Deiotarus had been loyal to the Liberators for a while, but by the time of the battle of Philippi he was back on Antony's side. He would remain loyal to his death, and his son Amyntas (and not his secretary, as Dio would mistakenly have it) would continue in his father's footsteps, as we shall see.

The reorganization of the Aegean area presented a different set of difficulties, but was nevertheless rather straightforward. The Thracians were already aligned, and mainland Greece had already welcomed him as we have seen, with chants and bacchanalia. Macedonia remained somewhat troublesome due to the presence of some Dalmatian tribesmen raiding across the borders, but they would be dealt with by Asinius Pollio the following year, and a strong contingent of seven legions would be stationed there permanently. Officially this would be for peacekeeping purposes, but we have already discussed the strategic importance of Macedonia and the via Egnatia as a bridge between the east and the west. It was an ideal place to station troops, ready to move east to fight on the Parthian border, or to be recalled to Italy if needs be. Even though it was non conflictual, the reorganization of the Greek area was demanding from a political and diplomatic standpoint because of the necessity of establishing an easily managed oligarchic control structure, which might have clashed with the local sensitivities and democratic traditions.[9]

Throughout this fundamental period of reconstruction and reorganization, Antony laid the foundations for what would become his broader political programme, which would be finalized over the course of the following five years. One of its key features would be the development of a network of local potentates, supported by a layer of capable administrators of Greco-Oriental heritage, fully conversant in the local languages and cultures, and which gave sufficient guarantees of loyalty to Antony and Rome. Many of these representatives would be given the Roman citizenship, a bargaining chip which Antony would use liberally to enfranchise them in order to constitute the backbone of a decentralized control structure. One example was Julius Caesar's freedman Demetrios, of proven intellect and capabilities, who would be sent to govern Cyprus, was soon to return under Cleopatra's crown, and would pay a great service to Antony with the capture of Labienus Jr.

This network reached deep into the fabric of these societies, and was certainly preferable to the traditional Roman approach to provincial government, and to the loose relationship with tributary kings seen so far, both in terms of results and in terms of acceptance by the locals. It was not unusual for these emissaries to develop such a bond with Antony and his vision that they added his name, Antonius, to theirs, as a sign of reverence and allegiance. One could say that winning loyalty for himself went hand in hand with strengthening loyalty to Rome. His generosity in reconstructing the coastal cities destroyed by Cassius, and the high level of autonomy awarded to the Greeks as well as the prerogative to organize in leagues as was their tradition, also contributed strongly.

His following travels took him to Cappadocia, where he backed up King Archelaus Sisena in a succession struggle, allegedly choosing to endorse him over his opponent because he supposedly had an affair with the young man's mother, the beautiful Glaphyra. To be true, Appian is not explicit on this specific matter, but there is other evidence, as we shall see, that news of the fling with the oriental queen made it to Rome and into the public domain. It might have made it to the ears of Fulvia, who saw her third husband drift away with other women in far away lands. It was later said that she even designed her next political moves to attract his attention back home. In the end, Antony's policies paid off. While he had to enforce his capillary taxation programme, he succeeded in fostering the peace and stability desperately needed for the east to recover its economic prosperity after being ravaged by years of uninterrupted conflicts and invasions. Antony had no intention of upsetting the order that the cunning Pompey Magnus had envisioned for the Asian provinces, based on client kings who could compensate Rome's shortcomings when it came to managing provinces. Further change could come once stability had been achieved, but in 40 BC the times were not right for too many waves of change. The order he was to enforce was going to outlast him, and the sovereigns he upheld would mostly remain successfully in office well into Octavian's principate. For example, while Antony was much criticized for the election of Archelaus to the throne of Cappadocia, due to his affair with Glaphyra, the king was to stay in office for fifty years, during which time his loyalty to Rome remained intact. Not all the interventions Antony made with the Greek and Eastern potentates were aimed at soothing and endearing. He also enforced discipline and punished questionable behaviour. For example, he did not hesitate to put to death Lachares of Sparta on charges of piracy. That would cost him the sympathy and the loyalty of the Spartans, who would later declare their support for Octavian, and Lachares' son Eurycles, who assumed the name of Caius Julius, and would lead them against Antony at Actium.

To Antony's intervention in Judaea we will return in greater detail in the next chapter, as this page is closely knit with the Parthian situation. Clearly here things were more complex because Antony was facing a divided nation, and both the Roman loyalists of John Hyrcanus, and the independentist Jewish faction were sending him envoys to see their claims satisfied. It will be shown how Antony would fully sponsor the future King Herod and the establishment of his dynasty.

As the winter approached, Antony left the bulk of his army in Bythinia, and headed for Syria followed only by his 1,000-strong Praetorian Guard, Rome's elite troops.

Egypt was next. The vivid memories of Cleopatra, the fascinating Cleopatra, were still fresh in Antony's mind, from her recent stay in Rome. Accordingly, he also remembered the arrogant ways that had made her so detested by all the Romans, without exception. On the contrary, Antony might have even found the snobbish ways of the queen an enhancement of her intriguing personality, and a challenge to his reputation of ladies' man. Let's not forget that Fulvia, his current wife, was considered a woman "nihili muliebre praeter corpus gerens", "who had nothing feminine except the (appearance of the) body", which suggests that Antony had emotional gaps to fill when it came to female companionship. As for all the predatory womanizing Antony was carrying out in Asia, it was purely opportunistic, and was a result of the enormous leverage he had. As such, none of it could have been intimately rewarding. When Antony was preparing to meet Cleopatra, it was fair for him to assume that Caesar's death would have made her demeanour more humble than previously, so he thought it a good idea to make her move from Alexandria to meet him in Tarsus, where he was heading. Having to respond to a summons would have been one more reminder for her of who was in charge.

It was so that he sent his aide Dellius to Egypt, to invite the snotty queen to meet the mighty Triumvir, to assuage her presumed guilt for not having helped the legitimate rulers of Rome during the latest stages of the Civil War, and for having sided with Cassius. The accusation was, of course, only another expedient from Mark Antony to make sure the last Ptolemaic queen was under his thumb and on her toes from the beginning of their discussions. We know, however, that she had actually done what she could to help the Caesarean side against the Liberators, which was to send her Gabinian soldiers to help Dolabella (although they had been intercepted by Cassius), and her ships to Antony across the Adriatic (although they had been wrecked by a storm).

There was, of course, one additional item on the agenda, and that was the degree to which she could contribute to the Roman treasury with Egyptian riches, no matter in what bad repair they were after all the splurging from her father

Ptolemy XII Auletes. By the time the two met, Cleopatra VII was 28 years of age, and already had a son, Ptolemy XV, also known as Cesarion, so as to leave no questions over the child's paternity. Appian is adamant that Antony had already noticed the legendary beauty of the young princess at the time of his exploits under Gabinius, and certainly there must have been many more occasions for the two to meet during the long period she spent in Rome before Caesar's murder. For all the myths that, over the centuries, have been cultivated around her stunning looks, there is no reliable indication on her actual appearance, other than the commonplace of the pronounced "Greek" nose that we can infer from statues and coinage. A large part of the Ptolemaic progeny, in order to mitigate the perverted effects of inbreeding in the brother-sister marriages, was obtained from royal concubines, some of which might have been Macedonian or Greek, and others Egyptian natives, or from other Middle Eastern stock. Forensic work carried out on the remains found in a noble burial in Ephesus, and attributed to the younger sister Arsinoe, suggested that the latter had some camitic features. But, for all we know, the four siblings that Ptolemy XII had fathered might have come from different mothers. Cleopatra might have had oriental traits, or, for that matter, she might have been a blonde, with the strong prevalence of Macedonian attributes.

What we know for sure is that the key to her legendary charms came from her intelligence, culture, and wits. She was an accomplished polyglot, the first of the Ptolemies to be fully conversant in Egyptian, along with eight or nine other languages, including the lesser known Troglodyte, Median, Parthian, Ethiopian, Hebrew, Syrian, Arabic, in addition to, of course, her native Greek and Macedonian dialect, plus some Latin, although she was not completely fluent in that language. She was, therefore, able to entertain all the ambassadors from neighbouring and vassal states in their native tongues. She was a capable sovereign, who had guided her country through some dire straits, including a famine only one year before, in 42 BC, when the annual flood of the Nile which gave its valley the legendary fertility had been irregular. She was impressive to the point of having influenced Julius Caesar into undertaking a number of innovative measures once he returned to Rome from the land of the pyramids: the opening of a public library based on the Alexandrine model, the completion of a population census, the reform of the Roman calendar based on astronomical observation, and the completion of public works based on the Egyptian model of river dikes. The commonplace image of the sexually insatiable temptress, the courtesan queen casting spells of lust on the Roman leaders was a remnant of the animosity directed at her by the Romans during her permanence, and, moreover, the result of a carefully orchestrated slander campaign at the hands of the Augustan scribes. The Romans had a lot of old poison in their teeth when it came to Cleopatra, and so Octavian's derogatory propaganda later fell on very fertile ground. But the reductive portrayal of this very capable queen as a luxurious courtesan is undeserved and entirely biased, for she was the only queen in her Dynasty able to formulate a vision of prosperity and independence for her kingdom, and to navigate effectively for many years through turbulent times.

The city of Tarsus, the capital of Cilicia, where Antony was waiting for her, lay on the banks of the river Cydnos, only a few miles inland from the Mediterranean coastline, so Cleopatra was able to sail upstream on the river, and make her grand appearance on the scene aboard her luxurious ship, causing all the Tarsian jaws to drop in unison, and all the locals to concur that Aphrodite, Goddess of beauty and love, had come to town to meet Dionysos. Cleopatra had not immediately responded to Antony's urgent summons. She was not the kind of woman meekly to do a man's bidding. Liz Taylor's sarcasm using the word "summon" in the 1961 "Cleopatra" is probably a perfect rendition of the reality, and it must have taken all of Q. Dellius' diplomatic skills to make her accept to travel east. What would have been pleonastic from Dellius is the recommendation that Plutarch reports him making to the alluring queen to look her best for the occasion! Finally, she decided to accept, and set sails in the summer of 41 BC.

Antony had erected a wooden Tribune to dominate the scene when she had arrived, but the appearance of her glamorous vessel immediately belittled his efforts, and he understood that dealings with the last of the Ptolemies were not going to be as unilateral as he had envisaged. When he invited her for dinner, she insisted on first inviting him aboard her royal barge, which must have resembled the floating palace of delights on which she had cruised on the Nile in the company of Caesar almost six years before. She amazed Antony with the incomparable beauty of the ornaments and the light effects with which she had adorned the boat, and we can imagine that the dinner and the entertainment were on a similar level as the surroundings. On such luxurious barges, of which she had a fleet, with their sails dyed purple and their high stern and castle gilded with gold, where the oarsmen rowed at the rhythm of flutes and bagpipes, one found libraries, gyms, and glamorous dining rooms. Many, in literature and movies, have portrayed in lyric terms the stupefying effects and the impact that they had on Antony, so it is not worth attempting to give yet another version here. It is clear that on the next day, when he returned the invitation, he was not able to make her walk knee deep in rose petals like she would do to her guests, and the best he could do in terms of preparation paled in front of Cleopatra's efforts, but Antony, who had a good sense of humour, openly conceded defeat with laughter, and derided the paucity and rusticity of his table and entertainment. Cleopatra's sophisticated choreography had been perfected over the millennia, and Egyptian sovereigns strived to surround themselves with a mystical aura, and position themselves in a divine space in the eyes of their subjects. Antony had at his disposal coarse soldiers, the municipal envoys of a trading port, and some wooden planks to erect a small stage. How he was hoping to impress the queen of Egypt and take command of the meeting that way remains one of the true mysteries of his life.

Antony followed the enticing queen back to Alexandria, but first he had to attend to some basic needs around the settlement of Syria and the exotic city of Palmyra. Palmyra was a city on the border of the Parthian Empire, which prospered thanks to the caravan traffic of the eastern trade routes which had to make stops there. Three hundred years later the city would reach its zenith under another rebel queen, Zenobia, who, after her husband Odhenatus had taught the Sassan kings (the heirs of the Parthians) a few lessons, went as far as conquering the land all the way to Egypt, before Emperor Aurelian defeated her and dragged her around Rome in his triumphal procession bound in golden chains to frame her legendary beauty. Antony's expedition was perhaps necessary as a demonstration of force, as the Palmyrenes were increasingly leaning towards Rome's arch-rival Parthia. The Parthians were, as we have seen, an imperialistic and conquering nation, and every time there was peace at home and they had a strong military, they dusted off their Syrian agenda and appeared as a menace at the border. At any rate, when the Romans approached, the inhabitants fled eastbound all the way to the river Euphrates, and did not return until Antony had left.

After this police operation, he left Syria with Decidius Saxa (Stones), one of the men he had entrusted with his avant guarde on the way to Philippi, and went to catch up with Cleopatra in Alexandria. With his arrival in the beautiful and thriving Hellenistic city, Antony opened a new chapter in his life, a chapter full of enjoyment, fun and greatly diverse and stimulating experiences. While Antony had had his share of fun in his days, it would have been limited to after hour tavern settings in his youth, and to the wild and depraved feasts with the raunchy and sleazy crowd of his entourage, maybe ending up a drinking brawl by handing old Cotyla a beating at the hands of his slaves, just for fun, as we have learned from Cicero. But in the classy, intellectually refined, and sophisticated company of Cleopatra, his leisurely occupations were raised to a completely different and previously unknown level.

After the Greek intermission in the winter of 42–41 BC, the period in Alexandria one year later was another break in Antony's worldwide restless pilgrimages, but the enjoyment of the interval was on a much grander scale. Under the Ptolemies the Egyptian capital had flourished as a cultural centre, a meeting place for scientists and intellectuals around the famous museum, and a hub for knowledge and scientific research unmatched in its day, and for many more centuries to come.

Antony had the good judgment to follow Cleopatra to Alexandria as a private citizen, and not as the representative of Rome, and he took the smallest possible and least noticeable bodyguard to escort him. And this was not, as his critics would claim, because he had abandoned Roman formalism in favour of Greek ways, but because he remembered what negative impact the sight of the Roman military uniforms had on the Alexandrines.

Antony and Cleopatra together formed a club, called the "Inimitable Livers", which was devoted to the quest for pleasure in all possible ways, including acting as a literary cenacle and a place for cultural and philosophical debate. The indulgence that the select few allowed themselves was to become legendary. One day, eight boars were seen roasting in the kitchen of the club at the same time. When a curious bystander asked why so much game was being prepared for only twelve guests, the answer was that the boars were all at different points of readiness, so that one would always be perfectly cooked whenever Antony wanted to dine. The club showed levels of refinement and decadence worthy of the famous banquet of Trimalchio in Petronius' "Satyricon", only possibly with far more refined table conversation. A playful Antony emerges from the lines of Appian and Dio. Everyone has heard the story of when the two were fishing from the royal ship, and Antony was sending divers to hook fish on his line, so that he would pull one up every time he threw it. But Cleopatra quickly outsmarted him and returned the ruse, by sending her own divers to hook, this time, a dried fish. It was then that Cleopatra tickled the ego of Mark Antony with her proverbial wits:

"You, my great Captain, you should leave the fishing rod to us, fishermen of Pharos and Canopos. You are a fisherman of cities, and kingdoms, and continents!"

Episodes like this amused everyone but proved to be real solace for the hardened heart of Antony, who, in Fulvia, had had a fighting companion, and a source of support politically, but was left with something to be desired in the romance and passion department. The complicity of the two even went as far as looking for cheap thrills in the streets of Alexandria at night, disguised as commoners, where Antony was on the receiving end of more than one bruising in a tavern brawl. Maybe he wanted to impress Cleopatra with his virile and soldierly ways, in an environment in which he was perfectly at home. And we know that she could be something of a chameleon in this respect: she accompanied him on hunting trips or to the gambling table and she was not above cracking crude jokes with her sensual lips. The lifestyle of the "Inimitable Livers", whose romantic involvement had become public knowledge, had to live up to the almost divine standards that the commoners would have expected from the queen and her companion. We will return to this matter in the next chapters.

During this first stay in Alexandria, or maybe immediately after Tarsus, Cleopatra obtained important concessions from Antony. The first thing was the immediate execution of her sister Arsinoe, who was held captive in the Temple of

Ephesus, where she was still revered as a queen by the priests. This 24-year-old Lagid, as we shall recall, had tried to seize power during the Alexandrian war, but instead ended up being dragged in chains through the streets to mark Caesar's triumph. The dispatching of siblings in order to secure one's own power was an established Hellenistic tradition, and the Ptolemies in no way departed from this time-honoured custom. Had Cleopatra taken care of the matter herself, probably nobody would have noticed or cared. She could have sent an Egyptian assassin to eliminate her sister quite easily. But Arsinoe was still Rome's war prisoner, so asking Antony to send one of his Centurions instead was a gesture of deference and respect. It also established the precedent of having obtained a favour. Arsinoe did not represent a real threat for Cleopatra, so her murder was just good housekeeping more than anything else. Antony was so zealous in the matter that he almost retaliated against the Ephesine clergy for having honoured Arsinoe more than was considered appropriate, and it took the intercession of the population to save the unlucky priests.

More importantly, Cleopatra obtained the return of the island of Cyprus to Egypt, after her father Ptolemy XII had handed it over to Cato and Brutus in 58 BC in exchange for the favours received, provoking the rage of the Alexandrines.

Meanwhile, in Rome, the state of mind was anything but serene. Dio's description of the arrival of news of the crushing defeat of Brutus at Philippi is filled with panic: Octavian was far from loved, despite the support of some diehard Caesarean veterans who had not forgotten their allegiance to his adoptive father, and neither was he trusted because of his obvious deviousness and ruthlessness. The return of the young man as an unchallenged despot was a very unsettling perspective for many. In order to reassure the rattled citizens, and possibly to pre-empt a revolt organized by Lepidus, Octavian had written a letter to the Senate reassuring everyone of his best intentions.

While Antony was busy in Asia, he did not neglect to make his presence felt in the Eternal City through his party allies and family. His brother Lucius, that same Lucius that Cicero had accused of being nothing more than a beast and had exposed to ridicule for having taken part in gladiatorial games, had been elected Consul for the year 41 BC. Theoretically, he had paired with a certain Publius Servilius, but in reality was sharing power only with Fulvia, who could finally exercise her power by working her puppets from behind the scenes. At this period, and for the first time in Roman history, we find coinage bearing the effigy of a woman, and this woman was Fulvia Flacca Bambula. She had been at Antony's side for years, of course, and had been especially visible in public affairs between 44 and 43 BC, a state of affairs which attracted Cicero's criticism. But now it was different: in Antony's absence, and with only a second-rate personality like Lucius around, she was playing first violin in the Antonian Party. But it was not just loyalty and a sense of duty to her absent husband which made her do this. The news of the affair with Glaphyra, and later the liaison with Cleopatra had quickly made it to Rome, and were public knowledge, to no lesser degree than the irrefutable evidence of the Triumvir's womanizing with Roman matrons at the apogee of his career. Accordingly, Fulvia's romantic attachment to Antony had probably waned. Fulvia simply enjoyed power for power's sake. While her relationship with Antony was not pure business, as the affinity between the two must certainly have been strong, and their partnership had been built on the basis of mutual appreciation, business surely came first.

This arrangement must have been an implicit covenant of their long and successful union, and nothing else could have been possible given Fulvia's personality, and her infamous track record with her previous two husbands.

From the beginning of their partnership, she used her influence and strength to further Antonian interests, beginning with the scoring of an undeserved triumph for Lucius, which was his thanks only to her intervention, after he conquered some insignificant mountain tribesmen. It is funny how, while Antony never got to celebrate a triumph, except for the mock-up one he awarded himself in Alexandria in 34 BC for conquering the Armenians, the same cannot be said for his barely significant brother.

Upon Octavian's return from Greece, it quickly became obvious that a clash between him and the duo Lucius – Fulvia was inevitable. True, Octavian was married to Fulvia's daughter Clodia, and the marriage had been arranged to seal a pact of non-aggression. But when it came to the allocation of the land between Antony's and Octavian's veterans, things quickly went downhill, so important was this matter in securing the troops' gratitude and loyalty. Land distribution was far from a noble endeavour, and its outcome had more to do with political opportunism and demagogy than with social justice: the process of the expropriation of the fields in the Po plain had begun again on a grand scale, and Rome was trading the potential unrest of the soldiers for the certain wrath of the dispossessed farmers. The evicted families took to rallying in the city, where their loud laments could be heard in the Forum. The veterans were abusing the situation by appropriating more land than they were entitled to and were taking premium plots instead of those assigned in the course of the lawful process. The disturbances, according to Dio, were such that many houses were burnt down, and the city was so perturbed that the rental prices suddenly dropped. In the beginning, Lucius and Fulvia had no choice but to go along with the process, concerned that Antony's legionaries would have suffered adverse discrimination in the apportionment of land and the creation of new colonies if they hadn't presided over the proceedings. We don't know for sure if this concern was justified, i.e. if the legionaries being dismissed from Octavian's ranks were receiving disproportionately preferential treatment thus justifying a strong reaction and the need for close supervision of the agents in charge of the process. In the end, either the young Caesar had a clear conscience and so he did not fear scrutiny, or he allowed some checks and balances to be introduced to eliminate all suspicions. But after a while, instead of continuing the daily power struggle on behalf of the Antonian military clientele, Lucius and Fulvia decided to change tack and embrace, or rather leverage, the cause of the expropriated landowners. This change was well thought out. The response from the rural midst was instantaneous, and the consensus generated spread by association onto Mark Antony, although in all likelihood he was not party to the initiative taken by his wife and brother. However, the pair was not so naive as to forget or neglect the interest of the veterans. Rather, they were re-directing their attention to the vast tracts of newly conquered land and wealth in the Asian provinces, which again reflected credit on Antony, who was in the process of making them more secure and hospitable. The veterans could re-settle in lands where they wouldn't have to fight an enraged occupant who was extremely reluctant to vacate his property. Instead, they could share in the fabulous new lands that Antony was organizing for the welfare of all.

Lucius Antonius had assumed the cognomen – self attributed, but highly symbolic – of *Pietas* (devotion, or piety), to represent, for all to see, his commitment to the cause and the interest of his absent brother. It is practically certain that if Cicero (who, as we know, did not hold the young man in high esteem) had not been decapitated almost three years earlier, he would have written a Fifteenth Philippic only to stigmatize or deride this initiative upon learning of its existence.

The consensus is almost unanimous that the Lucius – Fulvia duo did not act in co-ordination with or upon the orders of Antony. Appian has tried to ascribe the disturbances caused by Lucius to Antony's jealousy of Octavian, who was now harvesting the veterans' gratitude while his fellow Triumvir, the true winner at Philippi, was away in distant countries, his prolonged absence necessary for the good of the Republic. This point does not seem entirely fair, as we know how difficult it was for Octavian to keep the permanently mutinous soldiers in check, especially now that they had been made more aware of the weight they carried in public life by the gargantuan efforts made to settle them. They were becoming increasingly arrogant, to the point that Octavian himself had been made the object of violent attacks. Moreover, it seems that he had done whatever he could to reduce the adverse consequences of the confiscations: he tried to exempt all the properties of the senators, and the ones that had been given as a dowry, or that were individually smaller than a veteran's allotment. But he was tugging on the proverbial short blanket, and as soon as he took a step to mitigate the repercussion in one field, he would be confronted with a violent outburst on the other.

In order to highlight the uncertainty historians faced in trying to interpret Antony's position vis-à-vis Fulvia's and Lucius' initiative, it will suffice to say that when the situation started deteriorating, Octavian immediately sent one legion to Brundusium, southern Italy's main harbour, in case his colleague and father-in-law was actually behind the uprising, and was planning a landing in Italy with reinforcements for the two. The mistrust is fully understandable, but the lack of solid military intelligence is not, as the two sides would have deeply infiltrated the other camp with spies to pre-empt major actions such as sending a large military force. The fact is, Octavian himself was uncertain as to what Mark Antony's real intentions were, and whether he had really been an instigator of the war behind Lucius. Still, the scenario analysis of the situation that was quickly going to degenerate into the Perusian war, or Fulvian War, as it has also been dubbed, is quite fascinating. If we admit for a second that Antony was behind Fulvia and Lucius, he had a chance to snare Octavian in a Machiavellian political trap. The latter was facing political annihilation by popular discontent, outsmarted at his signature propaganda games, which he had played so shrewdly in the summer and fall of 44 BC against Antony, but who now risked being trampled underfoot in the double-edged stampede of the dispossessed landowners and the greedy legionaries. His weaknesses would have been exposed and his destiny as a political leader would have been sealed. At the same time Antony, the man who had sorted out the Asian provinces, ensuring the flow of financial resources to the Eternal City, would have been the one to save the day.

Octavian could also have walked one step deeper into the trap, and been stalemated in a long sequence of fights with Lucius and Fulvia, causing ongoing chaos in the peninsula. His inability to bring peace to the country would have had him branded as an inept and unreliable leader, capable of achievement only under the wing of seasoned mother hens like Antony, Hirtius, or Pansa. The Senate would have had to recall Mark Antony, who could have reined in his associates and relatives in no time at all, and restored peace. As a third alternative, Lucius could have defeated him, and of course this would have decisively strengthened the Antonian field. In sum, Antony had every chance of coming out on top after an escalation of domestic tension, the exception being, of course, the possibility of a crushing defeat inflicted on his wife and brother.

But this scenario analysis can be pushed one step further. Antony, looking at the events from a distance, with three outcomes out of four already in his favour, could also have survived and prospered even if Lucius and Fulvia were defeated simply by dissociating himself from them and their actions, as in fact was the case. However, was this to happen, the Antonian power base in Italy would have been weakened beyond the most pessimistic forecasts.

The turn taken by Fulvia and Lucius put even more pressure on the already beleaguered Octavian. Each time he made a concession to the veterans, the population would rise up in protest, and every time he returned a property, so would the soldiers. Things were spiralling out of control and in Rome some Centurions, sent by Octavian to placate some of the most unruly veterans, were slain in the riots, which were, once more, becoming a daily occurrence. Even some regular legions began an uprising, and it took two Antonian loyalists of the calibre of Calenus and Ventidius to mitigate the potential consequences. Initially, Lucius and Fulvia enjoyed a period of relative strength over the young Caesar. Fulvia was in a state of excitement, and was progressively yielding to her more belligerent instincts, to head into what soon became the Perusian war. As she rushed to arms, preparing for the eventual confrontation and stirring up the Italians against Octavian, she was seen running around yelling orders to her soldiers, with a sword at her side, actively participating in military life as if it were second nature to her, like a veteran military Tribune or Legate.

It was Fulvia in person who led the capture of the city of Praeneste, which she made her headquarters, and before the armed engagement she addressed the army lined up for battle. She must have felt young again, recalling the days when she was at the head of the urban gangs that she had inherited from her husband Clodius. She felt so sure of herself that she even snubbed the attempts of Octavian to meet with her and Lucius to negotiate. It was then that, short of options, Octavian instigated a march of soldiers to Rome who then proceeded to elect themselves judges of all the – many – land disputes that were pending a decision. Of course, these veterans, whom Fulvia called with disdain "*Senatores caligati*", or senators in army boots, easily found in their own favour, and were so arrogant as to record their decisions on tablets which they then entrusted to the Virgin Vestals, who in Rome acted as sacred record keepers. They also invited Lucius and Fulvia to parliament so they could explain to them their point of view on some fine juridical points. To be precise, the invitation was to meet to discuss their "differences". In one of the versions available, Lucius' scouts sent to inspect the meeting's grounds in Gabii, half way between Rome and Praeneste, were ambushed and killed, suggesting it was better for Fulvia and Lucius to politely take a rain check on the meeting. Instead of walking into the ambush, they set about completing their preparations for war. When open hostilities with Octavian began, they had rallied eight legions around their flag. Throughout the phase that was the prelude to the conflict, both sides pretended to be acting in accordance with Antony's desires and specific instructions. Octavian could produce documentation to show the terms of his agreement with the other Triumvir, while Lucius and Fulvia could claim to be complying to his most recent direct instructions, although this was probably not true. As already pointed out, we don't know for sure where Antony really stood. He was far away, possibly already in Egypt, and distracted. But it does not seem reasonable that he would have encouraged direct confrontation with Octavian, who had the potential to upset the equilibrium in Italy, without directly taking control of the situation himself or delegating leadership to his most capable generals and his best legions. It seems highly unlikely that he would have left such a situation in the hands of his inexperienced relatives.

Dio shows us a conciliatory and pacifist Octavian, and a belligerent couple, Lucius and Fulvia. Nevertheless, he swiftly made his arrangements for war. He recalled the troops he wanted to send to fight Sextus Pompey in Spain, and put a weak and increasingly indecisive Lepidus at the gates of Rome. At the same time, he built a strong strike force under the command of his friend, Marcus Vipsanius Agrippa (Agrippa), the eclectic genius that would make his fortune in war and in peace. Agrippa was nothing short of a genius, a gifted and imaginative leader, who certainly compensated for all of Octavian's weaknesses, and served him to the end of his days. Writes Velleius about him:

> "He was a man of distinguished character, unconquerable by toil, loss of sleep or danger, well disciplined in obedience, but to one man alone, yet eager to command the others. In whatever he did he knew no such thing as delay, but with him action went hand with thought."

The weak Lepidus was no match even for the incompetent Lucius, who stormed easily into Rome. From a legal standpoint, the situation could not have been more difficult to decipher. A lawfully elected Consul had taken the city by force, and was now advocating the abolition of the Triumvirate, which had also been established by law, but was at the same time upholding one of the Triumvirs (Antony) as the man deserving the gratitude of the Republic, and the primacy in the political life.

The Romans cheered at Lucius' intervention and saluted him as Imperator when he publicly stated that he was not pursuing Antony's interests, but he was there only as an opponent of the Triumvirate, an institution which had already served its purpose, and needed to be dissolved. Lucius positioned himself as the saviour of the traditional form of government, a claim that would have made Cicero have seizures if he had been alive. But the temporary success that Lucius enjoyed confirms what we have heard time and time again, that is, that the Romans were either doubtful of the young Caesar, or fearful of him, only expecting more bloody manhunts or financial prejudice. To be sure, in his race to take up arms Octavian had completely alienated the civilian population, and many more were looking up to Sextus Pompey even, who relentlessly strengthened his position, as a valid alternative to the obnoxious young man and the scarcely credible Consul Lucius Pietas. But between the two, it seems that Lucius was considered by far the lesser evil, especially since he was loudly advocating the return to the Republican tradition.[10]

When things went past the point of no return, the real war began. An immediate priority was securing the possession of central Italian towns, the most important being Nursia (Norcia), today the country's most celebrated producer of sausages and other pork derivatives, to the point that to this day the Italian word for "pork butcher" is "norcino". When Nursia capitulated to Octavian later that year, its inhabitants were left unharmed, yet they had the audacity to inscribe on the tombstones of the deas that they had fallen defending their freedom.

Unsurprisingly, Octavian failed to appreciate this, and was so angry that he demanded huge ransom payments which resulted in people preferring to emigrate and resettle in the south of Italy.

Fulvia tried to compensate for Lucius' lack of leadership, attempted to rally all the Antonian heavyweights mentioned and continued even to enlist soldiers, adding one legion borrowed from Plancus to reinforce Lucius' army. But her legendary activism was not enough to change the destiny of the war.

The inept Lucius, despite being at the head of a larger army, soon found himself sandwiched between Agrippa and the other Octavian General, Rufus, and was forced to retrench in the walled city of Perusia (Perugia) and withstand a long siege, which lasted for most of the winter of 41–40 BC. The period of the siege of Perusia is the topical point where the physical absence of Mark Antony was determinant because the coordination with the other Antonian heavy weight leaders was poor, and the Ventidiuses, the Pollios, the Calenuses did not intervene effectively in supporting Fulvia and Lucius, for lack of clear direction. It was so that the Perusian War took a turn that marked a sudden adverse change in the balance of power, and saw Octavian back at the top, while the Antonian colours in Italy suffered badly. It was during the desperate hours of the siege that Fulvia, from the Praeneste stronghold, following more reports of Antony's infidelity, probably first entertained the idea of jumping ship and joining the young Caesar, possibly even seducing the young man and thereby making him the fourth Roman political leader in her life. This hypothesis is extremely far-fetched, and might have just been one more attempt to denigrate and ridicule Fulvia and the whole Antonian cause for propaganda purposes later on. On the other hand, if it is true, and it has been commonly accepted by the historians of the period, this implies that she escalated a war to attract Antony back to Italy and away from his Asian distractions: his travels through Cilicia and Cappadocia and the charms of oriental queens, amongst other things. If so, she saw that her plans had not worked out, and the only alternative to defeat was to switch sides. Little it mattered that Octavian was married to her daughter Clodia; she thought that it was best to try to stay at the top. In fact, Octavian had dealt her a terrible blow, dissolving the marriage with Clodia, and sending her back to her fuming mother with a letter, in which he reassures her, adding insult to injury, that he was returning her in her original condition, that is untouched. Octavian did not subscribe to the idea of consorting with Fulvia, and his rejection took the form of a cruel epigram or sonnet, that was reported to us by the satirical poet Martial:

"Because Antony fucks Glaphyra, Fulvia has arranged this punishment for me: that I fuck her too. / That I fuck Fulvia? What if Manius begged me to bugger him? Would I? I don't think so, if I were sane / 'Either fuck or let's fight,' she says. Doesn't she know my prick is dearer to me than life itself? /

Let the trumpets blare!" Augustus, you certainly grant my clever little books pardon, / since you are the expert at speaking with Roman frankness."[11]

The raunchiness of the content and the form clashes with Octavian's typical composure, and it is probably the result of his prolonged exposure to a military environment during the siege. While his poetry might have been more suitable for the military barracks, the irony, as coarse as it was, must have had a devastating effect on Fulvia. The reference to the Glaphyra affair, at a time when Cleopatra was the centre of Antony's attention, coupled with his scornful rejection, was nothing less than a burning humiliation. Fulvia was still in Praeneste, and even though she was not physically in Perusia, she was the target of cruel mockery throughout the siege. In Roman times, projectiles, such as stones, which were exchanged during a siege, were also used to trade insults and irony, and archaeological research has uncovered many engraved projectiles addressing Fulvia along the same lines as the sonnets. The besieged Antonians returned the compliments to Octavian, picking on his alleged homosexuality or at least scarce virility.

The sequence of events leading to the end of Octavian's brief marriage to Clodia is uncertain. It is possible that Octavian had intended to untie the knot before the formal start of hostilities, and during the political skirmishes preceding it, and that this was a key contributor to Fulvia's exasperation and her decision to go ahead with the preparations for war.

The siege of Perusia lasted until mid-February 40 BC. When the starving city finally fell, Octavian gave the world yet more proof of his ruthless vengefulness, and 300 captives, most of whom were senators and knights, were dragged to an altar erected to Julius Caesar's memory, and slain there in cold blood. The city was razed to the ground and burned. Later, the survivors of the carnage were given the right to rebuild it, but with much lower walls around it, as a reminder of their association with treason. After the Perusia example, all the other central Italian towns that had sided with Fulvia considered it more prudent to rethink their position and yield to Octavian.

After the surrender of Perusia, Lucius was, surprisingly, left unharmed. Octavian thought it was more politically expedient to spare his life, and in fact later he was even sent to govern a small province in Spain. Reportedly[12] Lucius faced Octavian with great dignity, by telling him openly that his motive for waging war was not to side blindly with his brother, but to oppose his (Octavian's) oligarchic ambitions, and in the same way that he would have sided against Antony if he had been the one to distance himself from Republican principles. If this conversation really took place, it is hard to imagine how Lucius could have got away with this flimsy excuse, but it was at least consistent with the noble speeches he had given to the senators when he had marched into Rome a few months earlier. More likely, Octavian judged that the time was not right to go to war with Antony, and he recalled how enraged Antony had been at the execution of his other brother, Gaius, at the hands of Brutus and Hortensius.

The other Antonian clan members and closer associates considered it rightfully prudent to stay away from Octavian's knife. It was so that many of them either sailed to the east to reach Antony, or south, to apply for the protection of Sextus Pompey, still undisputed Lord of the Seas. For example, Antony's mother Julia met Sextus first, and it was the latter who encouraged her to continue her journey to meet her son, and possibly broach the subject of a possible alliance with the young admiral.

It is worth, at this point, examining the character of Sextus Pompey, who was a source of counter power to the Triumvirs for ten years, and who stalemated an enemy that could field twenty to thirty times his military force for over ten years. Velleius Paterculus gives a very unflattering portrait of the man:

> "A young man of scarce education (studis rudis), coarse (barbarus) in his speech, impulsive, quick in making decisions, nowhere similar to his father in loyalty, a freedman to his freedman and a slave to his slave,[13] envious of the illustrious, but ready to obey to the vilest."

Sextus will remain an important but enigmatic figure of the late Republic. While he survived and prospered while hugely outnumbered by his enemies for almost a decade, he was not visionary and strategic enough to assert himself as anything more than a nuisance. He remained on the fringe, scoring many small victories, but never capitalizing on his momentum to become a credible counter-power, leveraging his name and the weaknesses of Octavian. He was probably incapable of articulating a political programme beyond the establishment of his own power base, to which he felt entitled by birth, and for the death toll his family had paid to Caesarean Rome. It is perhaps for this reason that Antony never saw fit to fully consort with him against Octavian.

In the mercy shown by Octavian towards Lucius, and in his selectiveness in choosing the targets for his vengeance, we have to read a certain reverence for the absent Antony. His closest allies were able to get away with a slap on the wrist, whereas cruel vengeance was imposed on quite anonymous Perusians and other second rate figures of Equestrian census. As for Antony's historical flankers, Octavian did not try to pursue or engage them in battle, be it out of respect for Antony or risk management. If Lucius was not a fearsome figure, the leathered Ventidius, the charismatic Pollio, the shrewd Plancus, were of another stock altogether, and would have presented a more serious hurdle. They had been left out of the fighting, not intentionally but rather for reasons of bad organization, but there was no pressing need for Octavian to attack them, not even from a demonstrative point of view. It was so that shortly thereafter Plancus, the former

Proconsul of Gaul, sailed to join Antony with his soldiers, and so did Ventidius, who was to write several glorious pages of Rome's military history in the east, before his controversial retirement. Asinius Pollio, on the other hand, would be progressively sucked into Octavian's orbit, and put his refined intellect at the service of the cultural reconstruction that marked the early Principate of the new Augustus. The process of sponsorship of the best intellects of the regime would be carried out under the aegis of Octavian's close friend Mecaenas, and by extension to this day we call mecenatism the protection of artists and literates by enlightened capitalists.

It would not be accurate to say that the prejudice to Antony from the outcome of the Perusian war consisted mostly of the loss of political influence and the senator's count. Octavian was quick to mimic the shift of political equilibria into a transfusion of military forces. It was true that some of the Antonian diehards, such as Plancus and Ventidius, had been able to ferry substantial military forces to Antony's Asian stronghold but, numerically speaking, this was the exception rather than the rule. Two fully equipped legions had immediately opted to pass under the command of Agrippa. That left Antony's interests in the west relying mainly on Calenus, Proconsul in Gaul, who was at the head of a formidable force. But such was the play of destiny that Calenus fell ill and died at that very moment. His second in command was his inexperienced young son, who, in fear of retaliation, and of the sinister reputation of Octavian, handed over his army without any opposition, abandoning whatever was left of Antony's military power in the west.

Among those that fled Rome at that time was the noble Tiberius Claudius Nero, with his young wife Livia Drusilla, and their son named after the father. In a paradox of history, after Tiberius (the father) was pardoned, Livia would soon become Octavian's long-term wife, and Tiberius (the son), further to his adoption, would become the second Roman Emperor after Octavian Augustus.

Fulvia herself headed for Greece, to her exile in the final destination of Sicyon near Corinth, with a stop in Athens, where perhaps she met Antony. Appian puts Antony's mother Julia in the Greek capital at the same time. We can try to imagine the content of the exchanges between Antony and Fulvia, if their meeting actually took place. But even if they did not meet in Athens, we can be quite sure that Fulvia was going to try to reach him, even if it meant her crossing the Mediterranean, and intercepting him during his ongoing travels. She might have tried to use her presence and influence to harness the Triumvir's anger. After all, the power of her personality had always been her primary weapon of seduction. She might have tried to explain how the defeat in the war could have been put entirely on Lucius' account, on his poor generalship, and on his arrogance and inadequate preparation, rendering him incapable of organizing and federating the anti-Octavian forces in Italy. She might have given him a lot more colour and detail about the individual roles and responsibilities during the war, different angles and more information than Antony could have received piecemeal from the exiles that he had met in Egypt or in Tyre. She would probably have attempted to prove how events had forced her to take a specific course of action, and how all of her moves had been born from the sole aim to protect Antony's best interests. Even though her pride was hurt and she was angry at his unfaithfulness, and even with the knowledge that he was drifting away from her, she would not have played the jealousy or melodrama card, mentioning the Glaphyras and the Cleopatras, or letting her personal emotions and feelings show. Her anger would have shown, but only the anger and the frustration of a valiant General who has tried her best in battle, has been beaten due to the errors of others, and finally has to take the blame for the defeat in front of her commander in chief. The discussion would have centred on business. They would have caucused on what was left of the Antonian foothold in the boot and the western provinces, and on what was the best way forward to regain the upper ground and rapidly reconstruct a power base. How many influential senators and knights had been killed at or after Perusia, how many had fled, and who could step up to fill the huge gaps left open in the network of *clientes*. Finally and sadly, they would have coldly concurred that the best strategy for Antony was to take distance from everything that she and Lucius had done or said since Octavian's return to the Peninsula. Overall, Antony would almost certainly have been quite harsh with her, for having been part of a gamble that was backfiring beyond expectations, and was threatening to irreparably alter the power balances in the Roman world. In the end, his arm must have been firm as he pointed to her the way to the Purgatorium in the form of exile in the city of Sicyon, at least for the foreseeable future.

Fulvia died shortly after her arrival in Sicyon, of an unknown disease. Given the life expectancies of the time, this is not surprising *per se*. Nor have any of the sources, Greek and Roman alike, raised any suspicion of foul play being involved in her death. Fulvia's raging passions must have had a devastating effect on her general health, and we must not forget that she had just lived through eighteen months of enormous stress. However, the fact that her daughter Clodia also passed away in Sicyon at the same period, and also from unspecified causes, raises considerable doubts. After all, Fulvia, from Octavian's perspective, had proven to be a formidable opponent, more so than anybody else in Antony's camp. She was more ruthless and ambitious, capable and charismatic, and difficult to predict and control than anyone else. Unlike Fulvia, Antony had shown himself ready to compromise for the sake of the nation and collective welfare. It is generally agreed, however, that Fulvia could not see beyond her own self-interest and thirst for personal power. Also, if we look at her from Antony's point of view, as he prepared to disown her and rebuild his alliance with Octavian, her presence, even in exile, was an embarrassment, and would have always rekindled suspicions of his behind the scenes involvement in the Perusian "disturbances". Not to mention the risk of vengeful behaviour, always possible, because of his liaison with Cleopatra. A risk to one, and an embarrassment to the other, it seems pretty logical that, one way or another, Fulvia's days were numbered. It is certain that Antony had mixed feelings about the death of his second wife. This point of view is also sustained by Appian,[14] who says that while Antony thought that the departure of this "interfering woman" was for the best, he was nevertheless deeply affected because he felt partly responsible for not checking her more drastic impulses.

The exact sequence of events in this period is less than clear, but Plutarch points to two simultaneous wake-up calls that wrenched Antony from his state of bliss in Alexandria, and put him on the road again, not to return for several years. If we stay with Plutarch, the news of the end of the Perusian war and the intelligence of strong Parthian border activity arrived at the same time. More likely, the news from Italy made it to Egypt by mid-March 40 BC, while at that time the Parthian menace was not at its peak yet. We will recall how, right before the battle of Philippi, Cassius had sent Quintus Labienus to King Orodes to seek his help. For Labienus it was too late to change the course of history at Philippi, but not too late to take his revenge at the next available opportunity, so he had enrolled with Orodes as a military consultant of sorts, and he would lead the Parthian attack on Ionia and Lycia that would take place later in that year. Still, at the end of the winter of 41–40 BC Antony's attention was entirely focused on Italian events, and on how to limit the impact of the disastrous initiative of Lucius and Fulvia. One possibility, still according to Plutarch's interpretation, is that he had decided to tackle the Parthian menace first, and had set sails to the east at the head of a large fleet. But, once he reached Phoenicia, in the city of Tyre he received a message from Fulvia, asking him to meet her urgently, so he changed his mind and changed course for Greece with a squadron of 200 ships. Plutarch does not admit that the two actually met, but rather suggests that the news of her sudden and unexpected death made him change his plans one more time and head for Italy. In order to create more drama, in Shakespeare's "Antony and Cleopatra", the death of Fulvia is announced to Antony while still in Alexandria, and his mixed feelings are beautifully captured:

"There's a great spirit gone! Thus did I desire it /
    What our contempt doth often hurl from us
    We wish it ours again; the present pleasure /
    But revolution lowering does become
    The opposite of itself; she's good, being gone; /
    The hand could pluck her back that shov'd her on.
    I must from this enchanting Queen break off: /
    Ten thousands harms, more than the ills I know,
    My idleness doth hatch!"

Cleopatra, meanwhile, who had been playing the jealousy card all along, continued her mind-games in an attempt to keep Antony in Alexandria:

"Oh most false love!
 Where be the sacrest vials thou shouldst fill /
 With sorrowful water? Now I see, I see,/
 In Fulvia's death how mine receiv'd shall be!"

We trust that Antony had enjoyed his Alexandrian break, in the company of Cleopatra and the "Inimitable Livers", and whatever other pleasures he had savoured in the months between November 41 and February – March 40 BC, because after that date, no matter which version of events one chooses to accept, it is clear that his activities gathered pace and became frantic once again.

It does not seem probable though that by March 40 BC he had a Partian expedition ready, or that if he had, he would abort it in Tyre only because of Fulvia's lamentations. It would make more sense to assume that at that point the menace of Labienus on the horizon was not an immediate one, or was at least less pressing than the situation in Italy, which deserved immediate attention.

After Perusia, Octavian was pushing hard to further strengthen his position of dominance. Now that the relationship between the two Triumvirs was one of tension again, the Mediterranean Sea was back to being a major subject. One of the two independent naval powers in the *mare nostrum*, the one under Domitius Ahenobarbus, was already gravitating towards Antony's sphere of influence, and would soon make his intentions to support Antony formal. Octavian had made several attempts to conquer Sextus to no avail. And it was so that he opted for the pacific solution and put the diplomacy machine in motion, by marrying Scribonia, who was Sextus Pompey's niece, in addition to being Sulla's granddaughter.

On the way from Greece to Italy, Antony met the fleet of Domitius Ahenobarbus in the Adriatic waters. A truce and a possible alliance had been negotiated and contracted through intermediaries, but a meeting in person and with combat ready fleets in open waters was a different matter altogether from an intensity and riskiness standpoint. The Domitii had been a part of the conspiracy of the Ides of March. Domitius' father Lucius had faced Antony – and died – at Pharsalus. The son had invested himself in running a blockade in the Adriatic and the Ionian Sea to keep Antony and Octavian from ferrying their troops into Macedonia. On paper he was an unlikely ally. But finally Antony put his distrust to one side, and embraced his new partner, whose soldiers saluted Antony as their commander, although many on the Antonian side remained quite perplexed at seeing an aristocrat, a Caesaricide and one of the *boni vires* among their ranks.

Both continued their route towards Italy together, and approached landing near the heavily fortified Brundusium. Formally Octavian and Antony were not at war, although the tension between the two must have been palpable. But the presence of Domitius, so far a declared enemy, on Antony's side, triggered very hostile behaviour from the local garrison towards both. When Antony was denied the right to land, he besieged Brundusium, and started raiding the rest of the region of Apulia (Puglia), the heel of the Italian boot.

The forceful landing in Puglia again caused tensions to rise between the two Triumvirs and fighting, although on a reduced scale, continued. In these circumstances, Antony's reputation as an invincible military leader, earned at Philippi, gave him a clear edge. While he could not match the number of Octavian's legionaries, he fell back on his boldness and courage and with a small cavalry force attacked a mounted contingent four times larger, and took all the cavalrymen prisoners. With a clever stratagem he kept ferrying reinforcements from Greece undetected. Overall, his mere presence, fame, and personality were immensely intimidating for Octavian's legionaries. Even with just a small force at his disposal, Antony could have kept all of Octavian's forces in check if he had wanted to do so. At this point it is clear that a broad based movement in favour of appeasement emerged. In the narration from Appian it is incarnated by the wise Cocceius, but this call for peace must have had huge support, among the military and the civilians alike. Even the veterans, for whom Octavian was the flagpole carrier and the hostage at the same time, were feeling embarrassed by the hostile treatment that Antony had received at Brundusium. After all, by showing mercy when he had Fulvia and Lucius in his power, Octavian had left the door open for reconciliation. If Antony had refused the peace option offered, he would certainly have lost any goodwill he had with the veterans as the winner at Philippi.

Just like he had done in 44 BC when Antony was openly attacking him, Octavian was posing as conciliatory in order to win to his side those who were undecided. The interpretation of the events of the year 40 BC is not made easy by the Greek historians. Dio's narration diverges quite substantially from Appian's, and, for that matter, seems quite illogical. In his view, to begin with, Antony had given up the Parthian war and the protection of Syria and Palestine, first because of his laxness, bewitched and enslaved by the charms of Cleopatra as he was, and then because he had already decided to wage war against Octavian, beginning with the premeditated siege to Brundusium. In fact, common sense suggests that neither of the two Triumvirs would have been inclined towards a conflict at that particular time. There were at least three good reasons for that. First, there was still the menace of Sextus Pompey at large. Octavian had proven incapable of countering this menace, and, while there was no real threat to the mainland, the steady flow of grain towards Rome could have been impeded by it. Secondly, whoever had actively promoted another round of civil belligerence in 40 BC would have been hugely unpopular, and would have struggled to keep control of his side. Both historians echo the voices of the legionaries advocating reconciliation, and threatening to abandon Antony if he initiated a one-sided provocation. Thirdly, while Octavian had taken control of the armies of Gaul and was exerting hegemonic rule in the west, Antony was still a fearsome adversary for a well prepared war adventure. So strong had been his display of military leadership in Philippi that Octavian probably felt that his numerical prevalence was offset by the reverential fear that the other commanded, and he would rather not gamble his temporary advantage, but waited instead for a better opportunity where he could minimize the risks.

As one would have expected, the pressure to end the hostilities kept mounting, and the death of Fulvia provided a very convenient scapegoat, and an excuse to bury the proverbial axe.

At the same time, Pompey kept the pressure on and the diversion attacks coming, targeting Sardinia, and the coastal towns of Thurii and Cosentia. It would have appeared that the marriage of Octavian and Scribonia had not been sufficient to win Sextus' benevolence. On the contrary, it was commonplace to think that Antony was closely coordinating with Pompey, if not controlling him completely. This view emerges clearly from Plutarch. After the meeting of Pompey with the Triumvir's mother Julia, it seems Antony exercised a growing influence over him, to the point of ordering him to keep up his coastal raids.

Sextus was really the component that could have made the difference in the delicate balance in place, by throwing his weight in on Antony's side, and Octavian knew it. There is no evidence that between the Admiral in Chief and Antony there was anything more than an implicit understanding that Octavian's ascent to power should have been controlled. There is a range of nuances in all the accounts of the historians[15] on how this implicit coordination functioned, if at all, or if they were just on friendlier terms than in the past, or than with Octavian.

Eventually, after long intermediated negotiations, in the month of September, 40 BC, good sense prevailed and a formal reconciliation with Octavian took place in the city of Brundusium. Sextus Pompey temporarily relieved the pressure on southern Italy, and Domitius, the other naval random variable, was sent to govern Bythinia, in today's northern Turkey, so that the peace would not be sanctioned under the Damocles' sword represented by two hostile fleets surrounding Italy and threatening a complete embargo.

The transfer of power under the new arrangement further clarified the political landscape. The events of the previous eighteen months had altered the relative strength of the parts, and it is of no doubt that Antony had lost some leverage. For example, there was no reason for Octavian to let go of Gaul after the handover of the legions which had taken place with the young Calenus. It was so that the two Triumvirs divided the Roman world with the imaginary meridian crossing the Adriatic at a point in the northeast: the coastal town of Scodra. Antony would keep everything east of this meridian, including, of course, Egypt, albeit not formally a province, and Octavian everything to the west. As for Lepidus, who was gradually becoming a rounding error in the equation, he was confirmed as the ruler of the African provinces, which corresponded roughly to today's Tunisia and Libya. Antony could not have negotiated better terms. His main instrument to apply pressure on Octavian would have been a more robust alliance with Sextus, and the more intensive use of Domitius to threaten naval blockade and coastal raids. Both would certainly have been detrimental to the well being of the Roman people if used beyond the scope of small tactical expedients, and Antony would not have starved his fellow Roman citizens to gain more power. Furthermore, if he had done so he would have lost the hearts of the soldiers in Italy, who we know still looked up to him as the most authoritative leader, and who remained loyal and pledged their allegiance to him.

We must not discount the level of popularity that Sextus enjoyed, even as an enemy of Rome, or the credibility he had as an alternative to Octavian. It has to be remembered that many families felt themselves to be in his debt, for the many lives he had saved at the time of the proscriptions, and for the many that he had sheltered. Still, in those days, the defections were so numerous that the Virgin Vestals had been asked to make sacrifices for them to stop.

In order to complete the signing of the new treaty, more gestures of goodwill were needed, and more scapegoats had to be found, or, if you prefer, more pawns had to be sacrificed on the new altar of Peace. Luckily Fulvia had found a perfect time to die, exhausted by stress, fatigue, frustration, and, who knows, maybe a generous dose of poison. But a few more non-critical players were quickly identified as additional culprits to send under the knife as a highly symbolic gesture. Manius, the lieutenant that poured oil, had there been any need, on Fulvia's fire, was executed by Antony. Antony could not resign himself to the idea that Fulvia had done what she had done on her own initiative, no matter how unlikely it was that she would have acted under the influence of a third party rather than following her own instinct and wishes. Antony also turned in one of his fifth columnists to Octavian's side, Salvidienus Rufus, with whom he admitted having a secret deal, and it was now the turn of Octavian to put him to death. While Antony's anger towards Manius could have been justified, because of his contribution to Fulvia's fall, the sacrifice of his secret agent was perhaps proof of his good faith as blood sealed their new secret pact. Throughout Antony's life we struggle to find one instance where he had not been true to his word. The execution of Manius and the sacrifice of Salvidienus Rufus were more than token gestures: they were the consequence of Antony's scruples and of his unyielding desire to keep his faith. Octavian, on the other side, was true only to his interests, and his scruples ended exactly where his advantage began.

This time two more deeds served as stabilizers of the new alliance. One more time, family ties were considered the best way to build a strong bond between two rival leaders, and so the widower Antony married Octavian's half sister Octavia.

There was, of course, the precedent of the marriage between Octavian and Clodia, with the subsequent rejection and return of the spouse during the Perusian war. But this was not an insult so deadly that Antony could not obliterate it. After all, Clodia was not his daughter, but Clodius', who was nothing more than a juvenile acquaintance of his.

So important was this marriage that it was pronounced with the help of a special senatorial decree. By the time they married, Octavia was not in her prime by Roman standards any more. She was already 29 years old, and she was also a widow, her first husband Marcellus having died a few months before. She had two children already, and was pregnant with the third. In this case, the Roman law prescribed a *moratorium,* a suspension period in which a widow could not remarry, in order to leave no doubt over the child's paternity, hence the need for the Senate's intervention to grant a special dispensation. Octavia was to become one of the most important female figures of the early principate, universally praised for her virtues, and, as we shall see, the origin of many key figures of the Julio–Claudian dynasty. She was to become a loyal and faithful spouse for Antony, and would give him two daughters, both called, once again, Antonia. Further to the Treaty of Brundusium, Antony and Octavian were now reconciled again, and together minted coinage celebrating peace and harmony.

On a political level, the uncontrollable menace coming from Sextus Pompey had to be removed, as it represented too much of a threat for Octavian, and, given their friendly terms, gave too much leverage to Antony. The three men then, to the solace of the Italians, met on the promontory of Misenum in Campania to sign a peace treaty. In reality Sextus had slowed down the rhythm of his incursions into southern Italy, but never let his guard down and never completely lifted the naval block. The supply of grain to Rome had never properly resumed, so that bread, the staple of the Roman diet, was running short and hunger was beginning to plague the urban population. Hunger, as we know, has always been a bad advisor for the people throughout the course of history. Resentment towards Octavian was growing, and he had never been well-loved in the first place, for reasons including his failure to end tensions with Pompey in order to allow the flow of foodstuffs to resume. On the other hand, it was well known that Antony had a more pragmatic attitude and entertained friendlier terms with him, so he was open to the idea of bargaining for a peace accord. On one occasion, the rioting degenerated, and the young Caesar became the target of pelting rocks, putting his life in serious danger. Soldiers were called to disperse the rioters, but the situation quickly spiralled out of hand and many were killed, their bodies thrown into the Tiber. Antony, in an audacious move, intervened to save his young colleague's life. This is another clear example of how Antony could put his personal interest behind the common good, renouncing the elimination of his rival for the sake of peace and respect for the pact that they concluded. Still, that close call was maybe the trigger that convinced everyone that there could be no more procrastination over peace talks any more. The call for appeasement was heard coming from within the walls of Rome, and a meeting was arranged. Sextus Pompey's right hand man Libo was encouraged to make it all the way north from Sicily to the Gulf of Naples and he put his anchor down in front of the island of Ischia, while Antony and Octavian went to prepare to meet him in Baiae, slightly to the north, a popular vacation spot for the Romans, with a reputation for being a place for romantic or transgressive encounters. Besides the beautiful mansions of the senators, in Baia there was a huge estate which belonged to the Domitii Ahenobarbi. It was said that Emperor Nero had his Aunt Domitia killed to inherit her Baian estate, which was then the theatre of the murder of his mother Agrippinilla. To this day, the resort is known as Baia Domizia.

After Sextus had aligned all his key lieutenants to the idea of peace with Rome, the meeting could take place at Puteoli, on the Cape Misenum. The three men signed an all inclusive armistice and peace treaty, with full pardon for all the exiles, with the important exclusion of those that had participated in the murder of Caesar. Sextus had begun the bargaining with the aim of replacing Lepidus in the Triumvirate, but in the end he settled for being confirmed as the ruler of all the main Mediterranean islands, including Peloponnese. The two Triumvirs had taken minimal precautions for the meeting, and at one time they found themselves completely at Sextus' mercy, but he was true to his word and to his honour, and the meeting was carried out satisfactorily. Sextus started joking, saying that his ship was the only house he had left, a clear reference to the fact that Antony had seized his father's mansion in Rome while Master of Horse. When both Octavian and Antony were aboard his flagship, Menodorus whispered to Sextus that if they had just cut the rope of the anchor, he could have been the master of the whole Republic, instead of just the islands, to which Sextus replied that he should have just done it without telling him, but at that point it was too late, and he had to honour his word. In the future, Sextus would not always behave so ethically.

The scene of the formal conciliation between the two sides was marked by a huge outburst of enthusiasm and joy by the thousands of people who had come from Rome to witness the event, and who were watching the highly emotional moment from the shore or the docks of Puteoli. For those that were on the Pompeian side, it meant official pardon, and they did not have to consider themselves like stateless people any longer. For the Romans watching from the promontory, it meant the end of a hazardous conflict, food for their families back at home, but, for many, the possibility to embrace the many exiles that had joined Pompey over time. Many were devoured by the anxiety to learn if a long lost relative was still alive, or if he had died during his escape or in the many military engagements that had followed. Such was the excitement and the commotion that many died, either trampled or drowned after falling overboard.

Sextus was remunerated to his full satisfaction. He was made Consul and Augur, and he was paid an indemnity of 17 million dracmas, or 17 million *dinarii*, in addition to the land concessions already mentioned. In return, of course, he committed to securing a steady stream of provisions on to the peninsula, and to stop providing a safe haven for renegades and runaway slaves. All previous defectors would be pardoned, except, as usual, those who had played an active role in the assassination of Caesar.

The three parted ways, Pompey towards Sicily, Octavian towards Gaul, and Antony back to the east, to prepare for the Parthian expedition that had been put on hold for so many years.

If you want peace, prepare for war, said the old Roman adagio, which Octavian knew all too well. Now that he had taken some pressure off the Italian peninsula, he could have his friend Agrippa begin the construction of a military harbour right there in Baia, as well as the mobilization of a powerful fleet of battleships in preparation for a possible new naval conflict against Pompey, a possibility which became a reality shortly thereafter.

As was to be expected, peace with Sextus was short lived. The handover of the Peloponnese to Sextus never happened, apparently because Antony wanted to transfer control after the collection of the annual tribute, which would have been tantamount to transferring a share of stock after the annual dividend distribution. The refusal led to the rekindling of the incursions into southern Italy, and a return to the interruption of the supply lines.

Jealousy among Pompey's freedmen who had risen through the ranks and occupied important posts created some destabilization in his lines. Menodorus, one of the chief Pompeian admirals, and commander of Sardinia and Corsica, gave a nod and a wink in Octavian's direction to signal that he was ready for defection. This gave an opportunity to the Triumvirs to strike home with a coordinated attack on Sicily. Dio agrees[16] that the treason of this freedman was the cause that sparked further hostilities between Octavian and the young admiral. We do not know for sure if the latter had treacherously resumed hostile behaviour, in the form of piracy or coastal raids, or if he had opened his gates anew for renegades and runaway slaves. This might have been the case, or it might just have been propaganda to protect Octavian from the accusation of having unilaterally broken the truce.

Octavian wanted to organize a meeting with Antony to coordinate an all out attack, but the meeting never took place. Maybe this was because Antony felt he had a moral obligation to respect the peace treaty. He always acted with great integrity, after all, and he was uncompromising once he had given his word. Or maybe he was dissuaded by the sinister omens he saw in his camp during those days: one of his guards had been mauled by wild animals, and a wolf had been seen wandering around the same camp. Or, maybe yet, he saw in Octavian's intention the desire to eliminate another adversary quickly in order to accelerate his own rise to sole supremacy. Antony never sided openly with Sextus, but he probably took great exception to the outright aggression being carried out. He disapproved of the breakage of the Treaty of Misenum, and had no sympathy for Menodorus. He used to call him his fugitive slave, as he had been a former slave of Pompey Magnus, and technically he had acquired him with Pompey's estate in 49 BC.

Octavian was on his own, since Antony had not made himself available for the fighting. So he attacked from the east, while Menodorus, who by then had openly turned coat, attacked the island from the Tirrenian side. At the same time a sizeable infantry force descended all the way to Rhegium, the big toe of the Italian boot. Pompey gave command of the defensive operations to Menecrates, who held a grudge against Menodorus, and the feeling was mutual. When the two fleets met in the waters of Cumae, the two flagships carrying the two admirals went at each other like fighting cocks in a deadly bout, and as grappling irons bound them and gangplanks were crossed for the bravest to jump aboard the enemy ship, a flurry of arrows and javelins were exchanged. Both men ended up seriously wounded, with Menecrates diving in the sea to avoid capture and tragically drowning. But when the tally of sunken ships and dead sailors was made, it was in Pompey's favour, in spite of the loss, in just a few days, of his two most capable fleet commanders to treason and death. The Pompeian armada retreated after the day-long engagement, while the Republican ships remained in the coastal waters, where they were hit by a powerful storm. Many of the ships were wrecked, sunk or crushed against the Italian coast, and more than half of Octavian's force had been lost. At the same time, Pompey, safe in the harbour of Messana, had limited his damages substantially.

Appian, usually an aloof and non-emotional reporter of the events, in pure Thucididean fashion, for once gets carried away in depicting the scenes of panic among the seamen, either amidst the perils of the enraged sea, or on the beach after the wreckage, searching for the lost companions. In Cumae one of the largest naval battles of antiquity had taken place, so that the scale of the tragedy must have been enormous. If, for example, Octavian had lost sixty to seventy of his large vessels, the loss of life would have probably exceeded the 10,000 men.

Octavian was at the root of another large scale fiasco, and, not that there was much doubt about this in the first place, the dominance of Sextus Pompey over the seas was reinforced. The new Caesar headed back to Rome, surely "in low spirits".[17]

Once at home, he would have had to face the music for having broken the truce (since many would have considered his motives as a pretext), for having suffered yet another defeat, for exposing Italy to continuing famine, and for creating a further drain on financial resources for the reconstruction of the naval force that now languished at the bottom of the Tyrrhenian Sea.

Octavian was in a quandary, and had no choice but to fall back on Antony's military expertise and conduct a land attack. It was with this idea in mind that he left Maecenas for Athens to try to convince him to cooperate. It was not immediately clear why Antony accepted the proposition, and sailed from Athens with 300 ships, to the rescue of his unlikely partner. But he did not move until the spring of 37 BC, and by that time Octavian had made alternate plans, and perhaps wondered if he needed Antony's forces any more. For over a year, with Agrippa, he had been building a naval base in Baiae, after transforming a coastal lake into a protected harbour, and installing a powerful military fleet in its waters.

Antony, on the other hand, wanted to finish it off once and for all with the Parthians. The full vengeance of Crassus was now sixteen years overdue, and Ventidius had engaged with them several times victoriously, as we shall see in the next chapter, undermining their pride and their self confidence, and chasing them back outside the Roman provinces they had stormed in 40 BC.

The new meeting between the two men was held in Tarentum, on the Apulian coast on the Ionian Sea, and this time it was organized and facilitated by Octavia. She was a very active part of the negotiations, which ended with Antonius giving Octavian 120 ships with full crews for an invasion of Sicily, in exchange for 20,000 foot soldiers to be deployed in the Parthian invasion campaign, plus a special bodyguard of 1,000 chosen troops for Octavia. The elite force was the only counterpart that Antony was ever to receive from this deal.

It also has to be noted that, by that time, more than five years had elapsed since the meeting in Bononia which had set the ground rules for the functioning of the Second Triumvirate. Technically speaking, the lustrum (five year term) set by the Lex Pedia had expired, so that the two had to consult and deliberate over the extension of a second term in order to lawfully lead the Republic for another five year term. The general consensus among historians is that, since, in theory, the first five years had expired on 31 December 38 BC, this meeting that took place on 1 July 37 BC really did nothing more than ratify a status quo that was already six months old. But we have already witnessed many times how this kind of legal formalism was of paramount importance to the Roman mindset, and the three men went through the motions of formally renewing their mandate with a senatorial *imprimatur*. More betrothals marked the Treaty of Tarentum. Anthillus, the first born of Antony and Fulvia, the boy that as an infant had been given as a hostage to Brutus and Cassius after the Ides of March, was promised to Octavian's daughter Julia, barely two years old, born from his marriage to Scribonia. At the same time, Antony promised to Domitius Ahenobarbus the daughter he had had from his marriage with Octavia, also called Antonia, and still a toddler.

Towards the end of 38 BC, Octavian's wife Scribonia had given the young Caesar a daughter called Julia who, as an adult, would cause acute embarrassment to Octavian because of her promiscuous and immoral lifestyle. As the relationship with Sextus was, by that time, past the point of diplomatic repair, Octavian divorced her to marry Livia, the wife of T. Claudius Nero, already mother of one, as we have seen, and pregnant with the second child.

All was ready for the final aggression on the Mediterranean as well as the eastern front. In the remainder of this chapter we will deal with the war waged on Sextus Pompey, and in the following chapter we will deal specifically with the other front, in which Antony was more directly involved.

As he prepared for his n-th attack on the island of Sicily, Octavian had yet another change in his leadership line-up. He lost Menodorus, who visibly could not make up his mind on which side he was going to finish the war, and who returned to his old master, Pompey, with his seven best ships. Octavian at that point gave the command of field operations to Agrippa, who had earned his stripes on more than one occasion. At the same time, he enrolled Lepidus, and asked him to lead an attack from the African coast, and land in western Sicily. As an aside more than a major event for the outcome of the war, Menodorus switched sides back before the first arrow could be fired in the conflict, in the spring of 36 BC. Octavian, who was already suffering the consequences of yet another sea storm, accepted his return, but, obviously, he did not return him to his command, preferring to stick to the loyal Agrippa. His return, therefore, had no other consequence, apart from establishing beyond any doubt the absolute world record for changing sides during an armed conflict. Octavian's choice paid off, because the brilliant Agrippa immediately won an important naval battle in the waters of the Aeolian Islands, just north of the Straits of Messina. The defeat inflicted on the enemy left the Straits open for Octavian, who crossed over to the south, and landed in Taormina with the 120 ships he had received from Antony, for the first time making a break into the island with a heavy infantry landing. But, just as he was beginning to savour success, Octavian had to endure one more harsh disappointment. His ships were attacked and defeated by the rest of Sextus' fleet, so that his troops, already on Sicilian land, found themselves cut off and had to suffer heavy losses caused by the constant bombardment of stones, arrows, and javelins that the Pompeian light assault troops were hurling onto them as they marched north. One more time, Agrippa came to the rescue, so that in the end the two armies found themselves facing each other on Sicilian soil, ready for combat.

In the meantime Lepidus, on his way from Africa, had been hit by the same storm that had battered Octavian's ships on their way south from Campania, and he too had lost a considerable proportion of his force. Two major storms, so violent as to be able to wreck the big "fours" and "six" Roman warships that Agrippa had built, were a rarity in the Mediterranean summer. In fact, Lepidus' arrival had been even more eventful still, according to Appian, as his transport ships had been intercepted by Sextus, and his skippers had mistakenly sailed straight into the middle of the enemy squadron, so that many were sunk, and many of the soldiers of the two legions they were transporting died, either drowned or burned as their ships were set ablaze.

So bolstered was Pompey, that he began to think that some supernatural power was on his side when he was seaborne, and he went as far as trading his *paludamentum*, his classic red General's cloak, for a dark blue one, to signify that he considered himself an adept or son of Neptune, God of the Sea abyss. His coinage conveyed the same message, representing him with a flowing curly beard, and the three pronged fork. The arrival of Lepidus did not add much to Octavian's cause, but rather a bitter quarrel between the two over the former's status in his Triumviral rank, and the resurfacing of the suspicion of treason, or at least undue sympathies for Sextus Pompey that had already prevailed in 40 BC.

Once they faced each other on the mainland, the two armies spent a considerable amount of time in a game of hide and seek around Sicily, to no avail. It was then that Sextus took the initiative and challenged Octavian to battle where he felt strongest, that is, at sea. Arrogant as ever in his dark blue attire, his amazing track record on the water made him fearless. His ships, while smaller on average than the huge "liburnia" that Agrippa had built, were faster and easier to manoeuvre, and it was thanks to these two key features that he had always had an advantage over the Roman navy. But the ingenuity of Agrippa would come to the rescue before too long.

Perhaps there was never a true need for a formal gauntlet to be thrown on the water: Sextus was outnumbered on the land, and he could never have afforded anything but a naval battle. Here is how the resourceful Agrippa prepared for the battle with the formidable enemy. He had his ships armed with:

"the grab, a plank of wood two and a half metres long, shod with iron, with a ring at each end; to one of the rings was attached the grab, which was an iron claw, and to the other several ropes for winching in the grab when, after being fired from a catapult, it had hooked the enemy ship."[18]

The device, called *harpax*, was the evolution of the *corvus*, the harpooned moving bridge which the Romans had used since the first Punic war. The battle that was fought in front of the Sicilian shore, in front of thousands of civilians and soldiers holding their breaths as they waited for the final outcome, saw almost six hundred ships taking part in the action, barely recognizable from a distance, if it had not been for the colour of their towers. In the end, the device introduced by Agrippa made the difference, and a large portion of Sextus Pompey's fleet was sunk. The surviving seamen that had managed to reach the coast were immediately captured or killed by Octavian's soldiers who were patrolling the beaches nearby. In addition, the unexpected naval defeat had a disastrous effect on the morale of Pompey's land army, which shortly thereafter surrendered to Octavian *en masse*. As for Sextus himself, he had managed to salvage seventeen of his best ships from the disaster. He changed his military attire and his blue cloak for civilian clothing, and swiftly sailed to the east, perhaps confident of finding shelter with Antony, who had so far remained neutral. That would probably have been his best bet. After all, they had always maintained good relations, if not a secret alliance, and, as Appian points out, Sextus had welcomed Antony's mother Julia after Perusia. Octavian did not pursue him in his voyage towards the Greek islands, perhaps because he did not want to trespass into Antony's territorial waters. Or maybe we can envisage another reason since Lepidus was perpetrating an attempt to annex Sicily to his own domains, and he had begun with the raid and sack of the town of Messana. Lepidus was bitter and angry for having been progressively marginalized by Octavian. But when he finally confronted his nemesis, his overall lack of stature doomed him. His soldiers steadfastly refused another battle between Romans, and defected instantly to Octavian. A more hagiographical and theatrical version of the events is offered by Velleius,[19] who tells us of Octavian riding fearlessly by himself into Lepidus' camp, and intimidating him into surrender in a one on one confrontation. In either case, that was Lepidus' end. He conceded defeat, and obtained Octavian's pardon. He surrendered his military and provincial command, his post in the Triumvirate, and went back to Rome to live as a private citizen, other than for his religious office of *Pontifex Maximus*, which he had never abandoned. In one of history's paradoxes, he had to live among the many he had once proscribed, now pardoned, who were prospering in public life.

While Octavian was otherwise engaged, first by Lepidus and then by another mutiny of his greedy legions, Pompey had escaped to the Aegean Sea, where he spent some time reorganizing on the isle of Lesbos. Antony was not in Greece to welcome or confront him: he had already left for the first of his Parthian expeditions, and word was already spreading that the campaign was not meeting with huge success. The reported version from the official historiography is that Sextus, while fresh from a bloody defeat, was so blinded by his own arrogance that he could not resist the temptation to take advantage of Antony's temporary weakness, brought on by the defeats in Parthia, and implicitly by the resurgence of the love affair with Cleopatra that was adversely affecting his leadership skills. It is a very effective way of catching two birds with one stone, and tying the story together using the respective vices of the two men. It would appear that, in order to conquer his own part of the world, he was prepared to side with the Parthians, and discussions had already begun.

With the death of Sextus Pompey, which we shall narrate soon, and the forced withdrawal of Lepidus from the political scene, the last two alternative centres of power in Rome were eliminated. If this had happened at a different, earlier time, the outcome for Antony would have certainly been different. But these events took place at a low point of Antony's sinusoidal career, when he was in the middle of his Parthian setback, and he was not in a position to use them to his advantage. As for Sextus, while he had, for years, kept Octavian and Rome in a position of stalemate, he never followed through on his attacks to become more than a logistical disruption and a nuisance for the Republic. He never had the ambition or the audacity to capitalize on the current discontent and to propose himself as a true alternative to Octavian. Perhaps he would have done so if he had been able to break down the wall of Antony's integrity, but Antony would not compromise with his conscience after giving his word to Octavian.

When Sextus died, executed on Antony's orders, Octavian was overjoyed. He celebrated great honours for his fellow Triumvir. His kindness and his gratitude, as per usual, were of great propaganda value to him. One more time, he wished to display the maximum amount of goodwill towards Antony, especially now that, as we shall see in the following chapter, his colleague and rival was wading his way through various troubles, after the setbacks suffered in Parthia.

Chapter Seven

The New Alexander

The Parthian activity on the Syrian border, which culminated in a large scale invasion, caused a regional crisis that threatened to spread like wildfire and destabilize the *Pax Romana*, the Roman Peace underpinned by undisputed Roman control, which decades of war waged by the Republic had finally stabilized.

With the resurgence of the Parthian hazard, the first trouble that presented itself was that of Antigonous, the last prince of the Hasmonaean dynasty in Judaea, who took over after the deaths of his father Aristobulos and his older brother Alexander at the hands of the Pompeians, as described in the course of Chapter 3. The temporary conclusion of the hostilities in 53 BC had left John Hyrcanus in charge as High Priest, and Head of State, at least on a representative level, while another pro-Roman leader, Antipater, had been chosen by Gabinius and the Senate to act as Governor to oversee daily operations. Immediately, Antipater called on his two sons to administer Palestine. Phasael, the elder, was made Governor of Jerusalem and its immediate surroundings, while the younger, Herod, became King Herod the Great, founder of the Herodian dynasty, Governor of Galilee. As for Antigonous, the prevalence of the Caesarean party over the Pompeians did not further his cause, as he was pushed to the side and later exiled. In the years between Pharsalus and Philippi, the duo Hyrcanus – Antipater managed around the Roman presence, continuing their policy of allegiance to Rome, and even keeping the greedy Cassius at bay, satisfying his request for 7,000 gold talents. And while Antipater had done his best, with the help of Herod, Phasael, and their cousin Malicus, this had been a difficult task, as the vast majority of the population was extremely resentful of the Roman presence, and the growing fiscal pressure was, for sure, making things worse. But this was not all, as Cassius in his greedy rage had reduced into servitude the people of four Judaean cities, Goffa, Emmaus, Lydda, and Tamma, definitively wiping out whatever goodwill was left from years of benevolent and tolerant Roman government in Palestine. As a matter of fact, many of the special concessions from which the Jews benefitted, such as tax and military exemptions in compliance with religious rules, had been promulgated by Antony and Dolabella during their brief joint Consulship in 44 BC, and Josephus gives us ample excerpts of the decrees.[1] We have explained how Josephus was clearly intent on justifying his loyalty to Titus and the Flavians to his countrymen. In his insistent praise of Antony's deeds, we see him trying to find a tradition of benevolence and respect on the part of the Romans much earlier than the end of the first century AD. In this light, the deeds of Antony at the apogee of his career are an excellent case in point to prove his theorem. Already aware of the specific problems of this complex nation, or duly educated by Herod, Antony protected their interests not only at home in Judaea, but also in the Mediterranean coastal cities where they were a visible minority. Of course, both the ruling class and the masses had to be in line with the principles of the Pax Romana.

The Pharisee intelligentsia was constantly challenged by the masses, and Antipater was little more than a foreigner in the eyes of the Jewish people. In the meantime, the star of Herod was constantly on the rise, thanks in particular to some high profile victories over neighbouring populations causing trouble on the borders, and, as much as his father was loyal to Hyrcanus and aligned to his wishes, the future king was proving to be a maverick, and constantly provoked the High Priest. His temperament and ambition, of course, did not go unnoticed, and Cassius himself had in mind to associate him to his cause, and make him a Governor of the whole of Syria or, who knows, even a king of Judaea after the end of the Civil War. Malicus, a distant relative, but a first rated local personality, grew envious of the growing power of Antipater and his family, and eventually had him killed. Herod duly vindicated his father, with the blessing of Cassius. But, with the departure of his father, Herod was left as the strong man of the country, with full responsibility for protecting the borders of the Holy Land, which were subject to the usual provocations by their neighbours. Herod drove them out of Judaea, and also fended off an armed attempt by Antigonous to make a comeback. This attempt took place at almost the same time as the battle of Philippi, so just a few months before Antony made his return on the Judean scene, this time no longer as a young officer under Gabinius, but as the senior leader of the Roman Republic, with unlimited powers and charged with re-establishing central control. Immediately the anti-Herodian Jewish bloc sent emissaries to Antony, complaining about the young prince's violent and despotic ways. The pages from Joseph Flavius describing these events are not the easiest to follow or interpret.[2]

In his version of events, Herod managed to gain the upper hand thanks to a generous bribe for the Romans. This is not particularly credible. Judaea was a province, and a province that had complied with Cassius' will for that matter, so Antony could have exacted whatever sum of money he pleased, bribe or not. Perhaps a more realistic take on this would be that Antony was smart and far sighted enough to realize that the young man was probably the strongest, most capable (in military terms) and loyal ally who could govern the region on Rome's behalf. He was wise enough to forgive and forget his past allegiance to Cassius, and placed his absolute trust in him. As the sending of envoys from the opposite party continued, Antony turned to Hyrcanus for counsel. Hyrcanus advised Antony to rely on Herod and Phasael, and Antony made them both Tetrarchs, de facto confirming them in the roles they had been given by Antipater. Hyrcanus, maybe on account of his old age, kept reducing his sphere of influence to his religious offices. In preparation for his next and obvious career move, Herod married Mariamme, a niece of Hyrcanus, and was therefore now linked to the royal blood line.

A precarious equilibrium prevailed, but the religious factions that had supported Aristobulos in his struggle were all but appeased. On the contrary, it is likely that after the latest levies for funds they were more virulent than ever. It was in these circumstances that a 1,000-strong delegation was sent to meet Antony in Tyre. It was a vocal and unruly representation which caused Antony to lose his patience, and he immediately imprisoned the most vehement protestors and threatened to execute them. He eventually unleashed his legionaries against the envoys with the result that many lost their lives. This is one of the few documented episodes of violent repression carried out by Antony between 41 and 39 BC. It was neither an act of gratuitous and arbitrary violence, nor an act of vengeance against the local population. It was rather an act of retaliation and a police operation against a group that had proven hostile and rebellious against Rome on more than one occasion. It also coincided with Antony receiving the news of the Perusian debacle, and took place when he was preparing to head back to Italy via Greece. He must have been under considerable stress and had no time or appetite for a group of exalted rioters from a turbulent ethnicity.

In the spring / summer of 40 BC, when Antony had just left Alexandria, Parthian activity gathered pace, and the full scale invasion of Syria was about to begin. It would be led by the Satrap Barzaphranes, and by Prince Pacorus, son of the same King Orodes II who had annihilated Crassus. Leading their armies was that same Quintus Labienus that we have already met.

Dio,[3] in another act of deference to Augustan official historiography, says that the Parthians were encouraged to resume hostilities against the Roman dominion by Antony's perceived weakness, as he:

"had become her (Cleopatra's) slave, and was devoting all his time to love."

This claim has been sufficiently debunked in the previous chapter, so it would be redundant to further argue this point here. More rationally, we can infer that Pacorus was rather banking on the fact that the veterans from Philippi were exhausted, and, since many had served under the Tyrannicides and had been later enlisted by Antony, they were perhaps not unfailingly loyal. Labienus' campaign got off to a very good start, deploying such effective tactics as fast-mounted archer attacks combined with the intervention of their heavy, armoured cavalry, referred to in Greek as *cataphracts*, and they soon forced the Romans to retreat to their camp at Apamea.

Labienus then pulled the old propaganda warfare trick, bombarding the Roman camp with leaflets tied to arrows which incited the soldiers to desert. In the end, as expected, many did, and the subsequent surrender was complete. The young General Saxa, the brother of that Decidius Saxa who had opened the road to Philippi, was cruelly executed. In the end, the road to conquer Syria and its capital city Antioch was left open for the Parthians, and so was the one leading to Palestine. Labienus was becoming arrogant, as he superciliously held court in Antioch and began (him too!) to collect tributes from the coastal cities. He even assumed the name of Parthicus, as if he had conquered the Parthians as opposed to joining them. This may have been down to his youth as he was only in his late twenties at this time. The invasion had gradually taken the Parthians down the coast, and as far south as Cilicia, Ionia, and Lydia. In effect, the only coastal town of relevance that resisted was Tyre. The capture of Jerusalem, and the abduction of John Hyrcanus and his son Phasael, which we will describe below, took place at the same time.

Of course, in order to secure the newly obtained control over Syria, Barzaphranes and Pacorus could have used a more friendly neighbour than the philo-Roman Phasael, and especially Herod. Antigonous was a quite obvious choice for the Parthians. He was a legitimate member, and last survivor, of the deposed Hasmonean dynasty, and he was the much preferred option for the overwhelming majority of the people, as he was of pure Jewish ancestry, while Herod, albeit religiously devout, was partly Itumean, since his ancestry had his roots in modern day Lebanon. The Parthians saw an opportunity to capitalize on Jewish nationalism and anti-Roman sentiment, so it was easy for them to make a deal with Antigonus, and put him back on his father's throne in exchange for 1,000 talents of gold, and 500 women slaves. Antigonus had the weight of popular support behind him, thus facilitating the task. And, moreover, support for Antigonous' cause had also spread from the masses to Jerusalem's aristocratic circles, such as the "Sons of Baba", and even to the Pharisee leadership. But when the fighting actually started, Herod's military skills made the difference against the Parthians and the nationalistic Sadducees, and he was quickly able to gain the upper hand. But what military strength could not achieve was made possible by treason. Antigonous and Pacorus pretended to invite Hyrcanus and Phasael to parley, and then, in an unforgivable act of treachery, imprisoned them. Herod, caught by surprise, had no choice but to barricade himself in the fortress of Masada, the mountaintop castle that one hundred years later would see the heroic last stand of the zealots against Titus' XIII Legion and their mass suicide. Eventually, in a daring escape, he left for the mountains of his native Idumeia, which, while it was considered a foreign land for all intents and purposes, lay only 50 miles from Jerusalem.

The forceful combination of Parthian imperialism and Jewish nationalism had turned the tide against Roman interests in the Middle East. Pacorus handed

Hyrcanus and Phasael over to the cruel Antigonous. The High Priest, on his knees, humiliated himself in front of the new king, pleading for his life. His life was eventually spared, but the vicious Antigonous ripped his ears off with his teeth, the mutilation permanently disqualifying him from religious office. As for Phasael, he committed suicide in prison by smashing his head on a rock, thus preserving his dignity. Herod, defeated and devastated by the tragic ends of his brother and father, was now a prisoner in Parthia, but eventually found shelter in Alexandria, where Cleopatra gave him a warm welcome. It is interesting to recall at this point how Antipater had helped Gabinius and Antony on their Egyptian expedition, and how they had subsequently helped Cleopatra when she had been ousted by the regents of her child brother Ptolemy XIII. Cleopatra arranged for a ship for the future king of Israel, and he sailed to Italy to obtain the help of Antony and the Senate. It was so that Herod, following a passionate speech by Antony in which he praised his and his father's long time loyalty to Rome, and all the services rendered to the Republic, was appointed king of Judaea, the same title that the Parthians had just bestowed on Antigonous. Herod had gone for the second time in eighteen months to solicit Antony's help. It would also seem that Octavian played along, in the name of Antipater's track record in the service of his father Julius Caesar. In reality, the reader will recall how in 49–48 BC Caesar had played the Haesmonian card against the Pompeians, but later Herod's father had helped him sort out some other local disputes. According to Josephus, the outcome of his trip to Rome exceeded Herod's greatest expectations, as he could not have banked on a senatorial decree making him king. In the official tradition, the reign of the Herodiads in Judaea started on that day, which Antony and Herod spent together, celebrating sacrifices and registering the decision on the Capitol.[4]

The bond between the Triumvir and the Jewish king had been reinforced, and was sealed by a celebratory banquet held by Antony.

The reign of the founder of the Herodiad dynasty was on very weak grounds. His subjects would rather have a puppet king, crowned by the Parthian invader, than him, partly Lebanese, and of Roman sympathies. All of a sudden the invasion of Syria was no longer the only threat for Antony in the Near East, as Judaea had fallen in a Parthian-backed Civil War. Being entirely familiar with the old expansionist ambitions of the Parthian Empire, it was clear that dealing with the issue of border security could not be put off for much longer. Antony could no longer postpone decisive intervention, as he had been forced to do in the middle of the Perusian situation.

In order to meet the threat quickly, Antony, as we have seen, established his headquarters in Athens, so that he would be closer to the operational front. Again, Dio[5] criticizes him for alleged obnoxious behaviour, including his insistence on using the title of *neos Dionysos*, an attribute which, as we have seen, had a very different genesis from the one Dio subscribes to it.

The first offensive against the Parthians was entrusted to the faithful and experienced Ventidius. His campaigns in Syria began at the end of 38 BC, at a time when the relationship between Antony and Octavian was, at least on the surface, a harmonious one. Antony had resumed his role in the cult of Julius Caesar, which Octavian was manically promoting, as a forerunner to his own.

As he dispatched Ventidius to Syria, Antony established his headquarters in Athens, and for good reason. Athens was the centre of the Mediterranean at that time, and the best place from which to dominate the East, benefiting as it did from good connections, and reliable and easy access to all the key regions. It has been pointed out[6] how, while the winter spent in Alexandria had been a period of rest and relaxation, the one spent in Greece must have been a period of careful and thorough preparation for the decisive attack he was planning on Parthia in order to bring peace to the Roman eastern border for good. The description of his indolent or extravagant behaviour was really a distortion of the facts by Dio and Appian.

Ventidius was certainly not a flashy character. His origins could not have been more humble: as the reader will recall, in his youth he had been a prisoner in the Social War, and marched in chains behind Pompeius Strabo, Magnus' father. His early military exploits consisted of selling mules to the army, a profession which had earned him the nickname of "the muleteer". The Parthians, via Labienus, were certainly aware that Antony had not fielded a blue blood against them, and maybe derided his choice. Had they underestimated the threat the hardened veteran posed to them?

Antony ordered Ventidius not to attack Pacorus and the core of the Parthian army, but rather to halt their expansion in the Middle East, beginning with Cylicia and Lycia – Pamphilia. Ventidius landed on the Turkish coast, and, mimicking Caesar's and Antony's style, privileged surprise over mass invasion, and drove south towards Lycia with his light infantry alone. The strategy worked, because Ventidius was able to block Labienus with some second tier local troops before he could join forces with the remainder of the Parthian army. When the Parthians arrived in the area of Mount Amanus, they completely misjudged the situation. Instead of consulting with Labienus on the position of Ventidius, who in the meantime had conquered the highlands, they attacked directly; they had perhaps been rendered imprudent and arrogant by the memories of the great victory in Carrahe seventeen years earlier. So much time had elapsed since the Roman *gladia* had crossed with the Parthian spears, and Ventidius' legionaries felt they had something to prove. Charging downhill like an avalanche the Romans completely crushed their opponents, and over the next few days they did not let up: relentlessly harassing them with their ambushes to finish them off before they could re-group. So terrorized were his auxiliary troops, as they helplessly watched the Roman charges, that Labienus could do nothing to incite them to join the fighting, and he ended up going into hiding to wait for better days.

Numerous were those who tried to track down Labienus, no doubt because of the substantial reward that Antony had put on his head. Eventually it was a certain Demetrios, one of Caesar's old freedmen who had risen to Governor of Cyprus, who finally apprehended and no doubt executed him, as his name never surfaces again in the chronicles of the time.

After his spectacular success, Ventidius led his galvanized troops towards the Syrian border, and inflicted another tough defeat on the enemy, this time to Pacorus' Chief of Staff Barzaphranes, the conqueror of Palestine. The Parthians had to retreat substantially from Syria, and abandon Palestine to Ventidius, who immediately imposed a punitive tribute to Antigonous.

Antony was thrilled with the news of Ventidius' early success and with the spectacular and highly symbolic defeats of Labienus and Barzaphranes. Rome had been waiting for thirteen years to deal a blow to the pride of the Parthians and now they had.

Celebrations followed in Rome as well as in Athens. Plutarch highlights for us the next step of Antony's gradual transformation into a Greek or Hellenistic prince, describing how at the celebration games he was fully garbed in the Greek tradition, including the classic white shoes. He was clearly quite oblivious of his role as the representative of Rome and all the formalism that this required. While Appian simply states that when in Athens he got back to attending to State affairs, Dio, very much along the same lines as Plutarch, insists on the resurgence of his Dionysian persona, and on other unspecified extravagances. It has been reported that his extravagance went as far as representing a mock betrothal with the Goddess Athena! Overall, these pages from Plutarch and Dio seem to be too impregnated with Octavian's propaganda to be exploitable for the biographer, unless as an example of how such disinformation can distort reality. In truth, what had probably happened is that the adulatory Greeks had made the Roman a Gymnasiarch, or the president of the games, which would explain why he was attending the celebrations clad in the local attire. In all likelihood, the marriage with Athena was just an act of deference on the part of the Greeks towards his faithful wife Octavia, who had followed him to Greece, and, per protocol, was participating in all the public events. Nobody in their right mind would have conceived of arranging for him a marriage with someone else, let alone a Goddess, in the presence of his wife and Octavian's sister. The rest of the illations from Dio and Plutarch, for example on the Dionysian character of his coinage of the period, are purely the result of inflationary propaganda, and have been steadfastly refuted over time. What the Greeks did not take into account was Antony's very special interpretation of their act of deference. Antony accepted it gladly, and then he concluded that if he was to be engaged to the Goddess Athena, her namesake's city would have to give him a dowry. And so, he ordered the Athenians to pay him another tax of 1,000 talents.

Not content with his early victories, Ventidius had kept pressing the Parthians, probably going beyond his initial charter, and had beaten them three more times, each time getting closer to their homeland.

Ventidius had been extremely shrewd and resourceful to inflict such grave defeats on Pacorus and the rest of the Parthian force. He had come to realize that a certain Prince Conneus was double crossing him and was leaking intelligence to the enemy. He then lured him into a sense of security by giving him all sorts of innocuous information, and then, finally, gave him the wrong tip on the itinerary he was going to follow in his offensive march so that, after the bad intelligence was fed to Pacorus, he had him exactly where and when he wanted him, for the battle of Cyrrestica. The battle was an exact copy of the confrontation at Mount Amanus a few months earlier in late 39 BC, with Ventidius claiming the high ground early on, and then mowing down the Parthian cavalry with a sudden downhill infantry charge. The only notable and deadly variation was the intensive usage of slingers from Greece, Crete, and the Balearics, who could hurl a stone or lead projectile at a longer range than a Parthian arrow with firearm speed and accuracy. Between the rain of stones and the bloody finish at sword range, Cyrrestica was a complete slaughter. The casualties in the Parthian field now included no less than Pacorus himself, the son of King Orodes II, and brother-in-law of the king of Armenia Artavasdes. The loss of their crown prince, apparently a well loved member of the royal family and a true nobleman, was very demoralizing for the Parthians. The survivors escaped, and begged for shelter from the sympathetic king of Commagene, Antioch, who welcomed them in Samosata. It is at this point that some Greek historians postulate that the reason why Ventidius stopped short of total destruction of the Parthians was that he was afraid that Antony would have been jealous of his successes. But such reasoning has more than a whiff of Augustan propaganda about it. It was also – allegedly – for this reason that his subsequent actions were limited to attacking a flanker and besieging King Antioch in Samosata, on the banks of the river Euphrates, about 200 km inland from the Mediterranean. According to the official version of events, Ventidius deliberately delayed the conclusion of the siege, and dragged out the ransom negotiations, stuck at the sum of 1,000 talents, so that Antony had time to join him and take over the command of the operations. Antony's intervention was, however, ineffective, and the siege continued for much longer. The besieged Antioch grew confident that he could resist, and was able to renegotiate the ransom requested to avoid the rape and pillage of Samosata down to 300 talents.

A version of the events more favourable to Antony comes from Josephus, according to which the Triumvir struggled to make Samosata fall because of difficulties he encountered in finding reinforcements.

While his allies had rallied to the west, the road from the coast was blocked by a large Parthian mounted force, which nobody would confront. The bravest of the allies, or at least the one most eager to find favour with Antony, was Herod. He tricked the Parthians by sending his pack mules ahead of his cavalry, to draw the enemy out of their hiding place at the bottom of a deep gorge, then annihilated them. The road was open, and Antony could receive all the reinforcements and supplies he needed to reduce King Antioch and Samosata. The episode is reported by Dio, Plutarch, and Josephus with great consistency and attention to detail, indicating that, in all probability, the source for all three was Q. Dellius.

Soon after the town surrendered, Ventidius was sent home to celebrate a triumph for his victories. It was, of course, the first and only Roman triumph in terms of victories scored against the Parthians, and was not to be repeated until the days of Trajan, almost 140 years later. Plutarch rather bitterly concluded this chapter with the cynical remark that Antony and Octavian had secured more victories through the offices of others than by themselves. The supposed equanimity of the *par condicio* between the Triumvirs is a poor hiding place for his historical bias. True, Octavian had won at Mutina thanks to Hirtius and Pansa, at Philippi thanks to Antony, and in Sicily thanks to Agrippa, so, indeed, he hardly had a distinguished individual track record. But putting Antony on the same level as Octavian in this matter was to show a conspicuous lack of goodwill.

As for Ventidius, and the reasons for his repatriation, that is open to conjecture, but envy and jealousy can safely be ruled out as possible motives. Ventidius had been Antony's rescuer after Mutina, the first to join him after Perusia, and had always been ready to cover his back against Octavian. He had won him the gratitude of the Romans for defeating Labienus, killing Barzaphranes and Pacorus, liberating Syria and Palestine. Never, in any of the pages of the historians, have we found any evidence which could corroborate such petty claims. But Ventidius, back in Rome, died shortly after celebrating his triumph, in 38 BC. Again, this is open to conjecture, but it does not seem to be too far-fetched to imagine that the old soldier, certainly already in his sixties by then, had already started to show the signs of whatever infirmity was going to lead to his demise less than a year later, and that Antony sent him back to let him enjoy his recognition, and rest before his final physical decline.

The campaign, brilliantly conducted by Ventidius, put the Parthians on the defensive, and halted their plans for any future territorial expansion. They remained formidable on their home turf, but they had shown their limits once they were away from their natural boundaries.

This brings us to the month of March 38 BC and Antony's return to Italy at the head of 300 ships, summoned by Octavian to support him against Sextus Pompey, as we have described in the previous chapter.

Ventidius had rid the Near East of the Parthians, but the Roman order had not been fully restored yet, since Ventidius had not had time to deal fully with Antigonus. He had split his troops, sending the bulk of them to the siege of

Samosata to pursue the survivors of Cyrrestica, and the others to help Herod regain control of his kingdom. But, as we have seen, it was not enough, and Antigonous was still on his throne in Jerusalem. It was in this context that Antony sent another emerging talent from his military staff, Gaius Sossius, to finish off the work of his illustrious predecessor. The task was far from easy, because, as Dio pointed out,

"Those are terrible people when they are angered."[7]

Herod had come back and weakened Antigonous' resistance. He had been to Samosata to meet Antony and coordinate their actions. The young King Antigonous had it coming. He made a first mistake when he divided his forces, giving Herod the opportunity to annihilate one of his generals. He then barricaded in the citadel of Jerusalem, where his supporters fought strenuously, animated by religious and nationalistic feelings, and hatred for the Roman conquerors. In the end, any resistance was overcome, thanks too to famine and a four month long siege. The resistance had been so determined and fierce that the Romans themselves had nothing but admiration for these fighters, and Dio himself stresses how the defendants were at their posts of combat even "on the day of Saturn" i.e. during the Jewish Sabbath. The citadel of Jerusalem surrendered in April 37 BC, almost three years from when Herod had been made king by the Senate of Rome. Apparently, the young king manifested his gratitude towards Antony in a very tangible way. Here is Josephus on the subject:

"As soon as he took control over Jerusalem, he took all the treasures of the Kingdom, he expropriated the richest men, and, when he had amassed a large quantity of gold and silver, he used it to make gifts to Antony and his friends."[8]

During the Parthian invasion, Antigonous had had his Roman bodyguard massacred, so now his chances for pardon were nil. When he was finally defeated and apprehended by Sossius, Antony had him put to death, simply decapitated with an axe according to Josephus and Plutarch, or even tied up to a post and scourged prior to beheading according to Dio, but in any case, he was the first crowned head to fall at the hands of Antony, or any other Roman. While it was not customary to execute kings, we must recall that the Senate had recognized Herod as the rightful king of Judaea, so that Antigonus was seen as a usurper by the letter of the Roman law. He had been brave and gallant during the conflict, but when all was lost he had thrown himself at Sossius' feet imploring him to spare his life, provoking the Roman to call him "Antigone", distorting his name into that of Sophocles' tearful character.

The fortified area to the north west of the Temple of Jerusalem, the scene of Antigonous' last stand, was rebuilt by Herod later, with walls over 25 metres high, military barracks, and secret passages leading to the inner area of the Temple, and was called the Antonia, a name that was to last until after the days of Emperor Hadrian.[9]

Antony's participation, albeit unwilling, in Judaea's internal affairs was not over yet. When Herod appointed a new foreign born High Priest, Amonel, to replace Hyrcanus who was no longer fit for duty, Hyrcanus' daughter Alexandra attempted to use Antony and Cleopatra's influence to have her son Aristobulos, aged 16, named instead. Alexandra apparently counted on the incredible beauty of the young man to fascinate and seduce Antony. She went as far as offering to send the young man to the Triumvir, according to Josephus, with dubious intents. In the narration, Herod intervened diplomatically to stop this from happening, afraid of exposing such a beauty to the insatiable lust of the Roman, which was exactly Alexandra's plan in order to obtain more leverage with him. And, still according to Josephus, the suspicions that Herod harboured with regards to the sensual interests of his Roman friend were well grounded. It seems[10] that even Herod's beautiful spouse Mariamme tried to seduce Antony while he was in Egypt by sending him her own nude portrait, but he turned down such a flagrant invitation to avoid a sticky situation with Cleopatra. The story took an even more complicated turn with the arrival of Cleopatra on the Judaean scene. Herod temporarily yielded to Alexandra, and let the young Aristobulos ascend to the role of High Priest. But Alexandra was suspicious of the true intentions of Herod, and with good reason: she was thinking of making an escape for Egypt with her son.

Only weeks later, under the cover of festivities, the young Aristobulos was drowned in a swimming pool by the king's friends, who made it seem like a tragic accident. The desperate Alexandra wrote to Cleopatra, asking her to intervene through Antony. The Roman, already with his feet in the stirrups on his way to Armenia, summoned Herod to Laodicea to defend himself of all charges of involvement in this horrible murder. Herod left for Laodicea feeling ominous. He feared, along with many in his entourage, that Antony might convict him and have him killed. He was so concerned that he gave specific instructions to kill Mariamme if he died, so that she would not have had to yield to the sexual desire of another man, with a clear reference to the Triumvir. The pressure from Cleopatra, if any there was, did not influence the judgment of Mark Antony, and in the end he decided that he would not interfere with the internal affairs of Judaea, especially given Herod's merits in Antony's eyes, and Herod was let go. This whole passage in Josephus can be read as a suggestion that Cleopatra was trying very subtly to undermine Herod's position with Antony, and to take advantage of whatever domestic problems he might have had, in order to annex Judaea to her own crown, just as had been the case two centuries earlier. We have to bear in mind that Josephus was nothing short of an official imperial spokesperson, and therefore partly a victim of Augustan propaganda. While he falls prey to the usual stereotypes about Cleopatra, and of her sinister influence over Antony, he is somewhat more balanced than Dio or Plutarch when he writes:

> "She asked Antony to give her Judaea and Arabia, pushing him to take them from their Governments and Kings (and give them to her). Antony was so dominated by this woman, as it was apparent, that he appeared to obey to her every desire, not only for the intimacy which they shared, but also as if he had been under the influence of a drug. But the blatant injustice of her actions made him feel ashamed, and he held back from being so subdued to commit the gravest crimes."[11]

The year 37 BC saw a resurgence in Antony's love for Cleopatra. Antony, putting State affairs ahead of his passion for her, had been separated from Cleopatra since February or March 40 BC, and, for all we know, was guilty of no infidelities during that time. But it was then that, according to Plutarch:

> "the mischief that thus long had lain still, the passion for Cleopatra, which better thoughts had seemed to have lulled and charmed into oblivion, upon his approach to Syria, gathered strength again, and broke out into a flame. And, in fine, like Plato's restive and rebellious mule of the human soul, flinging off all good and wholesome counsel, and breaking fairly loose."

Antony sent Fonteius Capito to Egypt and had her join him in Syria. The pair met in Antioch, and Antony's infatuation was quickly rekindled. Perhaps the presence of their two twin children, Alexander Helios and Cleopatra Selene, born in December 40 BC, whom Antony was meeting for the first time, helped re-ignite the flame of his passion for her. If the first *coup de foudre* had ever subsided, the second had the effect of rewinding the clock to where things were in 40 BC, and the presence of the children made it all the more emotional. The "old calamity", to use Plutarch's metaphor, was back. There has been much debate on whether the formal Egyptian wedding between them was celebrated in this period, or over a year later in Alexandria, but the substance of things remains unchanged. However, there is no certainty on this point. From a Roman point of view, her return to favour signalled a turn for the worse, and the grants that had started in 40 BC with the return of Cyprus to Egypt resumed. Anti-Antonian propaganda permeates the Plutarchean narrative to a much greater extent than seen so far. Antony granted control over the Phoenicia, Celesyria, the part of Syria that borders Palestine, Judaea, Cilicia, and Nabatean Arabia to Cleopatra. In essence, he returned the borders of the Egyptian sphere of influence to where they had been under the first four Ptolemies, as we shall see in the next chapters, before domestic disturbances weakened the crown of the Nile. Land allocations were part of Antony's political project. He was not "donating" land to Cleopatra, as Octavian would have the Romans believe, because he had been bewitched and was infatuated. He was consolidating all the provinces and protectorates of the East which required more competent and effective management than was possible with the usual year-long political appointee, typically corrupt, who reported to a distant Senate, which had no real understanding of the local situation.

So Cleopatra came to control nominally, on Rome's behalf, all the Mediterranean coast from Africa to Syria, de facto covering the same reach as the first three Ptolemies.

The reorganization of the Asian provinces was progressing, following principles of realism and ease of control, and furthering the pan Asian vision that Antony was developing. In Asia Minor, the *status quo* was left largely unaffected by this last round of changes. The only changes worthy of note were the succession to the throne of Amyntas to Deiotarus in Galatia, and that of Archelaus Sisena in Cappadocia. As pointed out, both continued in the tradition of vassalage to Rome and loyalty to Antony. To the reliable client kings mentioned above, Antony added one more, Polemon of Ponthus. As pointed out earlier, Ponthus had been made into a province after the death of Mithridates VI. But in 37 BC Antony considered it was too far from Rome, and deserved a more decentralized control: it was so that the war lord Polemon, already running Cilicia for the Romans, was made king. He was an unfailingly loyal ally to Antony.

The reader will perhaps have a recollection of an inflamed Liz Taylor, in the Colossal from 1963, "Cleopatra", determined to get back to Antony / Richard Burton after his absence and for his marriage to Octavia, forcing him to his knees and dictating to him the list of the territories she wanted added to her kingdom. But the point that she makes, and that is historically accurate, is that Egypt represented an ideal control mechanism and could have been a decentralized control centre for Rome in the east. In fact, while Octavian had an easy time demonizing the "donations" to Cleopatra, any subsequent disapproval of the latter concessions would have been unjustified, as it would have been perfectly within the mandate or the prerogatives of the Triumvir to organize smaller provinces under the supervision of a Vassal State, such as Egypt would have been at the time. Egypt would have supplied the infrastructure that Rome had not yet been able to reproduce efficiently. In effect, merging much of the Near East with the Ptolemaic crown would have solidified the galaxy of vassal kingdoms into a more cohesive and manageable cluster. Egypt would also have been a powerful naval base, with its strong fleet ready to intervene wherever required. Annexing the Phoenician coast to Egypt would also have given the latter an endless supply of cider wood for shipbuilding, wood being scarce along the Nile, and thereby ensuring the constant renewal of their fleet.

However, during this period of restructuring, not all the Hellenistic potentates found Antony an enthusiastic patron. The ones which were found to be undeserving were mercilessly put out of business. Lisonia of Itureia, for example, seemed too chummy with the Parthians for Antony's liking and was executed, with the result that his small and mountainous kingdom swung between the control of Cleopatra and that of King Herod.

While Plutarch cites Judaea as one of the territories assigned to the Egyptian crown, Antony made a point of leaving his friend Herod all the latitude he needed to reign effectively over his people, in appreciation of the profound cultural and religious differences with the rest of the surrounding world, and to create a separate space without forcing an unnecessary and dangerous dependency on Egypt. As proof of his long sightedness, the Herodians would reign over the Holy Land for over one hundred years, thirty of which would be under Herod the Great.

The Spartans were among those who had to suffer. Their leader Lachares was apprehended by Antony for piracy and beheaded. As will be shown, this act of justice cost Antony the allegiance of his son Eurycles, who led his own countrymen against the Roman at Actium.

Discussing the reorganization of the Middle East, Plutarch reaches the apex of bad faith when he reprimands Antony for deposing and executing Antigonus. We would have thought that any Roman in his right state of mind would have rejoiced at the death of a sworn enemy of Rome, an enemy who had been leading a seditious people against the Senate of Rome (which had appointed Herod only one year before), who had been enthroned by none other than the Parthians, and who had made his fortune thanks to Syrian invasion. Still, according to Plutarch, "the turpitude that most displeased the Romans were the honours that were tributed to Cleopatra", as if to say that having freed up Judaea from the Parthians and their puppet king was something that would have displeased the Romans, as opposed to representing an accomplishment worthy of a Triumph for General Sossius, as it had, in fact, been. But there was one thing that the Romans would not forgive him: the public announcement of his paternity of his twin children, Alexander and Cleopatra, born in December 40 BC. Caesar had proudly done the same when Ptolemy XV, aka Cesarion, had been born, provoking the disapproval of his fellow citizens. And for once we must believe the official version, according to which Anthony proclaimed that his offspring were the foundation for generations of kings to come, as genuine, and not the product of enemy propaganda.

Another extremely far fetched anecdote born both of Augustan propaganda and Jewish national pride, relates that Cleopatra, as she escorted Antony towards the Euphrates and the Parthians, tried very explicitly to seduce Herod, in an attempt to hedge her bets in case of the possible downfall of Mark Antony, and that Herod, who despised her, not only sternly rejected her but at one point even planned to kill her to avenge his Roman friend and patron.

The Parthian campaign, one of the key episodes of Antony's life, is about to start, and we will have to follow it without Appian, one of the most reliable and impartial sources on the life of the Triumvir, who does not cover it. We will, therefore, have to tread carefully through the minefield of disinformation on which Dio and Plutarch had fed their unsympathetic commentaries. Fortunately, however, it seems that Plutarch resorted to the chronicles of General Quintus Dellius, one of the Triumvir's lieutenants, who was probably not a man of high moral principles (he had already served under Pompey and the Liberators, and had not joined Antony until after Philippi), but at least he had been a reliable eye witness, and his lost narration was extremely detailed.

The narratives of the Parthian expedition are abundant. This unusual bonanza of documents from the sources derives from the fact that historiography in Rome flourished under Emperor Trajan, who himself endeavoured to invade Parthia, so that the historical coverage of the previous attempts could have provided a good backdrop to make Trajan's expedition all the more glorious.

King Orodes II had been gravely affected by the loss of his son Pacorus, who had been killed in battle as he fought Ventidius. The following year, the old king was made to step down from the throne by his other son Phraates, who, to secure his right to the succession, had his father, and many of his next of kin, assassinated. As a result of the executions, many members of the Parthian elite felt unsafe and escaped overseas. Monases, a top rank personality of the Empire, was among those that went to seek shelter with Antony, who, only too happy to welcome an important enemy defector, appointed him to oversee some border cities. Phraates would not be deprived of such a prominent nobleman, so Antony sent Monases back to Parthia, but as an undercover agent, whose role was to ferment dissatisfaction/ destabilize the state. Mark Antony must have perceived that the hostile Empire was going through one of those prolonged periods of instability that had so frequently marked its history. The cruel succession and the many defections were clearly indicative of some level of internal destabilization.

As he took the initiative and began his advance, Antony used Monases as an ambassador, and demanded the return of Crassus' eagles, the insignia of the legions destroyed at Carrhae. The ambassador's instructions were to buy time to start making his way west.

Antony had carefully prepared the mission, which he hoped was going to deliver him to posterity as the greatest Roman hero of all times, and end the dualism with Octavian for good in the eyes of the Roman people and Senate. Maybe he had spent too long on preparations, or maybe the moment had passed, the decisive momentum that came with Ventidius' victories now lost, not to mention the temporary leadership void in Parthia. But in order to go and strike deep into enemy territories, he needed to arm more Italian legions, so that he did not have to rely too heavily on foreign auxiliaries, a dangerous bet in the extreme conditions he would have to face. But throughout 38 BC, in the heat of the Pompeian war, he could not have drafted any more recruits without draining young combatants from the domestic conflict.

But when he finally moved he was at the head of 60,000 Roman legionaries, plus 30,000 allied troops and cavalry, representing a total of 100,000 men. When they marched, they stomped their caligae on the ground and made the earth tremble all the way to the Indu Kush. Dionysos was marching to Asia again, and waves of fear swept the land.

Antony chose to enter Parthia, and the neighbouring state of Media, from the north west, concentrating his troops in the (allegedly friendly) kingdom of Armenia.

At this point, it is worth pausing to consider the status of Armenia in the Roman world and international equilibria. Armenia had reached the high point of its power and extension under King Tigranes II the Great, who, starting from a position of inferiority to the Parthians at the turn of the first century BC, had gradually consolidated his position and taken advantage, as we have seen in Chapter 2, of the prolonged weakness of the Seleucids. In the 80s, at the outbreak of the first Mithridatic War, he had also sided with Mithridates, king of Ponthus, against the Romans, albeit without really participating in military terms. When Mithridates escaped to Armenia after his defeat, the Roman general Lucullus demanded his expulsion. Tigranes defiantly refused, wanting to assert his independence, provoking, in return, a blitz attack on Armenian territory, the siege of his capital Tigranekert, and the defeat of his army. When he and Mithridates were able to stage a comeback and inflict on Lucullus a temporary defeat in 68 BC, as we have seen, it was Pompey Magnus' turn to take control of the operation. Pompey dealt with the situation effectively, and when Mithridates VI was finally put out of business, the old King Tigranes was mercifully allowed to retain his crown, although only once a payment of a 6,000 silver talent ransom had been made, and his son delivered as a hostage. Tigranes reigned until his death in 54 BC, just before the Crassus expedition. But the events as narrated explain why the "friendship" of the Armenians was not exactly the most spontaneous or reliable. In fact, the relative independence they had been granted came from Pompey's political design and opportunism rather than trust and confidence.

According to Dio,[12] Antony started the invasion of Media too late, when the Parthians were in a position to defend themselves and he could not count any more on the surprise effect. Allegedly, he was ill advised by the Armenian King Artavasdes, who shared with the king of Media (today's Western Azerbaijan) not only a first name, but also a fierce enmity which dated way back. While Sossius was helping Herod in taking back Palestine, another strong Antonian General, Canidius Crassus (Canidius), had forced Artavasdes into an alliance pact, and, evidently forcibly, into promising to make his cavalry available the day Antony wanted to bring the war to Parthia.

His plan was well thought out, and was the result of military analysis which had begun in the days of Julius Caesar, and was based on the reports by Cassius' survivors, and completed by Antony based on testimonies of the veterans of Ventidus' triumphs. He would also have had access to Labienus' surviving soldiers, captured by Ventidius, who had spent four or five years with the Parthians, and were well versed in local geography and fighting strategies. Given the configuration of the vast, open, desert-like regions that lie west of the Euphrates, the Parthians, strengthened by their superior cavalry, would have had a disproportionate advantage if Antony had followed in Cassius' footsteps. On the other hand, Ventidius had proven that in more mountainous regions the Parthians were easy prey to Roman military tactics. The Romans were not going to give up on stronger cavalry reinforcements, and King Artavasdes of Armenia was going to supply a mounted contingent of 16,000, which, if it had been delivered, would have further levelled the field. Antony could not afford the luxury of waiting for another Parthian expansion initiative westward. Ventidius had barely finished dealing with the noble and beloved Prince Pacorus, leaving the old Orodes shattered by his loss, than another generation of rambunctious leaders was already at the gates, announcing itself with a "night of the long knives" to wipe out the previous one. It was not a good omen for peace on the western front. The times were right to strike before the enemies regained their confidence and resumed their Syrian imperialism.

Antony took the shorter route towards the city of Phraaspes, the Median capital, which he wanted to besiege. He meant to capture it, spend the winter there, and then progress southward into Parthia during the following spring. Per his usual custom he made fast progress into Median territory, carrying important siege equipment to quickly reduce the Median town, while the carriages and pack animals of his supply column were left behind. Then, he also left the siege machines behind, as they would have slowed down his progress towards Phraaspes. This rushed attack was perhaps too ambitious and risky, as it opened Antony's side to an ambush on his baggage train, which Oppius Statianus was leading through the open plains. The baggage train was progressing through the Azerbaijani valleys when it was attacked by Median and Parthian mounted archers, and, not duly protected by cavalry, since the Armenians had not honoured their promise of support, it was totally destroyed. It has been reported that 10,000 Romans and auxiliaries died during the attack, which also cost Antony all of his siege equipment.

This was a major loss for the Antonians. His legionaries, now besieging Phraaspes, deprived of their supplies, had to split their time between fighting on the ramparts, and wandering off into the city to search for alternatives to their lost rations. The siege was dragging on at a slow pace because of the loss of the powerful

Roman siege machines, and they could not build new ones as wood was scarce in the Median high plains. Initially, they were just about able to cope, but disaster loomed because the soldiers had to go looking for food farther and farther from their camp and from the city walls, thus exposing themselves to enemy ambushes, with the Parthian archers picking off the Romans as they put down their shields and weakening the siege ring. Gradually, the weakening of the siege gave rise to the sudden breaks of the Phraaspans outside their walls. In reality, the search for food far from the city wall might have been an expedient to entice the Medians outside the city, and lure them into a fight in the open, as opposed to continuing the series of guerrilla episodes. On one remarkable occasion, a large regiment came out of the wall perimeter but, on being attacked by the Romans, coiled into a defensive semi-circular formation. The Romans, impressing the enemy with their disciplined battle tactics, quickly approached the point where they would be too close for arrows to be used effectively, and then attacked forcefully, but the Parthians withdrew without too much damage, and Antony came to realize that, even on a victorious day like this one, his side had inflicted minimal losses on the enemy, while the death toll after Statianus had reached 10,000 men. The disappointed Romans went back to the siege, and to their main camp. But with time, the besieged were becoming cockier, and were storming out of the city walls more brazenly, attacking the assault ramp that Antony's engineers were building, and terrorizing its defendants. So enraged was Antony on that occasion that he gave the order that the defendants of the ramp be decimated, and for a reduction in the rations of the others, to enforce fighting morale with iron fist discipline. It is one of the few reported episodes in Antony's life where frustration got the better of good leadership skills when managing his men, the other noteworthy one being the killing of the 300 mutineers in Brundusium in 43 BC.

Once again, the Parthians were proving to be a thorn in the side of the Romans, thanks in part to their unquestioned military skills and, even more so, to their capacity for deception, which they had got down to a fine art. Phraates played the deception card to perfection. The psychological pressure on the Romans was strong, as every day their enemies were riding past them, asking them why their stubborn commander would condemn so many brave fighters to certain death and suffering.

As Phraates sensed the frustration and fatigue in the Roman ranks, and aware that many soldiers were reluctant to fight during the impending cold season, he offered a truce, on the condition that the Romans withdraw immediately. Antony was uneasy as he negotiated the terms of the withdrawal with the arrogant Parthian king, who sat proudly on a golden throne while plucking at the string of his bow as if it was a guitar. Eventually he accepted to relieve the siege, not without a sense of guilt towards the 100,000 men who had enthusiastically followed him deep into enemy territory, and decided to head back to Armenia. The Parthian promised that he would give quarter to the retreating Romans all the way to Armenia, but did not yield to the request to return Crassus' silver eagles. Antony was so embarrassed that he did not want to break the news to the soldiers himself, but instead let Domitius Ahenobarbus, who had joined him from Ponthus, do it. The legionaries realized that Antony was not being arrogant or dismissive but that, simply, his pride was hurt, having failed in Rome's most glorious mission ever – the avenging of Crassus, a mission whose ambition would be matched, perhaps, only by Germanicus' punitive expedition after the disaster suffered at Teutoburg, and Trajan's campaign to Parthia.

The sources agree that Phraates never really meant to respect the terms of the truce, and that he had intended all along to prepare ambushes and traps along the 300 miles that divide the town of Phraaspes from the Armenian border.

The withdrawal was to prove a route of epic proportions, which could be compared to Napoleon's Russian retreat.

Antony could have had the opportunity to safely shorten his journey if he had progressed through the wide open plains on the west side of the country, but he would have paid huge home turf advantage to the Parthian mounted archers, and it could potentially have been Carrhae all over again.

Harassment by the enemy included contamination of the water sources, generally obstructing their progress by blocking the routes in one way or another and sudden cavalry raids.

Forced to cross narrow passages, exposed to continued ambushes, harassed by archers while procuring food, delayed in their progress by the sudden appearance of palisades and other obstacles, mislead by treacherous scouts into taking the wrong direction, prevented from refilling their empty canteens with water, the legionaries had to endure enormous hardship. Demoralized as they were, many were beginning to desert. But the Parthians made gruesome displays of the bodies of the deserters they had captured, thus deterring the others from doing the same. The hardened soldiers did not entirely lose spirit, and kept fighting back and inflicting losses, while the mounted Parthian archers still proved too elusive to be forced into a battle at close quarters, where the fury of the Romans could have been put to good use. At the n-th ambush suffered, the hardened Spanish legionaries of the III Legion were hit by a rainstorm of Parthian arrows. The specific training they had been given proved useful, and they braved the volley with their left knee on the ground, locking their large rectangular shields together, and forming the *testudo*, the impenetrable turtle formation, which absorbed the shock of the arrows or let them slide away to the side. Then, the unharmed Romans lay down and pretended to be dead, and the Parthians, duped, approached at close range, dismounted from their horses, unsheathed their cavalry sabres, and prepared to give the legionaries the mercy blow. But when they came within sword range, much to their surprise, they found themselves facing, without a shield for protection, the

25 inch steel blades of the Roman *gladia* held by the furious legionaries. It ended up in carnage, which, while it did not change the outcome of the campaign, at least consoled the Romans and helped them save face and make an honourable retreat. All there was left for Antony to do was to make haste to the north west, back to Armenia, transporting the many wounded and suffering, and rely for logistical support on King Artavasdes, who had proven to be unworthy of trust. Antony, as he progressed towards Armenia, leading, for the second time in his life, a defeated and demoralized army, was probably already planning to punish the Armenians for their lukewarm support, but, for the time being, he had to stay on good terms with them, as he still desperately needed to find temporary sanctuary, as well as whatever logistical help he could get from them, and the promise of shelter for the Romans for the cold and bitter winter months ahead.

Antony had carefully studied the Parthians, and by now had enough data to design a defensive strategy. He certainly treasured Ventidius' experience, and the memory of the mayhem that his Greek slingers had brought upon Pacorus at Cyrretica. It was so that the Roman army kept advancing through Media in a tight formation protected on all four sides by slingers and javelin throwers which kept the Parthians at bay. Also Crassus had tried to escape from Surena's trap in a compact square formation, but it was a hollow square, and without outside protection from the slingers, which probably made the difference. Plutarch's contribution at this point is very important to understand the effectiveness of Antony's strategy, and this we probably owe to him closely following the work of Q. Dellius, which would have focused on the resourcefulness and military ingenuity of the Romans. Dio, on the other hand, more subservient to the official Augustan party line, stresses only the magnitude of the losses, and some occasional episodes of bravery in combat, for sake of the good name of the Roman legions.

When the strategy adopted by Antony was beginning to yield results, and the enemy was suffering more losses than they were inflicting, and were considering abandoning the pursuit, the unpredictable happened. A young and inexperienced Tribune, Fabius Gallus, insisted, with a few cohorts, on pursuing a group of enemy soldiers that had been repelled. In his fervour, Gallus lost contact with the bulk of the army, and soon found himself surrounded by the enemy. When the other Generals realized that Gallus had been separated from the others, and that his men were sitting ducks, they started sending small groups of men to his rescue, who were then cut down immediately by the Parthian archers. This suicidal tactic was a crucial mistake, for which the Romans paid dearly. By the time Antony, who was leading the progress of the army from the front, realized what was happening in the rear, and could about turn and intervene, 3,000 legionaries lay dead, and 5,000 more were badly wounded, and would have needed to be transported, transforming the rest of the trip into an ordeal. Plutarch gives us one of his most lyrical pages on Antony's leadership qualities and how he inspired those enduring the most intense suffering to persevere in the face of asperity:

> "Antony went from tent to tent to visit and comfort the rest of them, and was not able to see his men without tears and a passion of grief. They, however, seized his hand with joyful faces, bidding him go and see to himself and not be concerned with them; they called him *imperator*, and said they were saved if he did well. To be true, never in all these times can history make mention of a general at the head of a more splendid army; whether you consider strength and youth, or patience and sufferance in labour and fatigues; but as for the obedience and affectionate respect they bore their general, and for the unanimous feeling among small and great alike, officers and common soldiers, to prefer his good opinion of them to their very lives and beings, in this part of military excellence, it is not possible that they had been surpassed by the very Roman of old. For this devotion, as I have said before, there were many reasons: the nobility of his birth, his eloquence, his frank and open manners, his liberal and magnificent habits, the familiarity in talking with everybody, and in this time particularly, his kindness in assisting and pitying the sick, joining in all their pains, and furnishing them with all things necessary, so that the sick and wounded were even more eager to serve than those who were whole and strong."

There is an open contradiction, this time between Antony's behaviour as described by Plutarch, who shows him grieving over his dying soldiers, and leading their progress as he tends personally to the wounded, and as represented by Dio.

> "As there were many dying and many unfit for duty, Antony did not want to know any longer of the individual cases, and ordered not to bring him any more news on the subject."

This is clearly at the antipodes of Plutarch's characterization, and we have possibly stumbled on one of the pages of Augustan disinformation which most vilifies Antony's image and where the description of his actions most lacks in credibility. Upon initiating the withdrawal, a Median scout offered to escort the Romans along a safer route, an itinerary which would have offered more opportunity for food and shelter. There has been debate on the origins of this scout, whether he was a local or if he had Italian heritage (maybe a survivor from Crassus' expedition), and to what extent his intervention was material in convincing Antony to take the mountain route. In reality, this scholarly point is irrelevant for the events. The existence and intervention of this scout, whether in good or bad faith, would have been only one more of the one million random variables that Antony had to manage during this perilous campaign, each one carrying a binary outcome in a blind-sighted choice. Antony had made the decision to stay away from the wind beaten plains, and there is no proof that things would have been any better if he had elected to do otherwise.

On his way south he crossed the flatter land between the Lake of Van and the Lake of Urmia, stayed east of Urmia and coasted the Sahand mountain range, heading directly towards today's city of Tabriz in northern Iran. He then planned to cross the Armenian border, marked by the river Shia Chai, in the area where the town of Jukfa is to be found today. The reader should be in no doubt that this was no walk in the park. The Sahand, at its highest point, reaches 3,700 m above sea level, and its rocky volcanic geological composition did not make for comfortable marching conditions at all. The relative proximity to the huge Uria lake (or to the Caspian Sea for that matter) was no guarantee of easy access to water, if the legionaries had to go as far as carrying water in their helmets. The fact is, Antony had to concede the enemy the home turf advantage, and yet he made the best use of his military expertise to limit the damage and the loss of life. If human error had not intervened, with the Gallus episode, which had been beyond his direct control, he would probably have avoided more than half the casualties.

But worse was yet to come. The slaughter of Gallus had reignited Parthian enthusiasm, and Phraates' men were preparing to attack again and take advantage of the fact that the Romans were now truly demoralized, malnourished and fatigued, carrying their wounded through the unfamiliar and inhospitable highlands of Western Azerbajian. The days of the Mutina retreat were back for Antony, with the notable difference that this time the enemies were definitely in his pursuit, and unwilling to let him off the hook, unlike Decimus Brutus and Octavian had been in 43 BC. Also Antony's psychological approach was different: in 43 BC his defeat could have been ascribed in large part to the politics of civil war: this was the outcome of a botched war of aggression, even if the constant risk represented by the Parthians had rendered it necessary.

Just like in the aftermath of Mutina, Antony stopped shaving as a sign of mourning, and stopped styling his hair with his signature curls, the hairstyle that made him so successful with the gentle sex. He traded his *paludamentum*, the red cloak, for a more sober and understated dark one. And, just like after Mutina, Plutarch saves his fondest words of appreciation for Antony, as if during his downturns the pain he experienced served a cathartic function, and redeemed him of the many faults on which most of the biography is centred.

The last stretch of the retreat was the most painful and the most fraught with danger. The starving legionaries, who had run out of grain, had taken to eating roots and grass. The hills of northern Iran had one more snare left, which was that some of these plants turned out to be highly poisonous, causing a dangerous condition known as "ergotism" which Caesar's troops had also suffered from in

Epyrum before Pharsalus. Those that had eaten the venomous plants were racked with excruciating pain and, in many cases, died. As the Armenian border was getting closer, rising panic was spreading through the Roman ranks, which were plagued by disease, and were desperately attempting to stave off the last attacks of the Parthian cavalry, and maybe even narrowly avoiding a last large scale ambush just thanks to Antony's last minute intuition. A desperate Antony, looking out to safety at the horizon, is said to have cried out "Ten Thousand!", re-living the adventure of the Greeks of Clearchus in Xenophont's Anabasis 400 years earlier, who, in a similar episode, were struggling to make it to safety on the shores of the Black Sea. And when the column made it to the river Araxes, which marked the fatidic border, they jumped in its turbulent and cold waters with the same enthusiasm with which the Greeks had run to the shores of Trabzon screaming "Thalassa! Thalassa!" (The Sea! The Sea!).

They were at the end of their ordeal, at least temporarily, and they had made it to a country which offered ample means of sustenance. Many soldiers, who could finally feed themselves properly after weeks of deprivation, fell prey to dysentery.

It is difficult to say to what extent Antony had made some serious errors of judgment in preparing the first Parthian campaign, or to what extent the narratives we have inherited are corrupted by the systematic Augustan misinformation which was disseminated after his death. But it would appear that leaving Oppius Statianus without defence, and thus losing the crucially important logistics chain, was the first and the largest, but not the only mistake made. For example, in the face of an enemy which was well prepared for attack, playing the element of surprise and rushing to the town of Phraaspes without the siege machines was possibly not the best call, and neither was, with hindsight, the season chosen to do so, with an arrival in the early fall making foraging more difficult. Again, this might have been different with the precious baggage. One more time, in a repeat performance of Crassus' experience, the last minute defection of the Armenian king, which had been tantamount to betrayal, depriving Antony of the promised 16,000 cavalry, had been decisive. Antony had to impassively hide his game and act graciously towards the treacherous King Artavasdes, but the time for retribution would soon come, as the traitor and his family would find out.

Even though the loss of life had been huge, the outcome had not been a humiliation. Plutarch, again no doubt educated by Dellius, stresses that the Romans had come out victorious in eighteen engagements with the enemy. Unfortunately, none had been decisive, and every time the Romans had the upper hand, the Parthians were able to avoid a massacre thanks to their horse-enabled mobility, whereas Antony could not keep his momentum going as a result of his scarce cavalry power. Antony had penetrated almost 500 km into enemy territory, if one counts the Armenian border as the beginning of his mission, while of course his soldiers had begun their journey from much further away, some from Syria, and some from Bythinia, crossing the whole of Cappadocia for another 800 km as the crow flies.

The first Parthian campaign closed at the very end of 36 BC, when Octavian had just returned home from Sicily, and Sextus Pompey had just dropped his anchor in the waters of Lesbos in the Aegean Sea.

Antony went to spend the end of the winter on the Mediterranean coast, and it has not been ascertained if he led the whole army with him, or if he left it in Armenia, planning to attack Parthia again in the following spring, and he moved only with a small contingent, maybe one or two cohorts of elite troops.

When the Romans tallied their losses, the total probably came to over 25,000 foot soldiers and 4,000 cavalry, maybe one fourth to one third of the force that had moved into Media. Still, over half of the losses had been caused by disease, malnourishment, poisoning, and fatigue, while the legionary eagles, the symbols of the Roman pride, were still on top of their flag poles, leading the way home.

Plutarch talks about another ordeal: a march which cost 8,000 lives, a very large number considering that no further combat has been recorded. This passage is extremely confusing, and no convincing explanation has been given. If the plan was to attack again in the following spring, why expose his extenuated army to another excruciating journey, only to do it in the opposite sense a few months later, especially since the logistics were guaranteed by the Armenians? Why wouldn't he have chosen to give his battered legionaries a chance to rest properly, tend to their wounds, recover from their fatigue and malnourishment, and repair their equipment? Furthermore, Antony knew already that he would have spent a period of time in Alexandria, and thus he would have left the bulk of the army behind. As a consequence, we could possibly infer that the 8,000 casualties refer to his retreat and they have already been counted in his calculation of total losses, so that Plutarch and his sources might have been confused and counted double.

As one would expect, it is not easy to arrive at an accurate estimate of the total number of dead taking all the historians into account. The number of casualties in Livy seems to coincide with all the other sources if we count the 8,000 that passed away in the harsh weather conditions upon returning to Armenia.

One can try to summarize and make sense of all of the sources as follows: Antony left with eighteen legions (Livy), some of which were at full strength, plus auxiliaries, so maybe he had 90,000 men, plus cavalry. The consensus is he lost 25,000 men, roughly half of which was in two major battles, the attack at Statianus and the baggage train, and the useless sacrifice of Gallus, which gives a total of 15,000 men. The balance of 10,000 plus cavalry died in the war of erosion led by the Parthians, or as a consequence of weather, famine, poisoning, or the wounds suffered.

Once he arrived at the coast, Antony was waiting impatiently for the arrival of Cleopatra, drinking profusely, looking as far as he could to the horizon waiting to see the square purple sail of the Egyptian royal barge approaching. He was, for sure, profoundly distressed: his sorrow at his defeat and the lives lost was compounded with worry at the news, by now fully confirmed, of Octavian's success in Sicily, and the consequent jubilation of Lepidus, and, finally, the recent arrival of Sextus Pompey in the area, as we have seen at the end of the preceding chapter. The official version of Antony's movements, at the time of the end of the first Parthian campaign, echoed by the Augustan historiography, was that he had hastily brought the end of the expedition to a close and had rushed west for the sole purpose of reuniting with Cleopatra, as opposed to regrouping his forces, and giving his distressed army a chance to rest for the winter. Livy is even more explicit:

> "Living a life of pleasure with Cleopatra, Mark Antony invaded Media quite late, and brought war to Parthia with eighteen legions and 16,000 horsemen; having lost two legions and failing to achieve success in any enterprise, he retreated, pursued by Parthians, and after immense confusion and great danger, reached Armenia, having covered in his flight 300 miles in twenty-one days. Because of tempest, he lost 8,000 men. Like the Parthian way that he had undertaken so unluckily, it was his own mistake that he encountered these storms, because he refused to spend the winter in Armenia, but he wanted to hurry to Cleopatra instead."[13]

Cleopatra eventually arrived, bringing supplies and cash, so that a bonus could be paid to the survivors of the botched invasion, to ease their sufferings for a while.

In 35 BC, Antony had scores to settle in the East even if Parthia had proven too difficult a target. The king of Armenia, Artavasdes, deserved punishment, for failing to honour his promise and withdrawing his support at the worst possible time and, moreover, when it was too late to make alternative arrangements. Antony had made a note of that and waited for a good opportunity for payback. But another important development could have changed the following events. The king of Media, Artavasdes, harboured a grudge against the Parthians, as well as against the Armenians. The trigger for his resentment towards Orodes had been over the sharing of the Roman spoils of war but, moreover, he was afraid that Media was going to be progressively squeezed between the two larger and more powerful neighbours. So, he sent Polemon, king of Ponthus, as an ambassador to Antony, to propose an alliance. Of course Antony was thrilled at this offer from a more motivated partner for a successive Parthian campaign, and at the same time he could have acted without the Armenians, and even retaliated against them for their spineless behaviour.

As Antony was preparing to cross the Syrian plains one more time and take the north west road to join up with the king of Media, he learned that his legitimate wife Octavia was travelling eastbound, bringing money, supplies, and some elite cohorts to the tune of 2,000 chosen men, nominally as a bodyguard, but really as more reinforcements for her husband. In reality, the deal Antony had struck with Octavian in Tarentum called for 20,000 men, but with the defiant attitude he had displayed Antony could only expect to be paid back in kind. Octavia's journey to the East can also be read as deliberate provocation from Octavian: he was certain that Antony would reject her, as Cleopatra was in the vicinity, and Antony had his mind set on following her to Alexandria. The rejection could have been a pretext for war. All this was taking place at a time when Antony was weaker politically as well as militarily, whereas Octavian was at the zenith of his career, after the defeat of Sextus Pompey and the ousting of Lepidus. The way things were going in Italy could only have added to Antony's level of discomfort. Octavian had been granted the honour of a golden statue in the Forum, atop a column adorned with the rostra, the ramming heads taken from Sextus Pompey's sunken ships. The Senate had voted the Tribunate for life for him, thus giving him sacred and inviolable status, and beginning the collapse of the principles of the separation of powers which had been the basis of the Republican order in Rome, another prelude to the instauration of the Principate.

As Octavian had expected, Octavia was asked by Antony to remain in Athens, allowing her brother to take full advantage and gain maximum publicity for this public insult. On the contrary, Octavia, demonstrating great political savvy and balance, did her best to placate her brother by proclaiming that the true scandal was not that Antony had snubbed her, but that the two most important men in the Republic were fighting over matters of women and jealousy. Octavia must have been a woman of extraordinary intelligence and sense of duty. Regardless of the propaganda, which deformed Cleopatra's personality traits, Octavia's noble behaviour was genuine, and can be backed up with facts. Instead of sailing back to Rome to play along to Octavian's tune, she remained in Antony's Athenian residence, where she dedicated herself not only to raising her own children from Antony, the two Antoniae sisters, but also the two children he had had from Fulvia. Later, after his death, in a rare example of devotion and piety, she would do the same with his children from Cleopatra. Chances are she would have also taken Cesarion under her maternal wing, if Octavian had not seen differently for his future. There is no doubt that such a noble and altruistic character deserved better. But there was more to her than her maternal instinct: even after her implicit repudiation, she continued to promote Antony's cause with her brother, and she stayed open for all Antonian family business, which involved maintaining contacts with the clientele that revolved around their household in Athens, just as if Antony had been there. Antony's body language was unmistakable, and so must have been his intention to burn all the bridges as he progressed in the realization of his political project. Still, it must have been difficult for Antony to part ways with Octavia. It has been shown that he knew the meaning of the word "gratitude", and his third wife certainly inspired his respect and admiration, for sure, albeit in a different way from the passionate Fulvia or the sophisticated Cleopatra, but certainly to the same level nevertheless. She had embraced his political cause, and had represented his interest effectively for over three years. She had smoothed over some hairy diplomatic situations, and shown great maturity and aplomb in dealing with the embarrassing lingering presence of Cleopatra in the background. She had given him two daughters, and we have to believe that, before "that mule" started kicking again, their union must have been happy and fulfilling. In the end, her presence was incompatible with Antony's project for the Greek Orient, a project that was hinged on Egypt as the motherland to govern effectively over that turbulent part of the world, which, as we have shown, for over 250 years had not found a stable political configuration, and which, in the Triumvir's view, could not have become a part of the Roman world without strong, decentralized control.

Octavia, being a woman of such undeniable virtues, where visible moral values met the charms of a refined and beautiful Roman matron, was a formidable competitor for Cleopatra. She also knew how to handle the situation with great style, probably exasperating Cleopatra, who reportedly was becoming prone to fits of jealousy and was throwing formidable tantrums at Antony. Perhaps Plutarch exaggerates her outbursts a little when he describes the 33-year-old queen acting like an adolescent. Here is Plutarch:

> "She feigned to be dying for love of Antony, bringing her body down by slender diet. When he entered the room, she fixed her eyes upon him in a rapture, and when he left, seemed to languish and half faint away. She took great pains that he should see her in tears, and, as soon as he noticed them, hastily dried them up and turned away, as if it were her wish that he should know nothing of it. All this was acted as he prepared for Media; and Cleopatra's creatures were not slow to forward the design, upbraiding Antony with his unfeeling, hard-hearted temper, letting a woman perish, whose soul depended on him and him alone."[14]

The image of Antony's struggling to contain and control Cleopatra's frequent and uncontrolled outbreaks of anger has become commonplace.

Of course, the ménage between the two must have been complex, with the queen cornered in an illicit relationship competing with a formal one, first with Fulvia and then with Octavia as a counterpart. Some concessions for the sake of peace keeping must have been made. Still, the portrayal of Antony that has him neglecting or mismanaging State affairs because he was blinded by his passion for Cleopatra, or extending huge and undeserved benefits to the Egyptian crown to appease her jealousy and her explosions of fury, is probably in large part an exaggeration, if not a total fabrication. As a counter argument, suffice to say that Antony did not see her in person for the entire time between his first departure from Alexandria in 40 BC, and the return from Parthia: a total of over three and a half years. This period does not suggest that Antony was on a short leash; on the contrary it proves that his dedication to State interests was first and foremost on his list of priorities, which included, in order, the solution to the Sextus Pompey issue, the reorganization of the Asian provinces, and the marriage to Octavia, which he hoped could have cemented the new world order.

In any case, whether it was because of the arrival of Octavia, or the pressure from Cleopatra, or maybe even because of his desire to prepare the new campaign as painstakingly as possible, Antony decided to revise his plans and postpone his second Parthian campaign from 35 BC to the following spring–summer of 34 BC. In all likelihood, this was a bad idea and a lost opportunity, as the end of 35 BC coincided with one of those frequent periods of weakness of the Parthian empire due to intestine fighting, which could have been better exploited by opportune timing. This crisis could have been related to the falling out with the Medians.

In the unlikely event that Antony was getting bored during the pause between the two wars on the eastern border, excitement arrived in the form of Sextus Pompey in the Aegean Sea. When he had escaped from Sicily, he had the firm intention of surrendering to Antony, thus becoming a political refugee, in the name of their history of reciprocal respect and tacit alliances. At best, Sextus could hope to be associated with Antony's fortunes as a subordinate partner, maybe contributing his naval warfare expertise to the partnership. But when he heard of Antony's downturn, he saw an opportunity to make his big comeback at Antony's expense.

At the beginning of 35 BC, as Antony was following Cleopatra to Alexandria, he sent envoys to King Phraates offering his willingness to cooperate with him, and also started probing other eastern kings, testing their interest in pursuing an alternate project to Antony's rule. He then sent his ambassadors to Antony, with a message which, in Appian's reconstruction, sounded like this:

"He (Sextus) prefers to join you in keeping the peace, and to fight under you, should that be necessary. This is not the first time he has made the offer. He made it while he still controlled Sicily and plundered Italy, at the time when he saved your mother's life and sent her to you. If you had accepted it, he would not have lost Sicily, nor would you have been defeated in the Parthian war... and you would now be Master of Italy, as well as the territories you then possessed. But although you failed to accept the offer... he now begs you not to be ensnared again and again by Octavian's words and by the family ties you have contracted with him, and remember that Octavian went to war with Sextus without any pretext, and in spite of having a treaty and family ties with him... You are now the only remaining obstacle to Octavian's acquisition of the sole power he so much desires."[15]

It would have been a magnificent speech, and all the fine political points were perfectly taken into account, in a brilliant political analysis, confirming many of the widespread suspicions which we have discussed in the course of Chapter 6. Unfortunately for Sextus, Antony's men had intercepted his envoys to Phraates, so that he was perfectly aware of his duplicity in the circumstance. Still, the ambassadors to Alexandria insisted on defending their master, pleading that the Parthian discussions were a hedge if Antony had not believed Sextus. In the end, surprisingly, Antony believed them, or pretended to believe them, maybe because, as Appian puts it,

"in every sphere of behaviour his character was straightforward, generous, and innocent."

This echoes words we have already heard from Plutarch, who maybe would have chosen words such as "prone to adulation", "naive", and "gullible". Whatever set of adjectives the reader chooses to endorse, Sextus had managed to buy himself some time, which he used to organize a landing in Asia, outsmart Governor Furnius' plot to overthrow him, enlist some retired veterans to fight for him, and attempt to seize the town of Cyzicus. The local garrison, stationed there to guard a gladiator training camp, reacted strongly and forced him to retire. But Sextus managed to bounce back, defeated Furnius, and started finding recruiting grounds with the Asian provincials, impoverished by the taxes Antony had levied, who would gladly fight for him as mercenaries. For a short period his fortunes rose, as he refilled his coffers by raiding the towns of Nicaea and Nicomedia. But the reinforcements sent by Antony kept arriving by sea, to the point where Sextus found himself facing a force much larger, and possibly better trained and armed, than the one he had managed to assemble. In the effort of concentrating all his fighters in one stronger land unit, Sextus burnt all his ships and armed the oarsmen, ready to give battle on land. By then, the best and brightest of his staff had understood that he did not stand a chance against the regular Roman troops, and, after having tried to dissuade him from continuing the fight, they negotiated their own peace terms with their opponents. Abandoned by most of his men, Sextus hastened through Bythinia towards Ponthus, planning eventually to escape to Armenia and possibly to Parthia, following in young Labienus' footprints. As desperate as he was, he even managed to inflict a defeat on his pursuers, Furnius, Titius, and the Galatian ally, King Aminthias, with a daring night attack. In the end though, when he understood that all was lost, he had to surrender. Officially, Antony had put Titius in command of the pursuit operations, but Sextus was very picky in his terms for surrender, and he would hand his sword only to the more distinguished Furnius, Titius being a B-list personality. When Furnius declined, respecting military procedure, Sextus spitefully preferred to deliver himself to

King Amyntas, choosing the anathema of surrender to a non-Roman than to a Roman of lesser distinction. When Titius received the order to put him to death, he must have done it with no regrets, mindful of the insult suffered.

Antony had transmitted his orders to Titius in this sense. But then, as was often the case with Antony, once he calmed down he reconsidered, maybe on account of their former friendship, or maybe just out of compassion, or maybe even because he thought that the name of Pompey could be useful for his cause. So, he wrote a second letter, telling his men to stay the execution. Unfortunately for Sextus, the postal service in those days was not entirely reliable, and the second letter arrived first, so that when the death warrant was received, Titius thought that it was the final word from Antony, and carried out the order.

When that axe fell, it marked the end of the distinguished line of the Pompeys, with its most turbulent representative. For all his shortcomings, and his lack of vision and charisma, which had confined him to the role of a nuisance more than an effective threat to the new order, during the days of the proscriptions he had managed to endear to himself such a large part of the population that when Titius showed up at the Circus in Rome, he was confronted by an angry mob and had to flee.

When in 34 BC the spring finally came, Antony could resume his focus on war. He had spent yet another winter in Alexandria, thus attracting Octavian's growing wrath, and one more time Cleopatra escorted him to Syria, and supposedly to the beginning of a new adventure. He was due to serve as Consul for that year, but this would have necessitated his presence in Rome, and therefore he decided not to serve. It was so that he resigned in favour of the hitherto unknown Afratinus. Octavian had also been gone from Rome for some time, first subjugating some rebellious tribes in Dalmatia, and then driving through Austria into the plains of Hungary to subdue the Pannonians. During both of these conflicts, he had clearly proved that he was developing great resolve and an iron fist, with enemies and his soldiers alike, maybe to show Rome that he was no longer the greenhorn who had to be carried around in a litter in Philippi, leaving the fighting to Antony. He had grown and matured, and his innate sense of politics and demagogy had blossomed. Not only had he repressed brigandage in Italy, but he had also made the spectacular promise to lay down all his powers upon Antony's return from Parthia – a promise which had won him the title of Tribune of the Plebs for life. One more major threshold on the way to totalitarian rule had been crossed: the separation of powers in Rome was beginning to crumble.

The second Parthian campaign, in reality, was to be only a punitive expedition against the traitor Artavasdes, whom Antony certainly held as partly responsible for the loss of over 25,000 Roman lives, as well as his political image and primacy in Rome. Under the pretext of preparing his second Parthian invasion, Anthony entered Armenia in the spring of 34 BC, accompanied by his 10-year-old son Anthillus.

He deceived the Armenian king with the offer of marrying his son Alexander Helios to an Armenian princess, and, to make the ruse more believable, he sent Dellius ahead to start the discussions. Upon his arrival, he lured Artavasdes into his camp, pretending to invite him to discuss the details of the betrothal. But then, once within his control, he had him arrested with his wife and children, and he sent them to Cleopatra in chains. When he paraded them in the streets of Alexandria, the restraints used were made of pure gold. Artaxes, his son, made a feeble attempt at resistance, but he was quickly overwhelmed by Canidius. From then onwards, Armenia was to remain only nominally a vassal state, headed by a puppet king from the Artavasdes family, but in reality it was operated as a province for all practical purposes. For centuries to come, the status of Armenia, an unwilling buffer between Rome and its Eastern foes, would remain as a question mark on the map of the Roman world. Antony was to be blamed for the deterioration in the relationship with the Armenians, but in reality he had inherited a situation which had been strained since the days of Lucullus and Pompey. Nevertheless, the abduction and execution of Artavasdes was to be considered by the historians as an act of treachery as opposed to retaliation for what had been suffered by Crassus and himself as a result of Armenian disloyalty. The annexation of Armenia, more or less formalized as it was, gave Antony more bargaining chips to secure the support of the Medians, and a piece of the kingdom went as a bounty to the faithful Polemon of Ponthus, who had facilitated the capture. The Median alliance, which was to be further secured by the marriage between Alexander Helios and a Median royal princess, was a smart idea: unfortunately, once Antony moved to war with Octavian, and withdrew his troops, the Parthians were quick to attack and subdue their neighbours once more.

As for the triumph itself, which was considered a huge scandal per se, Antony did not mean to depart from the most cherished of Rome's traditions. Nor had he wanted to check the box for himself and award himself an honour he had not enjoyed in a lifetime of military achievement. The procession must have had a dionysian twist, and probably ended in front of a glamorous platform supporting Isis-Cleopatra instead of Iuppiter Capitoline. It was therefore a piece of that carefully constructed puzzle of elements that would have given him more legitimacy in Egypt. For sure, the Alexandrians would not have had any appreciation for a Roman tradition. On the contrary, they would have thrived at the sight of the dionysiac warrior parading in their street like a victorious Pharaoh, reviving their glorious and not forgotten days under the early Ptolemies, and adding to the cult of their worshipped Queen Isis. The intention could not have been further from a Roman carnival, but it was meant to be framed in Antony's Egyptian politics and propaganda, on which we shall elaborate at the beginning of the next chapter.

Chapter Eight

The End of the New Dionysos

"Take but good note, and you shall see in him
The triple pillar of the world transform'd
Into a strumpet's fool, behold and see"
Shakespeare, Antony and Cleopatra, Act I, Scene 1

This is in essence the theorem of Augustan propaganda as expressed in the verses of the Bard, and in the strict Plutarch tradition. One of the three men in charge of the destinies of the world had become putty in the hands of an evil and manipulative foreign queen, and was now acting against Rome's interests. Perhaps the worst thing about this image which had been projected to his contemporaries is that Antony had fallen deliberately and knowingly into this trap which had been laid with insane passion and lust, and he does himself make the following comment about her:

"She is cunning past man's thought."

So he partially acknowledged that he had been seduced by the charms of the Egyptian *famme fatale*, who specialized in playing mind games.

Before we focus more closely on the final Alexandrian period of Antony's life, it will be beneficial to provide some historical context regarding the kingdom of Egypt under the Ptolemies, to better understand the background of Cleopatra VII and the scenario in which our Triumvir was projected into a quasi-monarchical role. Context is also important to understand how Antony adapted to Egypt, and how his assimilation into that society led to his decline in popularity at home, and created the hook on which Octavian was to hang his systematic slander campaign.

Ptolemy I Soter (the Saviour), the founder of the dynasty, had played a major role in the struggle that originated in the succession of Alexander the Great, and that continued for several decades. He had been the most important side of the triangle with Antigonos and Seleukos, the first to secure his borders, and to make some very important annexations to Egypt in the Eastern Mediterranean, extending his area of control all the way to the coastal part of Syria and the Phoenician cities.

At the climax of its initial geographic expansion, which was thanks to the victorious campaigns of his second successor Ptolemy III Euergetes (the

Benefactor), the Ptolemaic Empire controlled a fair portion of the Mediterranean coast, and ephemerally reached as far as northern Syria and even into Mesopotamia. The governance models realized by the two main Hellenistic empires, the Seleucid and the Ptolemaic, were essentially very similar in nature, and consisted of the superposition of a layer of Greek nobles and courtesans in central administrative roles, over the legacy structure inherited from the previous rulers. The Ptolemies had a remarkable advantage over the other Hellenistic kingdoms in terms of risk avoidance and self preservation, due to the fact that the kingdom of the Nile was much more centric in nature, and all of the land belonged to the crown, with minimal delegation of power to the periphery. This system was almost diametrically opposed to the model of the Persian satrapies, which were highly decentralized and were the norm in Syria and elsewhere. The rule of Egyptian satellite dominions was largely decoupled from the chain of command of the local military garrisons, which responded directly to the king, thus discouraging any centrifugal movements.

Initially striving to gain hegemony at sea after enduring a tough defeat at the hands of Demetrios Polyorketes in a naval battle, Ptolemy I and his early successors had to revise their imperialistic designs on the occupation of some coastal areas in the Mediterranean, which probably served more as a buffer between Egypt and the Seleucids.

The Ptolemies went to great lengths, in terms of their programme and propaganda, to follow in the footprints of Alexander the Great, and adhere formally to the basic principle of the divinity of the Pharaoh, an incarnation of Horus. Horus was the son of the sun God Amun-Ra, and recognized as such by the Gods, as demonstrated by his sacred right to sacrifice to them. Alexander had himself adopted Old Kingdom ceremonial rites and reinstated the old capital of Memphis as the main hub for the cult.

Alexander had also ended ten years of detested Persian rule, and positioned himself as the creator of rule and order from the chaos. The Oracle of Siwah, already, for 200 years, a place for syncretistic worship, had facilitated the linkage of the king to his divine ascendants. Accordingly, the political and social success of the early Ptolemies was due to their leverage with this religious connection and their nationalistic propaganda, which exploited anti–Persian feeling to unite the nation behind imperialistic and anti–Seleucid goals, and which enabled them to impose an economic policy to fund the war, always a subject of actuality with their eastern neighbour superpowers.

The traditional religious cult was soon identified as the means to endear intellectuals to the cause, since the intellectuals also happened to be the top layers of the clergy, and lavish donations were made to the temples and the traditional priesthood.

The embodiment of the religious principles, the application of the traditional Pharaoh's prerogatives, and the Macedonian kingship style introduced by Alexander, together contributed to shape the Ptolemaic brand of sovereignty. While the Ptolemies were not shy in the display of God-like luxury, they nevertheless demonstrated a certain level of social empathy that was hitherto unknown to their subjects, and was more in line with their expectations and needs, such as granting favours and bringing social justice, than was the norm with the traditional stiff and hieratic pharaonic rule.

We have already remarked how the dionysiac character of their religious propaganda started very early in their 290 year reign. The Greeks, on more than one occasion, had bought into the tradition of paying religious honours to the Ptolemies. The first three kings of the dynasties had altars and worship dedicated to them in Rhodes, Byzanthium, and Athens respectively, for the merits they had earned through military support. The dionysiac cult became especially visible under Ptolemy IV, who wanted to be referred to as New Dionysos, and who formally introduced a religious programme for the God's worship, while simultaneously trying to regulate those aspects of the cult that appeared to be too controversial and potentially dangerous.

Over time, all the religious propaganda efforts took the form of a real dynastic cult, which became increasingly focused on the reigning king and queen, who were frequently brother and sister, as the objects of divine worship. It was so that the cults of individual Ptolemies began to proliferate around Egypt, in a way that was unknown under all previous Egyptian dynasties. Just like Alexander had played the Siwah Oracle card to establish his divinity, the Ptolemies had to draw the Greeks and the Egyptians under their sceptre in one shared faith. The religious ideology outlined below is key to understanding the symbolism that Antony and Cleopatra had to adopt in their union.

The construction originated from the Serapeion, the Egyptian Pantheon in Memphis, seat of the cult, among others, of the Apis Bull, that later was the object of a theologically complex transmutation into a new divinity Apis-Osiris, also known as Sarapis. The Greeks in Egypt were quick to give this new God, which reunited characters of fertility and ruler over the Underworld, a dionysiac spin. As Sarapis / Osiris / Dionysos became identified with the king, by extension the Goddess Isis was identified in the reigning queen. The newly built Serapeum in the capital city of Alexandria became the centre for this new and powerful cult, which spread out across the Empire. So, to sum it all up, the mystical aura had spread out from Alexander (son of Zeus, Dionysos the Conqueror of Asia), to embrace all the Ptolemaic kings (Horus, sons of Amun–Ra), and eventually to cover the reigning couple (Osyris / Dionysos king and Isis his queen). But there is plenty of evidence that the Dionysos / Osiris identification was a lot older than the Ptolemaic period, and some evidence even points to mythical Egyptian origins for the God. Already, in the fifth century BC, the historian Herodotus leaves us in no doubt:

> "Osiris is he who is called Dionysos in the Greek tongue."[1]

And more:

> "For no Gods are worshipped by all Egyptians in common except Isis and Osiris, who they say is Dionysos; these are worshipped by all alike."[2]

And by the time we get to the period of our narrative, any remaining doubts have also been dispelled in the Greco-Roman world, as Diodorus Siculus affirms:

> "There is only the difference in names between the festivals of Bacchus and those of Osiris, between the Mysteries of Isis and those of Demeter."[3]

Plutarch himself wrote:

> "It is proper to identify Osiris with Dionysos."[4]

The list of commentators on this subject is, of course, longer still. So when a warrior who had already been saluted as the neos Dionysos in Greece made his appearance in Alexandria at the side of the reigning queen, nobody in the Mediterranean area, Rome included, could have conceived of another possible reaction than an immediate identification with Osiris, court ceremonial aside.

It is very much apparent, therefore, that Antonian propaganda revolving around the Osiris / Dionysos identification had, by necessity, to be powerful and very visible, but it was also perfectly logical and inevitable in the eyes of the Egyptian subjects as much as everyone else in the Greco-Roman world. If this had been the purpose, the association could not have been better suited for a programme of expansion and renewed imperialism in the East, thereby following in the footsteps of the early Ptolemies, as we shall briefly see: a God of conquest, a God of vengeance against his enemies, and a God that brings civilization and culture to the conquered populations.

If we briefly return to the developments of the Ptolemaic Empire, the expansionist policies of the first three Ptolemies came to a stop during the reign of the fourth, in a period dominated by court intrigue, powerful cunning chamberlains, and fighting over Syria and Asia Minor against the Seleucid kings, with alternate outcomes and fraught diplomacy. The partial successes of Ptolemy IV (self-appointed neos Dionysos himself) in the Syrian wars hid his weak and dissolute nature, and the progressive weakening of the State that was a prelude to the decline under his successor Ptolemy V. The period covering the first two decades of the second century BC saw the crisis of the empire accentuating, and marked a weakening of the reigning dynasty at a critical time. The triangle Ptolemies / Seleucids / Macedonians, which used to have the monopoly of power in the Eastern Mediterranean, had to make room for the growing importance and influence of Rome, which the Egyptians tried to leverage to secure their independence. Despite a political marriage between the young Ptolemy V and the Seleucid princess Cleopatra I, the trend for territorial losses for the Egyptian crown continued inexorably. The climax was reached under another child king, Ptolemy VI, when the inept court eunuchs acting as regents were crushed by the Seleucid King Antioch IV, who *de facto* at one point had Egypt under his thumb. It was then that Rome stepped onto the scene, as the Senate was growing weary of the increasing force of Antiochus' imperialism. A Roman ambassador, Popilius Laenas, intimated that the Syrian king should quit Egypt. It was sufficient for Laenas to draw a circle around Antiochus and warn him not to cross the line in the sand prior to committing to leave Egypt, to obtain his immediate withdrawal without military conflict, as the king was aware that the Roman legions were from a different mould from the Egyptian *oplites*. It was the year 168 BC.

Laenas, besides originating the popular expression of "the line in the sand" which is still in wide use, had created a bond of gratitude between the kingdom of the Nile and the Republic. The Egyptians acknowledged the military superiority of the Romans and progressed down the path of vassalage. The habit of resorting to the Senate to seek guidance and arbitration on succession matters, which we have seen taking place at the time of Ptolemy XII, had already begun shortly after the time of the events just exposed, when the two sibling rulers Ptolemy VI and Ptolemy VIII struggled for absolute and sole rule. On other occasions, Rome chose not to intervene directly, such as during the cruel Civil War that later saw Ptolemy VIII on the opposite side to his wife Cleopatra II, and the king chose to murder their first son to destabilize his spouse. After a brief period of prevalence by Cleopatra II, establishing the first precedent of feminine rule under the Ptolemies, the husband succeeded. The two were eventually reconciled and reverted to joint reign. The antagonism within the members of the dynasty was to continue, as their daughter Cleopatra III ousted her older brother Ptolemy IX, and placed her younger brother, Ptolemy X, on the throne and herself as co-regent.

Even from this oversimplified narration it is clear which DNA the first-century Ptolemies had inherited from their fathers, men and women alike, and which ruthless power culture prevailed at the Alexandrian court. They gave no hint of changing their ways over time either, Ptolemy X having his domineering mother killed after a falling out, much like Emperor Nero had his mother Agrippinilla, to whom he owed the adoption by Claudius and the subsequent elevation to the purple, killed 160 years later.

The Mithridatic wars in the 80s brought Egypt and Rome one more step closer. Ptolemy IX, back on the throne after his brother's death, bet on the right horse during those turbulent times, which otherwise might have easily seen Rome kicked out of the Eastern provinces, and renewed his loyalty to Sulla and Lucullus. At the same time, the Romans rescued the young Prince Ptolemy XI, held hostage by the Ponthic king. So Sulla was probably delighted when he got to enthrone the young prince, and marry him to his stepmother Cleopatra Berenice III. Hard to say if he was surprised at all, as he knew the Alexandrian ways well, when the young man had her assassinated so he could enjoy his reign alone. He did not enjoy it for long however, as the furious Egyptians, who loved the queen, immediately stormed the royal palace and lynched the young monarch.

We have now arrived at the period of time which is relevant to the life and times of Mark Antony, and which begins with the accession to the throne of Ptolemy XII Auletes, himself dubbed "Neos Dionysos" like some of his predecessors. The young king married his sister Cleopatra VI, in accordance with the tradition aimed at keeping other noble families away from the crown, and their first born was Berenice, the rebellious princess we met in Chapter 2. Since Sulla's days, the Roman view of Egypt had substantially evolved, and the annexation of the kingdom of the Nile as a province had been the subject of open debate for twenty years. This prompted Ptolemy XII to do his best to stay ahead of the game and always have on his payroll a substantial number of *optimates* opinion leaders, who would oppose the Roman expansionistic ambitions that would be to his detriment. Every ounce of gold that would cross the Mediterranean would prolong by one day or one week the dominance of the Ptolemies on the banks of the Nile. As we have briefly discussed earlier, bribes took a heavy toll on State finances, and made tough taxation necessary for Auletes to refill his coffers, so that a string of strikes, seditions, and open rebellions quickly followed. In the minds of the volatile and passionate Alexandrians, the Romans became the object of real hatred, as they were rightly identified as the beneficiaries of their tax proceeds, and the source of the threats of annexation and loss of independence. We have seen how Julius Caesar had to endure tough times because of this perception, and how quickly the Egyptians became inflamed against him.

When the First Triumvirate took control, the Egyptian agenda was managed even more decisively. During his Consulship, Caesar passed a law that sealed the final endorsement of Ptolemy XII as king, against the pledge for a huge sum of money to be paid to the Republic, as opposed to the pockets of influential senators. The Pharaoh was saluted as *amicus et socius Populi Romani*, friend and ally of the Roman people. But the deal Ptolemy XII obtained entailed his surrender of Cyprus, up until then a satellite kingdom of Egypt. Clodius, the Tribune, passed a law for its annexation to Rome, and the law was enforced by another first-tier player whose acquaintance the reader has already made, Cato the Younger. He and his nephew Brutus occupied the island, after the suicide in protest of its king. But the loss of the birthplace of Venus was too much for the Alexandrians, and Auletes had to flee to Rome in haste to avoid unpleasant personal consequences, where he appealed for the help of Pompey and the Senate. The ensuing events have already been covered, including the pivotal role played by Antony to put the king back on his throne.

By now, Roman involvement in Egypt was so deep that, in order to secure the payment of the sums promised to Rome, the Romans had to send the banker Rabirius Postumus. This businessman, who was closely connected to Crassus, was one of the financiers who had more skin in the game of Ptolemy XII's debt. Rabirius applied himself to the task so diligently that he had to be placed under special protection to save him from lynching at the hands of the locals. Later, upon his return to Rome, following a well consolidated tradition, he was tried for concussion, again a strong testament to his application and zeal in collecting from the Egyptians. The reader will not be surprised to learn that when his case was heard in front of the magistrates, he was defended by Cicero!

It was in 51 BC that Ptolemy XII, the last real Pharaoh of Egypt, died, leaving Cleopatra VII, by then 18 years old, as regent, to marry and reign jointly with the younger brother Ptolemy XIII. Her next husband, Marc Antony, was on his way back from Gaul, about to start serving as Augur and Tribune in Rome. Two years later, the shores of Alexandria saw the successive arrival of Pompey Magnus and Julius Caesar, as we have seen.

This historical digression has served the purpose of illustrating why Antony needed to make a clean break with the traditional image of the Romans in Egypt, and what he was to accomplish with the adoption of the dionysiac cliché as a part of his political design. As we shall see, this in turn would leave him open to heavy criticism in Rome, and to the eventual loss of consensus that would determine his final political decline, and consequent defeat. We will now return to our mainstream narration.

After the completion of the submission of Armenia, Antony, instead of following immediately with the invasion of Parthia, returned to Alexandria. The capture of Armenia did not, by any means, represent headline news for the Romans. Many still associated this country with the campaigns of Lucullus and Pompey, and, at the very best, what Antony had done could be considered a police operation, or an act of retaliation against an unfaithful subject king, but it did not give him the prestige of a foreign conqueror.

On the contrary, the general public in Rome was becoming increasingly influenced by the slander campaign conducted by Octavian, and progressively began taking its distance from Antony. Certainly, the treatment he had reserved for the noble and deserving Octavia had been there for all to see, and must have alienated from him the sympathies of more than one of his fellow citizens. Octavian was watching him closely, and was unforgiving in directing the attentions of the Roman citizens to whatever he did that could have been construed as an act of treason of the moral principles of the *Romanitas*, for lack of any deed that could have actually harmed the interests of the Republic. Certainly, when the Romans learned that Antony had celebrated a self-attributed triumph at the beginning of 33 BC in the streets of Alexandria, celebrating the conquest of Armenia, they must have been slack-jawed with disbelief. But other facts must also have compounded his problems and cost him the goodwill which he had previously enjoyed at home.

The marriage he had celebrated with Cleopatra, following the traditional Egyptian ceremonial, in 36 BC had been widely publicized. He was not ashamed of it: on the contrary, he openly admitted it, and even discussed it in his correspondence with Octavian, and certainly with the Senate too. This correspondence is lost to us, but it must have been widely accessible to the public, and Suetonius has left us ample excerpts. Antony was very aloof and matter-of-fact on the subject. It was his personal business, and it was the way he had decided he would run that part of the Roman world which had been entrusted to him by decision of the Triumvirate and the Senate. The marriage to Cleopatra was an important piece of his political design, as was integrating his view of his mandate as a Triumvir of the Republic. There has been debate over the date of this wedding. It has been suggested that it took place before the departure to Parthia, as the union might have been needed by Antony to raise finances for the war. Technically, that would have made him bigamous under Roman law, which did not allow polygamy, but the Hellenistic world tended to be more flexible on this subject matter.

Of course, there were very visible signs suggesting that he was in the process of founding an actual dynasty which would rule over the Roman East, in the name of Rome, but perhaps in a way which would better adapt to local customs and traditions. These intentions have already been partly discussed in Chapter 6. The years of the Alexandrine war were still too fresh in the memories of the Egyptians, and they would not have accepted Roman governance, which they associated with corruption and heavy taxation imposed by military strength, had it not come under the heavy disguise of local customs and shrouded with a veil of local sanctity. A cooperative Egypt would not exist in the Roman world without the *fumus* of a Ptolemaic restoration, and there would be no Roman Orient without Egypt, at least in the model that Antony had conceived. It was with this in mind that Mark Antony decided to play with the local deck of cards, and adopted the formal local ceremonial, inclusive of the Osiris-Dionysos syncretism, and of the mystical marriage to Cleopatra-Isis.

One of the key features of the Antonian vision was to embed in the Roman system a number of shrewd administrators of local or Greek heritage, who, thanks to a deep understanding of the specific situation, could have done a better job than short term Roman assignees, who, with their scarce knowledge of the local language and culture, would have had a hard time extracting money from the provincials. Antony's representatives made sure that his policies were followed, with maximum respect possible for local autonomy and empowerment. His decentralized superintendents were tied to the Roman world by the granting of citizenship, which at times raised an eyebrow in Rome. They, in return, would be renamed in deference to a project which signified loyalty and vassalage, but also adherence to the resuscitation of a vision to which the whole Greek Orient could proudly relate: that of Alexander the Great. As a youngster, Antony had witnessed first hand how the Republican provincial government system was intrinsically corrupt. Career politicians were peddling for a Proconsulate, moving to a distant foreign land with a court of administrative staff that had no further aim than to enrich itself for a period of one, or maybe two, years and then move on to the next land of pillage. It was bad enough for Sicily, Gaul, Spain. But in the cultural melting pot of the middle east, in the galaxy of the Hellenistic world, in the heterogeneous and complex world created by the disaggregation of the Persian Empire, by the meteoric passage of Alexander, by the 200 year struggle of the Ptolomies, the Seleucids, the Jewish dynasties, and the myriad of other attempts to build microcosms, it was out right impossible. When Antony, after Philippi, took over the task of reconstructing and integrating the East, he knew that he had to build something with much deeper foundations, well anchored in the ethnic, religious, and linguistic diversity of the world which lay east of the town of Scodra, where his responsibility began. He had probably made his plan and his rationale plenty clear to the Senate and the people of Rome, so that the misrepresentation of his political plan as a megalomaniac dream of Asian conquest was a masterpiece of deceit and bad faith. Nobody could have faked surprise and scandal in front of a formally communicated programme. Here is Cassius Dio on the topic:

"Furthermore, he did not make these declarations in Alexandria alone, but he communicated them in Rome, so that they would be confirmed by the Roman people."

Octavian would try to put a negative spin on events, but the Senate was neither blind to them, nor, for that matter, shocked or contrary. Nevertheless, the disinformation on what was being accomplished managed to find fertile grounds to spread its roots in Rome. The granting of Roman citizenship, which Antony had operated, was demonized, the reorganization of the provinces depicted as extravagant gifts, the plans for the Parthian borders branded with megalomaniac insanity, and later derided for the military fiasco.

In another spectacular display of his intentions, in the presence of a huge crowd reunited in the Gymnasium of Alexandria, Antony had placed in the arena two golden thrones for Cleopatra and himself, and, slightly below, three more thrones, to accommodate the twins Alexander Helios and Cleopatra Selene, plus Ptolemy Philadelphos, the baby that Antony and Cleopatra had had in 36 BC. Cleopatra had been called "Queen of Kings", with maybe some vague imperialistic hints, just like Ptolemy XV Cesarion, already associated to the crown of Egypt for many years, was dubbed "King of Kings". Caesar's unofficial son retained, with his mother, direct control over the land of the Nile, Cyprus, and Caelesyria. As for his half brother, Ptolemy Philadelphos, according to Dio, he was to receive Syria all the way to the Euphrates, while Cleopatra Selene would be queen of Libya and Cyrenaica, and Alexander Helios of Armenia and the lands beyond the Euphrates, which, in reality, had not been quite conquered yet. The young boy had been dressed as a Median king, wearing on his head the tiara, and the tall miter, as Antony had promised him in marriage to the Median princess Iotape, obtaining thereby the return of the eagles which Oppius Statianus had lost during the assault on the baggage train. On the same occasion, Cesarion was dressed as a Macedonian king, with a mantle and a wide rim hat, surmounted by a diadem. The two children, after hugging Cleopatra and Antony, were assigned bodyguards dressed to match their ceremonial attires.[5]

This apparently complex manoeuvre of assigning the Asian territories to children and adolescents, and calling his and Caesar's progeny kings and queens, was not just a display of arrogance or a PR stunt to impress the Egyptians. It was laying the foundations for a long lasting political vision of stability and peace, in line with a pan-Asian vision which might have resembled that of Alexander. Realizing this vision was not far fetched: if the Parthian threat could have been eradicated, nothing could have kept Antony from his visionary dream.

It is now clear why, upon his return to Egypt after the conquest of Armenia, Antony had no choice but to impose Roman control as a logical sequel of the best and most glorious pages of the Ptolomaic reign, including the dionysiac identification. All the earlier honours paid to him as a Dionysos incarnate could now be reutilized in accordance with local interpretation, and come to full fruition. If a Hollywood screenplay had been written for the occasion, it could not have been laid out better for Antony's purposes. The identification with Dionysos was as powerful as it had ever been with any of the Hellenistic kings which had inspired Antony's thinking. There was a mighty resemblance with the Greek tradition, and it fed beautifully into all the compassionate and merciful deeds which Antony had carried out in the years 41–37 BC. And now it was inspirational also in its Egyptian twist, as Antony was cast in the elaborate *mise en scene* which Cleopatra had no doubt directed for the benefit of the Alexandrine. The resulting imagery had no doubt been widely publicized throughout the Mediterranean, and must have been the object of curiosity and possibly reverence well beyond Egypt.

The fundamental question which the historians have left largely unanswered, after centuries of debate, is still that of the ultimate aim of Antony's political

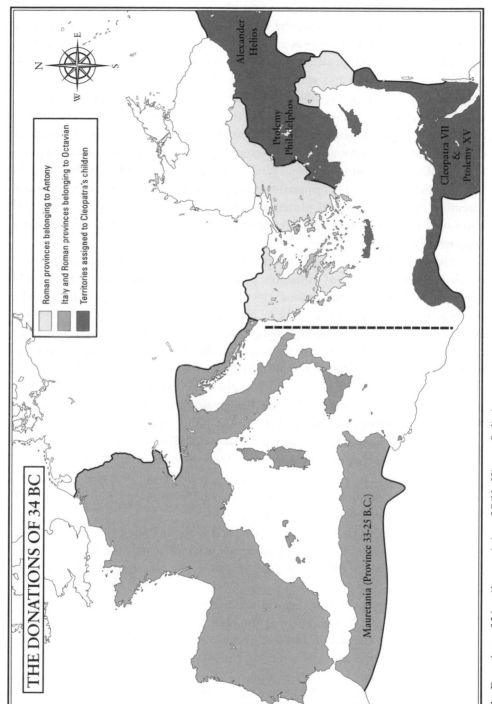

The Donations of 34 BC (*by permission of Bible History Online*)

construction. It remains to be ascertained whether the consolidation of all Rome's eastern domains around Egypt, the acceptance or even the active promotion of his image as the New Dionysos / Osiris as a powerful means of propaganda, and the continuing preparation for another war against the Parthians, were the preliminary steps to set up a springboard which would have made Antony the new Alexander, and stretched his dominions further East, or, if they were structuring and defensive moves, aimed at reinforcing the Eastern borders, without any further imperialistic goals. Much has been said on the role of Cleopatra as an instigator of aggressive policies, moved by her insatiable greed, as she actively peddled more territorial additions to her crown. While Augustan propaganda clearly points in the direction of pan-Asian imperialistic ambitions, logic directs us in the opposite direction, that is, the goal of protecting a minimum degree of independence and autonomy within the unavoidable logic of Roman control, but without unrealistic expansionist goals.

In the end, both Antony and Octavian were creating a robust governance model for their respective areas of influence. Their approach, though, was diametrically different, and reflected the personalities of the two. Octavian was pretending to be the beacon of Roman tradition. As he cumulated powers, and gradually chipped away at the separation of powers, progressively becoming more of an absolute ruler than his adoptive father had ever dreamed; he always remained in the grey zone of ambiguity, never formalizing his absolutism for the forty years to follow. In fact, it would take 103 years before, under Vespasian, the Senate would issue a law (De Imperio Vespasiani) to ratify what the Principate that had started with Octavian Augustus, or the Roman Empire, if the reader prefers, really meant, leapfrogging not only the first Emperor, but the whole Julio-Claudian dynasty.

Antony, on the other hand, was going to keep the reins of the East in his hands in a less intrusive, more flexible way, based on delegation, empowerment, and minimizing the visibility of Roman presence, which was mainly military in nature and vowed to the defence of the borders.

Antony in Alexandria adopted the full local look, including the trading of the gladium for the Asian sabre. He had adopted Greek attire on a full time basis, and, for the reasons already explained, did not disdain the poses typical of an oriental king.

As for the dionysiac-osiriac cult on which Antony was relying, it was clearly a double-edged sword. It was potent in the Hellenistic world, as we have seen. But it certainly looked suspicious and left Antony open to criticism and slander back at home, where, in the days when moral principles were more rigorously followed, it had been censored, limited, and almost banned by senatorial pronouncement. Furthermore, the names of the kings which it evoked did not resonate positively: they were either weak sovereigns who had struggled to survive, such as the late Ptolemies all the way to the XII Auletes, or unstable and overly ambitious warmongers such as Demetrios Polyorketes, or even declared enemies of Rome, such as Mithridates VI Eupator.

It was thus that Octavian exploited this weakness in Antony's political armour, and logically directed his attacks to it, with the ultimate intent of sufficiently stirring up Roman public opinion to gain widespread acceptance and support for the final war against him. The seeds of the propaganda patiently planted over the years were finally bearing fruit and tarnishing Antony's image at home beyond repair. It is hard to say if on the Dionysos-Osiris matter Octavian wanted to provoke an austere disapproval '*mos maiorum*', in the name of Roman tradition, or rather to expose Antony's religious policy to full ridicule. While the second possibility was not irrelevant, the first one was probably preponderant. The deification *per se* would not have been anathema in Rome, but things would have been seen under a different light in the case of a foreign and disapproved of deity. After the battle of Actium, and Antony's subsequent doom, upon taking direct control over Egypt, Octavian would have no shame in being saluted by his new oriental subjects as Zeus *Soter* (the Saviour), or *Eleuterios* (the Liberator), the latter a classic epithet used to address Dionysos. After all, Octavian had been the most active promoter of the cult of the Divine Julius Caesar, Divi Julii, as a means of self advancement. Antony knew perfectly well that these were not laughing matters, and his intention must have been to strike back hard, if he was behind the libel reported by Suetonius,[6] where Octavian was reported as having hosted a banquet, in which he and eleven of his friends posed as Gods and Goddesses, with the intent of promoting his image as Octavian-Apollo, in opposition to Antony – Dionysos/Osiris. The episode reported by Antony probably had no foundations in reality, because Octavian would not have incarnated an Apollo in a social function where there would have been a Zeus, senior to him in the Olympic rankings, in attendance.[7]

Still, as noted in a landmark scholarly article on this subject,[8] this type of counterpropaganda circulated by Antony could have done some severe damage, and Octavian was taking it extremely seriously. The proof is that, after the former's final defeat and death, the latter canvassed the Mediterranean to find and burn thousands of tracts distributed during Antony's campaign. The same article points to other interesting spins from Octavian's propaganda, whose traces can be found mainly in Dio and Plutarch, suggesting that either the divine support from Dionysos had abandoned Antony before the final showdown, or that the supernatural forces sustaining Octavian were stronger, and therefore systematically overpowered those of his opponents. Plutarch had been insistent on this aspect:

"It annoyed Antony that in all their amusements, on any trial of skill of fortune, Caesar should be constantly victorious. He (Antony) had with him an Egyptian diviner, one of those who calculate nativities, who, either to make his court to Cleopatra, or that by the rules of his art he found it to be so, openly declared to him, that though the fortune that attended him was bright and glorious, yet it was overshadowed by Caesar's; and advised him to keep himself as far distant as he could from the young man; "for your Genius", said he, "dreads his; when absent from his yours is proud and brave, but in his presence, unmanly and dejected" and incidents that occurred appeared to show that the Egyptian spoke truth. For whenever they cast lots for any playful purpose, or threw dice, Antony was still the loser; and repeatedly, when they fought game-cocks or quails, Caesar had the victory. That gave Antony a secret displeasure, and made him put the more confidence in the skill of the Egyptian."

Shakespeare had read Plutarch with great attention, and seized the power of the prophecy to give more intensity to the epilogue of Antony' life, like in his other plays. When Antony asks this fortune teller whose fortune will rise higher, Caesar's or his own, the answer is clear:

"Caesar's. /
Therefore, o Antony, stay not by his side: /
Thy demon, that thy spirit which keeps thee, is /
Noble, courageous, high, unmatchable, /
Where Caesar is not; but near him thy angel /
Becomes a fear, as being o'erpowered: therefore /
Make space enough between you."

And then:

"If thou dost play with him at any game, /
Thou art sure to lose; and of that natural luck /
He beats thee 'gainst the odds: Thy luster thickens /
When he shines by."

Notwithstanding all the efforts aimed at highlighting the religious aspects, the facet of Augustan propaganda which struck the deepest chord with the Romans and alienated the sympathies of Antony's fellow citizens, was the representation of the betrayal of Roman traditions. The Romans would not forgive him for having "gone native" with barbaric Eastern provincials. What was really making an impact in Rome were the speeches which sounded like the one that Octavian delivered to his soldiers before Actium, as reported by Dio:

"We would not lament upon seeing and hearing Antony himself: he has twice been Consul, ofter Imperator; along with me he has been entrusted with the superintendence of public affairs (the Triumvirate), he has had control over so many Cities and Legions, yet he now gives up all his ancestral ways of life and cultivates all those which are foreign and barbaric; he shows no respect for our laws and ancestral Gods, but worships that person (Cleopatra) as if she were some Isis or Selene, and calls their children Helios and Selene; finally he even calls himself Osiris or Dionysos, and from these (names), just as if he were lord of Earth and Sea, makes a present of whole islands and some of the continents."[9]

This was the best angle to carry out a political attack, and it would eventually succeed. While the religious issues were only a façade, what hit home was his obliviousness to his own heritage and natural loyalties, the obvious subservience to Cleopatra's whims, and his alleged liberality with the assets of the Republic.

Logically, after the religious politics, the betrayal of traditional values, the enslavement to a *regina meretrix*, whore queen, the next PR attack had to be centred on Antony's hearty tendency to over imbibe, which could be easily amplified by his association with the God of wine and libations. This stigmatization was not news for Antony. It had already been encountered numerous times in his life, and was widely used by Cicero in the Philippics to vilipend him. The Romans did not have to dig deep in their memories to find words and images which reflected this new wave of accusations of alcoholism, and now he was kept in a perennial state of drunken stupor by the malicious Cleopatra to keep him under her control. The attacks on the drunkenness target were delegated to the poets of the *régime*, especially Horace. This does not mean that the comments on Antony's drunkenness had not reached the general public; on the contrary, it proves it. Antony reacted to this new volley of slander with a pamphlet, called *De Ebrietate*, or *De Ebrietate Sua* (On Drunkenness, or, On His Own Drunkenness), as it is commonly known. This booklet, unfortunately lost for us, was far from being a light-hearted hymn to a white sin. It must have been a serious document of self exculpation, which, as we learn from Pliny, he composed a very short time before the battle of Actium, a time when Antony had no desire to be funny and write a pseudo philosophical dissertation on the pleasures of inebriation. As we have seen, Antony did not limit his actions to the issuance of defensive pamphlets, and returned propaganda blows line by line. Octavian's sexual behaviour and preferences were two of his favourite topics. Suetonius specifically points to Antony and his brother Lucius as the source of the gossip which had Octavian earning the adoption by Julius Caesar by prostituting himself to him, just like he had lain with Aulus Hirtius in Spain for 300,000 sesterces. The rumour went as far as indicating that the young man was used to softening his body hair with hot walnut shells, to make the contact with his pubescent body more pleasant. The rumours about the sexual relationship between Caesar and Octavian had started as soon as the adoption was announced. As one would imagine, the contributions to the debate on the foundations of the rumours themselves have been countless. All the custom made panegyric, first those of Nicolaus Damascenus, who insisted on Octavian's rigid and moralistic upbringing, and on how, since childhood, he had been a beacon of traditional values and behaviour. Nevertheless the fundamental question of whether his adoption would have been *avunculi stuprum meritum*[10] (by merit of the rape by his uncle) has gone to historiography without a clear answer.

The episode of the theatre appearance has already been quoted in these pages, and Octavian's penchant for young boys must have been an accepted truth, with no need of further substantiation to generate contempt. One day, Dellius complained about the quality of the wine served at Cleopatra's table, which tasted like vinegar to the sophisticated taste buds of the Roman, and he could not help making the point that Sarmentus in Rome was drinking the issue of the premium Falernum grapes. This Sarmentus:

> "was a boy of the kind that Caesar liked, and which the Romans called *deliciae* (pleasures)."

This description left little doubt about some of Octavian's preferences, which were evidently already in the public domain.

On the heterosexual front, Octavian too was guilty of immorality, but not, like Antony, because of a natural sexual exuberance, but because the bedchambers of the matrons with whom he lay were observatories from where he could obtain more political information or delations. Antony had also reported him for abducting the wife of a man of consular rank from a banquet, and bringing her back shortly thereafter in a state where:

> "her ears were very red, and her hair in great disorder."

The list reported by Suetonius goes on. Scribonia had been abandoned not because of political opportunity during the war with Sextus, but because of the pressure that one of his mistresses was putting on Octavian. And his friends, helping him exercise his infinite power, had become his pimps, stripping virtuous matrons and virgins naked to examine their bodies like they were slaves at the market, before sending them to lay with Octavian. The long and pointed stream of Antony's accusations also covered the modalities of his rushed marriage with Livia, for which a special derogation to the laws had to be granted, as she carried in her womb Drusus, the second son of T. Claudius Nero.

Octavian had sent him a letter in 33 BC, reproaching him publicly for the desertion of Octavia and the liaison with Cleopatra. And Antony:

"Why are you changed towards me? Because I lie with a Queen? She is my wife. Is this a new thing with me, or have I not done so for many years? And do you take freedom with Drusilla only? May health and happiness so attend you, as when you read this letter, you are not in dalliance with Tertulla, Terentilla, Rufilla, or Salva Titiscena, or all of them. What matters it to you where, or upon whom, you spend your manly vigour?"[11]

His reply made short work of his immoral behaviour, and likely created issues with Livia, who, it is fair to assume, being the dominating woman that she was, would not have appreciated the humiliation of having her husband's conjugal infidelity exposed.

We have already spoken of Antony's attacks on Octavian's origins, on the "Aricia" heritage, the moneylender "avum" (grandfather), and the family bakery, in Chapter 4, so they will not be discussed here again, but it is fair to assume that Antony lost no opportunity in refreshing Octavian's memory on the subject.

The accusation by Octavian of consorting with foreigners against the interests of Rome must have reached its intended targets as we find a retort in the Antonian counter-propaganda which was reported diligently by Suetonius:[12] in this specific case, the accusation that Octavian had promised his daughter Julia to Cotys, king of the untamed Dacians, who inhabited modern day Romania (thus the description of *Geticus*), instead of Antony's son Anthillus, as it had been agreed as a corollary of the Treaty of Tarentum in 37 BC. In the same passage, Suetonius, always in search of the juiciest gossip, tells us that the second part of Octavian's Dacian plan was to marry personally a daughter of the same king, in addition to his existing bride Livia. Of course the very idea of such a union ever taking place was ludicrous, but it is a sign of how far the mudslinging between the two had gone, and of how vicious the slander had become.

Close to Cleopatra as he was, Antony could not forget Cesarion, rubbing the Romans' noses in the fact that the young man was Caesar's biological son, who Caesar had recognized in front of the Senate, as opposed to an adopted one (Octavian). Antony had even called for the testimony of Matius and Oppius, Caesar's personal friends and eyewitnesses. This point was made by Antony only by mail, and not in person as Suetonius suggests,[13] as he would not have set foot in Rome in 33–32 BC, but the point was well taken nevertheless, and Octavian made a good note to address it when the opportunity presented itself.

Among the other attacks, Antony resurrected the accusations of unfairness in the allocation of land to the veterans, and of having favoured his own pet legions to the detriment of Antony's, an accusation which was reminiscent of the same charges brought by Lucius Antonius and Fulvia back in 41 BC. Of course, the problem was still outstanding, and Antony could legitimately hope that the accusation was going to resonate with many. The whole issue of the retired legionaries was a minefield. Antony could and certainly did reproach Octavian for the fact that his Parthian wars had been obstructed by Octavian's military recruitment in Italy during the war with Sextus, which had deprived him of the best reservoir of dependable legionaries.

Hitting one of the easiest targets, Antony had pointed insistently to Octavian's ineptitude and cowardice in battle. He had been far from the action in Mutina, bed ridden or hiding in a ditch at Philippi, and again in bed or otherwise absent at Naulochus against Sextus Pompey, where Agrippa had to lead his side by himself. There is more than a suspicion that the repression of the Istrian tribes and the invasion of Pannonia that Octavian carried out in 33–32 BC had been planned to add a few victorious episodes to his military CV, and build up his credibility as a war time leader. The echoes of the accusations that Antony was firing at the address of Octavian are found even in Plutarch, and it is certain that the epistolary exchanges which carried them must have been widely publicized in Rome by Antony's supporters. This was made possible by the fact that in Rome, even in the years 34–32 BC, there was still some degree of factional equilibrium between the pro- and the anti-Antonian parties. It will suffice to say that the Consuls for 32 BC were none other than Sossius and Domitius Ahenobarbus, hence two pure bred Antonians. We know that the two were very active in trying to keep Antony's most questionable deeds and behaviour away from the sight of the general public, whereas Octavian, of course, was trying to expose them as much as possible. The sudden sidelining of Lepidus was also a pretext for Antony's propaganda retaliation, and he possibly implied that the Sicilian rebellion might have been a fabrication. For sure, he complained of not having received any of the spoils of war after Sextus' defeat, in the form, for example, of a part of Sicily, while he had contributed to the victory with the 120 ships he had lent to Octavian. The latter replied sarcastically:

"Why does Antony want some of Sicily? He and his legions should have been satisfied with the newly conquered territories of Media and Parthia! Is not this enough to satiate them?"

This did not go down well at all with Antony. The bitterness was escalating to new levels, and war was ominous.

In the course of 33 BC, Antony travelled from Egypt to the East again, but still did not want to launch the much coveted Parthian invasion, probably meditating on the timing of the final showdown with Octavian. He visited Armenia again, and went to renew his vows of friendship with King Artavasdes of Media.

The consulship of Domitius and Sossius did result in an escalation of the tension. The two, Sossius more than his flamboyant colleague Domitius, were trading verbal blows with Octavian in the Senate on a daily basis, until the day when weapons were seen appearing at political rallies, and the pair decided it was more judicial to leave Rome and join Antony in Alexandria. Their escape precipitated events: those who were uncertain had to start openly taking sides, and the inevitable series of defections and treasons began. The two early noteworthy ones were that of Titius, the slayer of Sextus Pompey, and Plancus, another Antonian old time supporter since 43 BC, who publicly declared loyalty to Octavian. It should be emphasized that, by no means, until 32 BC, when the escape of Sossius from Rome precipitated events, did Antony intend any aggression towards Rome, but only a desire to carry out his programme as described. If, in Rome, Domitius and Sossius had been left unharmed, or unthreatened, the explosion of hostilities would have been, if not avoided, at least significantly delayed, and could not have been ascribed to Antony's initiative. He would have carried out his plan, and maybe launched his new Parthian attack, perhaps with more success this time thanks to the support of his Median ally, which was now his most Eastern outpost, bound to him by family links.

Both sides hastened the preliminaries for war. Antony moved on with the formal repudiation of Octavia, perhaps to pre-empt the same action from her on her brother's instigation, which was insistent and continuous. Octavia, with her usual dignity and composure, left Antony's Roman residence with all the children, except for Anthillus, the elder, who had followed his father to Media. Then he had a shadow Senate in Alexandria sanction the decision to proceed with hostilities. Octavian proceeded with the celebration of all those religious functions which were part of the pre-war ceremonial. He was very careful, though, in directing the formal declaration of war to Cleopatra, and not declaring Antony a "hostis", a public enemy, with respect for the sensitivities of all the many Antonian current or former loyalists still present in Rome.

It is at this point that Octavian produced the *coup de theatre* of the public reading of Antony's will and testament. Octavian went to the extreme measure of confiscating it from the Vestals, the sacred record keepers, to whom it had been entrusted: this was a highly illicit act, which under normal circumstances would have been deemed almost blasphemous, but once the assembly heard the content of the document, skilfully presented by Octavian, they were so enraged that they quickly forgot the procedural fault. Antony's will was the written transcription of all the visual manifestations of his programme. It went from the endorsement of Cesarion as a legitimate heir of Julius Caesar, to the attribution of their domains to his children, and, lastly, to proclaim his wish upon his death to be buried next to Cleopatra in Alexandria after his State funeral in Rome. The content was enough to convince the last vacillating few of Antony's dishonour, and to solidify the unanimous consensus around the decision for war. Soon, the Roman world would have but one master.

Just like before any other episode of the Civil Wars, omens abounded. Some were especially spectacular, like the arrival of an 85 ft dragon in Tuscany, which caused much havoc, or an earthquake which destroyed some of the colonies founded by Mark Antony. Others were less grandiose, but still worrisome, such as statues bleeding and sweating, or lightning striking temples. Others still might have gone unnoticed, such as a children's game in Rome, where the team impersonating the Antonians were defeated by their Octavianean opponents, but were nevertheless faithfully reported by the superstitious historians. While Dio reports omens and prodigies with notary-like precision, he also gives us an interesting angle on the remaining strong domestic opposition to Octavian. Some great fires which ravaged Rome and destroyed part of the Circus in those days should perhaps not be ascribed to supernatural intervention, but to groups of freedmen who had been made the object of another tax. Since the levy was only 8% of their net worth, the reader might conclude it was not worthy of systematic arson, and still lean towards the mystical interpretation. On the contrary, Dio hints that the popularity of Octavian was still quite low. For the year 32 BC, as an extraordinary measure for the financing of the war, the citizens of Rome, normally tax exempt, had to contribute to the public finances with 25% of their income for that year.

The initial enthusiastic response that Antony and Cleopatra obtained from the various oriental kingdoms to their rallying cry was evidence of the Roman's long sightedness and of his profound understanding of local politics and customs. Many of these vassal states would have gladly antagonized Rome, if given a chance of success, and sided with Antony and Cleopatra's counter power, as they were still mindful of what they had suffered because of the Republic over time. So they saw foreign allies flocking under their standards very rapidly, and joining the sixteen legions which Antony had ordered Canidius to lead from Armenia to the coast, crossing the 2,200 km of mountainous country. Cleopatra was a powerful symbol, who could act as a catalyst for the whole Orient, and the liaisons that Antony had worked at establishing between 40 and 37 BC could now be tapped for support. When the preparations were complete, Antony could count on King Bocchus of Lybia, Tarcondemus from Cilicia, Archelaus from Cappadocia, Philadelphus from Paphlagonia, Mithridates from Commagene, Sedala from Thracia, Polemon from Ponthus, Malchus from Arabia, and, of course, Herod from Judaea. With his most recent recruit, Artavasdes from Media, they were all ready to fight Rome, inspired by the ideal of pan-Asian independence, under the crest of Dionysos.

When Antony counted the men he was going to take to war, he must not have been far from the 100,000 units. He had summoned nineteen legions, but probably all well below full force, for a total of maybe 60,000 trained Roman soldiers. The rest was a composite force, resulting from all his allies' contributions, just like

Pompey Magnus had at Pharsalus. Maybe Antony's later decisions were influenced by a lack of confidence he may well have had in these fighters, again, very much like Pompey. The difference with the precedent was that Antony exerted a firm control over his vassal kings, at least initially, and he was not likely to let them influence his decisions, like Pompey had to do.

Antony had gathered a gigantic fleet, which at one point must have been 800 vessels strong, including many forms of transport, and 200 battle ships sent by Cleopatra. The massive fleet moved from Ephesus, where it had been reunited, into the Aegean Sea, and made a first stopover on the island of Samos, which for a few days resonated with enthusiasm, music, and chanting, before heading for Athens. The period spent in Ephesus and the apparent waste of time in music and shows on the island of Samos were probably intended as a bonding exercise for the heterogeneous company which had rallied around Antony and Cleopatra. The dionysiac symbolism of this was one more catalyst to make this composite force stick together under one powerful symbol. It was for this reason that companies of dionysiac actors and musicians provided the spectacular backdrop for those few days, and were meant to fire a collective enthusiasm.

Cleopatra could not be dissuaded from participating in the expedition. The Ephesians had bestowed upon her great honours on her arrival, and saluted her as their queen. After all, her contributions to the war had been greater than all the other kings'. Either Antony still very much valued her power as a symbol, or maybe she exerted on him an influence strong enough to dissuade him from sending her home. Once in Athens, she claimed and obtained greater honours than those reserved for Octavia six years before. In general, the key men in Antony's closest circle were uneasy with her presence, considering her to be a distraction for him, as she demanded attention. Some even felt endangered by her presence alone because of her mood swings and unpredictable reactions. Regardless of her undisputed brain power, for these Roman generals on the Antonian side, who had grown up in the male and chauvinistic environment of the Roman army, the presence of an opinionated and arrogant oriental woman was an element of disruption. The resulting tension would have very negative consequences on the conduct of the war, as we shall see. Roman misogyny was not the only danger, and some put up with the queen better than others, for the sake of the financial resources she contributed. But some of the Hellenistic kings could not abide her proximity. Herod, to name one, was a clear Type A personality with whom she was incompatible in close quarters.

The Greek islands in the Adriatic were the first area of war interest. In the fall of 32 BC, Antony had sailed all the way to Kerkyra (today's Corfu) with a large squadron, but then decided to avoid the confrontation with the Octavianean fleet patrolling those waters, and returned to Greece, after scattering around most of his fleet to control the Adriatic coastline, and the many islands, such as Ithaca, Cephalonia, and

Zacyntus, that guarded access to Greece. For him, an invasion of Italy was out of the question, at least for the near and medium term, and pushing too far north was not a risk worth taking. Some[14] have read the early abandonment of the plan to invade Italy as the result of Cleopatra's influence, an effort on her part to keep Antony's attention away from Rome born of an irrational and possessive instinct. In all likelihood, it was a realistic assessment of the probabilities of success which dissuaded Antony, who probably came to this decision without any influence from a third party.

It was so that the area between Corfu and the two islands of Paxos and Antipaxos became the hub for Octavian's naval force. Antony then established his base camp further south. About 80 km down the Greek coast, the shoreline retreats by about 15 km inland, and forms the gulf of Ambracia, which has a very narrow mouth. The village of Actium lay near these straits, and it was in the bay of Ambracia that Antony had gathered together his fleet, and set up camp. Just south of the straits lies the island of Leucos, initially another protection for Antony, but which would eventually be captured by Agrippa, and become another springboard for Octavian's attacks. Antony's camp was on an ideally placed hilltop, protected by a strong wall, while at the same time dominating the bay where 500 ships had dropped anchor, and the open waters of the Adriatic that spread before Actium. To further strengthen his position, the Antonians erected two towers guarding the mouth of the strait. Antony himself joined his naval base at the end of the winter by land from Patrae, taking with him the majority of the remaining land forces in Greece. It is not entirely clear what Antony's real intentions were when he chose to establish his defensive line so far to the south.

Octavian's landing in Epyrum, in the vicinity of Panormus, roughly at the same latitude as Otranto at the southern tip of Puglia, had been unimpeded. Practically the whole of Epyrum was abandoned in his hands, and, with it, the access to the strategic via Egnatia. Moving his troops quickly onto this east – west superhighway, Octavian at some point could have rapidly crossed the Macedonian mountains to gain easy access to land to attack the East. The best explanation[15] for this apparent mistake is that Antony had no other options but to execute a prudent defensive strategy, attracting Octavian away from Italy before striking hard for his destruction. His alliance with Cleopatra precluded an invasion of Italy. The Romans had tolerated the arrival of the legions of Lucius Sulla marching up the Appian Way to the gates of Rome, but there was not a chance, no matter how detested Octavian might have been, that they would have accepted the return of Antony at the head of a multi-ethnic force and with an oriental queen at his side. So all he could do was lure Octavian away from home, giving him the false sense of security that Greece would have easily fallen. Certainly, he was counting on the discontentment in Italy, and on the precarious financial situation his opponent was facing. It was not unlikely that at some point mutinous thoughts would have begun to infiltrate Octavian's ranks, and generate some defections in Antony's favour, also thanks to the deep pockets of

Cleopatra, which could have supplied financial muscle to sustain a prolonged war effort. Antony's surrender of his northern outposts, such as the island of Corfu, could have been interpreted as a desire to reduce the breadth of his engagement and wait for better days. There was certainly some merit in this type of thinking. When Octavian, again serving as a Consul alongside Valerius Messalla Corvino (a man who would become a smaller scale Mecaenas, and the grandfather of the famous Empress Messalina), sailed to Greece to take control of operations, he took with him the majority of the Senate, certainly in a display of cohesiveness, but mainly in an attempt to better control them in his absence, perhaps fearing a *coup* while he was away.

At the beginning of the war, Octavian's situation was far from secure. His fleet, patrolling the Greek coastline, had no safe shelter from stormy weather. Had his ships been wrecked by a storm, his land army would have been marooned in Epyrum, and would have been easy prey for Antony's land forces. But in the period between late 32 BC and the spring of 31 BC the pendulum of destiny swung decisively in Octavian's favour. While he did not commit any major errors in conducting the war, Antony found himself on a path of forced decisions, and the victim of events outside his direct control. While initially he enjoyed the favour of the odds and the enthusiasm pervading the ranks of his coalition, the inherent structural limitations of his alliance were fully revealed and materialized into strategic weaknesses, before he could leverage to his advantage the full extent of the problems which Octavian was facing. Antony was playing with several degrees of freedom missing in his strategy, and, after making the first move into the Adriatic, soon found himself on his heels, deprived of initiative and momentum.

While Antony enjoyed a well defended position, Octavian had taken the advantage in these preliminary phases of the confrontations in two different ways. First of all, Antony had not dared take the war to Italy, so Octavian was not subjected to the psychological consequences of an enemy invasion. Secondly, while he had landed much to the north, he had quickly moved to the south, and established his base in the peninsula which ends in the straits of Actium, a position which was ideally placed to survey his enemy, and which allowed him to take his time to wear down Antony with a series of nerve wrecking skirmishes, and then reap the fruits of his propaganda campaign in the way of defections. The landmark examples of Titius and Plancus were still very fresh, and certainly had caused hesitation and wariness in Antony's camp. This is why Antony was the more eager of the two to engage rapidly and seek a swift solution. He had challenged Octavian to an individual duel with taunts that their age difference was no advantage. Then, he challenged him to a pitched battle in the plain of Pharsalus, where Caesar had defeated Pompey eighteen years earlier. Octavian did not bite the bait, knowing that Antony was all the more dangerous in a traditional field battle, and kept waiting for the defections to come. Two setbacks suffered by the Antonian side accelerated the process of the erosion of their morale. On the nearby front, the defector Titius defeated Antony's cavalry in the valley of the Louros River, which divided the two encampments inland. Antony was trying to force the land engagement by blocking Octavian's access to fresh water sources, but in the end he had to abandon this project. But the real surprise move was the attack on Antony's southern front, with an incursion led by Agrippa which resulted in him conquering the city of Patrae, on the north eastern coast of Peloponnese. At the same time, the island of Leucades, just south of the gulf of Ambracia, fell to Octavian, so that now Antony's base was sandwiched between enemy territories. The faithful Sossius came out of the bay and inflicted a defeat at sea on one of Octavian's admirals, Arruntius, but did not even have the time to celebrate, because Agrippa arrived promptly, and, in turn, beat him. Even before attacking Patrae, Octavian had struck first blood with a small scale and swift attack on Meton, on the thin peninsula which constitutes the western finger of the Peloponnesian hand, half way between Cape Tanarum and Patrae. It was defended by King Bocchus of Mauretania, who died in its defence. After these demonstrative and surgical raids, a steady stream of defections began. The city of Corinth, on the western Peloponnese coast, revolted against Antony immediately after the fall of Patrae. Actually, the defections on Antony's side had started much earlier, since 32 BC, when the Spartans, led by Eurycles, whose father Antony had decapitated for piracy, had abandoned him, followed by the inhabitants of Berytus, modern Beyrouth, which had rebelled against Cleopatra. Patrae, Corinth, Spartha: the control over Peloponnese was lost, the ring around Antony was closing, and, with it, his access to reinforcements and provisions was becoming more problematic by the day. Soon after, it was King Philadelphos of Paphlagonia who jumped ship. While the nerve of Antony's coalition had been shaken by the early setbacks and by an opportunistic weighing up of the possible outcomes of the war, more were to abandon Antony because of their profound incompatibility with Cleopatra.

That Dellius turned coat could have been easily expected. He had fought for Dolabella, Cassius, and Antony already, and another change should not have surprised anyone. The last and most representative personality to jump sides was Domitius Ahenobarbus, only to die of natural causes only days after his escape from Antony's camp. Mark Antony even saw him escaping on a small boat at night, and in an impulsion of generosity, not only let him go unharmed, but also sent him another boat carrying all the personal belongings he had left behind. It is important to point out that those who betrayed Antony were accepted in Octavian's camp, but not necessarily welcomed with enthusiasm by their historical opponents. There was certainly, for example, a big difference between the welcome reserved for Asinius Pollio, and the one that went to Munatius Plancus, who, according to Velleius,[16] had switched sides:

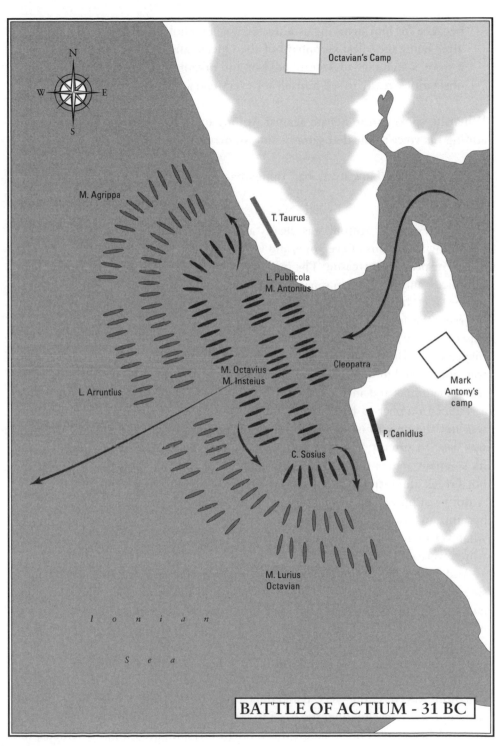

Octavian's Camp

M. Agrippa

T. Taurus

L. Publicola
M. Antonius

Cleopatra

M. Octavius
M. Insteius

Mark
Antony's
camp

L. Arruntius

P. Canidius

C. Sosius

M. Lurius
Octavian

I o n i a n

S e a

BATTLE OF ACTIUM - 31 BC

The Battle of Actium

"because for him behaving as a traitor was a pathological state of the mind, after being the vilest sycophant of the Queen, and a client worth less than a slave, a secretary to Antony, advisor and organizer of the most disgusting obscenities, ready to sell himself for every end and at any occasion."

When he spoke in the Senate against Antony upon his return to Rome, happily adding his voice to the derogatory choir, someone commented:

"By Hercules! How many bad things has Antony done the day before you deserted him!"

If we believe Dio,[17] Antony was deeply affected by the defections, to the point of becoming suspicious of everyone, and very forceful in stomping out every instance of real or presumed treason. The first to pay with their lives were the Arabic King Jamblicus and the Roman senator Postumus, followed shortly by King Amyntas, who we met during the pursuit of Sextus Pompey. While we can accept, to different degrees, the level of discouragement that affected Antony, it is undeniable that this time he was being dealt a generous dose of the psychological warfare he had dispensed to Brutus and Cassius at Philippi. The bleeding of men from his army was not limited to senior leaders either; it reached frightening proportions in the legionary ranks and in the crews of his ships, and soon he could only count on a reduced number of battle ships due to the scarcity of oarsmen. And defection was not the only cause of the thinning of his lines. While the gulf of Ambracia was easy to protect, the very nature of its geography made it insalubrious, and its stagnant waters fostered the transmission of disease. With the arrival of the hot Greek summer the problem was exacerbated, and grew exponentially when Antony's supply chain was disrupted by the loss of Peloponnese, and malnutrition became an issue. Soon, Antony was obliged to resort to forceful drafting of whatever manpower he could find locally to operate the oars of his ships, many of which were still inoperable.

And when the enemy embarked on more severe provocations, lining up a sizeable naval squadron in front of the mouth of the Gulf of Ambracia, Antony had to come up with a clever but very risky ruse. He dressed as many oarsmen as he could find in full soldier's combat gear, while all the unmanned oars were being held up as if the ships were ready to move and counterattack. This was enough to instil sufficient fear in the enemy for them to back away for the moment.

The problem remained; as the end of summer approached, the manpower situation was reaching very dangerous proportions, and, while the stalemate situation was consolidating, the need to force a military solution was becoming a pressing necessity. The situation was a tough one and, according to Velleius, the odds at this point were overwhelmingly in favour of Octavian, due to the fitness and motivation of his men and officers. Both sides, for the reasons listed above, had an interest in bringing the stalemate to an end and concluding the war.

Sometime around the end of August 31 BC, the war council of the Antonians must have experienced moments of extreme tension, while the strong southern winds that swept the south Adriatic made operating the ships problematic. Canidius, representing traditional military expertise and common sense, pushed for a retreat to inland Greece, maybe heading north east towards Thracia. After all, there was an outstanding promise from Dicome, king of the Dacians, to come to the help of the Antonians with a powerful army. Their initial numerical superiority had evaporated over time, due to desertion and disease, and, at the most, they could have fielded 300 warships in full combat gear. Plus, not to be forgotten, Octavian's admirals, and Agrippa in particular, had already had plenty of opportunity to cut their teeth at naval battles during the war with Sextus Pompey. The best seaman on Antony's side had been Domitius Ahenobarbus but he, if we can use the expression, also had just jumped ship! Canidius explained how their best option was a retreat, waiting for better times to fight on land. Cleopatra, however, advocated breaking out at sea, as Plutarch suggests, because she was already thinking of making a run for Egypt. The intervention of Cleopatra at this point of the decision on the course of the war has become another centrepiece for the post war propaganda, and a commonplace to highlight Antony's weakness when faced with her whims. The same biographer reports the episode of an old Centurion kneeling in front of Antony and begging him to give battle on land, where he and his men felt comfortable fighting and winning, and not aboard ships, which were suited for Phoenicians and Egyptians. Antony probably just gave the Centurion a pat on the back and moved on. From this episode, and from others, such as forgiving the escaping Domitius, it is possible to capture a very specific angle of the imperial propaganda, and at the same time the indelible legacy of honour and loyalty that Antony left behind, and which followed him in the eyes of his supporters. Even in his current predicament, he commanded a huge amount of respect, and his men were still ready to die for him. What had weakened him was the proximity with Cleopatra, who was clouding his judgment, and with whom not even his closest aides would accept to associate. The final stages of the Civil Wars, the years 33–31 BC, have been disjointed from all the preceding episodes, as they do not oppose Roman leaders and armies. They see the clash between Rome and a rebellious eastern coalition led by Cleopatra, with the intervention of some misguided Romans, Antony first among them. Appian ends his "Civil War" with the death of Sextus Pompey, and the period of interest of this chapter was the subject of a totally separate work, unfortunately lost for us. In this way, Octavian later would have had an easier task of forgiving all the stragglers, and furthermore, of pardoning them and offering them a re-entry passport to become a part of the *Pax Augusta*.

As for the naval battle, the idea that Cleopatra was either pushing Antony for an all-out battle at sea because she felt like going yachting on a beautiful September day, or because she was planning her own escape, is really best avoided. Plutarch might seem to suggest these options, but they are an oversimplification and a misrepresentation of the underlying reality, which was a plan more worthy of the brainy queen. Dio captures her thoughts much better. What she really wanted to achieve was a naval break through the enemy fleet, using the impetus of their larger ships, and to head for safety in Egypt with the best part of their forces, and the large treasure she carried with her. For sure, the Greek permanence in 32–31 BC had been a setback. Still, they would have salvaged the best part of their army and fleet, while the experienced Canidius could have marched the rest to the East, maybe reuniting with the Dacians. Once in the safety of Alexandria, the extent of the Ptolemaic treasures would have made all the difference. A new, more powerful army could have been recruited and trained, while at the same time Octavian would have been struggling to keep his legions in check, with many months of pay in arrears, and, what's more, they were well aware of how shaky their perspective of ultimate settlement was upon retirement. Octavian was not going to be able to pursue the fleeing Antonians, so they would have had a long time to reorganize. Furthermore, Antony also had a reserve of eleven legions, albeit under full force, which were stationed in other parts of the Mediterranean basin, but which could have been unleashed in later bouts. In sum, the very idea of Antony yielding to the caprices of Cleopatra, who wanted a naval battle because she was foolishly convinced of the superiority of her ships, is a pure misconception. Never the Roman or his Egyptian queen would be so naive, but they made a different decision and had a very pragmatic plan in mind.

When, in the last days of August 31 BC, Antony embarked his troops and prepared to give battle, he could only find rowers for fewer than 300 ships. He boarded 20,000 legionaries, and 2,000 archers and slingers, on which he counted to bombard the enemy ships from the height of his much taller and larger Egyptian vessels. The rest of the army watched from the shore, while Antony burned all the remaining ships he could not use, so that they could not be added to Octavian's fleet, already 400 galleys strong. The young Caesar chose to embark over 40,000 men, but of course they would be spread out over a much larger number of smaller ships. As pointed out, the average size of the ships which Antony had at his disposal at Actium was way larger than the average trireme of the late Republican period.

The trireme was the standard battleship of the first century BC. The three orders of oars of different length were the best engineering solution to give the vessel sufficient speed, resistance, and ideal mass to make the best use of the ram, host soldiers, and carry ballistae to throw missiles during the engagement at long range, and retain some key features of manoeuvrability. The ramming was the most important strategy prior to the boarding: the men aboard a ship would run to the prow at the time of impact to balance the ship forward, and try to inflict the damage below the flotation line. If this was not possible, the blunt form of the ram would have caused a huge shock throughout the enemy ship as a prelude to the attack at close quarters. The ram could be positioned to hit the enemy ship below the flotation line, in order to sink it, or above, in order to hook it. A good skipper could also direct the blow higher or lower with the speed of the galley, and by moving the soldiers at the time of impact to the front or the back as they were ballast. A typical trireme would have a total crew of about 180 rowers, plus maybe another eighty between attendants for the catapults or foot soldiers for the eventual boarding of the enemy ships. Larger ships did not have more orders of oars, but simply more than one man on the same oar. A quinquireme, or a "five", for instance would have had two men per oar in the two upper orders, and maybe one in the lower order, for a total of 300 rowers, and could easily carry another 150 armed men. The Egyptians were masters at building even much larger ships, "ten" and above, so the reader can extrapolate the humongous size they reached, the manpower they required, and the difficulties that they encountered when manoeuvring. Of course they had their advantages. Their hull was very strong, partly because it was reinforced by a complex system of internal beams and external metal braces, and a smaller combat ship would never contemplate ramming it. At the most, as an alternate strategy, an Augustan trireme attacking an Antonian ship of a higher order could have attempted a diagonal attack, trying to mow down the protruding oars, and leaving the larger vessel inoperable. Or, several triremes could have ganged up on a larger ship, attacking it from all sides so it could then be directly boarded or set on fire with burning arrows and ignited projectiles.

The strong winds which had been sweeping the Adriatic finally subsided, and the time for the battle came. As a final omen, at dawn on 2 September 31 BC as he walked around his camp, Octavian met a peasant leading a donkey. When asked, the man told Octavian that his name was Fortunate, and that of his donkey was Victorious. It was so that Octavian after the battle, in addition to founding the coastal town of Nikopolis, had a bronze monument built, portraying a man and his donkey.

In the speech he delivered to his troops before the battle on 2 September, as reported by Dio,[18] Antony shows strong reliance on the "size effect", as well as the relative quality of leadership. It is possibly the historian's attempt to rationalize the course of the battle.

"They are inferior to us in number of soldiers, in financial resources, and in type of weapons available. But they are especially inferior in what pertains to the age and experience of their commander. He is very weak physically, and he has never won a fight, land or sea. There is no doubt that even at Philippi I won, and he has been defeated! … As for the fleet, they cannot measure to us. Look for yourself, the size and height of our ships, for which, even if the enemy fleet had the same number of boats than ours, they could do no harm to us, either ramming or attacking to the sides. The sheer size would make any attack pointless. Who will dare get near our ships, with so many archers, and slingers, and soldiers striking from the towers?"

There was some merit in this thinking, if this is what Antony actually thought and said in his address to the soldiers. After all, Sextus Pompey in Naulochus had been defeated by larger ships, which harpooned his swifter triremes and dragged them close to Octavian's ships like fish on a hook. In fact, many of those ships might still have been in service, so that the similarity in average size between the two fleets might have been significant, and the disparity quoted by the historians the fruit of dramatization.

Octavian's speech was in all likelihood a summary of the years of his mudslinging campaign, and Dio's transcript provides a very clear checklist of all the key propaganda points.

"Do not consider Antony a Roma, but an Egyptian; do not call him Antony, but Serapeion; do not think of him as a former Consul or Imperator, but a gymnasiarch; he has chosen all of those things to these, and refusing all the noble titles of his homeland, he has become like another cymbal player from Canobus."[19]

The conclusion of the speech suggests that Antony's intentions were obvious to Octavian, and the following quotation is a classic example of Dio letting the truth transpire, while trying to uphold the official propaganda version:

"They have loaded all their valuables aboard their ships, to save them with themselves, if they can. Since they confess to be weaker than us by placing on their ships the prices of victory, we don't have to let them get away, but stop them here and strip them of their possessions."

Early in the morning, as Antony's ships occupied the mouth of the straits and prepared their exit for battle, a light sea breeze was blowing in their faces.

The Octavianean fleet was commanded by Agrippa, as one would have expected. Agrippa himself commanded the left wing, to the north, followed by Arruntium in the centre, and Lurius, the man who had lost Sardinia to Sextus Pompey, on the right. As for Octavian, he positioned himself on the far right, closing the exit south to the Ionian Sea.

That morning, contrary to standard battle procedure, Antony had the crews embark all the sails. This must have sounded strange to the soldiers, as the large, heavy sails would have just been in the way during the fighting. Antony's reasoning was that they might have come in handy for the pursuit of the escaping enemies but, in reality, the plan was to use them for their own escape towards Egypt, after they had broken through the enemy lines, and they had reached the high seas and favourable winds.

Antony knew that he was outnumbered, and that the enemy ships were on average faster and easier to manoeuvre. If he was to avoid trouble, he had to keep his squadrons tight, and avoid having his lines infiltrated or outflanked. He moved his 240 ships forwards, organized in four squadrons of sixty ships each. While the best ships were kept on the wings, just like the most experienced legions in a land battle, the centre was double deep, with Cleopatra herself, aboard the flagship, called "Antonia", in the second line.

As for Antony, he did not directly command any part of the fleet either, but rather initially kept moving around the whole battle line, inspecting the deployment of his squadrons from a liburnian, a small ship powered by fifty men, on one order of oars. If his ships were to break through Octavian's lines, he needed to generate maximum impetus and momentum, and keep his formation as compact as possible. He was well aware that every one of his large ships that got separated from the rest of the fleet would have fallen prey to the swarming of the smaller and more agile enemies. After making sure that his squadrons were sufficiently tight, Antony abandoned his liburnian, and took his place on his flagship, probably a "ten", on the right hand side of the front, under the command of Publicola, and facing Agrippa himself. His left flank was under the command of the faithful Sossius, the conqueror of Jerusalem, and the centre was under a Marcus Octavius, a former Pompeian general, who in the past, prior to serving under Antony, had successfully confronted Dolabella and Gaius Antonius.

Under the eyes of Canidius' troops, who were watching the battle from the shore, the Antonian fleet stood motionless at the mouth of the straits, facing the enemy, who was also completely still one mile away. The entire morning of 2 September 31 BC was spent in this mutual observation. But around noontime, as is normal in the Adriatic summer, a strong breeze started blowing from west – northwest, against the Antonians. This was not going to help Antony's plans: in order to take a southern route he had to clear the island of Leucas, which obstructed the direct trajectory from Actium to the open Adriatic and eventually Egypt. With a more easterly wind, he could have more easily cleared the blockade, staying closer to the coast, and beaten the attempts of the oar powered enemy ships to pursue them. Unfortunately for him, the ships of the period, and especially Antony's, with their bulky hull and square sails, were entirely incapable of reaching a decent speed in a bowline trajectory, i.e. advancing close to the wind, which would have been necessary to gain the high seas. With a different wind direction, the momentum of their escape would have been unstoppable. Under the present circumstances,

Antony had no alternative but to attack to force his way, which he did, beginning with moving forward Sossius' left wing. Agrippa initially pretended to fall back under the pressure, but it was a ruse to suck in the enemy and bag him within his formation, and at the same time make them lose their initial impetus. Then, once Antony's lines had stretched sufficiently, he counterattacked in the expected fashion with coordinated assaults from several vessels aimed at isolating and immobilizing the larger ships.

Actium marked the end of an era in naval warfare and engineering where size made the difference, and the ramming power of a well manned "six", "eight", or "ten", or their superior firepower from numerous men standing on taller towers, was a guarantee of success, just as Agrippa had defeated Sextus in Sicily. This time Agrippa's lower order galleys were taking turns at directing their attacks from different directions on Antony's crafts, like a pride of lions on a buffalo, forcing it to final exhaustion and capture. This is the traditional reading and interpretation of the battle, where the much celebrated advantage of the larger ships turned into a burden, and their clumsiness and slowness were a huge hindrance. This view may need to be modified to a certain extent, as it may have been taken to an extreme by the usual imperial propaganda, aimed at giving Antony better odds before the battle, in order to make Octavian's victory seem all the more heroic and epic. Archaeological work has pointed to the possibility that the two fleets were a lot more similar in size than the historians would have us believe, and that Antony might have had only a limited number of ships of class "six", "eight" or "ten". Even without the comfort of archaeological research, after all, it is sure that Cleopatra had contributed with no more than 20 or 25% of the fleet which had sailed from Ephesos the previous year, including several transport ships. On the other hand, it is also a fact that Agrippa had defeated Sextus Pompey thanks to the larger size of his ships, which harpooned the lighter triremes and pulled them like fish on a hook.

All the sources agree that at some point in the early afternoon, while the battle was still raging and its outcome was still uncertain, Cleopatra's squadron, which up until that moment had remained behind the front line, took advantage of a gap in the opposite ranks and cleared its way into the open Adriatic. Still according to the traditional account, it was then that Antony, evidently surprised by Cleopatra's flight, could not abide the sight of his queen abandoning him, and himself deserted the battle aboard a faster "five", reached Cleopatra, and then boarded her flagship. Antony's escape gave the final blow to the morale of his soldiers, who were then destroyed by Agrippa, while Antony, filled with shame, and sitting at the prow of the ship, his face buried in the palms of his hands, abandoned himself to a state of profound melancholy. This traditional version of events served beautifully as the final case in point to conclude and prove beyond doubt the propaganda theorem, which has been discussed several times here. One could not put it in clearer words than Plutarch himself:

"Here it was that Antony showed to all the world that he was no longer actuated by the thoughts and the motives of a commander or a man, or indeed by his own judgment at all, and what was once said as a jest, that the soul of lovers lives in someone else's body, he proved to be a serious truth. For, as if he had been born part of her, and must move with her whatsoever she went, as soon as he saw her ship sailing away, he abandoned all that were fighting and spending their lives for him, and put himself aboard a galley of five ranks of oars … to follow her that had so well begun his ruin, and would hereafter accomplish it."

A few thoughts immediately come to mind. The image of Cleopatra spreading her sails to pass the blockade at full speed is puzzling. The wind was picking up and we have no evidence that it had turned to the east. If it had, it could not have facilitated their escape towards Peloponnese. An easterly wind would have forced them on a slower course and made the pursuit from Octavian much easier. So the initial part of Cleopatra's break must have been oar powered. In conclusion, it seems entirely probable that Cleopatra's escape was not the result of the Ptolemaic queen seizing a random opportunity, but rather the centrepiece of Antony's main battle plan. Cleopatra, the treasures she carried on board her ship, and the wealth of Egypt, were the cornerstone of his project to bounce back and launch another war campaign in the near future. Had Cleopatra fallen into Octavian's hands, the probability of this happening would have seriously decreased. The way Antony eventually deployed his forces was aimed at engaging all the enemy battleships, possibly leveraging the size advantage, and absorbing enough of the pressure, to let Cleopatra and the second squadron in the double deep centre sneak through the enemy lines relatively undisturbed. We can compare his tactics to what an American football team does when "running the ball", with a defensive line tackling all the opponents to let a fast man run through the gaps skilfully created. Accordingly, his own subsequent escape would have been carefully planned. Prior to making their run for the open seas, the ships of her squadron quickly discharged at sea all the heavy combat towers, the protective metal braces, and all the other ballast still on board. This interpretation is perfectly coherent with the war council discussions which have been reported by Dio. Of course, this view would be incompatible with the romanticized view of a panicked Cleopatra who abandons the waters of Actium, followed by an Antony crazed by passion. This is even more incompatible with the implication of Octavian's speech reported by Dio, that it was clear to everyone that Antony wanted to give battle at sea only to facilitate their escape with the precious content of their ships. In other words, if the battle plan had been to let Cleopatra escape from the start, there is no logic in accusing her of cowardice and feminine weakness when she had perfectly accomplished her plan.

The accusations from Dio embellish the propaganda case against her, but are in open contradiction with what had been illustrated a few pages earlier.

Eurycles the Spartan, the most perseverant in Antony's pursuit, or maybe the one with the fittest rowers, after much yelling at Antony's address, finally diverted his attention from the flagship to the precious cargo of two other galleys in the squadron, leaving little doubt about the interest in what Cleopatra was transporting aboard her vessels.

Once out of immediate danger, on their way across the Mediterranean Antony and Cleopatra made a stopover at Cape Tainarum in Laconia, the south eastern tip of Peloponnese, and therefore in the territory of their Spartan enemies. Tainarum also had a place in Greek mythology for being one of the two horns of Aedes, or the Roman Pluto, God of the underworld, so that the area was ridden with temples to worship this sinister divinity. And here, no matter how prostrated by despair, humiliation, and fear for his impending end, Antony shows us again his altruism and generosity, his first thoughts going to his friends, to whom he sent a merchant ship loaded with valuables, to help them hide from Octavian, with the sole result that:

> "They refused his kindness with tears in their eyes, he comforted them with
> all the goodness and the humanity imaginable, entreating them to leave him
> …"

The battle of Actium had ended later that day with the total defeat of Antony's forces, but the outcome was probably not dependant on his flight. The idea of the Antonians losing morale and being overwhelmed as a consequence of a leadership void must be rejected. Plutarch tells us very clearly that most of them did not even realize that their commander had left, given the length of the fighting front, the smoke from the burning ships, the screaming of the fighters, the moaning of the oarsmen under cruel effort. Few could have spotted the flagship sailing away in the middle of a fight involving 650 ships, 60,000 soldiers, and an enormous number of rowers. The cruel fight continued for hours, in spite of the best efforts of Octavian, who wanted to spare as many ships and lives as possible for future use, and who kept frenetically running around the battle line yelling at the Antonians that their leader had left, and that surrender was the best option. The systematic refusal to do that led to intensified bombardment with ignited ballistae projectiles, and the burning of many more ships, leading to the complete annihilation of Antony's fleet. It was not until late in the day that the survivors started raising the oars in sign of surrender.

While no account exists of the extent of Antony's losses, it has been estimated that maybe ninety ships from the Eastern armada made it safely to Egypt. Of the remaining 150 which were destroyed in the battle, one must add those that had been lost in the preliminary fights, and those which Antony had deliberately burned because they were unmanned and to subtract them from enemy usage. In the end, Octavian could have collected well over 300 ramming heads from enemy ships sunk or destroyed, with which he built a war memorial. As for the loss of life, estimates range from the low of 5,000 according to Plutarch, who was maybe referring to fighters alone, and not drowned rowers, to highs of 12,000 and more. All things considered, these losses are not staggering if compared to the overall size of the army that Antony had under his command. If his plan had worked, and if Canidius had been able to march through Macedonia and reunite with the other legions in Asia, Antony's position would have been serious but not irreparably compromised. But the one major factor which Antony had not taken into account in his plans was the devastating psychological effect on his land forces of witnessing the destruction of their comrades at sea. After standing true to their duty for seven days, the appeal of Octavian's pardon versus a long and perilous journey across Greece, Thrace, and Asia followed by more wars, became increasingly attractive. As had happened many times in the course of the Civil Wars, pragmatism eventually prevailed, and, once they were reassured that their units would not be disbanded and that they would retain rights to their pay in arrears and bonuses, the majority of the legionaries surrendered, not before having seen Canidius, who had seen the writing on the wall, escape under the cover of darkness.

Antony had committed a fatal mistake. Not everybody can spring back from such a defeat, and lead men through a difficult retreat, with a strong enemy in pursuit. Antony had done it after Mutina, and had done it again in Media, but there was no way he could have delegated such a delicate exercise of leadership, which would have required all his special charisma in order to avoid the dissolution of that loyalty which had miraculously survived the onslaught of enemy propaganda, the hardship endured, and the problematic presence of Cleopatra. It is impossible to say if Antony's presence with the 40,000 men watching from the shore would have changed the eventual outcome, but for sure it would have improved the probability of success. The fact remains that, far from obeying an irrational impulse to be with Cleopatra at all costs, Antony was executing a very precise plan, a plan which miscalculated the importance of the human bond between soldiers and commander. As a true paradox, Antony had lost the war not in the waters of Actium, but on his very own turf of soldierly brotherhood and inspiring leadership.

Many think of Actium not only as the conclusion of the Civil Wars and the beginning of the Roman Empire, but also as a final clash of civilizations, and the prevalence of the Roman west against the rebellious east. This is untrue. What died in Actium was Antony's dream of a Greco-Roman east built on the backbone of Egypt, and governed with a formula better tailored to the local cultures and heritage, with a less intrusive Romanizing presence, which strove to obtain a more sincere allegiance which could have lasted longer and presented a better defence against foreign threats such as the Parthians. We don't know if Antony had had an intuition of what would eventually lead to the separation of the two souls which lived in the body of the Roman Empire, and which took place three centuries later. But there is perhaps enough evidence to conclude that he had conceived a smarter form of imperialism than what Rome had shown to date. Proof of the robustness of his project is that the shrewd Octavian Augustus may have eliminated Antony, but not what he had built during his ten year Asian spell, except of course for the dynastic vision, and the regional kingship layer made up by his own and Cleopatra's offspring. The Polemos, the Amyntas, the Archelauses, and eventually also the Herods, kowtowed to the new Augustus, and got away with the same arrangement they had made previously with Antony.

Here is the account of Josephus of the meeting between Herod and Octavian, where the king of the Jews did not try to be apologetic or ask for mercy, but rather:

> "he gave a frank explanation of the past without trying to exculpate himself. He confessed to Caesar that he had had a great friendship for Antony, and had done whatever he could to help his cause. He had not participated actively in his campaign because he was at war with the Arabs, but he had sent him money and provisions, although maybe not as much as he should have done… When a man recognizes to be the friend of another, and he is conscious that the other is his benefactor, he has to share in his dangers, risking with him his life and his belongings."

In sum, Herod concluded, all he could do was to advise him to get rid of Cleopatra, as:

> "if rid of her, it would have been easier for him to retain his power and find a compromise with you instead of remaining enemies. But he did not listen, preferring his ill advised imprudence, bad for him, good for you. But if now you are angry with Antony, and you condemn my attention for him, I will never deny what I have done so far, or be ashamed to admit openly my loyalty to him. If you… see how I behave towards my benefactors… with the benefit of this experience you will know who I am."

This passionate and bold speech won Herod the benevolence of Caesar Augustus, and, of course, his crown.

In the meantime, the news from Actium was spreading around the Mediterranean like brushfire. In Rome, it had been the privilege of Cicero's son Marcus to announce the news in the Forum. But the news also travelled to the east. When Antony's envoys reached the camp of the reserve legions in Cyrenaica, the eastern part of Libya, under the command of a Pinarius Scarpus, for the sake of avoiding any misunderstanding with Octavian they were swiftly put to death, and Scarpus swore loyalty to the young Caesar immediately. The quick contagion of betrayal had deprived Antony of all his backup troops in a matter of weeks.

Octavian could not organize a full scale pursuit of the fugitives right away. He had first to go back to Italy and take care of the periodic outbursts of the veterans and dispossessed villagers. Possibly he did not have the means or the intention to honour his promise to all the Antonians who had surrendered at Actium, and who now had augmented the ranks of the dissatisfied.

Cleopatra had arrived in Alexandria, after a first landing in Cyrenaica, the prows of her ships adorned with flowers, and to the usual sound of bagpipes and flutes, as if the battle had been won. She could not go back to Alexandria with her feathers down, as she knew well that her subjects would have been unforgiving, and she was in jeopardy of ending up like her father Ptolemy XII, only this time with Octavian instead of Gabinius ready to intervene. Once home, she thought well of eliminating all those she considered potentially dangerous once the truth had been divulged. Their money was furtively taken away, and the funds of some wealthy temples were also confiscated, in order to rapidly constitute a large war chest.

The war chest theorem was in line with pre-Actium thinking, but this time the suggestion from Dio that Cleopatra preferred to negotiate her own peace terms, and the gold that she was stockpiling was going to serve as a ransom, also seems very credible. The conveyance to Octavian of a golden sceptre, crown, and throne, would have been a signal of her willingness to bow to the winner. Apparently, a negotiation took place, with Cleopatra, as a goodwill gesture, handing over a minor Caesaricide who had found sanctuary in Alexandria. Antony, on the other hand, was less willing to give up, given the realistic assessment of his chances of survival. His last attempts to organize his last stand were only demonstrative. Herod, before deserting his side, had recommended that he kill Cleopatra and then surrender, but Antony was way too proud for such an eventuality. The last draft to arms for the final defence saw the enrolment of many youths, including Cesarion and Anthillus, who wore the uniforms of the ephebes, the children-soldiers of ancient Greece. Hope is the last to die, but neither of the Egyptian rulers thought their chances of survival were high. Antony had trained one of his freedmen to assist him in his suicide by sword. As for Cleopatra, portrayed by the Greek historians as delusionally confident of being able to seduce the young Octavian, she had her servants and courtesans mobilized to identify the most painless way to die, and the poison which would guarantee the most serene departure. To this end, the pace of the executions of convicted criminals, on the basis of research, increased in Alexandria, until, after several unsatisfactory attempts, the bite of the asp, which caused numbness and gentle drowsiness before death, was found to be suitable, and it is believed that detailed arrangements were made accordingly. Indeed, the use of criminals to test poisons was an old Egyptian consuetude, so there should have been a sufficient body of knowledge on the subject, but we can only assume that Cleopatra wanted to see the results confirmed with her own eyes.

Another theory which found credit with Plutarch and Dio is that the money was to finance yet another attempt to flee Egypt, and it seems that Cleopatra had ordered some of her ships to be carried over land into the Red Sea. But the Arabic tribesmen, sent by the Roman Governor of Syria, set fire to them before her plan could take shape.

Antony remained in Cyrenaica longer than his queen, alone with his thoughts, and a few friends, such as the rhetoricians Aristocrates and Lucilius, the man who had turned himself into Antony's hands at Philippi to favour the escape and suicide of Brutus. When even the head of his local garrison defected, he turned back to Alexandria in a profound depression, fuelled by the insurgence of misanthropic feelings. His closest friends had jumped on the winner's ship, and Cleopatra was trying desperately to get herself a deal where she could, if not keep her crown, obtain a dignified retirement. It was so that Antony went to live in partial seclusion on the island of Pharos, in Alexandria, meditating on injustice and ingratitude of mankind. He had called his last residence the Timoneum, after the famous Athenian misanthropist Timon. It was not until the news of more defections reached him, and the standards of the Roman legions appeared on the horizon, with Gallus at the head of the four legions formerly led by Scarpus from the west, and Octavian himself from the east, that he left this humble retreat and joined Cleopatra in the royal palace of Alexandria, to go down in style, with a last hooray. The club of the "Inimitable Livers" was dissolved, to be replaced by a sinister association, just as decadent as the first, in the quest for refined pleasures, but this time with a nihilistic and dark flavour. For days the royal palace sounded of song and dance like in its most splendid days. Cleopatra's own anniversary was celebrated in an understated fashion, whatever this might have meant in the context, but for Antony's the party was lavish, the guests walking away enriched by the party favours.

The conclusion of the ordeal for Antony and Cleopatra had to be postponed by a few months. Agrippa was struggling to keep the situation under control in Italy, and he had sent for Octavian; the latter would not delegate the last act to Gallus, or anybody else for that matter. It is not clear either if the various exchanges of envoys took place before his trip to Rome, after, or both. Per Plutarch, there might have been as many as three steps in the negotiation, one of which included Anthillus, who had begun his short life as a hostage in the hands of the Caesaricides. It seems impossible that Antony tried to bargain for his life, asking Octavian to let him retire as a private citizen in Athens. Antony was no Lepidus, and his pretend or real naivety did not stretch that far. This humiliating posture clashes so strongly with everything he had stood for in his lifetime, that it can only be yet another product of imperial propaganda, trying to belittle him one more time. Even if he had accepted to kneel down in front of the young Caesar, there was absolutely not a chance he could have been spared, at the risk of finding him at the head of a resurrected and nostalgic Antonian side a couple of years later. By the same token, the eventuality of Cleopatra negotiating her way out of her current predicament seems quite unlikely. It seems just another expedient way to burn in the eyes of the Romans the image of a devious woman, ready to abandon the man she had enslaved as soon as she saw a decent way out, and at the same time to give Octavian a way to look magnanimous and merciful in victory, ready to spare her life, if not to pardon her.

Just like Antony, Cleopatra could not have been so delusional as to expect such favourable treatment. She knew perfectly well that she would have had to follow Octavian's triumph, golden chains being the last jewel that she would have worn, while pride would not have contributed to adorning her legendary beauty any more. As for the continuation of the house of the Ptolemies, if Octavian had contemplated leaving them in place, he would never have accepted one of Cleopatra's offspring. Admitting the very existence of Cesarion as a son of Julius Caesar would have jeopardized the robustness of Octavian's claim to succession, and it was unthinkable. As for her other children, they were Antony's, and succession was equally out of discussion. But Plutarch insists on these frequent exchanges of envoys (and that Octavian had even gone as far as showing signs of infatuation for the Egyptian) whose role may have been to induce her to give up her resistance or to dissuade her from any ideas of suicide she might have been harbouring. Antony had an outburst of rage against one of Octavian's freedmen, which the new Caesar was sending to Cleopatra as a negotiator. He had him tied up and whipped, and then retorted maliciously to Octavian:

"You have my freedman Hipparcus with you. If you want, tie him up and scourge him, so we shall be even."

The sarcasm lay in the fact that this freedman was one of those which had most recently jumped ship.

Spring came, and the Roman armies came closer to Alexandria. Antony, with the few remaining troops at his disposal, had to tackle them on both the eastern and the western front. Gallus had gone all the way to Paretonius, on the Egyptian border, and captured easily whatever ships were left. The city had a strong strategic importance, as it guarded the access to the land of the Nile. Antony had tried to recapture it, without success, and he tried to address citizens and soldiers in the attempt to win them back to his cause, as the western legions had already fought for him. But Gallus had the trumpets blare so loud that they covered his voice.

On the other front, Pelusium had fallen, that same Pelusium which Antony had conquered as a young field commander under Gabinius. Actually, the official version is that Cleopatra had ordered the garrison commander to give it up without fighting, to simplify Octavian's access to Alexandria, as a surrender deal had already been made. In her duplicity, Cleopatra was formally encouraging the inhabitants to defend the city, while in secret she was ordering them to give it up, and avoid any armed confrontation. Then, to cover her tracks, Cleopatra had handed over the unfortunate general, and his family, for Antony to exercise his revenge and find an outlet for his frustration.

The appearance of Octavian on the eastern front, at the outskirts of Alexandria, close to the hippodrome, caused Antony to shift his attention away from Cyrenaica. The opportunity to go down with one more glorious gesture presented itself, as the legionaries exhausted from the crossing of the Egyptian deserts were a target within reach even for the scarce forces left at his disposal. Even now that everything was lost, Antony must have glowed when he saw the chance to savour one last time the sweet taste of victory, to snap out of his state of melancholy and depression, and to think of something other than his preparations for suicide and tallying up the daily list of betrayals and defections. He rounded up a small cavalry squadron and raided the Roman camp, leading the charge himself, just like he did twenty-seven years before on the very same scene, inflicting a defeat on those who had almost totally annihilated him. That cavalry charge was to be his swan song: he was in high spirits when he went back to the palace, proud as a peacock, cheerfully announcing his victory. He took with him the soldiers who had most distinguished themselves, and Cleopatra honoured him with a golden helmet and a golden breastplate, both of huge value. But, as one more memento of the predicament in which they found themselves, that same soldier defected to Octavian the same night, taking the precious gifts with him. It was a bittersweet ending, with the last disillusionment from one of the last to show him devotion, loyalty, and honour, the values which Antony most cherished, and which were the most out of place in the context of the Civil Wars of Rome. Before this nameless soldier, the last to show unyielding commitment to him had been a group of gladiators in Cyzicus on the Marmara Sea, who had invited him to join them to go down gloriously at their head. The recording of this event is one of the few last tributes from Plutarch to Antony, and to his way of inspiring others and leading the humblest, sometimes the men one would least expect.

But the simple betrayal of men could not be enough to mark the ending of a man of the stature of Mark Antony, a man who had been vested with a supernatural identity in Egypt and in the east at large. There had to be a religious or mystical endorsement of his fall. Dionysos could not be associated with the fall of his protégé and emulator. At night, strange noises were heard.

"That night, it is related, about the middle of it, when the whole city was in a deep silence and general sadness, expecting the events of the next day, on a sudden was heard the sound of all sorts of instruments, and voices singing in tune, and the cry of a crowd of people singing and dancing, like a troop of bacchanals on its way. This tumultuous procession seems to take its course right through the middle of the city to the gate nearest the enemy; here it became loudest and suddenly passed out. People who reflected considered it to signify that Bacchus, the God whom Antony had always made his study to copy and imitate, had now forsaken him."

After his friends, after his soldiers, now Dionysos himself was deserting Antony. Now, returned to the dimension of a mere mortal, he could finally go to meet his fate. His *daimons*, after being beaten by Octavian's, had yielded to a stronger power, which was now dominating the mystical sphere after conquering the battlefield. The last sight of a battlefield for Antony would be that of his remaining battle ships raising their oars in surrender in the harbour of Alexandria.

The theory which relates that Cleopatra had gone into hiding in the area of the royal enclosure of Alexandria, which had been transformed into her mausoleum, and was at the origin of the rumour that she had already committed suicide so that Antony would have dispatched himself at once, and left her in a better position to negotiate her way out, certainly adds pathos to the tragic ending of the story, but is totally irrelevant to Antony's decision to end his life. It only piles up tragedy upon tragedy, disillusionment after disillusionment, not to mention the imperial propaganda implications of such a display of callousness towards the man to whom she had given three children and ten years of her life. Whoever came up with this rumour, he or she will have earned the eternal gratitude of numerous poets and (screen) playwrights.

With the surrender of the last semblance of a military force to oppose Octavian, and hours away from his capture, with Roman soldiers already walking around the royal palace of Alexandria, Antony finally saw that the moment to put an end to his life had come. He had chosen and trained one of his freed slaves, Eros, to stab him to death. It would seem that this Eros (Love, in Greek, but in the sense of carnal versus brotherly or spiritual love) was not even from the upper echelons of the slave society. It was common in Rome to call the slaves that were especially designated to perform sexual favours for their masters with such names (Love, Pleasure, Lust). But Eros pre-empted the intentions of his master and stabbed himself to death in front of Antony.

That was the cruellest and the noblest of all treasons at the same time, but it also provided an example which Antony could ignore; he extracted his sword, which Shakespeare depicts as the gladium which had once belonged to Julius Caesar, and fell on it, in the solitude of one of the rooms of the palace.

Driving a sword through one's body is a messy affair, and survival instincts make the work all the more difficult. He managed to inflict on himself a deadly wound, and it was clear to those who found him that death was going to come slowly by internal bleeding, but certainly not immediately. But why give in to such contempt for ritual suicide as Plutarch does:

> "Antony took himself out of the world in a cowardly, pitiful, and ignoble manner, but still in time to prevent the enemy having their person in his power."

Other Romans were praised for their stoic disregard for pain and death, such as Cato Minor, Cassius, Brutus, hosts of Pompeians, among the most recent. So why single out probably the greatest idealist of all for disdain, in what was univocally considered the most dignified way out for a Roman noble, and for a man of arms, if not to add to an already long list of unfair judgments and comments which have been passed on one of the men that truly made profound and irreversible changes possible in antiquity, and who had been inches away from making more dramatic change possible, if only the stars had been a little better aligned for him?

Learning that Cleopatra was still alive, he demanded to be taken to her. But as she had triggered a complex lock mechanism which blocked the entrance to her mausoleum, he could not be brought to her entering by the front door, and his bleeding body had to be hoisted from the balcony with ropes and pulleys, certainly an undignified exit from the earthly world, but perhaps some black humour on Antony's part, intended to remind his foes of their accusations of visiting another lover, Curio, by climbing up to his balcony in the middle of the night.

Shortly thereafter, Marcus Antonius, cavalry commander, military Legate, Quaestor, Augur, Master of Horse, Consul, Proconsul, Enemy of the State, Triumvir, last Leader of the Hellenistic world, exhaled his last breath between the arms of his lawfully wedded wife, Cleopatra VII Thea Philopater of the house of Lagos.

It was the first day of August, as the month was renamed after Octavian Caesar's honorific name, of the year 30 BC.

Chapter Nine

The Aftermath, the Offspring, and the Legacy

> *"With thy sharp teeth this knot intrinsicate*
> *Of life at once untie: poor venomous fool*
> *Be angry, and dispatch."*
>
> Shakespeare, Antony and Cleopatra

Under the strict surveillance of the Augustan envoys, Cleopatra staged her departure carefully. She weighed up, if there had been a need, one more time, her real chances of saving crown, family, and dignity, simply by kowtowing in front of the new Princeps, and accepting to be dragged in front of the cheering crowd of the Romans. While held under house arrest, it was not difficult to have a "venomous fool" smuggled to her, not before having sent Octavian a sealed message, asking him to bury her in the mausoleum expressly prepared, next to Antony. She passed away eleven days after Mark Antony.

The majority of the sources accept the version of the asp delivered in a basket under a layer of figs, while others opt for a vase as the vessel for transportation, and the possibility of poison having been self injected by a hairpin is also mentioned. Tradition would have it that the reptile was never found in Cleopatra's quarters, to the joy of animal rights activists, but its tracks were spotted in the sand outside the window, so we can be reassured that the co-protagonist of that last scene made it home safe and sound. Contrary to popular belief, the snake known as "Cleopatra's Asp" is not the small Egyptian cobra, whose toxicity is powerful and painful, but rather a short and thick horned viper, whose bite causes blood coagulation and organ failure in a quasi lethargic and relatively painless way. Altogether, modern science has confirmed that the choice could not have been better. Also, by Roman standards, she had gone down in style. Roman suicide etiquette did not request the brutality of the sword for the honourable death of women, as was the case with the dying Plancina stabbing herself in front of her husband and encouraging him with "Piso, it does not hurt!" Her suicide finally redeemed her partially, even in Rome, where she was detested as the epitome of all evil, and the embodiment of everything a true Roman should abhor. In death, as it has been recently put:[1]

> "by the Roman definition she had at last done something right; finally it was to her credit that she had defied the expectations of her sex."

What she could not secure was the pardon for her two older children. For Cesarion, for the succession issues exposed above, surviving Cleopatra had never been an option that could be remotely conceived. He had been formally associated to the crown of Egypt, and for all practical purposes he was a foreign monarch who had been at war against Rome. Also, he and Anthillus had worn arms, as they had been enrolled as Ephebs. That was probably enough for Anthillus also: in addition the boy had recently formally come of age, too soon for Roman customs, and he had dropped the child's tunic to wear the adult toga, adorned by purple. In the remote eventuality that Octavian had even needed an excuse to put them to death, these facts alone would have amply sufficed.

Cesarion, aged 17, maybe made it to the coast of the Red Sea, where a ship had been prepared for his escape to India. Either he was intercepted, given away by his tutor Theodorus under promise of reward, or maybe he even made it overseas, and was later convinced by another tutor, Rhodon, to return under promise of amnesty. As one of Augustus' teachers put it, too many Caesars is not good.

The tutor Theodorus also handed over the 14-year-old Antyllus to be brutally beheaded by Roman soldiers. Maybe his last mission as a diplomatic envoy to Octavian, if it had ever taken place, had given him too much unwanted visibility, or bad vibrations had gone around at the wrong time. When a precious pendant fell from his neck, Theodorus was swift to pick it up and put it in his belt. We will never know if the report that Octavian had him tried and crucified for theft was founded, or whether it was yet another piece of propaganda aimed at showing that imperial justice had no tolerance for delators. Plutarch reports that the boy was already showing, at a young age, the unmistakable traits of the generosity of the Antonii. The biographer gives us a cameo of him bestowing a huge amount of valuable vases to a physician, mimicking the gestures of Creticus, and his silver tray given to a needy friend, and many anecdotes from Antony's life along the same lines which have been faithfully reported by Plutarch. Maybe more of the genetic message would have manifested itself if the boy had been given a chance to grow up to full manhood.

The death of Anthillus did not stomp out the genetic message of the Antonii to the classical world. In fact, for the irony of fate, Antony's offspring spread out in many of the ruling houses of the Mediterranean and Roman world, albeit in a very different form from that which Antony had envisioned. We can try to briefly reconstruct how Antony's lineage continued to spread out in history.

The character of Antonia Hybrida Minor, Antony's cousin and first wife, has not been discussed much throughout this narration. It has been mentioned how Antony had arranged for her daughter, Antonia, to marry the tycoon Pythodorus of Tralles, in order to secure financing for the first Parthian campaign. The Roman Senate had frowned at the initiative, although it was a part of the Triumvir's broader plan for the Greek east. The couple had a daughter, called Pythodorida, who married Antony's old friend and companion of adventures Polemon, king of Ponthus, already a

279 The Aftermath, the Offspring, and the Legacy

widower. Polemon had been confirmed in office by Octavian. The success of Antony's granddaughter did not stop within the boundaries of Ponthus: after Polemon passed away, she married Archelaus of Cappadocia, another fervent Antonian until Actium, and, as the reader will recall, a son of the beautiful Glaphyra, the alleged mistress of the Triumvir during his Asian roaming in 41 BC.

While the latter marriage was childless, and at the death of Archelaus she went back to Ponthus, her first marriage started a long line of Roman vassal kings and queens. Her first son Zeno became the king of Armenia (!) under the name of Artaxias III, and was raised to the throne by none other than Germanicus, the Julio-Claudian hero born of Livia, Octavian's wife, and Antonia Minor, the second daughter of Antony and Octavia. Germanicus had crowned, among much cheering of approval in the Senate House, his fourth-degree nephew. At his death, he had no successors and the crown of Armenia passed on, but that did not end the propagation of the Antonii in the area.

The second son of Phytodora became Polemon II of Ponthus, and reigned over the vassal state, upholding loyalty to Rome, until his death in AD 74. He left no heir.

A different destiny was in store for her third born child, named Antonia Tryphaena. She married the prince of Thrace Cotys VIII, the son of that Cotys which, according to Antonian propaganda, Octavian wanted to marry to his daughter Julia, as opposed to her first fiancé Antonius Anthillus. She survived the inevitable dynastic struggle thanks to the patronage of Emperor Tiberius, and she gave birth to four children, who reigned over Thrace, the Cimmerian (or Roman) Bosphorus, and Lesser Armenia. The Antonian descendants kept reigning more or less successfully in this Greco-Romanized Crimea, well into the fourth century BC. Their success, and the relative success of this kingdom, depended critically on the integration of neighbouring populations, including marriages with Persian princes.

As for the children Antony fathered with Fulvia, we have already discussed the tragic destiny of Anthillus, fallen under the executioner's axe at 17 years of age.

His younger brother Jullus Antonius would have a very different destiny. He was raised under the generous and maternal care of Octavia, who, as we have seen, stretched her wing to also take in Cleopatra's children after Antony's death. Over time, Octavia's generosity went as far as succeeding in putting Jullus in Octavian Augustus's good graces, and introducing him into the cursus honorum. He made Quaestor, then Consul, and eventually Proconsul for Asia. Eventually he became a very influential presence in the palace, and he married Claudia Marcella, from the imperial clan. His influence was his perdition. Julia the Elder, the only daughter of Octavian and Scribonia, soon started manifesting the signs of her predatory sexual exuberance, which would take her to previously unheard of extremes of licentiousness. Her voracity would reach a high point when she "had a passenger on board", i.e. during one of her frequent pregnancies, and had no risk of falling pregnant anew. She was so bold as to consume her illicit sex acts in her litter in the Forum at night, by the same *rostra* where her father was announcing new laws on public morality. With her in mind, Octavian Augustus was soon to say:

"Oh if I had never married or had children!"

When the pressure mounted on her, she probably approached Jullus for protection from the wrath of her father, but he too became the last of a long string of lovers. In the end, Augustus sent her into solitary confinement on the small island of Pandataria (today's Ventotene), with her mother. Some of her lovers were also exiled, but Jullus had no such luck, and was forced to commit suicide. He had three children, Lucius, Gaius, and Julla. None of them had any claim to fame. Lucius prospered under Tiberius, and his son married the daughter of the cruel and infamous Pretorian Prefect, Sejanus. Antony's legacy from the Fulvia side was thus extinguished within two generations.

Rather than following the order of Antony's children by birth date, I have chosen here to follow that of the official wives, so that the noble Octavia comes before Cleopatra. Octavia bore Antony two daughters, both called Antonia, following, as we have seen, a very deeply rooted tradition and a fundamental lack of imagination that ran in the family. Both were welcome in Rome, allowed to receive the inheritance of Mark Antony, and were to become the originators of the two main Julio Claudian branches.

The first, Antonia the Elder, born in 39 BC, had been betrothed to Lucius Domitius Ahenobarbus, son of Gneus, Antony's ally until Actium, who had died of fever just after his defection and before the battle. The father's abandonment of the Antonian camp was not enough to change Octavia's mind about the wedding, which was celebrated in 25 BC. Their union bore three children, Domitia Lepida Maior, Gneus Domitius Ahenobarbus, and Domitia Lepida Minor. All three would have great impact on the Roman scene, and not all for the right reasons. Lucius himself showed the worst traits of the Domitii, their rashness, cruelty, and at times, savagery, which, in the following generations, would overpower the kindness, nobility, and composure of both Antony and Octavia, qualities which one could also find in both Antoniae. Lucius, during his term as an Aedil and Quaestor, distinguished himself for extravagance, organizing the bloodiest shows of wild beasts and gladiators, provoking the disapproval of Augustus, and showing a maniacal passion for chariot races, which he would transmit to his more famous grandson, Emperor Nero.

Of the three children, Domitia the Elder's children did not distinguish themselves other than for mildly successful political careers. Her husband, Decimus Agrippa, fell during the crazy witch hunt operated by Tiberius, while she managed to survive under Gaius' (Caligula) and Claudius' principate, remaining as an authoritative figure in the palace, and holding her ground with the other powerful clan women. She did not, though, survive the reign of Nero, her nephew, who had a predilection for her beautiful estate in Baia. Her doctors killed her with a lethal dose of laxatives, a most undignified death for such a noble woman. The estate would be the theatre of the murder of Nero's mother, Agrippinilla.

The second born, Gneus Domitius Ahenobarbus, also inherited all the ruthlessness and cruelty that run in the Domitii. He killed for his own pleasure, and was dishonest and corrupt in business, which did not prevent him from ascending to Consulship under Tiberius in 32 BC. Most importantly, he married his cousin, from the Antonia Minor line, Agrippinilla. Together, they would have one son, Lucius, who Claudius would adopt, when he married Agrippinilla himself, and who would assume the name of Nero, as we have discussed earlier. The key character traits of the preceding Domitii revealed themselves in their purest form in this Antonii descendant, alongside the taste for chariot racing inherited from his paternal grandfather.

Domitia Lepida Minor also had some relevance in the maze which is the Julio-Claudian family tree. She married a Valerius Messalla Corvino, son of the other by the same name who had been a strong opponent of Antony in the last stages of his career. Their daughter Valeria Messalina, of legendary beauty and depravity, would obliterate the sexual exploits of Julia the Elder, raising the bar to heights unknown even to the most experienced courtesans. This would not, however, be an obstacle to her being raised to the purple as the wife of Emperor Claudius, to whom she bore two children, widely known as Octavia and Britannicus. Neither of them survived Nero's paranoia and jealousy: Britannicus was poisoned while dining at the palace's children table, his inevitable fate maybe accelerated by having called the future Emperor to his face by his real name, Domitius. The sweet and compassionate Octavia was also killed by the envoys of her cousin, who had her tied to a chair and had her wrists slashed open until she bled to her death. The last child of Domitia Minor was called Faustus Cornelius Sulla Felix, after his father, adding another major family liaison to an already crowded family tree. This branch of the offspring from Antonia Maior did not go very far either. Under Nero, he fell into disgrace and was initially exiled, until the ferocious Prefect Tigellinus sent a squad to kill him. The consensus is that he was not a personality that could have made it to the limelight or really concerned Nero.

The history of the offspring of the second daughter of Antony and Octavia is even more interesting and picturesque. Technically, as the title of Antonia the Elder under Roman onomatology rules would have gone to the daughter of Antonia Hybrida, as opposed to this Antonia's older sister, she should be called Antonia Tertia (Third). After the death of Antony, she was raised by her mother Octavia along with all the other siblings and half-siblings that Antony had fathered. When she came of age, she was married to Nero Claudius Drusus, Emperor Tiberius' brother. She bore him, in order, the great Roman hero Germanicus,

Livilla, and the future Emperor Claudius. It is amazing to see how deeply Antony's genes penetrated the Julio-Claudians, deeper than Octavian and Julius Caesar individually.

Germanicus was showing the traits of idealistic heroism and individual bravery that his great maternal grandfather had possessed. Unfortunately, a plot by the envious Calpurnius and his wife Plancina brought an early end to his life, possibly under the instigation of Tiberius, envious of the immense popularity that Gemanicus enjoyed. The tracks of the murder were carefully covered with the suicide of the murderous couple, and the truth will never be known. But the story is not over. Germanicus had married Agrippina the Elder, daughter of Marcus Vipsanius Agrippa, and the sex fiend Julia the Elder, Octavian Augustus' only daughter. The genes of Antony, his enemy Octavian, and his military nemesis Agrippa had finally met. The outcomes, in the mysteries of genetics, were numerous: Nero (not to be confused with the Emperor) and Drusus were put to death by starvation by the raving Tiberius, the latter ending up chewing the mattress in his cell. The main characters though were Gaius, who went down in history as Emperor Caligula, and his younger sister Agrippina, the mother of Emperor Nero, who we have just met, plus their younger sisters, Julia Drusilla, maybe Caligula's incestuous lover, and Julia Livilla. Half of the combinations that intervened between the turbocharged lineages would have been a detonator powerful enough to terminate the first dynasty of the Roman Empire. The story of each of these characters is picturesque and depraved at the same time, and this is not the place to go through the listing of the most resounding names. In terms of the continuation of the Antonian genealogy, Gaius gave his contribution to stomping out his relatives by killing Tiberius Gemellus, his nephew, son of his aunt Livilla. As for the other children, neither Julia Drusilla nor Julia Livilla had any children of their own.

Germanicus' sister Livilla, the second daughter of Antonia Minor (or Tertia) and Drusus, also distinguished herself for her ambition and ruthlessness. Seduced by the despicable Sejanus, she was accused of plotting with him to overthrow Tiberius. When it came to settling the scores, Tiberius did not hand his niece to the executioner, but rather to her mother Antonia, who punished her too with death by starvation, a recurrent punishment during the reign of Tiberius.

The third son of Antonia Minor was Emperor Claudius, who succeeded Gaius (Caligula) when the latter's career was terminated by a palace plot, ending his bloodthirsty extravagances. Claudius married three times. The second marriage, with the famous Valeria Messalina, and the children it bore, has already been discussed in the pages above, and so has the one with Agrippinilla, sister of Caligula, former wife of Gneus Domitius, and mother of Lucius Domitius (Nero). After the adoption of Nero and his ascension to the throne were secured, Agrippinilla dispatched Claudius by a poisoned mushroom and successive doses of lethal substances by enema when the first attempt by mushroom failed.

We are left now with the three children Antony had fathered with Cleopatra, the cornerstone of his dynastic dream. All three were critical in the short term for Octavian to be able to give evidence of his clemency and mercy. They were all spared, at least initially.

Of course, the elder, Alexander Helios, the King of Armenia, Media, and Parthia, could not keep his engagement to Princess Iotape of Media. The most likely version of his fate is that he died of disease at a young age, and without descendants. The same happened, in all probability, to his younger brother Ptolemy Philadelphos.

Greater success was going to come to Cleopatra Selene, Alexander's twin sister, queen of Libya and Cyrenaica. Like her siblings, regardless of their maternity, she was raised in the loving care of Octavia, and she was remarkable for her beauty and intelligence. When she came of age, she was married to Juba II of Numidia. Numidia was no longer a kingdom at the time. It had ceased being one after the battle of Thapsos, when Caesar had defeated Juba's father and his elephant mounted troops. King Juba, an old Pompeian, had committed suicide after the defeat, but his son had been taken to Rome, where he had been raised as a Roman.

For reasons of political opportunity, giving Numidia back to the young Juba was not possible, but soon Octavian Augustus had a different idea. When Bocchus, king of Mauretania, had died a few years earlier, his kingdom had been transformed into a province. It was so that Mauretania became anew a client kingdom, under the command of Juba. Cleopatra Selene was then given to Juba in marriage, bringing him a huge dowry supplied by Augustus. By then, both of her brothers had died. Once in Mauretania, Cleopatra proved to be a valuable partner and an enlightened queen, promoting arts and architecture, and contributing to the development of the capital Cesarea (modern Cherchell in Algeria), which soon had buildings that could rival in beauty any other Middle Eastern city. Three hundred years later another queen who would stand up to Rome, Zenobia, queen of Palmyra, would claim descent from her.

Juba and Cleopatra Selene had a son, who was called Ptolemy of Mauretania. He too reigned successfully as a client king, and he entertained excellent relations with Rome. Things went well and he was able to continue in the footsteps of his parents. He was instrumental in keeping the Berber tribes in neighbouring Numidia in check. He was attributed high honours by the Senate, who called him king, ally, and friend. All went well for him until the day he was invited by Emperor Caligula on a State visit. The young king had the audacity to arrive at the gladiatorial games wearing a magnificent purple cloak, an imperial prerogative at the time. That was enough to trigger the jealousy of Caligula, his second cousin, who had him immediately arrested and put to death. He became the first recorded fashion victim in the Antonian genealogy, and the last of the Ptolemies at the same time.

Bibliography

Appian, The Civil Wars, Penguin Classics 1980, Trad. By John Carter

G.P. Baker, Sulla the Fortunate, Roman General and Dictator, Cooper Square Press 1928

Cassius Dio, History of Rome, BUR 1996

Cicero, Orationes In Verrem, BUR 1992

Cicero, Orationes Philippicae, BUR 2003

Cicero, Ad Atticum, UTET 1998

E. Cantarella, Secondo natura, BUR 1988

F. Chamoux, Marc Antoine – Dernier prince de l'orient Grec, Arthaud 1976

M.P. Charlesworth, Some Fragments of the Propaganda of Mark Antony, The Classical Quarterly, 1933

A. Everitt, Cicero, Random House 2003

R. M. Errington, A History of the Hellenistic World, Blackwell 2008

R. Hard, The Routledge handbook of Greek Mythology, Routledge 2004

G. Hölbs, A History of the Ptolemaic Empire, Routledge

E. Golz–Huzar, Mark Antony, A Biography, Univ. of Minnesota, 1978

C. Julius Caesar, Le guerre in Gallia (De Bello Gallico) Mondadori, 1987

C. Julius Caesar, De Bello Civili, Barbera 1998

Josephus Flavius, Antichità Giudaiche, UTET 1998

Josephus Flavius, Le Guerre Giudaiche (Bellum Iudaeorum), UTET 1995

A. Keaveney, Sulla, The Last Republican, Routledge 1982

T. Livy, Ab Urbe Condita Periochae

J.G. Manning, The Last Pharaohs – Egypt under the Ptolemies 305–30, Princeton 2010

Plutarch, Antony, 2010 ebookslib.com

Plutarch, Brutus, 2010 ebookslib.com

Plutarch, Comparison of Demetrios and Antony, 2010 ebookslib.com

G. Sampson, The Defeat of Rome in the East, Casemate 2008

K. Scott, Octavian's propaganda and Antony's De Sua Ebrietate, Review of Archaeology XIX, 1924

R. Seager, Pompey the Great, Blackwell 1979

S. Sheppard, Actium 31 BC, Osprey 2009

S. Sheppard, Philippi 42 BC, Osprey 2008

P. Southern, Mark Antony, Tempus 1998

P. Southern, Augustus, Routledge 1998

A. Spinosa, Cleopatra, Mondadori 1992

G. Suetonius Tranquillus, The lives of the XII Caesars, Penguin Books 1979

R. Syme, The Roman Revolution, Oxford 1939

Goldsworthy, Caesar: Life of a Colossus, Yale University Press 2006

Goldsworthy, The Complete Roman Army, Thames and Hudson 2003

C. Velleius Paterculus, Historiae, BUR, 1997

Florus, Epitome of Roman History, Loeb Classical Library 1929 (translated by E.S. Forster)

Notes

Introduction
1. II, 21
2. L. Anneus Florus 74–130 AD
3. L. Anneus Florus, Epitome, 4, XI
4. Appian, The Civil Wars
5. F. Chamoux, Marc Antoine, Dernier prince de l'Orient Grec
6. Philippics, II
7. A Jewish general during an anti-Roman rebellion, Josephus had been cornered in a cave with forty of his companions. He convinced them to perform collective suicide by killing each other, volunteering to be the last to go. Rather than suiciding when his turn came, he surrendered, and became part of the entourage of Vespasian, and his son Titus, later acting as a negotiator during the siege of Jerusalem. He then took to the historical work being discussed
8. Ref to main text on Herod's pledge to Augustus after Antony's death in 30 BC
9. Little good it did to him, as he will die at the siege of Mutina (Modena) in 43 BC fighting against the Antonian troops, after having been lured to the Octavian side by Cicero
10. GM Masselli, Introduction to "De Bello Civile", Barbera 2008
11. Drusus and the future emperor Tiberius

Chapter 1
1. And the second born was invariably called Gaius
2. A Praetor was a magistrate created to relieve the Consuls of some duties. Praetors could exercise military command or imperium (Praetorium imperium), provincial governorship (praetorian potestas), or judiciary power (praetorium ius)
3. Consulship was the highest elected political office of the Roman Republic. Consuls held effectively the executive power, and often assumed military command at war time. There were two Consuls elected at a time, each holding veto power on the colleague, and they stayed in office for one year.
4. Censors were very powerful magistrates that could be chosen only between former Consuls. Besides supervising all the census functions, they would supervise the album, or registrar of citizens that could be admitted to the Senate, and review their eligibility in view of their morality
5. Consuls at the onset of the Republic inherited all the powers of the Kings. Over time they passed Censorship to Censors, and Judicial to Praetors, to remain, in fact, Chief Executive alone, with overall Imperium, or military command. They were the highest magistrates, and could overrule all others, except the Tribunes of the Plebs. The two Consuls stayed in office for a year, and gave their name to the year they presided
6. Interestingly enough, the following one was the "Lucio Silla", reestablishing the *par condicio* between the two arch-rivals on the musical front

7. Latifondia were the huge estentions of farmland that concentrated in the hands of few as small, family agricultural enterprises became less competitive and economically viable. Over the centuries, but beginning from the Roman days in Sicily, this changed the rural population from small entrepreneurs-farmers into impoverished farm hands at the service of large landowners. This continued in Italy until reforms were introduced at the end of the twentieth century

8. A Proconsul was a Governor, or a provincial commander, holding the Imperium, or military command for the legions stationed in that province at the same time. The main prerequisite for the role was having held the Imperium before, as a Praetor or Consul

9. It is extremely hard to find a logical consistency between political field and marriages in the upper echelons of Roman society. For example, Caesar's first wife was a Cornelia, granddaughter of Marian tyrant Cinna. But when she died prematurely, he married Pompeia Sulla, granddaughter of the deceased dictator

10. A Quaestor in the Roman Republic was a magistrate supervising financial affairs, and it was one of the early steps in the cursus honorum

11. Cassius Dio, XXXVII, 39

12. Dante, Inferno XXVIII

13. For a thorough discussion of the matter see E. Cantarella "Secondo natura", 200X

14. A Quaestor was a financial official supervising fiscal and treasury affairs, both in the civil and in the military field. Quaestorship was one of the necessary steps in the "cursus honorum" or public career. A questor was automatically enrolled in the Senate

15. De domo sua (On his own house)

16. Plutarch, Life, 10, 6

17. Clodius might have held an inconsistent posture towards the Triumvirate: per Appian (CIV, II, 14) Caesar was wielding him as a weapon against Cicero, who was "blackening the compact of the three men, to secure sole power"

18. F. Chamoux, others

19. "Conquered Greece captured her ferocious victor, and brought the Arts in rural Latium" Epistulae II,1

20. P. Southern, Mark Antony, Tempus 1998

Chapter 2

1. Josephus, Jewish Antiquities, 13, 367–394

2. Herrington, 13

3. In 53 they came to blows in the Forum, with Antony having the upper hand and chasing Clodius with a sword until he could hide in a librarian store

4. Cassius Dio, XXXVII, 44

5. P. Southern, Mark Antony, Chapter I

6. Livy, 8

7. Life, 3, 9

8. Cassius Dio XXXIX

Chapter 3

1. Interestingly enough, Antony spoke for the Accusation, and Cicero for the Defence. But in the intimidating setting of the trial, Cicero staged his poorest performance ever, so that Milo was exiled to Massilia. He later published a better speech than the one he had delivered

during the trial, so that a sarcastic Milo thanked him for the delay in producing his defence, thanks to which he was enjoying the delicious sea snappers in his new home town

2. In the Sixth Philippic Cicero would refer to him as a "saviour of Rome "
3. A. Goldsworthy, Ceasar, Life of a Colossul, Ch. XVII
4. Antonius, V, 5
5. Appian, Civil War, II, 59
6. Cassius Dio, XLI, 48,2
7. Appian, The Civil War II, 66
8. Phil II, 29
9. I came, I saw, I conquered
10. Suetonius, Caesar
11. G.P. Baker, Sulla the Fortunate
12. Cassius Dio XLII, 29
13. Cassius Dio XLII, 31, 1–2
14. Antony, 12, 1
15. Cassius Dio, XLII, 27
16. Quote
17. Appian, Civil War, II, 107. In all likelihood Caesar had already planned to a reasonable extent of detail his Parthian campaign. Anticipating a prolonged absence, he had assigned the key Republican magistracies for several years out, in order to guarantee seamless succession in his absence, even in the case of prolonged gaps in communication
18. Phil II, xxx
19. Cicero, Phil II, xx
20. XLVI
21. F. Chamoux: "Marc Antoine, dernier Price de l'Orient Grec"
22. XLIV, 6

Chapter 4

1. This fact itself strongly contradicts Plutarch as for the alleged attempt from Trebonius in winning Antony to the conspirators' cause. Trebonius intervention on the Ides would have made Mark Antony all the more suspicious
2. Civil War, II, 119
3. Civil War II, 135
4. The *lictores* were a traditional honour guard awarded to Consuls. This institution was most likely of Etruscan heritage. They carried the *fasces*, bundled rods with an axe in the middle, to symbolize that the Consuls could inflict punishment to varying degrees. The *fasces* became the symbol of fascism in the twentieth century
5. XLIV, 34–35
6. Bel Civ III, 4
7. The legionaries of the V Alaudae, the heros of Thapsos had received the same privilege
8. « inquilinus civis urbis Romae » Sallust, Bellum Catilinae
9. Appian, Civil War, III, 20
10. Although Suetonius implies that Octavian applied a sensible haircut to Caesar's intentions
11. Cic., Phil III, 13
12. Quod bene cogitasti aliquando, laudo ; quod non indicasti, gratias ago ; quod non fecisti, ignosco ; virum res illa quaerebat

13. Di immortales nobis haec praesidia dederunt : Urbi Caesarem, Brutum Galliae
14. Ad Atticum, X, 4,5
15. Ad Atticum, X, 7,5
16. See pag. YY
17. Civ. Wars III, 63
18. XLVI, 31
19. Chamoux, IV
20. To the point that Cleopatra sent him reinforcements all the way from Egypt – reinforcements that never made it on time to save him from defeat and suicide in Laodicea
21. Appian, Civ. Wars III, 26
22. Cassius Dio, XLVI, 38–40

Chapter 5

1. Aug, II
2. Ann, 1, 10
3. Cassius Dio, XLV, 12
4. Dio, XLVII, 1
5. Civ War IV, 5
6. Antonius, 19, 4
7. Hist Rom II, LXVII
8. Aug, 37,1
9. Hist, Rom. II, LXVI
10. XLVII, 7
11. Civ Wars IV, 30
12. Appian, Civ. War, IV, 124
13. Aug, 13

Chapter 6

1. Aug 13
2. Antonius, 24, 15
3. Appian, Civ. War, V, 5
4. Plutarch
5. Appian, Civ. War, V, 6–7
6. Antony, 34,12
7. Hölbl, Chapter II
8. Josephus, Jewish Antiquities, XIV, 306–320
9. See Golz-Huzar Ch. X
10. Appian, Civ, V, 31
11. "Quod futuit Glaphiram Antonius, hanc mihi poenam / Fulvia constituit, se quoque uti futuam / Fulviam ego ut futuam? Qui si me Manus oret / Pedicem, faciam ? Non puto, si sapiam / « Aut futue aut pugnemus » ait. Quod, quat mihi vita / Carior est ipsa mentula? Signa canent ! / Absolvis lepidos nimirun, Auguste, libellos / Qui scis Romana simplicitate loqui"
12. Appian, Civ War V
13. This comment refers to the fact that some of his closest aides were former slaves of Pompey Magnus, his father

14. Civ War V, 59
15. Plutarch 32,5 ; Appian, V, 65, Dio, Velleius
16. XLVIII, 45
17. Appian, Civil War, V, 92
18. Appian, Civ War, V, 118
19. C. Velleius Paterculus, Historiae Romanae LXXIX

Chapter 7

1. Ant. Jud 14., 290
2. Jewish Wars, 1, 13
3. XLVIII, 24
4. Ant Jud, XIV, 388
5. XLVIII, 39
6. Chamoux, Marc Antoine Ch 7
7. XLIX, 23
8. Ant Iud, XIV, 5
9. Ant 5–2, and BJ 4–2
10. Bel Jud I, 439
11. Ant Iud, XV, 93
12. XLIX, 23
13. Livy, Periochae CXXX
14. Plutarch, Life 53
15. Civ War V, 133

Chapter 8

1. Historiae, 2.42
2. Historiae, 2.144
3. Diodorus Siculus, *The Library of History*, 1.13
4. Plutarch, On Isis and Osiris, 28
5. Plutarch, Ant 54,10
6. Aug LXX
7. MP Charlesworth, 1933
8. K. Scott, Octavian's propaganda and Antony's De Sua Ebrietate, Review of Archeology XIX, 1924
9. Dio, L, 25, 2–4
10. Aug, 68
11. Quote
12. Aug, 63
13. Di. Jul 52,2
14. Golz–Huzar, Ch. VII
15. S. Sheppard, Actium 31 BC, Osprey 2009
16. LXXXIII
17. L, 13
18. L, 18, 5–6
19. Dio, L, 26

Chapter 9

1. S. Schiff, Cleopatra, A life, 2010

Index

Discover Your History

Ancestors • Heritage • Memories

Each issue of *Discover Your History* presents special features and regular articles on a huge variety of topics about our social history and heritage – such as our ancestors, childhood memories, military history, British culinary traditions, transport history, our rural and industrial past, health, houses, fashions, pastimes and leisure ... and much more.

Historic pictures show how we and our ancestors have lived and the changing shape of our towns, villages and landscape in Britain and beyond.

Special tips and links help you discover more about researching family and local history. Spotlights on fascinating museums, history blogs and history societies also offer plenty of scope to become more involved.

Keep up to date with news and events that celebrate our history, and reviews of the latest books and media releases.

Discover Your History presents aspects of the past partly through the eyes and voices of those who were there.

FREE BOOK WHEN YOU SUBSCRIBE TO *Discover Your History*

UK only

Discover Your History is in all good newsagents and also available on subscription for six or twelve issues. For more details on how to take out a subscription and how to choose your free book, call 01778 392013 or visit **www.discoveryourhistory.net**